Peter Norton's DOS 6 Guide

10th Anniversary Edition

Peter Norton's DOS 6 Guide

10th Anniversary Edition

Peter Norton

New York   London   Toronto   Sydney   Tokyo   Singapore

Acknowledgments

Special thanks to Judi Fernandez for her masterful work on this completely new edition.

Thanks also to my literary agent, Bill Gladstone at Waterside Productions; to Michael Sprague at Brady Publishing for his dedication and enthusiasm for the project; and to Donna Tabler, Scott Clark, and Kevin Goldstein for their invaluable assistance.

Their contributions are greatly appreciated.

Credits

Publisher
Michael Violano

Acquisitions Director
Jono Hardjowirogo

Managing Editor
Kelly D. Dobbs

Developmental Editor
Michael Sprague

Copy Editors
Jo Anna Arnott
Gregory R. Robertson

Editorial Assistant
Lisa Rose

Book Designer
Michele Laseau

Cover Designer
HUB Graphics

Production Team
Katy Bodenmiller
Paula Carroll
Christine Cook
Mitzi Gianakos
Dennis Clay Hager
Howard Jones
John Kane
Sean Medlock
Roger S. Morgan
Angela M. Pozdol
Linda Quigley
Michelle M. Self
Susan Shepard
Greg Simsic
Suzanne G. Snyder
Alyssa Yesh

Overview

Contents

Introduction

Many new personal computer users try to ignore DOS. They concentrate on learning just the one or two applications they work with every day. A word processor or database manager, however, can't locate and correct errors in the disk directory structure; these programs can't rescue a file that you deleted by mistake, and they can't detect and remove a virus that has infected your hard disk. The more you know about DOS, the safer your data will be. You also can significantly improve the overall performance of your system with DOS. For example, you can make your applications run faster, and you can squeeze almost twice as much data onto your hard disk.

What You Will Learn

In this book, you learn how to do the following:

- Upgrade your system to DOS 6.

- Use DOS's on-line help system.

- Protect your system from viruses.

- Protect your data from accidental deletions.

- Manage your disks, directories, and files by using DOS Shell or the DOS command prompt.

- Set up DOS Shell to make your everyday tasks easier.

- Use several programs at the same time under the DOS Shell.

- Use DOS's full-screen editor to create and modify text files.

- Write your own simple programs.

- Understand and take full advantage of the CONFIG.SYS file.

- Use DOS 6's new backup system to protect and restore your files.

● Optimize the way your system uses memory (especially if you have a 386 or 486).

● Optimize your hard disk; you can minimize the time it takes to read and write data as well as double the amount of usable space.

At the back of the book, you will find a complete command reference for all the DOS commands and device drivers. With DOS 6, Microsoft decided to cut down on the amount of printed documentation. Most of the commands and device drivers are described only in the on-line help system, and that information is often incomplete. When you are ready to move beyond the basics and dig into the nuts and bolts of DOS commands and drivers, you will find the Command Reference and the Appendix, "Device Drivers," two of your best resources.

This book explains the DOS basics as well as the major new utilities released with DOS 6, such as DoubleSpace and MEMMAKER. Whether you are a new DOS user or have just upgraded from an earlier DOS version, you will find all the information you need to get started with your new operating system.

Conventions Used in This Book

The following conventions are used in this book:

italics

Expressions in italics indicate variables to be replaced by specific values. In the example, "CHKDSK creates generic file names in the form FILE*xxxx*.CHK," the *xxxx* indicates four characters that change from file name to file name. The actual file names generated by CHKDSK are FILE0000.CHK, FILE0001.CHK, FILE0002.CHK, and so on. (Italics also are used when introducing new terms and occasionally for emphasis.)

ALL CAPS

In regular text, commands, file names, directory paths, drive names, and program names are shown in all caps to make them stand out from the context. For example, the expression "the copy program" refers to any program that makes a copy, but "the COPY program" refers specifically to the DOS program named COPY.

Commands are shown in all caps even though DOS usually ignores case. You can enter commands in any mixture of cases, and many users prefer to work with all lowercase characters. The few places in which DOS is case-sensitive are pointed out in the appropriate chapters.

Hyphenated key

Key combinations separated by a hyphen indicate that you press and hold down the first key while you press the second key. For example, Ctrl-Break indicates that you press and hold down the Ctrl key while pressing the Break key.

`Special typeface`

Screen displays and on-screen messages appear in a monospace typeface.

Filespecs

The expression *filespec* is used to indicate the conglomeration of elements that identifies a file or set of files. It can include a drive name, a path, a filename, and/or an extension. The file name and the extension can have *wildcard* characters. In many cases, a drive name alone is sufficient; all files in the current directory of that drive are implied. In other cases, you may find it necessary to include a path, a file name, and perhaps an extension to identify the file(s) you want.

This icon is your cue to "check out" the information presented. These tips usually provide an alternative method of accomplishing a task or a way to make the task easier.

This note icon indicates an interesting fact or subject related to the topic currently being discussed.

As you navigate through the book, this icon acts much like a Yield sign—warning you of potential dangers and sharp curves. Pay close attention to the information presented.

Getting Acquainted

Includes

Getting Acquainted with Your System

Getting Acquainted with DOS

How DOS Organizes Data

Setting Up Your System

Getting Acquainted with Your System

1

Introduction

Your personal computer system isn't just hardware; it also is the software that makes the system work for you, the data it processes, the media where it stores information, and, most important of all, you.

Your Hardware

Hardware refers to the physical pieces of your system: at the very least, the system unit, monitor, and keyboard. You probably also have a mouse and printer and maybe a few bells and whistles.

The System Unit

The *system unit* houses the heart of your computer. This unit is where the microprocessor chip, disk drives, and the power supply are located. IBM personal computers and their clones are made to be opened by their owners, so feel free to take the case off but don't touch or remove anything unless you know exactly what you're doing.

To open your system unit, unplug it (very important), remove the screws around the outside edge of the back panel, and slide the entire case forward. Figure 1.1 shows the insides of a typical system unit.

Figure 1.1.
The system unit from the inside.

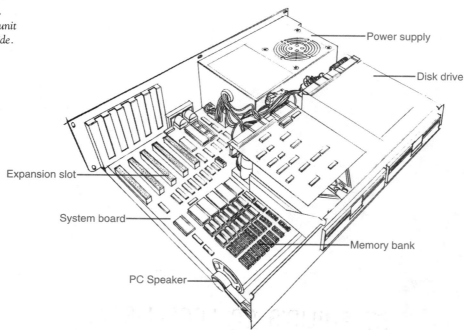

Power supply

Disk drive

Expansion slot

System board

Memory bank

PC Speaker

While the case is open, vacuum or blow out the dust.

Inside, you see the system board, the power supply, some expansion boards, the disk drives, and lots of ribbon cables. The system board is the large circuit card that everything else plugs into. It holds the microprocessor module, banks of memory chips, maybe some other chips, and all the circuitry to connect them.

The Microprocessor

The *microprocessor* provides the brains of your computer, an amazing conglomeration of electronic circuits microminiaturized into a single silicon chip. The microprocessor executes the program commands that make up a word processor, a CAD/CAM system, a solitaire game, and the many other programs that run on your computer. You usually can't see the chip because it is encased in a plastic module that plugs into the system board. You should be able to see the module on your system board—probably near the center. Figure 1.2 shows what the newer modules look like.

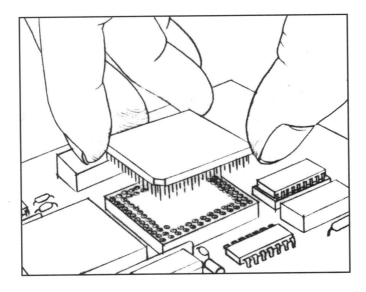

Figure 1.2.
A microprocessor module.

The terms *286*, *386*, and so on, refer to the type of microprocessor your system contains. The original IBM PCs and XTs and their clones featured Intel Corporation's 8088 microprocessor. ATs use the 80286 chip, known familiarly as the *286*. Newer machines contain 386 or 486 chips; by the time you read this book, the next generation may have entered the marketplace. Each new microprocessor more than doubles the capacity and speed of its predecessor. Suffixes such as the *SX* in *386SX* indicate variations of the chip's basic architecture.

Coprocessor

Your system also might have a mathematics coprocessor. The coprocessor handles math better than the main processor does, significantly speeding up programs that must do a lot of heavy calculating. Surprisingly, spreadsheets and scientific calculators aren't the only beneficiaries. A great deal of math is required to control margins, to manage fonts, to position the cursor in a drawing or document, to zoom in and out of a drawing, and so on. Programs such as word processors, desktop publishers, and graphic developers may speed up noticeably when you install a coprocessor—if they're designed to use that coprocessor.

Memory

Your *memory* component stores the programs and data currently in use. This component provides short-term, high-speed storage closely linked to the microprocessor for fast retrieval. However, most memory requires a constant supply of electricity to hold data. When the computer's power goes out, intentionally or accidentally, the memory component drops its data. This data loss also happens when you reboot DOS, even if you don't turn the power off to do so.

Many people find memory the most confusing component in their computer system—both to understand and to control. Chapters 30 and 31 explain in detail terms such as *RAM*, *ROM*, *extended memory*, and *expanded memory*. These chapters also show you how to get the most out of your system's memory with DOS.

Buses

In computer terms, a *bus* is a circuit that carries data from one component to another. For example, a bus transfers data between memory and the microprocessor. Even the simplest operations, such as adding two numbers, involve several data transfers, so the size and speed of a computer's buses have enormous impact on the overall speed of the computer.

For example, a 386 has 32-bit architecture, meaning that its basic data storage unit—called a *word*—can hold 32 digits. A full 386 machine (the 386DX) includes 32-bit buses, so data can be transferred a whole word at a time. A 386SX, however, saves money by using 16-bit buses internally, so it takes two trips to transfer a complete word. Therefore, a 386SX is cheaper but slower than a 386DX.

CMOS and Its Battery

The CMOS (*complementary metal-oxide semiconductor*, pronounced "sea-moss") module first appeared in 286s to retain information about the computer's hardware configuration. This information becomes crucial during the startup process, because if the system doesn't know what type of hardware it has, it can't read the disk drives, and it can't load DOS.

Because the CMOS must retain its information when the computer's power goes out, a small battery provides it with constant power. Most new computers have a lithium battery with a life expectancy of several years. When the battery dies, you see CMOS error messages when you try to boot. You can still boot by running your hardware's SETUP program and manually setting the drive types, the date, and the time. Your hardware manuals should tell you how to use the SETUP program; if not, call your dealer or the manufacturer. When you get the battery replaced, your technician may substitute a regular battery pack for the lithium battery. Regular batteries don't last as long, but you can replace them yourself. The CMOS battery also supplies your clock/calendar chip so that the time and date remain current when the power goes out.

Now is a good time to prepare for a CMOS battery failure. Your hard drive is identified by a code number. If you don't know that code number, you can't complete the SETUP program and boot your computer. Write down your code number and attach it to your system unit. If your hardware manual doesn't tell you the number, DOS 6 includes a diagnostic program called MSD that can tell you what it is. Start MSD and look in the disk drive section for the message `CMOS type nnn.`

Jumpers and Dip Switches

Jumpers and dip switches weren't developed just to torture innocent PC owners (see fig. 1.3). They are designed to make your hardware more flexible by reconfiguring it when you change its basic setup. For example, if you add more memory, you may have to reset a dip switch to tell the system how much memory is present. If you change from a lithium battery to a battery pack, you probably have to change a jumper to redirect the circuit to the new power source. You shouldn't change jumpers or dip switches without knowing exactly what you're doing. Your hardware manual probably has instructions on what needs to be done. If you can't figure it out, see your dealer or repair technician.

Figure 1.3.
A jumper (inset)
and a dip switch.

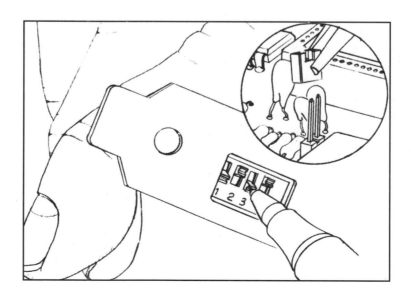

Printers often have dip switches, which are used to select options such as the default font, vertical spacing, and the emulation of a standard printer.

Keyboard

Your keyboard works much like a typewriter, but with some important differences. In addition to the regular typing area, it has function keys, a keypad, and some special-purpose keys.

Function Keys

The function keys are labeled F1, F2, and so on and are located to the left of the typing area or across the top. You may have 10 or 12 of them. Each program uses the function keys for whatever it wants; throughout this book, you will learn what they do in DOS, but they have different functions in Windows, WordPerfect, Lotus 1-2-3, and every other program you use.

With many programs, F1 brings help information to the screen.

The Keypad

The keypad has two functions. When NumLock is on, it works like a 10-key adder. The numbers appear in the uppercase positions on the key caps. When NumLock is off, the keypad becomes a cursor-movement pad. (The *cursor* is the indicator on your monitor screen showing where the next character will be typed.) The cursor movements appear in the lowercase positions on the key caps; only the white keys have cursor-movement functions, but the 5 key has none. What these keys do depends on the program currently in control, but generally, you can count on the up-arrow key moving the cursor toward the top of the screen, the left-arrow key moving the cursor to the left, and so on. The gray keys on the keypad have only one function, which works whether NumLock is on or off.

Extra Cursor Keys

An enhanced keyboard (often called a 101-key or 102-key keyboard) has an extra set of cursor-movement keys so that you can leave the keypad locked in the numeric position. Again, the meaning of these keys, and whether or not they duplicate the functions of the keypad keys, depends on the program with which you are working.

The Locking Keys

Your keyboard has three locking keys: NumLock, ScrollLock, and CapsLock. *NumLock* locks the keypad into uppercase (numerics) or lowercase (cursor movement) functions. *ScrollLock* has no function with most software. *CapsLock* locks the letter keys into uppercase (capitals). Unlike Shift Lock on a regular typewriter, CapsLock has no effect on number or symbol keys (or any other keys).

A locking key is a *toggle* key; press this key once to turn it on. It stays on until you press it again.

The Shifting Keys

Your keyboard has three shifting keys—Shift, Ctrl, and Alt—that produce no characters of their own but which alter the function of other keys. For example, in a word processing program, the unshifted G key probably types the lowercase letter "g." If you press Shift with G, which is written as Shift-G, an uppercase "G" probably results. Ctrl-G may have some other function, as may Alt-G, Shift-Ctrl-G, Shift-Alt-G, Ctrl-Alt-G, and Shift-Ctrl-Alt-G. Using various combinations of the shifting keys, a program can assign eight different functions to one key.

The Shift key generally reverses the effect of a locking key. If CapsLock is on for a word processor, the unshifted G key probably types an uppercase "G," and Shift-G types a lowercase "g." The same is true for the keypad; if it's set for numeric functions, Shift produces the cursor functions and vice versa.

In many programs, Shift-Tab tabs backwards, to the preceding tab stop or column.

Special-Purpose Keys

Several of your keyboard keys have special purposes for your system. The *Pause* key generally interrupts the current program until you press any other key, at which time the program continues where it left off. The same key, when pressed with Ctrl, generates a Break signal that kills the current program (although in many programs, you can't do this). The PrintScreen key (which may be Shift-PrintScreen on your keyboard) generally prints whatever is on your screen, although it may have trouble if your screen is currently in graphics mode. The *Esc* key generally cancels whatever is happening without actually killing the current program.

The Typematic Feature

The character and cursor-movement keys repeat themselves if you hold them down. For example, you can type a row of asterisks by holding down the * key. Some programs, such as Windows and DOS, enable you to adjust how long you have to hold a key down before it starts repeating, and how fast it repeats.

Your Mouse

Your keyboard enables you to interact with all programs, but graphical programs such as Windows also work with a mouse. A mouse enables you to accomplish functions visually instead of verbally. You point to the thing you want to do and click a button. You actually can grab an object and drag it around on-screen. It's often faster and easier to accomplish tasks using a mouse.

Your mouse comes with a vocabulary of its own:

- **Pointer**. The graphic symbol on your screen that indicates where the mouse is; the pointer moves as you move the mouse. Each program decides what symbols to use as mouse pointers. To point at an object, move the pointer close to or on top of the object.

- **Click**. To click, you press and release a mouse button without moving the mouse. Generally, you click the left button, but some functions need the right button or both buttons together. To click an object, point to it and click.

- **Double-click**. To double-click, you click twice in rapid succession without moving the mouse. Many programs enable you to define how rapidly you have to click to send a double-click instead of two individual clicks.

- **Drag**. To drag an object, you point at the object and press and hold down the appropriate mouse button while you move the mouse so that the object also moves. When the object reaches the desired new location, you release the mouse button to drop it there. (This technique also is called *drag-and-drop*.)

Software

The term *software* refers to programs, without which your computer would be a large lump gathering dust in the corner. Two primary categories of software exist: system and application. The difference between them lies in whether they solve a problem within the computer system or in the external, work-a-day world of the user.

System Software

System software controls your computer system and its resources: memory, the disk drives, and the microprocessor. System software includes operating systems such as DOS, shells such as Windows, device drivers, and *utilities*—separate programs that help you manage your system. The DOS package includes dozens of utilities to do such things as format disks, manage disk directories, copy files, and print files.

Application Software

Application software turns your computer into a work tool. Application software includes programs such as word processors, spreadsheets, and database managers. An application program helps you *apply* your computer system to problems outside the computer.

You may occasionally hear the term *firmware*—system software built into the computer so that it becomes an integral part of the hardware. Most software comes and goes as needed, residing permanently only on disk. Firmware, however, is always present in the computer, usually because it provides such basic system functions as reading the keyboard.

Your Disks

You use disks for permanent storage of your programs and data. You keep the programs and data you use most often on your hard disk because it is fast and holds a lot more data than a floppy disk. Floppy disks generally are used for transferring data between two computers—for example, when you buy a software package and for long-term, off-line storage.

DOS assigns single-letter names to your disk drives. Your first floppy drive is called A. If you have a second floppy drive, it's called B; otherwise, drive A also is called drive B. Your first hard drive is C. Additional hard drives are named D, E, and so on. Other types of drives, such as RAM drives and network drives, receive higher letters. In commands, you often have to put a colon after a drive name to distinguish it from some other type of name. For example, to format the floppy disk in drive A, you must enter the following command:

FORMAT A:

Whether it's a hard disk, a floppy, or something in-between (such as a floptical diskette or a Bernoulli box), a computer disk consists of a round platter that spins, much like an audio disk. It uses magnetic technology to record data in concentric circles called *tracks*.

Each recording surface on the disk has its own read-write head. The arm that holds the head moves back and forth over the surface of the disk to locate a desired track. Then the disk drive waits for the desired area to spin under the head and reads or writes the data as appropriate. Because the disk spins so fast, the drive can't read or write just one character or one number, so it divides the tracks into *sectors* and reads or writes one sector at a time. The disks in common use today have 512-byte sectors.

Not all of the disk can store data; some of the disk must hold system information. Every sector has an *address*, which is a number that identifies it. Each sector address appears in an area preceding the sector; the drive hardware reads the sector addresses to locate the sector it wants.

Also stored with the sector address is a special value called a CRC (which stands for *cyclic redundancy check*) that helps to validate the data in the sector. When it writes data in a sector, the drive controller performs a special calculation on the data to arrive at the CRC value, which it stores with the sector address. When the drive controller reads a sector, it recalculates the CRC value and compares it to the stored one. If they don't match, the drive controller knows that something is wrong with the data and refuses to use it; you see an error message on your monitor when this happens.

Disk data goes bad for a variety of reasons. A disk could have manufacturing defects that were too slight to be detected and blocked out during formatting; such defects sometimes crop up after DOS has stored data on the disk. In addition, the magnetic spots that represent the data sometimes begin to drift after a while; if they drift far enough, the data can no longer be read. But the most common cause of data loss on disks is mishandling by users. You can protect your disks by following these sensible guidelines:

- Never expose them to magnetism; you must avoid not only those obvious magnets attached to your refrigerator but also audio speakers, telephone receivers, most screwdrivers, magnetic paper clip holders, and even electrical wires.

- Keep your computer and its disks in a clean environment. Dust, smoke, and other ambient particles can prevent a drive from reading a disk.

- Keep disks cool and dry.

- Never touch the recording surface.

- For a 5.25-inch floppy, don't write on the stick-on label after attaching it to the disk. Also, don't bend it.

Your Data

Whether it's a doctoral dissertation, a client database, a five-year plan, or the great American novel, your data is one of the most crucial parts of your system. The hardware, software, and media can be replaced. But it could be very difficult, if not impossible, to replace your data unless you keep a good system of backup copies, as explained in Chapter 24.

You probably have heard the terms *bits* and *bytes*. *Bit* stands for "binary digit," which is the way computers represent data internally. A binary digit can have only two values, 0 and 1, so it can be represented in a computer by a magnetized or demagnetized spot on a disk, an electric pulse or no pulse in a circuit, and so on.

To create meaningful data out of 1s and 0s, eight bits are grouped into a *byte*. When a byte is used to store numeric data, it can handle any value between 0 (binary 00000000) and 255 (binary 11111111); bytes are grouped together to represent larger numbers. When a byte is used to store character data, it can hold one character. Your personal computer uses the American Standard Code for Information Interchange (ASCII, which is pronounced ASK-key) to represent characters as binary bytes. For example, the binary number 01111001 represents a lowercase "y" in ASCII.

ASCII code is based on 7 bits, not 8. The high-order bit (on the left) is always 0, so only 128 characters are possible in ASCII code. All the lowercase and uppercase letters in the American English alphabet, the 10 digits, and a collection of symbols (such as the period and the comma) are included in the 128 characters. Today's word processors and other text-based software need more characters, and they assign values to the remaining 128 byte values, the ones from 10000000 to 11111111. The problem is, those *extended* characters aren't standardized, so one program may treat 10001010 as an ë, and another may treat it as an ç. In fact, the same program may interpret it differently depending on which font is in use.

The capacity of a computer's disks or memory is expressed in kilobytes, megabytes, and gigabytes. In the outside world, *kilo* means 1,000, but in computers, where everything must be based on powers of 2, it means 1,024 (that's 2^{10}). So a 360K disk holds 368,640 bytes. A megabyte is 1,024 kilobytes or 1,048,576 bytes, so an 80M hard disk holds 83,886,080 bytes. A gigabyte is 1,024 megabytes or 1,073,741,824 bytes, so 4 gigabytes of memory holds 4,294,967,296 bytes. For convenience's sake, you can think of a kilobyte as a thousand bytes, a megabyte as a million bytes, and a gigabyte as a billion bytes. In the near future, you may be measuring memory in terabytes, which is more than a trillion bytes.

The User

In general terms, the person who operates a personal computer is referred to as the *user*—that's you. The rest of your system depends on you to tell it what to do and when to do it. The real purpose of this book is to help you make intelligent decisions about managing your hardware, software, data, and storage media. The key to doing that lies in understanding how your system works, what can go wrong, how you can use the tools that DOS provides to prevent problems as well as to recover from them, and occasionally, when to turn to outside sources for help.

Getting Acquainted with DOS

2

Introduction

The better you understand DOS, the more control you will have over your computer.

What Is DOS?

An operating system makes it possible for you to use your computer. It provides the interface between you, the hardware, and the software. The Disk Operating System (DOS) was developed by IBM and Microsoft for the original IBM PC computers. Throughout the last 10 years or so, as the IBM personal computers and their clones have evolved into today's 386 and 486 machines, DOS has grown along with them. The latest version of DOS, called DOS 6, is much more sophisticated and powerful than the original DOS, but it also is a lot easier to use.

DOS has three main functions: it manages your system's resources (such as memory and the disks); it provides the interface through which you interact with your computer; and it enables you to manage your system.

What Does DOS Do?

As soon as you boot, DOS seizes control of every part of your system except one. You, the user, are in control of DOS.

Two User Interfaces

Take a look at how you interact with and control DOS. You can choose between two methods: the traditional DOS command prompt and DOS Shell.

The Command Prompt

The command prompt has been around since DOS 1, and it has more than its share of shortcomings—both major and minor. However, many people still prefer to work at the DOS command prompt. Figure 2.1 shows an example of a command prompt interaction. DOS displays the command prompt—a brief message saying, in effect, "I'm ready for your next command." In the figure, the user entered a command requesting a listing of the files on drive A, and DOS invoked the DIR program to display the listing. Then DOS displayed the next command prompt.

Command prompt

```
C:\>DIR A:          Command
    Volume in drive A has no label
    Volume Serial Number is 252B-0FEA
    Directory of A:\

SACK-EGA SEC     37178 12-24-91   8:54p
SACK-TDY SEC     50784 12-24-91   8:54p
DEMO         <DIR>      02-23-93  10:37p      Result of command
        3 file(s)        87962 bytes
                        908800 bytes free

C:\>
    Next command prompt
```

Figure 2.1.
*Sample command
prompt interaction.*

For many people, the major problem with the command prompt lies with the commands. Intelligence in software is often measured buy its capability to comprehend free-form language, and by that standard DOS is pretty dumb. You must speak to it in much the same way as you would a well-trained dog—with a limited vocabulary and a strict syntax. For example, the command in figure 2.1 would have failed if the user had said LIST or SHOW DIR or even DIRECTORY instead of DIR. It also would have produced a different result if the user had omitted the colon after the A.

It's easy to get commands wrong, and even experienced users have to look up commands they don't work with every day. DOS 6 includes an on-line help system so that you can look up commands without leaving your computer.

If you can't find the information you want from DOS, a complete command reference is located at the back of this book.

Another major problem with the command prompt is that DOS doesn't always provide as much feedback as you would like. The following is another sample command interaction in which a user asks DOS to delete all files ending in BAK:

```
C:\>DEL *.BAK
C:\>
```

DOS erased the files but displayed no message about how many files were erased, what their names were, whether any BAK file couldn't be erased, and so on. Even a simple "Done" would be better than absolutely nothing. You get much better feedback from the other user interface, the DOS Shell.

DOS Shell

The last few years have witnessed the growth in popularity of graphic user interfaces (GUI), which are oriented more toward the mouse than the keyboard. Instead of typing a command, you choose it from a menu. You can examine a directory and click the files with which you want to work. When you delete them, you see the files disappear from the list. When you move or copy files, you see the results on your screen. Many actions can be done without even using a menu. You can drag files around on-screen to accomplish your work. These types of actions are more natural for most people than entering commands with a strict vocabulary and syntax.

DOS first introduced its graphic user interface—called the DOS Shell—with DOS 4. The Shell was significantly improved with DOS 5; DOS 6 made no major changes to it. Figure 2.2 shows an example of the DOS Shell screen. You can see the drive list, directory tree, and file list. The menus are at the top; you have to pull them down to select commands. At the bottom are more commands that enable you to start up programs by clicking them.

Figure 2.2.
Sample DOS Shell screen.

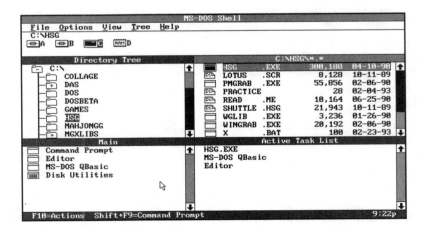

At the command prompt, you can execute only one command at a time. The next command prompt doesn't appear until the preceding program terminates (except for memory-resident programs, which are in a class of their own). In DOS Shell, you can launch several programs and switch back and forth among them; this technique is called *task swapping*. Notice the Active Task List in the lower right corner of figure 2.2. It shows that three programs are currently loaded: HSG.EXE, MS-DOS QBasic, and Editor.

An example should help to explain why you would want to swap tasks. Suppose that you are working on a document with your word processor when you realize you need some information from a spreadsheet.

If you are working at the command prompt, where task swapping is not available:

1. Exit your word processor (being sure to save the document).

2. Open the spreadsheet program.

3. Open the desired worksheet.

4. Find the needed data and copy it by hand.

5. Close the spreadsheet.

6. Open the word processor.

7. Open the document.

8. Find your former place in the document.

9. Enter the data from the spreadsheet.

Now suppose that you're working in DOS Shell with task swapping. The task is much simpler and faster:

1. Switch from the word processor to the DOS Shell screen. (Leave the word processor running and the document open.)

2. Start up the spreadsheet program.

3. Open the desired worksheet.

4. Find the needed data and copy it by hand.

5. Switch back to the word processor; you'll return to the same place in the same document you left.

6. Enter the spreadsheet data.

Now that the spreadsheet is open, the next time you want to consult it, it is even easier:

1. Switch directly from the word processor to the open worksheet. (You don't have to go through the Shell screen.)

2. Find the desired data and copy it by hand.

3. Switch back to the word processor document.

4. Enter the spreadsheet data.

Many people who have been using DOS since its early days prefer the command prompt because they are used to it. However, new users will find the Shell much easier to learn and use, at least at first. As you become more familiar with DOS, however, you'll find yourself learning more and more commands, because you have a lot more control over DOS when you can use its commands. This book shows you how to use both the Shell (in the early chapters) and the command prompt (in the later chapters).

DOS Features

DOS provides facilities to help you with the tasks you must do every day, such as manage files, as well as the less common tasks that you may have to do when trouble develops in your system.

Entering Commands

When you're working at the command prompt, DOS helps you out in many ways:

- The DOSKEY program enables you to record, recall, and edit all your commands rather than having to type everything from scratch. In addition, this program enables you to turn complex commands into easy ones.

- You can display documentation on your monitor to help you with command usage and syntax.

- You can design your own command prompt.

- If a command produces so much output that it won't fit on one screen, you can break it into pages.

- You can redirect command messages from the screen to a file, a printer, or someplace else. You can even feed it to another command as input.

- You can cause a command to be repeated for a set of files.

Disk and Data Management

One of DOS's major functions is to manage your disks so that all programs use the same storage techniques on all disks and a well-coordinated system results. Any software that runs under DOS doesn't read or write on your disks directly; the software asks DOS to do it. Most of the time, you aren't even aware that DOS is doing this for you—it works behind the scenes.

Most of the time, you access your disk files through your favorite applications, such as your word processor or database manager. However, DOS gives you a lot of facilities that most applications don't:

- It provides several commands to manage disks. For example, you can prepare a new disk for use with the FORMAT program and make a backup copy of a complete floppy disk with the DISKCOPY program.

- DOS uses a system of directories to track where files are stored on the disks. You can create and manage directories with such commands as MD (make a directory), DIR (display a directory), and RD (remove a directory).

- Perhaps the largest category of DOS commands helps you manage your files. You can copy them, view them, print them, delete them, and sort them. An editor (called EDIT) enables you to create and edit simple files.

- In case you lose track of a file, which happens more than you may think, especially with a large hard disk, you can search for it by name or by its contents.

Protecting and Recovering Your Data

Literally millions of people have used personal computers in the past 10 years or so, and they have discovered literally hundreds of ways to lose data. Some methods are quite easy, such as deleting the wrong files; others take real dedication. One friend's kid decided to drop a few coins in that interesting looking slot in Daddy's new computer; another friend tried to remove the label from a 5.25-inch disk with a razor blade; and another friend put a valuable disk exactly where she would find it in the morning—attached to the refrigerator with a magnet.

User mistakes are not the only way to lose data. Hardware and media malfunctions probably account for most problems, and viruses are gaining in (un)popularity.

Every new version of DOS adds a few new facilities to help you protect your data against loss and to recover it when that becomes necessary. DOS 6 now includes the following facilities:

- You can preserve information about deleted files for a few days so that you can undelete them (get them back) if you change your mind.

- Microsoft Anti-Virus detects and removes computer viruses, hopefully before they have time to do any damage.

- Every disk must be formatted before you use it, but sometimes you accidentally format a disk that already contains data. You can unformat disks to recover the former data on them.

- You can write-protect individual files to prevent them from being changed or deleted.

- You can hide files so that others can't see them in your directory lists.

- If bad data gets into a disk's directories and tables, DOS can't find some files even though the files are perfectly fine. The CHKDSK program can identify and fix such problems.

- Perhaps most important of all (because you can't possibly prevent all data loss), DOS 6 makes it easy for you to make backup copies of your important files. If you do this regularly, you can recover from any loss, including having your entire computer stolen or melted in a fire.

> DOS gives you the tools to protect your data, but it's up to you to use them. This book shows you how.

Memory Management

Memory is another area where DOS is always at work behind the scenes, controlling access to the lowest portion of memory, called *conventional memory*, where your programs run. DOS also can control other areas of memory in 286 and higher machines. DOS 6 includes commands and facilities to do the following:

- Manage the memory area beyond conventional memory.

- Load software into parts of memory that were once reserved for system use only; this practice gives you a lot more room in conventional memory.

- Display reports on your current memory usage and availability.

- Configure your system to get the most out of the memory space you have.

System Efficiency

DOS includes several features to make your system run faster and to give yourself more disk space:

- DOS's DEFRAG program reorganizes your disk data for the fastest possible access. You should run DEFRAG regularly to keep your hard disk in tip-top shape.

- You can create RAM drives that work much faster than real drives. A RAM drive uses a memory area to simulate a disk drive—without any moving parts.

- DOS's DoubleSpace facility compresses the data on a disk so that you can store nearly twice the normal capacity. For example, if you have a 40M hard disk, you may be able to store 80M or more on it.

- DOS's SmartDrive program duplicates disk data in memory so that DOS can read and write in memory instead of the disk. This duplication makes all your programs run faster because they aren't impeded by the relative slowness of the disk drive.

The Batch Facility

DOS enables you to create your own programs, called *batch programs*, by combining DOS commands. You don't have to be a programmer to write batch programs; many people who know absolutely nothing about real programming write batch programs.

You can use any commands in a batch program; in addition, DOS provides several special commands:

- You can test a condition (such as whether the AUTOEXEC.BAT file exists) and decide what command to execute next based on the result.

- You can display messages to the user.

- You can read a character from the keyboard and decide what to do next, based on what the user typed.

Hardware Management

DOS also is responsible for most interactions with your hardware. Many applications do not access your keyboard, monitor, or printer directly but ask DOS to do it for them. (This is not a hard and fast rule, however.)

DOS interacts with hardware through *device drivers*, programs that actually control the devices. For example, when a program wants to print a line on the printer, the printer driver adds in the codes that position the print head, select the font, print the data, and so on. Drivers make DOS more flexible in the types of hardware it can access. If hardware management was built into DOS, the operating system would be able to handle only those printers, monitors, and keyboards already built into the operating system. By using drivers instead, DOS can access any piece of hardware for which you have a driver.

DOS comes with basic drivers for keyboards, printers, and monitors. Your other hardware should supply its own drivers (and hopefully instructions on how to install them).

DOS gives you the ability to do the following:

- Install device drivers as part of the boot process.

- Control the communications settings (baud rate, etc.) on your serial port.

- Set up your hardware to display and print non-English characters, such as ñ.

- Use a device other than the keyboard-monitor combination to communicate between the user and DOS.

- Fine-tune a variety of hardware settings for the best system performance.

Miscellaneous Services

DOS includes a variety of other facilities:

- DOS includes features that make installing DOS 6 easy; you can even uninstall the operating system if it doesn't work out for you.

- You may have some software designed for an earlier version of DOS that refuses to run with DOS 6. You can set up DOS 6 to lie about its version number to such programs.

- You can set the system date and time through DOS.

- The POWER program preserves your laptop's battery.

What's New in DOS 6?

If you're already familiar with DOS 5, you may be curious as to what's new in DOS 6. The basics of DOS have stayed the same. DOS 6 adds a handful of new utilities to make your job easier:

- **DoubleSpace**. Compresses data so that you can squeeze nearly twice as much onto a disk.

- **INTERLNK**. Enables you to hook up two computers with a cable and copy files directly from one to the other.

- **Anti-Virus**. Detects and removes viruses from your system. (A DOS and a Windows version are included in the DOS 6 package.)

- **MEMMAKER**. Makes loading drivers and TSRs into upper memory blocks easier. Essentially, it does all the decision-making for you.

- **DEFRAG**. Reorganizes a disk to eliminate file fragmentation.

- **POWER**. Saves battery power in your laptop.

In addition to the new utilities, DOS has improved a number of older ones:

- **BACKUP**. The old DOS BACKUP program has been completely replaced with a new, graphic facility that has many more features and is a lot easier to work with. A DOS version and a Windows version of the backup program are included in DOS 6. (The old RESTORE is still available so that you can restore from backups you made in an earlier version of DOS.)

- **UNDELETE**. DOS 6's UNDELETE includes Delete Sentry, which preserves deleted files for a few days. This safety feature makes it much easier to recover files accurately. DOS and Windows versions of UNDELETE are included in DOS 6.

- **DEVICEHIGH and LOADHIGH**. These two commands now include switches that enable you to control exactly where a TSR is loaded in upper memory. The new MEMMAKER program determines the best location for each TSR and creates the DEVICEHIGH and LOADHIGH commands for you.

- **On-line command help**. A completely new command help utility provides complete on-line documentation for DOS commands (not just the format summaries that DOS 5 provided).

How DOS Organizes Data

3

Introduction

When you know how DOS organizes data on disks, you have a better chance of working with it instead of fighting it.

Files

W hen you want to store something on a disk, you have to place it in a *file*. A file is somewhat like a piece of paper in a file folder. It might contain a letter, a database, a spreadsheet, a graphic, a chapter, a program, a font, or some other item.

Filespecs

In DOS, every file must have a file name up to eight characters long. You can use letters, digits, and the following symbols:

　_ ^ $ ~ ! # % & - { } ( ) @ ' '

DOS does not see any difference between uppercase and lowercase letters. The names TechData, TECHDATA, and techdata are all the same; DOS stores the name as TECHDATA no matter how you type it.

> The following special file names are reserved for DOS's use: CLOCK$, CON, AUX, COM1 through COM4, LPT1 through LPT3, NUL, and PRN.

The 8-character file name is just part of a *filespec* (an abbreviation for "file specifier"). The filespec also can have an *extension* of up to three letters, which is connected to the file name by a dot, as in TECHDATA.JUN or DESIGN.1. It's common practice, but not a requirement, to use extensions to identify file types. Microsoft Word, for example, adds the extension DOC to every document file it creates, DOS uses TXT for ASCII files, and HotShot Graphics uses HSG for its graphics files.

Life is less complicated if you avoid using your application's extensions for other files. If you use Microsoft Word, for example, you shouldn't use the DOC extension for files you create with DOS's EDIT program, because Microsoft Word incorrectly will include them in its list of available files.

DOS attaches special meaning to the following extensions, and you would be wise to avoid using them for other types of files:

COM	One type of executable program file
EXE	Another type of executable program file
BIN	Another type of executable program file
SYS	One type of device driver
BAT	A batch program file

Global Filespecs

When you want to access a specific file, you reference it by its filespec. The filespec TECHDATA.JUN, for example, refers to just one file. But sometimes it's convenient to process a whole group of related files, and you can often do this by using a *global filespec*. A global filespec contains *wildcard characters* that stand for any other characters. The DOS wildcard characters are ? and *.

The ? Wildcard

The ? character matches any single character except a blank. The global filespec TR?CK, for example, matches TRACK, TRICK, and TRUCK, but not TRCK or TRUELUCK. Note that it also doesn't match TRACK.100, TRICK.DAT, or any other filespec with an extension, because TR?CK specifies no extension. TRACK.?00 matches TRACK.000 through TRACK.900 along with names such as TRACK.A00 and TRACK.$00.

When the question mark comes at the *end* of the file name or extension, it also matches a blank. The global filespec GRAD?, for example, matches GRAD as well as GRADE and GRADY. VORP.NL? matches VORP.NLA, VORP.NLX, and VORP.NL.

You can use more than one question mark in a global filespec. The name ?ART??.?? matches any filespec containing ART in the second, third, and fourth character positions, up to two more characters in the file name itself, and up to two characters in the extension. ?ART??.?? will match PART1, CARTER.JE, and MART.T but not ARTS.23, DEPART, PARTINGS.1, or MART.DAT.

Suppose that you want to delete all your chapter files from the disk. They all start with CHAP and are followed by one or two digits and the DOC extension (as in CHAP1.DOC through CHAP15.DOC). You can use the global filespec CHAP??.DOC in the deletion command.

A global filespec like this one can access files you didn't intend. This filespec, for example, will delete CHAPIN.DOC and CHAP.DOC if they happen to exist.

The * Wildcard

The * wildcard matches any number of characters, including blanks. The global filespec TR* matches TR, TRY, TREK, TRIAD, TRADER, TRUDEAU, and TRIPTALK, but not TRUST.ME, because no extension is specified. The global filespec CHAP01.* matches any file that has CHAP01 as the file name and any extension (including a blank extension).

▶ ▶ ▶ ▶ ▶ ▶ ▶ ▶

The most global filespec of all is * * or ????????.???, which matches every filespec.

You can use up to two asterisks in a global filespec, one in the file name itself and one in the extension. DOS ignores any characters following an asterisk in either part of the filespec. Therefore, RE*.T* is a legitimate global filespec, but *RE*.TMP is not. In fact (and unfortunately), there's no direct way in DOS to specify a global filespec containing the letters RE (for example) anywhere in the name.

Suppose that you want to delete all files starting with CHAP in the current directory, with any extension. You can use the global filespec CHAP*.* in your deletion command.

Once again, be aware that this filespec may delete more files than you intended.

Attributes

Every file has four attributes: read-only, hidden, system, and archive. These attributes control how DOS and other programs access the files.

Do not trust attributes alone to protect your files from accidental or malicious damage. Many programs ignore or override the attributes. Furthermore, anyone who knows DOS basics knows how to change a file's attributes.

Read-Only

When the *read-only* attribute is turned on, the file should not be modified or deleted. Most of the DOS utilities display an `Access denied` message if you try to modify or delete a file with a positive read-only attribute. (You will see some exceptions later in this book.) Most other programs also respect the read-only attribute, but you should be aware that some programs don't.

Even though the read-only attribute can't do much when someone wants to damage a file on purpose, it is good protection against accidental erasure. The DOS DEL command, for example, refuses to erase a read-only file, and the DOS COPY command refuses to overwrite it with another file.

Hidden

A positive *hidden* attribute means that a program should ignore the file when looking for files to process. The DIR command, for example, normally will not list a hidden file (but you can override that). The DEL command will not delete a hidden file because it can't "see" it; you get a `File not found` message instead. Only the most uninformed DOS users, however, will be unable to find a file simply because it is hidden. Here again, the attribute is mostly a protection against accident rather than maliciousness.

System

The *system* attribute combines the read-only and hidden attributes; a system file normally can't be modified or erased, and normally it can't be "seen" by programs when searching for files.

Not too many people use the system attribute. In fact, until DOS 5, you couldn't control the attribute yourself, because Microsoft saw no need for ordinary users to do that. DOS's primary program files, IO.SYS and MSDOS.SYS, which must reside in specific locations on a boot disk for DOS to work, have the system attribute. Other system programs may have a few system files; very few applications need to protect their files this way.

Archive

The *archive* attribute indicates that a file has been modified since the last time you made back-up copies. This attribute signifies that the file needs to be backed up (archived). DOS's BACKUP program, and most other back-up programs, can se-lect files to be backed up based on their archive attributes. They turn the archive attribute off after making a back-up copy because now the file doesn't need to be archived.

DOS automatically turns a file's archive attribute on when it creates the file or modifies it in any way. Both these actions mean that the file needs to be archived in the next back-up cycle. You also can turn a file's archive attribute on and off manu-ally to control whether the next back-up cycle picks up the file. You may not want to back up your software files, for example, because you have the original disks. When you install software, DOS automatically marks all those new files with the archive attribute. You can remove the archive attributes to avoid including those files in the next back-up run.

Directories

DOS uses directories to keep track of files. A *directory* is somewhat like a telephone book, but instead of name, address, and phone number, each entry contains these items:

File name

Extension

File size

Date last modified

Time last modified

Starting location of the file on the disk

Attributes

DOS uses this information to locate each file. You also can view a directory to see what files it contains. A typical listing looks like this:

```
FLOOD3    DOC      42496  10-06-93    7:52p
FLOOD3    STY        640  10-06-93    7:52p
TREAT     DOC     116608  10-04-93    7:56p
FLOOD1    DOC     140416  10-04-93    8:01p
BUDDY1    DOC      94080  10-02-93    8:15p
ALLBUDDY  SAM     257727  09-30-93    8:36a
```

Each line describes one file. You can see its file name, extension, size (in bytes), and the date and time it was last modified. In a listing of this type, DOS doesn't show you the attributes or the starting location on disk.

The Root Directory

Every disk must have at least one directory, called the *root directory*, which must be located in the first track. DOS installs the root directory when it prepares the disk. The root directory can have a limited number of entries, determined by the size of the disk. On a hard disk, you probably will need more directory space than the root directory permits. The next section explains how you can get that space.

The Directory Tree

You can create your own directories that are *subdirectories* of the root directory. A subdirectory acts something like a file folder; you group related files together in it to keep them separated from other files and to make them relatively easy to find. For example, you may want to create subdirectories on your hard disk for all your major programs: DOS, Windows, your word processing application, your spreadsheet, and so on. You can create as many subdirectories as you want.

A subdirectory also can have subdirectories, which in turn can have subdirectories. Your word processing subdirectory, for example, may have subdirectories for correspondence, artwork, style sheets, the chapters in a report you're working on, and so on.

A disk's entire directory structure looks something like an upside-down tree, with the root directory at the top, branching into a first level of subdirectories, which in turn branch into a second level of subdirectories, and so on. Figure 3.1 shows an example of a disk directory structure. You can see the root directory at the top; its name is always \ (a backslash). DOS assigns this name, and you can't change it. The subdirectories have names just like files do, including an extension if you want.

Figure 3.1.
A sample directory tree.

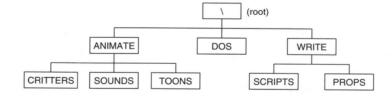

 Subdirectories can have attributes just as files do, but this feature is not used much.

When a directory has subdirectories, the directory is called a *parent*, and the subdirectories are its *children*. In figure 3.1, ANIMATE is the parent of CRITTERS, SOUNDS, and TOONS. They are the children of ANIMATE.

 In general, try to keep your files in subdirectories, not the root directory. Not only is space in the root directory limited, but in some cases the UNFORMAT program can't recover files in the root directory, should that become necessary.

When you list a directory, its subdirectories appear with `<DIR>` in the size column. The date and time show when the directory was created, not when it was last modified. Here's a sample directory listing:

.		`<DIR>`		10-05-93	10:32p
..		`<DIR>`		10-05-93	10:32p
FLOOD3	DOC		42496	10-06-93	7:52p
JULY		`<DIR>`		10-07-93	10:38p
FLOOD3	STY		640	10-06-93	7:52p
TREAT	DOC		116608	10-06-93	7:56p
FLOOD1	DOC		140416	10-06-93	8:01p
BUDDY1	DOC		94080	10-06-93	8:15p
JUNE		`<DIR>`		10-15-93	10:38p

This directory contains five files and four directory entries. JULY and JUNE are its children. The two directory entries at the top appear in every subdirectory to help DOS keep track of the directory tree. The first one, identified by a single period, always refers to this directory itself. The second entry, identified by two periods, always refers to this directory's parent. You can't see the parent directory's real name, but you can see that it was created on October 5, 1993, at 10:32 p.m. What you can't see, but DOS can, are the starting locations for these two directories, which help DOS link the directories together.

You can use the names . and .. to refer to the current directory and its parent, respectively. Sometimes that's easier than typing out the directory's real name.

The Current Directory

Every one of your drives has a *default directory*. This is the directory that DOS accesses if you reference that drive but don't specify which directory to use. If you copy a file to drive A without specifying a directory, for example, DOS copies the file to the default directory on drive A. When you boot, the root directory on each drive becomes the default directory for that drive. But you can make any directory you want the default; you learn how in Chapter 6.

In addition, one drive is always the current drive; DOS accesses this drive when you don't specify another one. If you copy a file to the directory named BACKUPS without specifying the drive, for example, DOS assumes that BACKUPS is on the current drive.

When you boot, the boot drive becomes the current drive, but you can change to any other drive; you learn how in Chapter 6.

The *current directory* is the default directory on the current drive. This is the directory DOS accesses when you specify neither a drive nor a directory. If you enter a command to delete PCLIST.TXT without specifying a drive or directory, for example, DOS looks for it in the current directory.

Usually, the DOS command prompt shows the name of the current directory, so you always know which directory you're about to access. In the DOS Shell, you know the current directory because it's the one that's displayed on-screen.

Path Names

When you want to access a nondefault directory, you must use its *path name*. The path name shows DOS how to get to the desired directory. The path name may include a drive name (if you don't want the current drive) and a series of directory names separated by backslashes. For example, the following expression is the correct path name for the TOONS directory in figure 3.1:

C:\ANIMATE\TOONS

This name tells DOS to go to drive C, start at the root directory (the first backslash), find its child named ANIMATE, and find ANIMATE's child named TOONS. You can omit the C: at the beginning of this path name if C is the current drive.

You also can start a path at the current or default directory instead of the root directory. Suppose that the current directory is C:\, and you want to use the TOONS directory. This path name will do it:

ANIMATE\TOONS

Because the path name doesn't start with a backslash for the root directory, DOS knows to start with the current directory. If the current drive is A and you want to access TOONS on drive C, all you have to do is add the drive name to the path:

C:ANIMATE\TOONS

Here again, because the root directory is not specified as the starting point, DOS starts with the default directory on the specified drive.

Now suppose that TOONS is the current directory and you want to get to CRITTERS. You can start at the root directory, as follows:

\ANIMATE\CRITTERS

But DOS offers you a shortcut. You're allowed to use the .. name to tell DOS to start with the current directory's parent, as in:

..\CRITTERS

Paths in Filespecs

A filespec can include a path name along with the file name and extension to completely identify the location of the desired file. If the current directory is C:\ANIMATE and you want to access the file named NEWBUMPS in A:\SOUNDS, you use this filespec:

A:\SOUNDS\NEWBUMPS

Allocation Units and the File Allocation Table

You have seen that your disk drive divides tracks into sectors and reads and writes one sector at a time. But if DOS had to keep track of every sector in every file on a disk, its system tables would take up more room than the files themselves. To accomplish this task, DOS groups sectors together into *allocation units* (also called *clusters*) and keeps track of the allocation units instead. This helps keep its system tables down to a reasonable size.

The size of an allocation unit depends on the overall size of the disk; DOS decides on the best size when it formats the disk. Disks have one or two sectors per allocation unit. A high-capacity hard drive may have four or more sectors per allocation unit.

Because DOS tracks allocation units instead of sectors, it can't assign part of an allocation unit to a file. It always allocates file space in whole allocation units; that's why they call it an *allocation* unit. Even if a file contains only one byte, DOS gives it a complete allocation unit; the rest of the space in the allocation unit, which is called *slack*, is wasted. But if the file expands, there's plenty of room for it. When the file expands beyond the first allocation unit, DOS assigns it a second complete allocation unit.

Obviously, allocation units waste space, but DOS has to find the best trade-off between wasting space in slack and taking up too much space tracking small allocation units.

The DOS allocation unit system yields some apparent disparities that confuse many DOS users. For example, when you copy a small file (say, 200 bytes) from a disk with 1K allocation units to a hard disk with 4K allocation units, the file's size is still 200 bytes, but it uses up 4K of space on the hard disk. If you try to copy a group of 20 small files whose file sizes add up to less than 1K, you may not have enough space for them on the hard drive, even though it has 40K available.

This section looks at how DOS keeps track of a file's allocation units. Figure 3.2 shows an example of a *file allocation table* (FAT); this is DOS's system table. It contains one entry for every allocation unit on the disk.

Figure 3.2.
A sample file
allocation table.

		EOP	0	0	6	10	EOF
EOF	11	EOF	13	14	15	16	EOF
0	0	BAD	20	21	EOF	23	24
37	0	0	0	0	0	31	32
33	34	35	36	54	38	39	40

Each allocation unit on the drive has a numeric address, from 2 to whatever. The file's directory entry shows the address of the first allocation unit in the file. In the FAT, the entry for that allocation unit shows the address of the next allocation unit. That entry shows the address of the next allocation unit. This pattern continues until you reach the last allocation unit in the file, which contains a special code that means "end-of-file." Because the FAT entries link to each other in chain-like fashion, the set of entries for one file is called a *file chain*.

Suppose that the directory entry for GROWTH92.DB shows that it starts in allocation unit 5. Find allocation unit 5 in the FAT in figure 3.2 (remember that allocation unit numbers start with 2, not 1). You see that it contains a 6, so 6 is the next allocation unit. Allocation unit 6 chains to 10, and 10 chains to 11. Allocation unit 11 shows the end-of-file mark. This file, then, occupies four allocation units. That should be confirmed by the file's actual size, which is stored in the directory entry.

The GROWTH92.DB example also demonstrates a *fragmented* file. Its allocation units are in two chunks, or fragments. DOS frequently fragments files to use up available space on the disk. Fragmentation is especially likely to occur when you expand a file. For example, if you expand GROWTH92.DB so that it needs another allocation unit, it can't expand into allocation unit 12 because that currently belongs to another file. It has to use the next available allocation unit, indicated by a 0 in the FAT entry, in this case allocation unit 15. Thus, another fragment is born.

Many files need only one allocation unit. Suppose that the file named ALLISON.MEM starts in allocation unit 2. In the sample FAT, allocation unit 2 contains the EOF mark; this is the only allocation unit in the file.

Because the FAT is so important to controlling both the files and the empty space on a disk, DOS maintains two identical FATs—one as a backup of the other. Every time you create a new file or expand or contract an existing one, DOS needs to update both FATs. If you interrupt it before it can complete the update, you throw the FATs out of whack, and you may not be able to access your files correctly. To avoid this problem, don't reboot or turn the power off when a drive light is on (unless you want to interrupt a virus at work).

How DOS Deletes a File

When you ask DOS to delete a file, it doesn't erase the file's data from the disk immediately. All it does is put a special delete code in the first character of the file's directory entry and change the file's FAT entries to 0. This makes the directory entry and allocation units available to other files. When you expand another file, it may take up one or more of the released allocation units, destroying that much of the deleted file's data. When you create a new file, it may use the deleted file's directory entry and some of its former allocation units. Eventually, all trace of the former file disappears, but it may take a while. In the meantime, the possibility exists that you can undelete all or part of the file's data. Chapter 27 discusses the DOS UNDELETE facility.

Putting It All Together

Knowing how DOS stores your data can help you make better decisions when you're working at your PC. When creating a set of files, for example, you may want to give them names that fit well in a global filespec, such as MONTH1.DAT through MONTH12.DAT instead of JANUARY.DAT through DECEMBER.DAT. You now know to check the drive lights before shutting off your PC.

You're also better equipped to understand how many of the DOS utilities work. Later chapters discuss programs that undelete files, unformat disks, defragment files, and so on.

Setting Up Your System

4

Introduction

This chapter guides you through the installation process if you are upgrading from an earlier version of DOS.

T his chapter assumes that you are upgrading to DOS 6 from an earlier version of DOS. If you are changing to DOS 6 from OS/2, the procedures you should follow are explained in your user's guide. This chapter also assumes that your boot drive is drive C and that your current version of DOS is installed in the directory named C:\DOS; if not, you need to adapt the various commands shown in the instructions to use your boot drive name and DOS directory name.

The SETUP program needs to make changes to your partition table, to replace your DOS system files, and to add about 4M of data to your boot drive. The program can fail if it can't work with your hard drive accurately or if you are using software that isn't compatible with SETUP (such as an anti-virus monitor that doesn't let programs write to the partition table). The following steps help to prepare your system for SETUP and to protect your current system in case SETUP fails.

1. You can use the installation disks in drive A or B. If you need double-density disks (360K or 720K) instead of high-density, you must send for them using the coupon at the back of the user's guide.

2. Make sure that you have 4M of empty space on your boot drive. If not, delete enough files to make the room. If you can't delete that many files, move some files to floppy disks while you install DOS and then restore the files to the hard drive. (If your boot drive is compressed, the space must be available on the compressed drive, not the host drive.)

3. Back up your boot drive using your current backup program. If you can, back up all files, including program files. If SETUP fails and you need to restore the hard drive, all the files you need will be in one place.

4. Make an emergency startup disk for your current DOS version by formatting a floppy disk in drive A using the following command:

   FORMAT A: /S

This procedure will destroy any data currently on the floppy disk.

5. In case SETUP fails, you need to enter the following commands. These commands copy the files necessary to restore the hard drive:

```
COPY C:\DOS\FDISK.COM A:
COPY C:\DOS\FORMAT.COM A:
COPY C:\DOS\RESTORE.EXE A:
```

Put the emergency startup disk in a safe place; hopefully, you will never have to use it. When DOS 6 is safely installed and running properly, it will no longer be valid as it is set up for your earlier version of DOS.

6. Unless you have compressed your hard drive with a disk compression program, SETUP will create an Uninstall disk that you can use to return to your former DOS version if anything goes wrong. Make sure that you have a blank floppy disk that fits in your drive A. The disk can be unformatted or formatted, but it must not contain any data. (If drive A is a 360K drive, you need two disks.)

If your hard drive is compressed, you can't uninstall DOS 6. Therefore, it is doubly important that you back up your boot drive and make the emergency startup disk described in steps 4 and 5.

7. Disable any program that might try to display a message on-screen while SETUP is running. For example, if you use a pop-up alarm to remind you of appointments, you should turn it off.

8. Disable all disk caching, deletion protection, and anti-virus programs. Programs of this type can prevent SETUP from working properly. (You don't need to disable DOS's SmartDrive.) If your CONFIG.SYS and AUTOEXEC.BAT files load such programs, follow these steps to unload them:

   a. Use an ASCII editor such as DOS 5's EDIT to open C:\CONFIG.SYS for editing. (If you use your word processor, be sure to work on the file in ASCII mode; don't treat it as a document file.)

   b. Insert the word **REM** in front of every command that loads a disk-caching, deletion-protection, or anti-virus program.

   c. Save the file.

   d. Do the same thing in C:\AUTOEXEC.BAT.

e. Exit the editor.

f. Press Ctrl-Alt-Delete to reboot.

Rebooting should remove the indicated programs from memory.

9. Exit DOS Shell or Windows. You must run SETUP from the DOS command prompt.

10. If you use Windows, decide whether you want to install the DOS or Windows versions of UNDELETE, BACKUP, and Anti-Virus. You really need only one version of BACKUP and Anti-Virus, but it makes some sense to install both versions of UNDELETE for the following two reasons:

   - You can do an immediate UNDELETE no matter where you're working; if you're not using Delete Sentry, it's very important not to start up Windows when you need to delete a file.

   - The Windows version has some features that the DOS version doesn't have.

Running SETUP

To start SETUP, insert disk #1 in the appropriate drive and type one of these commands:

A:SETUP

or

B:SETUP

SETUP displays information and instructions on your video screen. After choosing which versions of UNDELETE, BACKUP, and Anti-Virus you want to install, you probably do not have to make any more decisions. However, you do have to insert disks upon request.

If SETUP encounters problems, it probably will ask for the Uninstall disk so that it can restore your former DOS version. The chapter titled "Diagnosing and Solving Problems" in your user's guide includes procedures for dealing with the common SETUP problems. If you can't make SETUP work, contact Microsoft's Product Support Services for help; the user's guide tells you how to contact them.

If SETUP leaves your boot drive in an unusable state, you may need to reformat it and restore its files. This procedure involves running FDISK, FORMAT, and RESTORE. If you followed the recommended procedures in this chapter, you have the necessary data to do that. You probably need to get an experienced DOS user to help you set up your hard disk again.

What Did SETUP Do?

The SETUP program replaced the old files in your C:\DOS directory with the DOS 6 versions. It moved the old files to a directory called OLD_DOS.1; preserving these files enables you to uninstall if you find that necessary. Any files in the C:\DOS directory that were not replaced by DOS 6 were not touched. Any files you happened to store in C:\DOS are unharmed. In addition, some of the older DOS programs that have been dropped from DOS 6, such as RECOVER and ASSIGN, live on in your DOS directory. DOS 6 has dropped these programs for good reason. Most of them were pretty much extinct, replaced by better ones. The RECOVER program caused too many problems; in fact, it had become infamous. When you decide to keep DOS, you might want to delete these files from your C:\DOS directory; you will not need them, and with DOS 6, they are just taking up space.

4201.CPI

4208.CPI

5202.CPI

ASSIGN.COM

COMP.EXE

EDLIN.EXE

EXE2BIN.EXE

GRAFTABL.COM

JOIN.EXE

LCD.CPI

MIRROR.COM

MSHERC.COM

PRINTER.SYS

RECOVER.EXE

SMARTDRV.SYS

Additional Documentation

You will find some TXT files in your DOS directory that supplement the user's guide. You should take a look at each TXT file to see whether it contains anything about your system.

To view TXT files:

1. Enter the following command at the DOS command prompt:

   ```
   DIR C:\DOS\*.TXT /OD
   ```

   This command lists all the TXT files in the DOS directory in chronological order. If any files have a date before October 1992, they are from your earlier DOS version and are no longer pertinent. You can delete or ignore them.

2. Follow these steps for each file that you want to read:

   a. Enter the following command:

   ```
   EDIT C:\DOS\filename.TXT
   ```

   This command opens the file in DOS's editor.

   b. Press PgDn and PgUp to move around in the file.

   c. To print the file, press Alt-F followed by a P. (See Chapter 20 to print just part of the file.)

   d. Press Alt-F, press X, and then press Y to exit the editor.

Scanning for Viruses

As soon as you have DOS 6 up and running, why not take advantage of one of its most powerful new features, Microsoft Anti-Virus? If you have never scanned your system for viruses, you should do so immediately, even if your system is new. (If you have been using another virus program fairly regularly, you can safely skip this section.) You learn how to use Anti-Virus in Chapter 26.

To scan for viruses using the DOS version of Anti-Virus:

1. At the DOS command prompt, type the following command and press Enter:

   ```
   MSAV /L /C /P /F
   ```

   This command causes all your local drives, except for floppy drives, to be scanned for viruses. If any viruses are found, they are removed. A report is displayed at the end.

2. If the report shows that any viruses were detected, shut down your system and read Chapter 26 immediately.

To scan for viruses using the Windows version of Anti-Virus:

1. Start Windows.

2. Open the Microsoft Tools group. The MWAV (Microsoft Windows Anti-Virus) icon should be there.

3. Open the MWAV item. (The Anti-Virus window should open.)

4. Select all your local nonfloppy drives.

5. Press the Detect and Clean button.

6. If any viruses are reported, press the Stop button, exit Anti-Virus, close any other programs that are running, exit Windows, and shut down your system. Read Chapter 26 immediately.

Starting Delete Sentry

DOS 6 includes another new feature that you should install right away. Delete Sentry protects your deleted files for a few days so that you can undelete them easily. Delete Sentry is explained in Chapter 27, but you should set it up now.

To set up Delete Sentry from the DOS command prompt:

1. Type the following command and press Enter:

   ```
   EDIT C:\AUTOEXEC.BAT
   ```

   This command opens the AUTOEXEC.BAT file for editing by DOS's editor.

2. Press the down-arrow key to move the cursor to the first blank line in the file.

3. Type the following command on the blank line:

   ```
   UNDELETE /SC
   ```

   This command starts Delete Sentry to protect drive C. If you have more than one hard drive, add an /Sdrive switch for each one. For example, if you have drives C, D, and E, the command would appear as follows:

   ```
   UNDELETE /SC /SD /SE
   ```

4. Press Alt-F, press X, and then press Y. This keystroke sequence exits the editor and saves the changes in AUTOEXEC.BAT.

5. Remove any disk in drive A and press Ctrl-Alt-Del to reboot your system. Delete Sentry will be installed during booting.

To set up Delete Sentry from Windows:

1. Start Windows.

2. Open the Microsoft Tools group window; the UNDEL icon should be there.

3. Open UNDEL. The Microsoft Undelete window should open.

4. Pull down the Options menu and choose the Configure Delete Protection command. The Configure Delete Protection dialog box opens.

5. Click the Delete Sentry radio button. Then click OK. This procedure opens the Configure Delete Sentry dialog box.

6. Press the Drives button to open the Choose Drives for Delete Sentry dialog box.

7. Select all your hard drives and press OK several times to return to the main Microsoft Undelete window.

8. Exit Undelete. Close any other programs and exit Windows.

9. Remove any disk from drive A and press Ctrl-Alt-Del to reboot DOS. Delete Sentry will be installed during booting.

Now that Delete Sentry is installed, you should find it easy to undelete files if that becomes necessary. Chapters 9 and 27 explain how.

Making an Emergency Startup Disk

Now that DOS 6 is up and running, you need to make an emergency boot disk for DOS 6. You may find it handy some day when your hard drive fails. Follow steps 3 and 4 under "Getting Ready for Installation" earlier in this chapter to make the disk. You could reuse the same disk you used before because you don't need that one any more.

Uninstalling DOS 6

If your hard disk was not compressed, SETUP recorded uninstall information so that you could return to your former DOS version. If you have a program that will not run under DOS 6, you may find it necessary to return to your earlier version while you resolve the problem. (This procedure might involve upgrading the program to a version compatible with DOS 6.)

You can't uninstall DOS 6 if you have repartitioned or reformatted your boot drive, deleted or moved DOS's two system files (MSDOS.SYS and IO.SYS), deleted the OLD_DOS.1 directory, run DELOLDOS, run DoubleSpace, or run a third-party compression program.

To uninstall DOS 6:

1. Insert the Uninstall disk in drive A.

2. Reboot.

3. Follow the instructions on your screen.

DELOLDOS

When you are sure that you want to keep DOS 6, the program named DELOLDOS removes the former version from your hard drive, which will free up several megabytes of space. Enter the following command:

DELOLDOS

After you run DELOLDOS, you can't uninstall DOS 6.

II

DOS Shell

Includes

Working with the Shell

Managing Directories

Selecting Files

Copying and Moving
Files

Deleting and Undeleting
Files

Additional File
Management

Working with Programs

Customizing the Shell

Getting Acquainted with the DOS Shell

5

Introduction

DOS Shell makes working with DOS not only easier but also much more powerful.

The Shell's graphic user interface is almost, but not quite, intuitive.

Why Use the Shell?

DOS Shell is DOS's graphic user interface. It enables you to see the drive and directory you're working with and makes it easy to manage disks, directories, and files as well as to start programs such as the DOS editor or your favorite game. You interact with the Shell by using your mouse or your keyboard, selecting items from lists, choosing commands from menus, and choosing options in dialog boxes. You can even drag files around to move or copy them from one place to another.

The Shell offers a number of features that aren't available at the command prompt. Some of them can be important time savers as well as safety features. For example, the Shell warns you if a copied file is about to overwrite an existing file; you can cancel the copy if you want. As another example, the command prompt's COPY program quits in midstream if a target diskette becomes too full, but the Shell's COPY feature lets you insert another diskette and continue copying without losing your place.

Perhaps the most important Shell innovation is task swapping, which enables you to start several programs at once and switch around among them. This can save you mounds of time and frustration if you need to consult a spreadsheet while working on a document, for example, or to make some room on the hard drive before saving the graphic that you have just spent two hours developing.

Still, you don't really need the Shell if you have a more sophisticated third-party shell such as Norton Desktop for DOS or a true multitasking program such as Windows. If you have one of these programs, you can safely skip to Part III of this book.

Starting the Shell

You start the Shell by typing **DOSSHELL** at the command prompt and pressing the Enter key.

To make DOS Shell start up automatically every time you boot, insert the DOSSHELL command as the *last* command (that's important) in your AUTOEXEC.BAT file. Chapter 21 explains more about AUTOEXEC.BAT and how to insert commands in it.

DOS Shell's Screen and Features

Figure 5.1 shows what DOS Shell's screen looks like the first time you start it up after installing DOS, except the contents of your lists will be different. Someone already may have tailored your screen so that it looks quite different from this example. You learn how to tailor your Shell screen in Chapter 12.

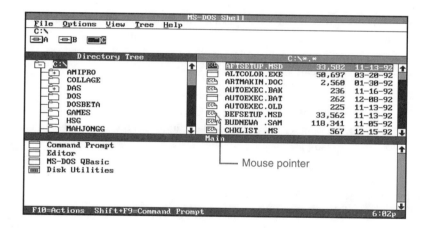

Figure 5.1.
The original DOS Shell Screen.

You can choose from two display modes for the Shell screen: graphics and text. Graphics mode, shown in figure 5.1, includes icons and a graphics mouse pointer (the outline arrow near the center of the screen). Text mode looks plainer; it provides the same information, but the mouse pointer takes the shape of a rectangular block and there are no icons. Dull as it is, text mode may work better on your monitor. You also can vary the number of lines per screen, depending on the capabilities of your monitor. Twenty-five lines are standard, but you can pack a lot more information onto the screen if your monitor can display it clearly.

The *title bar* indicates that you are working with MS-DOS Shell. The *menu bar* offers five pull-down menus: File, Options, View, Tree, and Help. Each menu contains a list of commands you can apply to the directories or files shown on the screen. For example, if you select some files in the file list, choosing the File Delete command deletes those files.

This book shows the name of the menu as the first word of a menu command. That is, File Delete refers to the Delete command on the File menu, and Options File Display Options refers to the File Display Options command on the Options menu.

The *current directory* displays the path name of the currently selected directory—the directory whose files appear in the file list. The current directory is C:\ in figure 5.1.

The *drive list* shows all the disk drives available to you, including RAM drives and logged-on network drives. If you're using DoubleSpace, it shows you both the compressed drive and the host drive. The highlight marks the currently selected drive (C in fig. 5.1). In graphics mode, each icon indicates the drive type. In text mode, drive names appear in square brackets without indicating the drive type.

The *directory tree* displays the directory structure for the selected directory. In the example, you can see that the root directory is C:\, and its children are AMIPRO, COLLAGE, DAS, DOS, and so on. The highlight indicates the current directory, which is C:\ in the example.

In its default status, the directory tree displays only the first level of subdirectories. Directories marked with plus signs (+) have children you can't see. Chapter 6 explains how to display them.

The text mode directory tree looks much like the graphics mode tree except that square brackets appear in place of the file folder icons.

The *file list* shows the files in the currently selected directory. You see an icon in graphics mode that indicates the type of file (program or data), the file name, its size, and the date it was last modified. The highlight marks currently selected files. In the example in figure 5.1, if you choose the File Delete command right now, you will delete the AFTSETUP.MSD file. Text mode displays no icons and indicates selected files with arrowheads.

The *program list* shows programs that you can execute merely by choosing them from this list. You can start the DOS full screen editor, for example, by choosing Editor from the list in figure 5.1. This is often the easiest way to execute a program in DOS.

Maneuvering on the Shell Screen

On the Shell screen, one of these areas is always active: drive list, directory tree, file list, or program list. You activate an area by moving the cursor into it, which highlights its title bar. In the drive list—which doesn't have a title bar—the current drive is highlighted. The active area becomes the focus of any commands you execute; in fact, some menus change their contents as you move the cursor from area to area. For example, the Tree menu disappears when you activate the program list because none of its commands pertain to that area, but it reappears when you activate another area.

The Tab and Shift-Tab keys move the cursor from area to area. Tab cycles through the areas from top to bottom, left to right. Shift-Tab reverses the cycling direction.

To activate an area by using the keyboard, repeatedly press Tab or Shift-Tab until you reach the area you want.

If you use a mouse, you don't really need to activate an area in a separate move. Clicking an item automatically activates its area.

Scrolling Around in Lists

Sometimes a list doesn't fit in the available space, and you have to scroll to see it all. Table 5.1 shows the keys you use for scrolling. If you hold a scrolling key down, it starts repeating so that you scroll "on the run" in the indicated direction.

Table 5.1. Scrolling with the Keyboard

Key	Function
Up-arrow	Scrolls up one line
Down-arrow	Scrolls down one line
Home	Scrolls to the first line

continues

Table 5.1. continued

Key	Function
End	Scrolls to the last line
Page Up	Scrolls up one page
Page Down	Scrolls down one page
character	Scrolls to the next file starting with that character

Scrolling with the mouse requires the scroll bar. The *scroll box* always indicates the position of the current page within the entire list (even when you're scrolling from the keyboard). Holding down the mouse button on the arrow icons or the dark part of the bar scrolls on the run in the indicated direction.

There's a major difference between scrolling with the keyboard and scrolling with the mouse. When you scroll with the keyboard, the cursor moves up or down in the list, changing the item that's selected. But the mouse scrolls the list itself, not the cursor. (If you scroll *up*, the list moves *down* so that you can see more lines at the top.) In fact, the cursor actually disappears from view if you scroll far enough. Scrolling with the mouse never changes the selected item; you must click another item to change the selection. Sometimes you want to change the selection as you scroll; sometimes you don't. After you get used to the difference, you will choose the keyboard or mouse, depending on which is faster for you.

Working with Menus

Figure 5.2 shows an example of a pulled-down menu. You can pull one down by using either the keyboard or the mouse.

There are several ways to pull down a menu when using the keyboard. One of the easiest ways is to press Alt-*initial-letter* (the first letter of the menu name). For example, press Alt-F to pull down the File menu.

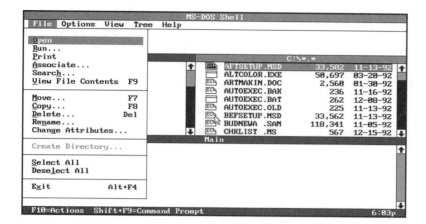

Figure 5.2.
A sample menu.

After a menu is down, you can move to neighboring ones with the right- and left-arrow keys.

To pull down a menu when using a mouse, click the desired name in the menu bar.

Dimmed Commands

Some commands on the menu may appear dimmed (printed in gray). Dimmed commands are not available because some required condition for using them has not been met. In figure 5.2, for example, the Create Directory command appears dimmed because the directory tree isn't active.

To choose a menu command when using a mouse, click the command.

Some commands have hot keys listed next to them; these are keys you can press to execute the command without pulling down the menu. Hot keys often provide the easiest and fastest way to execute a menu command. For example, you can delete files by selecting them in the file list and pressing the Del key.

Hot keys work regardless of whether you pull down the menu first.

61

To choose a menu command by using the keyboard:

1. Type the highlighted letter in the desired command.

or

1. Press the down-arrow and up-arrow keys to highlight the desired command.

2. Press Enter.

Sometimes after you pull down a menu, you realize that you don't want it after all. You can cancel the menu without choosing a command.

To cancel a menu when using the keyboard: Press Esc.

To cancel a menu by using a mouse: Click the menu name again.

> Clicking a blank menu line or anywhere outside the menu cancels the menu, but you may accidentally select something else. That's why it's recommended that you click the same menu name to cancel a menu.

Dialog Boxes

Some menu items conclude with an ellipsis (...). These commands open dialog boxes like the one in figure 5.3 to collect additional information. This particular dialog box appears when you choose Options Display; yours may be somewhat different, depending on your type of monitor.

> Chapter 12 explains the display options. The dialog box used here is an example only.

After a dialog box opens, you must respond to it. You can't pull down any menus, select items from the main Shell screen, or perform any other actions until you complete or cancel the dialog box. (However, you can ask for help information about the dialog box.)

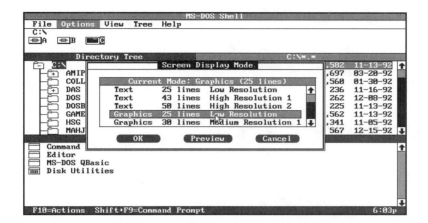

Figure 5.3.
A sample
dialog box.

Command Buttons

Every dialog box has at least one *command button*, which causes some kind of action to take place. Many dialog boxes have an OK button and a Cancel button. Clicking OK puts your dialog choices into effect and closes the dialog box. In the example in figure 5.3, choosing Text 25 Lines Low Resolution and pressing OK closes the dialog box and switches the screen to text display mode.

Clicking the Cancel button closes the dialog box without putting your dialog box choices into effect. In the example, if you choose Text 25 Lines Low Resolution but press the Cancel button, the dialog box will close without changing the current screen display mode.

Other command buttons also may be present. In the example, clicking the Preview button shows you what the selected mode looks like without closing the dialog box.

To press a command button when using the keyboard:

1. Press Tab or Shift-Tab until the cursor highlights the desired command button.

2. Press Enter.

To select a command button by using the mouse: Click the desired button.

The Esc (escape) key has the same effect as the Cancel button.

To cancel a dialog when using the keyboard: Press Esc.

To cancel a dialog by using the mouse: Click Cancel.

Selecting a Drive

You can change the current drive just by selecting another one. The directory tree and file list change to show the new information. The first time you select a drive after booting, DOS reads its directory structure from the disk. You see a message while this happens. From then on, DOS Shell remembers the directory structure. If you switch away from that drive and then return to it, the directory tree and file list reappear much faster because DOS doesn't have to reread them. But sometimes you have made changes to the structure that DOS Shell isn't aware of. Then you need to force the Shell to reread the structure from the drive itself. This is called *refreshing* the drive.

To select a drive when using the keyboard, press Ctrl-*drive-letter* to select the drive (without refreshing), no matter what area is active.

Alternatively, you can do the following:

1. Activate the drive list.

2. Press the right-arrow or left-arrow key to highlight the desired drive name.

3. Press space bar to select the drive without refreshing it.

or

3. Press Enter to select and refresh the drive.

To select a drive by using the mouse, click the desired drive if you don't want to refresh it. Alternatively, double-click the desired drive to refresh it.

To refresh the current drive:

Press F5 or choose View Refresh (no matter what area is active).

You also can press Ctrl-F5 to refresh just the current directory without refreshing the entire drive. In addition, sometimes the Shell screen becomes messed up with part of a leftover image. Press Shift-F5 or choose View Repaint Screen to clean up the screen without refreshing the current drive.

Using DOS Shell's On-Line Help

The next few chapters explain the basics of using DOS Shell. You also have a complete on-line help system available to you when you're working at your computer. It will help you remember what you have read here. There are two paths into the help system: the F1 key and the Help menu.

Context-Sensitive Help

You can press F1 at any time when using DOS Shell. The help system tries to figure out the best topic for what you're working on, as determined by the location of the cursor. Figure 5.4, for example, shows the help topic that appears if you press F1 while the Screen Display Mode dialog box, shown in figure 5.3, is open. As you can see, it attempts to explain what this dialog box is all about.

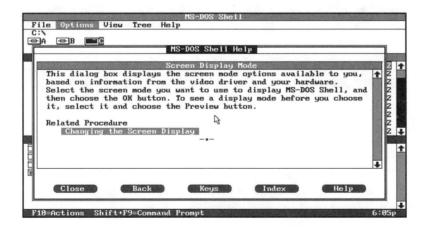

Figure 5.4.
A sample help topic.

If the cursor is in the file list when you press F1, the help system displays information about using the file list. If the cursor is in a menu, the selected topic explains the highlighted command. This type of help is called *context-sensitive* because it's responding to the context (location) of the cursor.

After you have entered the help system through context-sensitive help, however, you have access to the entire system, just as if you had started from the Help menu. The command buttons at the bottom of the help window provide a path to the rest of the system. You learn how to use them in the following sections.

The Help Menu

The other way to enter the help system is through the Help menu, which offers a number of help categories (see fig. 5.5).

Figure 5.5.
The Help menu.

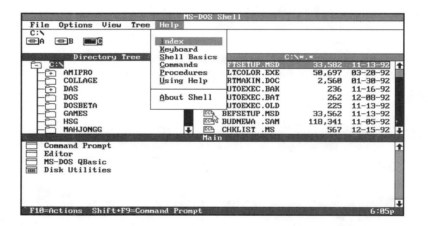

The Help Index

The help index provides a general index to all the topics in the help system (see fig. 5.6). It groups the topics into several categories, such as Keyboard Help, Commands Help, and Procedures Help. There's even a category on how to use the help system itself. You can scroll and select the topic that interests you. Many topics in this index lead to more detailed indexes.

To select a topic, tab to it and press Enter or double-click it.

You also can access the help index by choosing the Index button in any help system window.

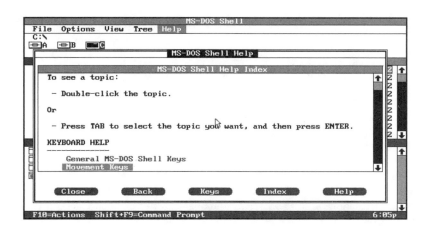

Figure 5.6.
The help index.

Other Help Options

The other commands in the top portion of the **Help** menu duplicate portions of the help index, enabling you to access the category closest to your needs. These detailed indexes are the following:

Keyboard	Lists topics on keyboard use with the DOS Shell, such as Movement Keys and File List Keys. This Keys Index also can be accessed by pressing the Keys command button in any help window.
Shell Basics	Lists general topics on using the Shell, such as Dialog Boxes and the Program List.
Commands	Lists topics on the Shell menus and their commands, such as the File Menu and the Tree Menu.
Procedures	Provides access to step-by-step procedures for how to do things in the Shell. For example, you can see how to use the file list and how to run programs.

Using Help	Lists topics on the help system itself, such as Using Help Buttons and Using Help Menu Commands. You can access this same index by pressing the Help button on any help system window.

About Shell

The About Shell command appears below the dividing line in the Help menu because it's quite different from the other Help options. Choosing this command opens a box that shows your DOS version number—to two decimal places. If you call Microsoft for technical support on DOS, you may be asked for this number.

Maneuvering in the Help System

When you're looking at a help window, whether it's an index or a topic, you can scroll up and down in it by using the same scrolling methods you use with lists. Any text displayed in color provides a link to another index or topic; select it the same way you select a topic in a help index. (On black-and-white monitors, such text is highlighted instead of in color.)

The help system keeps track of the windows that you view and you can revisit former ones by pressing the Back button, which appears in every window. Press Esc or choose Close to exit the help system and return to the DOS Shell screen.

Unlike other help systems, you can't keep the help window on-screen while you work on the Shell screen, nor can you move or resize the help window.

Exiting DOS Shell

You can exit DOS Shell temporarily or permanently. A temporary exit takes you to the DOS command prompt so that you can enter some commands without closing down the Shell; when you return to the Shell, the screen appears just as you left it. A permanent exit also goes to the DOS command prompt, but it closes down the Shell. If you restart the Shell, it will be in its initial state again.

To exit the Shell temporarily: Press Shift-F9.

The status line contains a reminder that this hot key takes you to the command prompt.

To return to the Shell after a temporary exit; enter the following command at the DOS prompt:

```
EXIT
```

To exit the Shell permanently, choose File Exit or press F3.

Managing Directories

6

Introduction

The Shell's directory tree makes it easy to create, delete, and otherwise manage directories.

Selecting Directories

Selecting a directory makes it the current directory. Its files appear in the file list, and any File menu commands pertain to it. If you exit the Shell, you will see it listed in the command prompt as the current directory.

To select a directory:

Click it or move the cursor to it.

> Check the Keys Index in the help system if you forget how to move the cursor in the directory tree without a mouse.

Ctrl-F5 refreshes the current directory without refreshing the entire drive. You may need to do this if you made a temporary exit to the DOS command prompt, made some changes to the directory, and then returned to the Shell.

Collapsing and Expanding the Directory Tree

After you have created a few dozen directories on your hard disk, in four or five levels, it can become difficult to find your way around in the tree. Most of the time, you can find the branches you want to work with a lot easier if the lower levels of subdirectories don't appear. The Tree menu gives you control over the branches that appear (see fig. 6.1).

> In the directory tree, a plus sign indicates a directory with unseen children; you can expand this directory to display its children. A minus sign indicates a directory with at least one child displayed; you can collapse it to hide its children.
>
> You may not have to activate the directory tree to expand or contract it. The Tree menu and its hotkeys also work on the current directory when either the drive list or the file list is active.

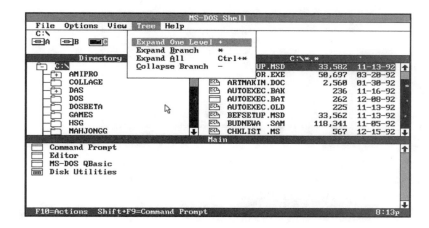

Figure 6.1.
The Tree menu.

To display a directory's immediate children (one level only), click the plus sign. Alternatively, select the directory and press the + key or choose Tree Expand One Level.

To display an entire branch (all levels):

1. Select the parent directory.

2. Press * or choose Tree Expand Branch.

To expand the entire tree, press Ctrl-* or choose Tree Expand All.

To collapse a branch, click the minus sign. Alternatively, select the parent of the branch and then press the – key or choose Tree Collapse Branch.

If you want to collapse the entire tree for some reason, just collapse the root directory.

Renaming Directories

You may find it necessary to rename a directory on occasion. Figure 6.2 shows the dialog box that opens when you choose File Rename while the cursor is in the directory tree. The current directory's name appears in the Current Name field.

Figure 6.2.
The Rename
Directory dialog box.

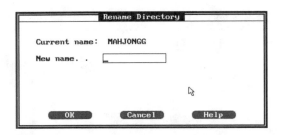

File Rename is not available when the root directory is selected because you're not allowed to rename the root directory.

To rename a directory:

1. Activate the directory tree.

2. Select the directory to be renamed.

3. Choose File Rename.

4. Make sure that Current Name shows the correct directory name. (If not, press Cancel and try again.)

5. Type the new name in the New Name box.

6. Press OK.

DOS Shell shows each level of the directory tree in alphabetic order, so the renamed directory may move to a new place under its parent directory.

Each directory name must be unique within its parent directory. It can't duplicate either another directory name or a file name in the same parent. If you try to assign a nonunique name, the dialog box shown in figure 6.3 opens. This multipurpose dialog box often appears in DOS Shell when something goes wrong, so its wording may seem a little general. In this case, `Access denied` means that you tried to assign an invalid name to the directory. You must select one of the two options or Cancel.

When you're trying to rename a directory, the first option, `Skip this file or directory and continue`, has the same effect as Cancel. It cancels the Rename command and returns to the Shell screen. (You will see situations later where this option has a different effect than Cancel.) You may want to choose this option to take another look at the directory tree and the file list before trying again.

Figure 6.3.
The Access Denied
dialog box.

The second option, `Try this file or directory again`, returns to the Rename Directory dialog box so that you can try another name right away.

To choose an option in the Access Denied dialog box, double-click the option or highlight the option and press OK.

You can highlight an option by typing its number.

Creating Directories

If you need to create a new directory, you can do it right in the directory tree. Figure 6.4 shows the dialog box that opens when you select File Create Directory. This command is available only when the cursor is in the directory tree.

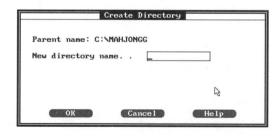

Figure 6.4.
The Create
Directory
dialog box.

To create a new directory:

1. Activate the directory tree.

2. Select the desired parent directory.

3. Choose File Create Directory.

4. Make sure that the Parent name field is correct. (If not, press Cancel and try again.)

5. Enter the desired name in the New Directory Name box.

6. Press OK.

You should see the new directory appear underneath the selected parent in the directory tree. If you entered an invalid name, however, the Access Denied dialog box opens and you must choose to cancel the command or try again.

Deleting Directories

A directory must be completely empty before you can delete it by using DOS Shell, which means that the directory must contain neither files nor subdirectories. If you want to delete an entire branch, you have to start at the lowest level and work your way up. Figure 6.5 shows the dialog box that opens when you choose the File Delete command with a directory selected.

Figure 6.5.
The Delete
Directory
Confirmation
dialog box.

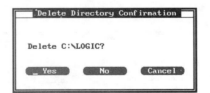

Be sure to select the desired item before choosing File Delete or pressing the Del key. If DOS Shell's delete confirmation feature is disabled, all selected items will be deleted before you get a chance to change your mind.

To delete a directory:

1. Activate the directory tree.

2. Select the directory to be deleted.

3. Delete all the files in the directory. (Chapter 9 explains how.)

4. Choose File Delete or press the Del key.

5. If the Delete Directory Confirmation dialog box opens, make sure that it displays the correct directory name. If so, press Yes. (If not, press No or Cancel.)

You should see the selected directory disappear from the directory tree; the next higher directory becomes selected.

If the selected directory isn't empty, the dialog box shown in figure 6.6 opens. This is often a surprise, because it can happen when you thought the directory was empty. In fact, the directory may contain files and subdirectories that you can't see in the current directory tree or file list.

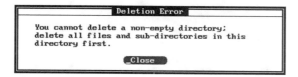

Figure 6.6.
The Deletion Error
dialog box.

You already have seen how to display unseen subdirectories. If the directory you want to delete has a plus sign next to it, display and delete its subdirectories before trying to delete that directory.

A directory also may have files that you can't see. By default, DOS Shell does not display hidden and system files. If the message in the file list reads No files match the file specifier instead of No files in selected directory, the directory has files you can't see. You learn how to display and delete them in Chapter 9.

> You may be able to undelete a directory and its files if you change your mind. Chapter 9 explains how.

For the Future

Every once in a while you want to do something to a directory that isn't possible in the Shell.

- *Deleting a nonempty directory*. Being forced to empty a directory before deleting it can be annoying. At the command prompt, you can delete a single directory or an entire branch without deleting the files first. Chapter 15 shows you how.

- *Hiding a directory*. It would be nice to be able to have directories that only you know about. To a certain extent, you can hide directories at the command prompt, but not in the Shell. Chapter 15 explains how.

- *Moving or copying a directory*. You can't move or copy a directory directly in the Shell. You have to create a directory and move or copy the files to it. But you can copy a directory at the command prompt. Chapter 15 shows you how.

Selecting Files

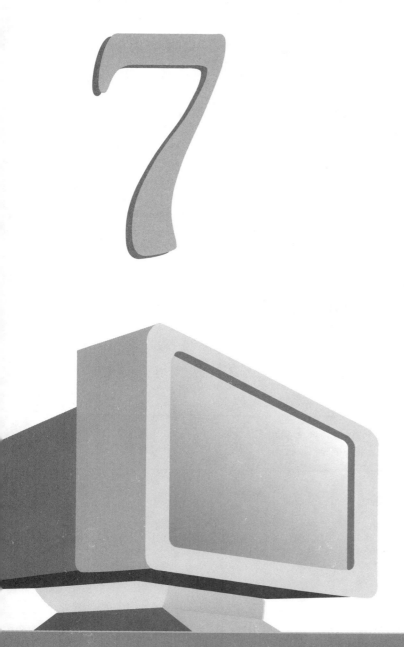

Introduction

In the Shell, you select files in the file list to be processed by File menu commands such as Print, Copy, and Delete.

Selecting a Single File

You often will want to process just one file at a time. For example, you may want to view or print a single file. Selecting one file is as easy as selecting a directory—click the file or move the cursor to it. The file that's highlighted is the one that's selected; this file becomes the target of any File menu command you invoke while the file list is active.

Selecting Multiple Files

Sometimes it's handy to select a group of files for processing. Unlike the command prompt, the Shell enables you to select files with unrelated names. At the command prompt, you have to come up with a global filespec that selects just the files you want and no others. This is sometimes impossible to do in one step. But in the Shell, you can select whatever files you want, regardless of their names. There's quite a difference, though, in how you select multiple files with the mouse and with the keyboard.

Selecting Multiple Files with the Mouse

The technique you use to select multiple files with the mouse depends on whether the files you want are adjacent to each other in the file list.

Scrolling with the mouse does not affect file selection, but scrolling with the keyboard does, because it moves the cursor.

To select adjacent files with the mouse:

1. Click the first file.

2. Hold down Shift and click the last file.

Shift-Click selects all the files between the currently selected file and the file on which you press Shift-Click. You can create the range of selected files from the top down or the bottom up; you can start by selecting either the first file or the last file in the range and then Shift-Click the other end of the range.

Shift-Click does not move the cursor, which remains on the first file in the range. You can adjust the other end of the range by using Shift-Click again.

To select nonadjacent files with a mouse:

1. Click the first file.

2. Hold down Ctrl and click each subsequent file.

Ctrl-Click selects a file without deselecting any other files.

If you want to select a mixed group of files, some adjacent and some not, you can combine the two methods. But take care not to inadvertently deselect the files you already have selected. This precaution means that after you have selected the first range of files, you have to use Ctrl-Click to select the rest, even if there is another adjacent range, because Ctrl-Click is the only way to select files with the mouse without deselecting all others.

To select a mixture of adjacent and nonadjacent files:

1. Click the first file in a range of adjacent files.

2. Shift-Click the last file in the range. (The range is now selected.)

3. Ctrl-Click each additional file to be selected.

Deselecting Files with the Mouse

Deselecting means removing the selection status of a file so that it is no longer selected. Selecting any individual file without using Ctrl or Shift deselects all other files. If you want to deselect an individual file without deselecting them all, Ctrl-Click the file. Ctrl-Click toggles individual file selection on and off without affecting any other selected files.

Suppose that you want to select all but one file in an adjacent range. You can select the entire range with Shift-Click and then deselect the individual file with Ctrl-Click.

Selecting Multiple Files with the Keyboard

Again, there's a difference between how you select a range of adjacent files and how you select nonadjacent files.

To select a range of adjacent files with the keyboard:

1. Move the cursor to the first file in the range.

2. Hold down Shift and move the cursor to the last file in the range.

You can use any method to move the cursor while you hold down the Shift key: the up- and down-arrow keys, PgUp or PgDn, Home or End, or the first letter of the file name. You also can adjust the end of the range by holding down Shift while you move the cursor again. Suppose that you want to select all the files in the list except the first and the last. You can select the second file, press Shift-End to select the rest of the list, and then press Shift-up arrow to deselect the last file.

Selecting any individual file deselects the range, so be sure not to move the cursor without Shift until you're ready to deselect the range.

To deselect a range of files:

Move the cursor without holding down Shift.

To select nonadjacent files when using the keyboard, you must use a special file selection mode called *Add mode*. Add mode enables you to move the cursor in the file list without selecting or deselecting files. The Shift-F8 key combination toggles Add mode on and off; when it's on, the word ADD appears in the status line.

To select nonadjacent files when using the keyboard:

1. Select the first file.

2. Press Shift-F8 to enter Add mode. (The word ADD appears on the status line.)

3. Move the cursor to the next file to be selected.

4. Press the space bar to select it.

5. Repeat steps 3 and 4 to select all desired files.

6. Press Shift-F8 to exit Add mode.

When you're in Add mode, you also can select a range of files by holding down Shift while you move the cursor. Alternatively, you can select one end of the range, move the cursor to the other end of the range, and press Shift-space bar. It's possible to select multiple ranges in Add mode because moving the cursor does not deselect files.

You don't have to exit Add mode before processing the selected files. For example, you can press the Del key to delete all the selected files and then select some more files and choose File Print.

To deselect an individual file in Add mode:

1. Move the cursor to the file.

2. Press the space bar.

The space bar acts as a selection toggle in Add mode, just as Ctrl-Click does when you're using a mouse.

Selecting and Deselecting All Files

The File menu enables you to select or deselect all files with the Select All and Deselect All commands. Their hot keys, however, are much faster.

To select all files, press Ctrl-/.

Selecting all files selects only those files that are showing in the file list. If hidden and system files are not displayed, for example, they are not selected.

To deselect all files, press Ctrl-\.

Actually, this action deselects all but one file. The file the cursor is on remains selected.

Identifying Selected Files

When you have selected multiple files, the file list indicates which files are selected, which are not selected, and where the cursor is. Figure 7.1 shows how the list might look in graphics mode, and figure 7.2 shows how the list might look in text mode.

Figure 7.1.
A sample file list in graphics mode with multiple files selected.

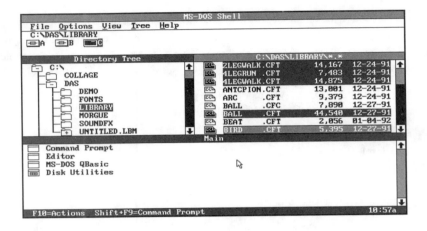

Figure 7.2.
A sample file list in text mode with multiple files selected.

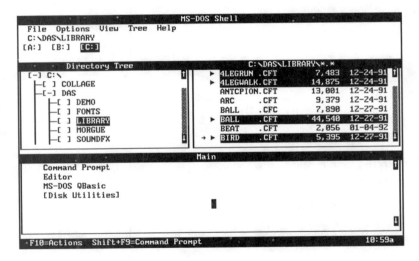

In graphics mode, a selected file has both its entry and its icon highlighted. The position of the cursor is indicated by a highlighted entry only. If the cursor is on a selected file, you can see it on a color monitor because it's a lighter color and has a black box around it. Monochrome monitors make it difficult to find the cursor when it's on a selected file in graphics mode. In figure 7.1, the cursor is located on the BIRD.CFT file.

In text mode, arrowheads indicate selected files; their entries also are highlighted. The smaller arrow indicates the location of the cursor, which also highlights the entry. It's actually easier to find the cursor on a monochrome monitor in text mode because the arrow provides an additional clue.

When No Files Are Selected

It's possible in the Shell to deselect all files. All you have to do is deselect the last remaining selection by using Ctrl-Click or the space bar. When you do this, most of the commands on the File menu go dim (see fig. 7.3). To make the commands available again, select a file.

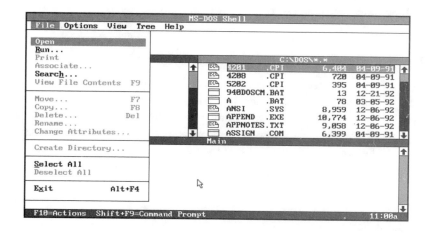

Figure 7.3.
The File menu
when no files
are selected.

Selecting across Directories

So far, you have been selecting files in one directory only. But you can select files in more than one directory and process them all at the same time. This is one advantage over the command prompt interface, which can process multiple directories on a limited basis only.

You can select files from multiple directories by turning on the Select Across Directories feature. As long as it's on, changing directories does not deselect the files in the preceding directory.

Select Across Directories can be a very dangerous feature. For example, it can cause you to delete more files than you intended. It's a good idea to turn this feature on only to perform an isolated task and then immediately turn it off again.

Select Across Directories is a toggle. Select it once and you turn the feature on; select it again to turn it off. When it's on, a bullet appears next to the command in the Options menu. Unfortunately, this is the only clue that Select Across Directories is on, and you cannot see it unless you pull down the Options menu.

To turn on Select Across Directories, choose Options Select Across Directories.

To turn off Select Across Directories, choose Options Select Across Directories.

When Select Across Directories is on, you select files in one directory as normal. Then change directories and select more files. The files in the first directory remain selected. You can continue to change directories and select files until you have selected all the files you want to process in one command. Then choose the command you want. If the command displays a list of the files to be processed, check it very carefully. It's easy to select more files than you intended with this feature.

For the Future

When you're accustomed to selecting files at the basic level, you may want to try some of the more advanced techniques. You can limit the contents of the file list not only by attribute but also by file name. In addition, you can display all the files on a disk in one file list and select files from that list. You also can display two separate file lists from which to select files. All these techniques are explained in later chapters.

8 Copying and Moving Files in the DOS Shell

Introduction

It's amazing how often you must copy or move files. DOS Shell makes it easy and (almost) safe.

Using Replacement Confirmation

It seems like the most innocent task possible, but copying or moving files can actually be dangerous—you stand the chance of losing data without even knowing it. When the destination directory (the directory to receive the file) already contains a file of the same name, DOS replaces that file with the new copy. It can't evaluate whether the files are identical or are even two versions of the same file; if the name's the same, DOS replaces it. This is referred to as "clobbering" the file.

DOS's UNDELETE command can't recover a file that was clobbered by a COPY or MOVE. (But the Norton Utilities's Unerase program can.)

When you're working at the command prompt, DOS clobbers files without warning. But the Shell warns you. This is one of the big advantages of the Shell.

Figure 8.1 shows the dialog box that opens when you choose the Options Confirmation command. The second item, Confirm on Replace, controls whether the Shell warns you before replacing a file.

Figure 8.1.
Confirmation
dialog box.

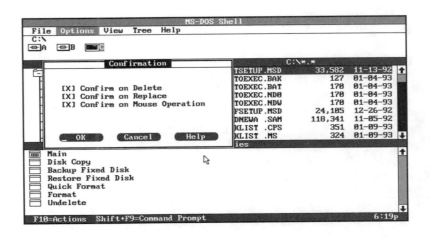

This dialog box contains check boxes. You toggle an item on or off by selecting it. The X indicates that it's on.

To turn replacement confirmation on or off:

1. Choose Options Confirmation.

2. Click Confirm on Replace or move the cursor to Confirm on Replace and press the space bar.

3. Select OK.

You would be wise to keep replacement confirmation on at all times. Turn it off only for an isolated task when you actually intend to clobber some files and don't want to be bothered confirming each one. Turn this feature on again as soon as possible.

Copying a Single File

When you copy a file to a different directory, you can give it a new name or let it keep its original name. But when you copy a file to the same directory, you must give it a new name, because a directory can't have two files with the same name.

Figure 8.2 shows the dialog box that opens when you choose the File Copy command (or press its hot key, F8). The name of the current directory appears in the To box. If you want to make a copy in the same directory, you must add a filespec to the directory name. Or you can change the path to copy the file to a different directory, with or without a new file name. If you omit the filespec, the copy receives the same name as the original.

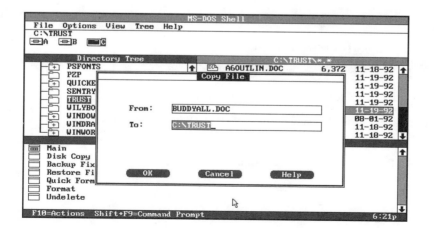

Figure 8.2.
Copy File
dialog box.

The Copy File dialog box uses a text box to collect information from you. When the dialog box first appears, DOS highlights all the text in the To box, indicating that it is selected. The first character you type automatically replaces the entire field.

The From box looks like a text box, and you can place the cursor in it, but DOS beeps if you try to type in it.

If, for example, the default value is C:\TRUST and you want to replace it with A:\, all you must do is type **A** and the C:\TRUST disappears. Suppose that, instead, you want to change C:\TRUST to C:\TRUST\OLDFORMS. If you press a horizontal cursor key first (left arrow, right arrow, Home, or End), the highlight disappears. The End and right-arrow keys leave the cursor where it is (at the end); the Home and left-arrow keys move the cursor to the beginning. Either way, you're ready to start editing.

Continue pressing the left- or right-arrow keys to position the cursor where you want it. (After the highlight disappears, pressing the left-arrow and right-arrow keys move one character at a time.) DOS inserts whatever you type at the cursor. So, to change C:\TRUST to C:\TRUST\OLDFORMS, you could press End and type **\OLDFORMS**.

Another way to start editing is to click the position where you want to place the cursor, and you're ready to go.

To copy a file to the same directory:

1. Select the file.

2. Choose File Copy or press F8 (the file list must be active).

3. Check the file name in the From box. (If it's wrong, press Cancel and try again.)

4. Press End to move the cursor to the end of the text in the To box.

5. Add a file name to the path.

6. Press OK.

To copy a file to a different directory:

1. Select the file.

2. Choose File Copy or press F8 (the file list must be active).

3. Check the file name in the From box. (If it's wrong, press Cancel and try again.)

4. Edit or replace the path in the To box.

5. Add a filespec if you want to give the copy a new name.

6. Press OK.

If the name of the copy duplicates an existing file name and you're using Confirm on Replace, the Replace File Confirmation dialog box, shown in figure 8.3, appears. It shows you the names, dates, and sizes of both files to help you decide what to do. Select Yes to make the replacement or No or Cancel to cancel it.

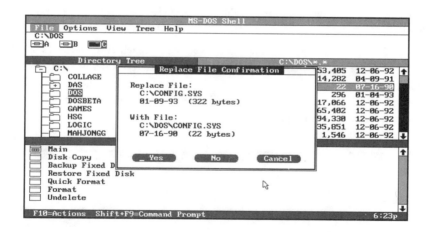

Figure 8.3.
Replace File
Confirmation
dialog box.

Moving a Single File

Moving a file is similar to copying it, except DOS removes it from the source directory. You must, of course, move the file to a different directory; moving it to the same directory makes no sense.

To move a file:

1. Select the file.

2. Choose File Move or press F7 (the file list must be active).

3. Check the file name in the From box. (If it's wrong, press Cancel and try again.)

4. Edit or replace the default path in the To box.

5. Add a filespec if you want to give the file a new name.

6. Select OK.

Copying and Moving Multiple Files

When you select multiple files to move or copy, you can't rename them. They must keep their original names, and that means that you must copy or move them to another directory.

Figure 8.4 shows what the Copy File dialog box looks like when you select multiple files. You can see the last couple of file names in the From box, but you must scroll to see the rest. To be safe, you should examine all the names before continuing. Remember that it's easy in the Shell to select more files than you intended, especially when you're selecting across directories.

Figure 8.4.
Copying multiple files.

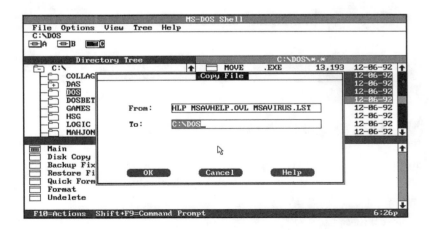

To scroll in the From box:

1. Press the up-arrow key or click the box to put the cursor in it.

2. Press Home, End, and the left- and right-arrow keys as needed.

The rest of the procedure is just like copying or moving a single file to another directory, except that you can't add a new file name.

To move or copy multiple files:

1. Select the files (make sure that no other files are selected).

2. Choose File Copy (F8) or File Move (F7).

3. Scroll through the list in the From box. (If it's not correct, press Cancel and try again.)

4. Edit or replace the text in the To box to identify the destination directory.

5. Select OK.

If the Replace File Confirmation dialog box appears (see fig. 8.3), No and Cancel have different effects. As always, Cancel ends the entire command; no more files are copied. But No cancels only the current file; DOS continues with the next file in the list.

Dragging Files

Now that you know the hard way to move and copy files, you should learn the easy way. You can select the files you want and then drag them to a new location. You must drag them to a different directory, and you can't rename them.

To drag files, select them first and then point to any selected file, hold the mouse button down, and move the pointer to the desired directory (in the directory tree) or drive (in the drive list). If the destination directory is on a different drive, DOS automatically copies the files to that drive, but if the directory is on the same drive, DOS moves them. You can have DOS copy files by holding down the Ctrl key while you drag them. Use the Alt key while dragging to move files.

The Shell gives you many visual clues to confirm what you're doing. The mouse pointer becomes a single file icon when you're dragging one file or a bunch of file icons when you're dragging more than one. As you move the pointer across areas where you can't drop files (such as the program list), the pointer turns into a "No" symbol—a circle with a line through it. When it becomes a file icon again, you have reached a legitimate destination. In addition, the message line displays `Cancel` when you can't drop the files and `Move files to directory` or `Copy files to directory` when you can.

> You can scroll the directory tree while you're dragging files. Just move the mouse pointer to the arrows on the scroll bar, and you see the list scroll.

To move files to another directory on the same drive:

1. Scroll the directory tree and expand subdirectories as needed to reveal the desired destination directory.

2. Select the files.

3. Drag any selected file to the desired destination directory (in the directory tree).

4. Drop the files by releasing the mouse button.

5. Confirm the move, if necessary.

To move files to a different drive:

1. Select the destination drive (in the drive list).

2. Select the destination directory (in the directory tree) to make it the default directory for the drive.

3. Select the source drive (in the drive list).

4. Select the files to be moved.

5. Press Alt and drag any selected file to the desired drive (in the drive list).

6. Drop the files by releasing the mouse button.

7. Release the Alt key.

8. Confirm the move, if necessary.

To copy files to another directory on the same drive:

1. Scroll the directory tree and expand subdirectories as needed to reveal the desired destination directory.

2. Select the files.

3. Press Ctrl and drag any selected file to the desired target directory (in the directory tree).

4. Drop the files by releasing the mouse button.

5. Release the Ctrl key.

6. Confirm the copy, if necessary.

To copy files to a different drive:

1. Select the destination drive (in the drive list).

2. Select the destination directory (in the directory tree) to make it the default directory for the drive.

3. Select the source drive (in the drive list).

4. Select the files to be copied.

5. Drag any selected file to the desired drive (in the drive list).

6. Drop the files by releasing the mouse button.

7. Confirm the copy, if necessary.

Keep your eye on the message line. If it displays Move when you want to copy, or vice versa, you can press Ctrl or Alt to change the procedure in mid-drag. You don't have to start over.

If, in the Confirmation dialog box (see fig. 8.1), you have set the Confirm on Mouse Operation option to on, when you drag files, a dialog box asks whether you're sure that you want to move or copy the files. Choose Yes to complete the operation or No to cancel it. This confirmation feature is not nearly so important as Confirm on Replace. Keep it on if you like a chance to change your mind; for example, if you frequently mix moves with copies or drop files in the wrong place, you may appreciate a confirmation step. But if the extra step irritates you, go ahead and turn it off.

You may notice as you drag files around that you can drop them on program files in the file list. Chapter 11 explains what happens when you do this.

Alternate Views

You can set the Shell screen up to be more helpful when you're dragging files. Figure 8.5 shows what it looks like without the program list. The larger directory tree could make it easier to reach a destination directory.

Figure 8.5.
Eliminating the
Program List.

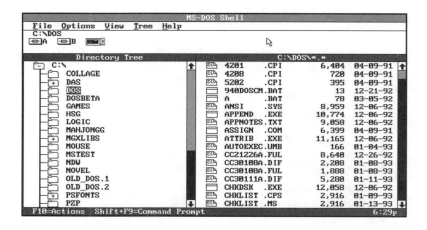

To eliminate the program list, choose View Single File List.

Figure 8.6 shows another view of the Shell screen, in which you can see two directories. You can set up the source directory in the top half of the screen and the target directory in the bottom half. This view comes in particularly handy when two drives are involved, as shown in the example, but it can even be helpful with two directories on the *same drive*. *This view* has the added bonus of letting you see what files already exist in the destination directory.

To view two directories at once:

1. Choose View Dual File Lists.

2. In the bottom half of the screen, select the desired drive and directory.

To return to the usual view, choose View File/Program Lists.

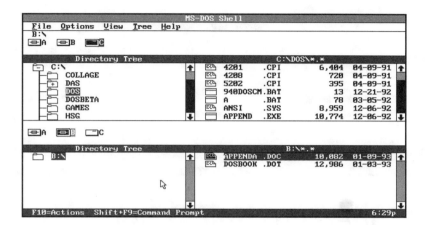

Figure 8.6.
Dual file lists.

Understanding Some Copy Facts

When DOS copies a file, it also copies the source file's date and time stamp rather than assigning the current date and time to the new copy. The reason is that the date and time stamp identifies the file's version—for example, the version created on March 13th at 3:10 p.m. As long as you don't revise either copy, they both have the same date and time stamp and you know they're identical. When you revise one or the other, the date and time stamps no longer match, and you can see not only that they're different, but also which one is newer.

DOS Shell can be a little too forgiving when copying and moving files with hidden, system, and read-only attributes. The Shell ignores a source file's attributes, even if that means removing a hidden or read-only file from the source directory. Apparently, it's OK as long as a copy exists somewhere. Perhaps even worse, the Shell replaces a hidden or system file in the destination directory without warning you about the attribute.

When the Shell is about to clobber a read-only file, a confirmation box mentions (in parentheses) the read-only attribute (see fig. 8.7). This box appears whether Confirm on Replace is on, but it doesn't prevent you from clobbering the file.

97

Figure 8.7.
Read-only warning.

Understanding What Can Go Wrong

A number of problems can crop up when you're moving or copying files. Most of them result in some kind of error message. The following sections discuss some of these problems.

Dimmed Commands

If you can't choose File Copy or File Move, or F7 or F8 merely beep at you, either you didn't select a file or you didn't activate the file list. You activate the file list or select a file to make the commands available.

If you can choose the command but no dialog box opens, you're in the program list, not the file list. Press Esc to end the current command. Then activate the file list and try again.

Write Protection

A write-protected disk can't be written to, and you see the `Access Denied` message if you try to move or copy a file to it. You can solve this problem by changing disks or removing the write-protection. Then choose option 1 to continue (it won't skip any files.)

Nonexistent Directory

When you specify a name, such as C:\FORTRAN\CODE, CODE could be either a file or a subdirectory. DOS finds out which by looking in the C:\FORTRAN directory. But what if CODE doesn't appear in the directory? DOS assumes that it's a file name and that you want to create a new file.

Figure 8.8.
Copy File window.

But if you're moving or copying more than one file, you're not allowed to specify a new file name. So DOS Shell displays the message `You have more than one file selected` in the dialog box. What this message really means is, "The name you entered doesn't exist, so I'm assuming that it's a file name." If you really meant it to be a directory path, correct the name and try again.

Forgetting To Rename a File

If you forget to supply a new file name when copying a file to the same directory, you see a dialog box that displays the message `File can't be copied to itself`. The same thing happens if you try to move a file to its own directory. The only thing you can do is cancel the operation and start over, being more careful to type the correct destination and filespec.

Full Target Disk

If the destination disk doesn't have enough room for the new files, DOS displays the message `The disk is full`. If the destination is a hard disk, you must cancel the operation while you figure out what to do. But if you're copying or moving to a disk, you can change the disk and select option 1 to continue with the copy operation (it won't skip any files).

By the way, this is another significant advantage of the Shell over the command prompt. At the command prompt, DOS's COPY command quits when it encounters a `disk full` error. In the process, it loses track of which files it has already copied, making it nearly impossible to continue the copy operation with a second disk. With the Shell, you can keep going.

Miscellaneous Problems

You can encounter many other problems when you are moving and copying files. You might, for example, type a drive or directory name that doesn't exist or drag files to an empty disk drive. A disk might be damaged—so might a hard drive, for that matter. In every case, the Shell displays some kind of message and gives you the chance to fix the problem. These messages usually aren't as cryptic as `Access denied` and `You have more than one file selected`, so you should be able to figure out what the problem is and what you can do about it. If you end up copying files to the wrong destination, don't worry; the next chapter shows you how to delete and undelete them.

Deleting and Undeleting Files

9

Introduction

Deleting files is easy (sometimes it's too easy). With DOS 6, you can finally undelete files with near 100-percent accuracy. This chapter explains the process.

Deleting a Single File

Deleting a file is as simple as selecting the file and pressing the Del key (or choosing File Delete). If Confirm on Delete is on, a dialog box asks whether you want to delete the file. Without Confirm on Delete, DOS deletes files the instant you press the Del key.

Because it's easy to select the wrong file or bump the Del key without meaning to, you would be wise to keep Confirm on Delete on. If you want to turn it off to delete a group of files without having to bother with confirmation, be sure to turn it back on again immediately.

To toggle Confirm on Delete on and off:

1. Choose Options Confirmation.

2. Select Confirm on Delete.

Deleting Multiple Files

To delete multiple files, select them all. Make sure that no others are selected—watch out particularly when you're selecting across directories. When you press Del, the dialog box shown in figure 9.1 is displayed. You should scroll through the list to make sure that it's correct.

Figure 9.1.
Delete dialog box.

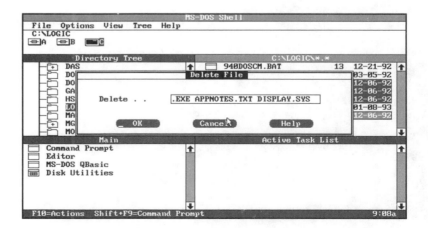

When you select OK, a confirmation dialog box appears for each selected file if
Confirm on Delete is on. You must choose Yes or No for each file. No bypasses that
file and goes on to the next file in the list. Select Cancel to stop the entire process.

The delete confirmation feature gives you a second chance to notice that you have
selected a file you didn't intend to delete. Many people become impatient and start
rapidly choosing Yes without reading the file name in each confirmation box. If you
do that, you're more likely to delete a file accidentally.

If a file is read-only, the Shell displays the dialog box shown in figure 9.2. Notice
that this is only a warning. You can delete the file even though it's read-only.

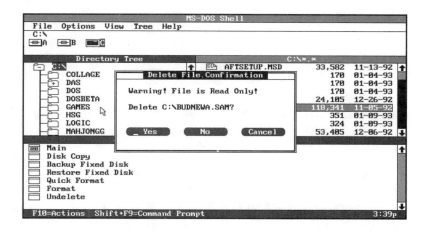

Figure 9.2.
The Delete File
Confirmation
dialog box.

On the other hand, if you're trying to delete files from a write-protected disk, you
see the Write Protection Warning dialog box, shown in figure 9.3. You can't delete
the files as long as the disk is write-protected. If you want to delete the files, you
must remove the write protection.

Understanding the UNDELETE Feature

In spite of all DOS Shell's precautions, everyone deletes the wrong files occasionally. Even more common is changing your mind after you intentionally delete a file.

DOS's UNDELETE facility helps you recover a file after you have deleted it. DOS 6 includes a new and more sophisticated UNDELETE program that offers three levels of protection and recovery: Delete Sentry, deletion-tracking, and DOS directory entries, which are explained in the following sections.

Figure 9.3.
The Delete File
dialog box warns
you when a file is
write-protected.

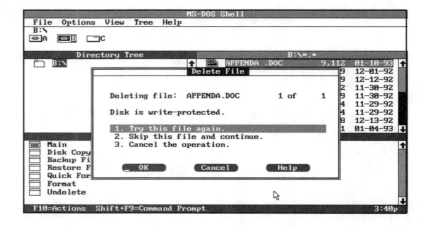

UNDELETE is not really a Shell feature, but you can start it from the Shell's program list. UNDELETE's messages don't have the same "feel" as Shell functions, such as File Move and File Copy. The messages are black-and-white and nongraphic—no icons, menus, or dialog boxes. UNDELETE displays information for you to read and asks you simple yes-or-no questions. Beyond that, you can't interact with the information you see on the screen.

This chapter shows you the basics of UNDELETE. Chapter 27 digs into the details of what it does and how to use it.

Delete Sentry

The Delete Sentry method offers the highest level of protection and recovery. It preserves deleted files in its own directory (called SENTRY) for a while so that you can undelete them with 100-percent reliability. Chapter 4 explains how to set up Delete Sentry.

Deletion-Tracking

Deletion-tracking is not quite as powerful as Delete Sentry. When you delete a file, deletion-tracking records the file's directory and FAT entries in a deletion-tracking file. But because deletion-tracking doesn't preserve the deleted file itself, DOS might reuse some of the file's clusters before you try to undelete the file. UNDELETE can recover whatever is left. That might be the entire file, some of it, or nothing.

DOS Directory Entries

If you're not using Delete Sentry or deletion-tracking, UNDELETE can still search a directory for deleted entries. This is the least reliable method, because if the desired directory entry has been overwritten, the file can't be recovered. Even if the entry still exists, it indicates only the first cluster in the file, and UNDELETE has to guess at the remaining clusters. This is a chancy process and often fails or produces the wrong results, especially if the file was fragmented.

In some cases, the directory entry still exists, but the first cluster has been reused. Then UNDELETE can't recover any of the file using the DOS directory method.

Starting UNDELETE

You can start UNDELETE from the Shell's program list. The program list is divided into groups of related programs. You display and work with one group at a time. The name of the current group appears in the program list's title bar.

> Chapter 11 shows you how to create and manage program groups and program items.

By default, the Main group appears when you first start the Shell. This group is much like the root directory on a hard disk; DOS creates it, it sits at the top of a tree-like structure, and you can't delete or rename it. The Main group contains subgroups, which are its children; they, in turn, can contain subgroups.

In graphics mode, you can tell the difference between a child group and a program item in the program list because they have different icons. In text mode, group names appear in square brackets.

DOS Shell also creates a subgroup, called Disk Utilities, that contains utilities for managing disks and files. The UNDELETE program appears in the Disk Utilities group. To see the Disk Utilities group, you must open it. (This is the same technique you use in the drive list to refresh a drive.) To open the Disk Utilities group, double-click Disk Utilities in the Main group or move the cursor to Disk Utilities and press Enter.

When you open the Disk Utilities group, its name appears in the Program List title bar, and you see items, such as Disk Copy, Quick Format, and UNDELETE. The Main group name appears at the top, providing a path back to the parent group.

Figure 9.4 shows the UNDELETE dialog box, which appears when you open UNDELETE. This dialog box enables you to enter parameters for the UNDELETE command. The default parameter, /LIST, causes UNDELETE to simply list all the files available for recovery from the current directory. It does not actually undelete any files. This is a good first step in recovering files, because it allows you to scan the entire list and decide exactly which files you want to recover.

Figure 9.4.
The Undelete dialog box.

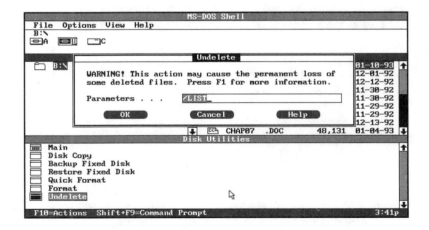

If you select OK without modifying the text box, the DOS Shell screen disappears, the command prompt screen appears, and you see a set of messages that looks something like this:

```
UNDELETE - A delete protection facility
Copyright (C) 1987-1993 Central Point Software, Inc.
All rights reserved.
Directory: C:\
File Specifications: *.*

    Searching Delete Sentry control file....
    Delete Sentry control file contains 5 deleted files.

Deletion-tracking file not found.

    MS-DOS directory contains 5 deleted files.
    Of those, 5 files may be recovered.

Using the Delete Sentry method.
X BAT 32 12-08-92 1:35p ...A Deleted: 12-21-92 10:52a
N6OUTLIN TXT 16413 11-11-92 11:07a ...A Deleted: 12-21-92 10:52a
N6CONTNT TXT 5843 3-20-92 2:00a ...A Deleted: 12-21-92 10:53a
N6CHAPS TXT 104448 3-20-92 2:00a ...A Deleted: 12-21-92 10:53a
N6PACKAG TXT 64666 3-20-92 2:00a ...A Deleted: 12-21-92 10:53a

[Press any key to return to DOS Shell...]
```

You can see that UNDELETE found five files using the Delete Sentry method and five deleted files in the MS-DOS directory. (There is no deletion-tracking information because the example system used Delete Sentry instead of deletion-tracking.) UNDELETE went ahead with the Delete Sentry method and displayed the files that it could recover. Then it terminated itself automatically. Because the /LIST parameter was used, no files were recovered.

The final message tells you to press a key to return to DOS Shell. As long as you don't press a key, you can examine the message from UNDELETE. When you press a key, the screen clears, and the DOS Shell screen returns.

Any time DOS asks you to press any key, press a character key, a cursor key, or a function key. The other keys (such as the Shift keys) have no effect.

Undeleting Delete Sentry Files

When you remove the /LIST parameter from the UNDELETE dialog box, UNDELETE gives you the chance to recover any files it discovers in SENTRY. Instead of listing all the files, UNDELETE presents one file at a time and asks whether you want to undelete it, as follows:

```
UNDELETE - A delete protection facility
Copyright (C) 1987-1993 Central Point Software, Inc.
All rights reserved.
Directory: C:\
File Specifications: *.*

Searching Delete Sentry control file....
    Delete Sentry control file contains 5 deleted files.

Deletion-tracking file not found.

    MS-DOS directory contains 5 deleted files.
    Of those, 5 files may be recovered.

Using the Delete Sentry method.
    Searching Delete Sentry control file....
X BAT 32 12-08-92 1:35p ...A Deleted: 12-21-92 10:52a
This file can be 100% undeleted. UNDELETE (Y/N)?
```

If you already have reviewed the complete list of files with the /LIST parameter and know which files you want to undelete, it's easy to answer Y or N to each file in turn. Press Esc after you have undeleted the last file you want.

> You can add a filespec to the UNDELETE command (type it in the text box) to limit the files that UNDELETE considers. ***.BAT**, for example, lists only BAT files, and **X.BAT** lists only files named X.BAT (there could be more than one of them).

To undelete files using the Delete Sentry method:

1. Open the Disk Utilities group.

2. Open the UNDELETE item. (The UNDELETE dialog box appears with the /LIST parameter in the text box.)

3. Select OK. (UNDELETE displays a list of all the files available for recovery by the Delete Sentry method.)

4. Decide which file(s) you want to undelete.

5. Press a key to return to DOS Shell.

6. Open the UNDELETE item again.

7. Press the Del key to delete the /LIST parameter from the dialog box.

8. Select OK.

9. For each file that UNDELETE asks you about, press Y to undelete it or N to skip it.

10. When you have recovered all the files you want, press Esc.

11. Press any key to return to DOS Shell.

The next section explains how to recover files if you have been using deletion-tracking instead of Delete Sentry.

Undeleting Deletion-Tracking Files

UNDELETE favors the Delete Sentry method, but when Delete Sentry is not available, UNDELETE automatically turns to deletion-tracking, if it is available. With the /LIST parameter, UNDELETE lists the files available for recovery by the deletion-tracking method. When you delete the /LIST parameter, the messages look something like this:

```
UNDELETE - A delete protection facility
Copyright (C) 1987-1993 Central Point Software, Inc.
All rights reserved.
Directory: C:\LOGIC
```

```
File Specifications: *.*

    Delete Sentry control file not found.

    Searching deletion-tracking file....
    Deletion-tracking file contains 2 deleted files.
    Of those, 2 files have all clusters available,
              0 files have some clusters available,
              0 files have no clusters available.

    MS-DOS directory contains 1 deleted files.
    Of those, 1 files may be recovered.
Using the Deletion-tracking method.
    Searching deletion-tracking file....
X BAT 62 11-13-92 3:27p .... Deleted: 12-21-92 12:00p
All the clusters for this file are available. UNDELETE (Y/N)?
```

You press Y for each file you want to recover, N for each file you don't, and Esc when you're ready to quit.

Because deletion-tracking is less reliable than Delete Sentry, you might run into situations in which only part of the file can be recovered. You must decide whether you want to recover part of the file. If you keep your backups up-to-date, you're better off restoring the file from its backup copy. But if you don't have a valid backup of a text file, a word processing document, or a database, it makes sense to recover part of it using UNDELETE—you can fill in the missing parts to complete the file, which is considerably better than retyping it from scratch. But files that aren't based on text, such as spreadsheets or graphics files, are useless when only partially recovered.

> Never partially recover a program file (COM, EXE, BIN, or OVL). Running it could actually damage other programs and their data. If you need to recover a deleted program file, reinstall it from its original program disks or restore it from your backup disks.

To undelete files using the deletion-tracking method:

1. Open the Disk Utilities group.

2. Open the UNDELETE item. The UNDELETE dialog box opens with the /LIST parameter in the text box.

3. Select OK. (UNDELETE displays a list of all the files available for recovery by the deletion-tracking method.)

4. Decide which file(s) you want to undelete.

5. Press a key to return to DOS Shell.

6. Open the UNDELETE item again.

7. Press the Del key to delete the /LIST parameter from the dialog box.

8. Select OK.

9. For each file that UNDELETE asks you about, press Y to undelete it or N to skip it.

10. When you have recovered all the files you want, press Esc.

11. Press any key to return to DOS Shell.

Undeleting Files from the DOS Directory

If you haven't been using either Delete Sentry or deletion-tracking, UNDELETE searches the directory for deleted entries. The /LIST parameter produces messages that look something like this:

```
UNDELETE - A delete protection facility
Copyright (C) 1987-1993 Central Point Software, Inc.
All rights reserved.
Directory: C:\LOGIC
File Specifications: *.*

    Delete Sentry control file not found.

    Deletion-tracking file not found.

    MS-DOS directory contains 3 deleted files.
    Of those, 2 files may be recovered.

Using the MS-DOS directory method.
    ** ?DOC0070 TMP     13721 12-21-92 12:38p ...A
       ?DOC1D78 TMP     13751 12-21-92 12:34p ...A
              ?BAT         57 12-21-92 12:30p ...A
```

111

```
"**" indicates the first cluster of the file
is unavailable and cannot be recovered

with the UNDELETE command.
```

Several details in this list are different from the earlier lists. Most outstanding is that note about the first cluster not being available. The deleted directory entry indicates where the first cluster was, but UNDELETE can tell from the FAT that some other file is now using that cluster. In this recovery method, without the first cluster, UNDELETE can't recover any of the file.

Notice also that the first character of each file name is a question mark (?). That's the character that DOS overwrote when it deleted the file. Because the directory entry is the only information UNDELETE has for this file, it doesn't know what the first character used to be. UNDELETE asks you to supply a first character when you recover the file, as you will see shortly.

Another difference from the other methods is that UNDELETE doesn't show the date and time of the deletion. Without either Delete Sentry or deletion-tracking, the deletion date and time are not known. You must go by the date and time of the last modification to determine which file(s) you want.

Finally, notice the files with strange names like ?DOC0070.TMP. These are temporary files created and deleted by applications such as Microsoft Word without your knowledge. Delete Sentry and deletion-tracking ignore such files, but they show up in the deleted directory entries. You also might find several versions of the same file, with different dates, times, and sizes. This is the result of continually saving a file while editing it; each time you saved a new version, the old one was deleted.

When you enter the UNDELETE command without /LIST, the response looks something like this:

```
UNDELETE - A delete protection facility
Copyright (C) 1987-1993 Central Point Software, Inc.
All rights reserved.
Directory: C:\LOGIC
File Specifications: *.* Delete Sentry control file not found.

    Deletion-tracking file not found.

    MS-DOS directory contains 3 deleted files.
    Of those, 2 files may be recovered.

Using the MS-DOS directory method.
    ** ?DOC0C09 TMP 16805 12-21-92 4:28p ...A
```

```
Starting cluster is unavailable. This file cannot be recovered
with the UNDELETE command. Press any key to continue.
    ?DOC1E5C TMP 15271 12-21-92 4:20p ...A UNDELETE (Y/N)?
```

UNDELETE told you about the unrecoverable file and then went on to list the next file. When you press Y to undelete a file, UNDELETE displays a message like the following:

```
Please type the first character for ?REELIMB.PIC:
```

You don't have to restore the original file name. If, for example, the file was named TREELIMB.PIC before, you might choose to call it FREELIMB.PIC now. In fact, you can't use a first character that duplicates an existing file name or subdirectory name in the same directory. If you do, you see this message:

```
A file name with that first character already exists.
Press any key and then re-type the first character.
```

To undelete files using the DOS directory method:

1. Open the Disk Utilities group.

2. Open the UNDELETE item. (The UNDELETE dialog box opens with the / LIST parameter in the text box.)

3. Select OK. (UNDELETE displays a list of all the files available for recovery by the directory method.)

4. Decide which file(s) you want to undelete.

5. Press a key to return to DOS Shell.

6. Open the UNDELETE item again.

7. Press the Del key to delete the /LIST parameter from the dialog box.

8. Select OK.

9. For each file that UNDELETE asks you about, press Y to undelete it or N to skip it.

10. If you press Y, type a first character for the file.

11. Repeat steps 9 and 10 until you have recovered all the files you want.

12. Press Esc.

13. Press a key to return to DOS Shell.

Understanding What Can Go Wrong

The biggest problem you can run into using UNDELETE is that you can't find the file you want, even if you're using Delete Sentry. If you wait too long to recover the file, it might be purged from Delete Sentry or the deletion-tracking file. Chapter 27 explains some techniques that might still recover the file.

Additional File Management

10

Introduction

One reason for learning DOS is that it lets you do things that you can't do through your applications, such as assigning attributes to files and renaming files.

Managing Attributes

You have seen how a file's attributes are supposed to control the way programs handle it (although even DOS programs don't always comply). Table 10.1 lists various attributes and their purposes:

Table 10.1. File Attributes

Attribute	Function
Archive	Indicates that the file needs to be backed up.
Read-Only	Prevents the file from being modified or erased.
Hidden	Prevents the file from showing up in the directory.
System	Combines hidden and system characteristics.

You can view and change a file's attributes through the Shell.

Viewing Attributes

Figure 10.1 shows the Show Information dialog box that opens when you choose Show Information from the Options menu. This dialog box gives you some statistics about the current file, the entire set of selected files, the current directory, and the current drive. The file displayed in the first section is the file you most recently selected or deselected. If, for example, you selected AFTSETUP.MSD, BEFSETUP.MSD, and SDVXD.386 and then deselected BEFSETUP.MSD, the File section would give you information about BEFSETUP.MSD (but the Selected section would tell you about the two selected files). The file list doesn't have to be active for this command to be available.

The Attr field shows the status of the four attributes. When the letters r (read-only), h (hidden), s (system), or a (archive) are displayed, it indicates that their respective attributes are on. A dot means that an attribute is off. In figure 10.1, all attributes are off.

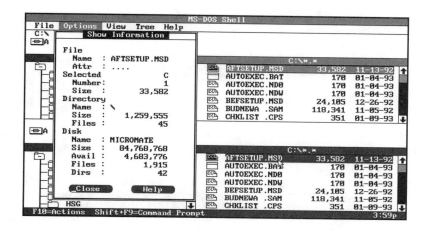

Figure 10.1.
Show Information dialog box.

To view a file's attributes:

1. Select the file.

2. Choose Options Show Information. You can see what attributes, if any, are on by looking at the Attr field.

3. Choose Close to return to the Shell screen.

Changing Attributes

Figure 10.2 shows the Change Attributes dialog box. When only one file is selected, this dialog box shows the current attributes of that file (Read only, in the figure). You toggle attributes on and off by selecting them.

To change a single file's attributes:

1. Select the file in the file list.

2. Choose File Change Attributes. (The file list must be active.)

3. Click an attribute to toggle it on or off. Or you can use the Tab key to move to an attribute and press the space bar to toggle it on or off.

4. When all the attributes are set as you want them, select OK.

Figure 10.2.
*Change Attributes
dialog box.*

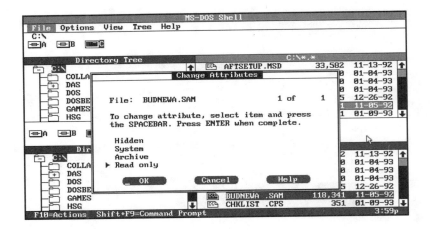

Changing Multiple Attributes

When you choose File Change Attributes with multiple files selected, the Change Attributes dialog box shown in figure 10.3 is displayed.

Figure 10.3.
*Changing the
attributes of
multiple files.*

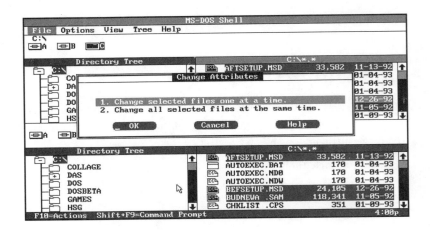

You must choose between two options. If you decide to change the selected files one at a time, the dialog box shown in figure 10.2 appears for each selected file. You can see in the upper right corner of this dialog box how many files are selected and which one you're currently working on (4 of 7, for example). If you decide to change all the selected files at once, DOS immediately clears all their attributes. Then it displays the dialog box shown in figure 10.2 (without the first line) so that you can set the attributes for the entire group.

To set the same attributes for a group of files:

1. Select all the files (and deselect all others).

2. Choose File Change Attributes. (The file list must be active.)

3. Choose option 2 (change all selected files at the same time).

4. Select the desired attributes.

5. Choose OK.

If you want to set a specific attribute for a group of files without changing their other attributes, process the files one at a time. If you choose to do them all at once, DOS automatically clears all their current attributes.

Renaming Files

It's pretty simple to rename a file. When you choose File Rename, a dialog box appears in which you enter a new name for the file. When multiple files are selected, the same dialog box appears again and again until all the files are renamed. You can't rename them all at once in the Shell.

To rename one or more files:

1. Select the files.

2. Choose the File Rename command (the file list must be active).

3. In the dialog box, make sure that the file's current name is correct. (If not, press Cancel and try again.)

4. Type the new name and select OK.

5. Repeat steps 3 and 4 until all the files have been renamed.

When the Shell screen returns, the renamed files move to their new positions in the file list's alphabetical order.

Understanding What Can Go Wrong

If you specify an existing name for either a file or a subdirectory, you see the `Access denied` message. If you choose option 1, the current file is not renamed, but DOS shows you the next selected file (if any). Choose option 2 for a second chance to rename the current file.

For the Future

You can't perform a group rename in the Shell, but you can at the command prompt. You can, for example, rename all *.SAV files to *.OLD. This procedure would rename PLANE.SAV to PLANE.OLD, BOAT.SAV to BOAT.OLD, and so on. This example is fairly straightforward, but group renames can be tricky and have unexpected results. When you're ready to learn more about this procedure, look up the REN command in the Command Reference at the back of this book.

Viewing Text Files

Sometimes, it is convenient to see the contents of a file while working with the Shell. You can always view a data file by starting up the application that created it. But it's often faster and easier to view it through the Shell, which doesn't have to be loaded. Of course, when you view a file through the Shell, you can't edit it as you can when you start up the file's application.

The Shell's file viewer takes over the entire screen (see fig. 10.4). You can scroll in the file with the cursor keys. (Enter acts like PgDn, as you can see by the note on the message line.) There aren't any scroll bars, but you can scroll with the mouse by clicking PgUp, PgDn, ↑, and ↓ in the message at the top of the screen.

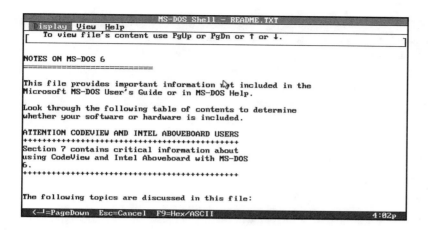

Figure 10.4.
Viewing a file
in the Shell.

The file viewer offers two short menus along with the usual Help menu. The Display menu contains two commands, Ascii and Hex, which control how the Shell displays data. Ascii displays the file as text, as shown in the example. Hex displays the bytes stored in the file in hexadecimal, which means something to programmers but nothing to almost everyone else. You don't really need the Display menu to switch back and forth from ASCII to Hex mode; the F9 key toggles between them. There's a reminder on the message line to this effect.

The Shell automatically displays text files in ASCII mode and all other types of files in hex mode.

The View menu contains two commands: Repaint Screen and Restore View. Repaint Screen (Shift-F5) does the same thing it does on the Shell menu; it cleans up a messy screen. The Restore View command (Esc) exits the viewer and returns to the Shell screen. (Notice the reminder Esc=Cancel on the message line.)

Printing Text Files

You also can print ASCII text files through DOS Shell, but the PRINT program must be initialized before you start up the Shell. You must do this from the command prompt.

PRINT installs a small TSR (terminate-and-stay-resident program), and it's always best to install TSRs without DOS Shell or Windows running. So, you should either initialize PRINT before you start Windows or DOS Shell or permanently exit Windows or the Shell before initializing PRINT.

When you enter the first PRINT command after booting, PRINT asks you what device you want to use by displaying the following prompt:

```
C:\>PRINT
Name of list device [PRN]:
```

[PRN] identifies the device PRINT will use if you press Enter without typing another device name. PRN refers to the standard print device that's attached to the first parallel printer port (named LPT1). If you want to use that device, and most people do, just press Enter. Otherwise, type the name of the device (such as LPT2 or COM1) and then press Enter.

Next, PRINT displays the following messages:

```
Resident part of PRINT installed
PRINT queue is empty
```

The first message tells you that PRINT has been initialized; the TSR has been loaded in memory. It stays in memory until you reboot, and the PRINT program continues to use the device you specified in the initial command. (You can't change the device without booting.) The second message indicates that you are not currently printing any files.

To initialize the PRINT program:

1. Exit the Shell or Windows, if necessary.

2. Enter **PRINT** at the command prompt.

3. To use the standard printer attached to LPT1, press Enter. Otherwise, type the name of the print device and press Enter.

If you'll be using PRINT on a regular basis, you can place the command to initialize it in AUTOEXEC.BAT so that it's initialized every time you boot.

Printing through the Shell

Once you have initialized the PRINT program, you can print ASCII text files through the Shell's File Print command. PRINT does its work in the background, which enables you to continue to work on other tasks, stealing just a little time here and there to send a character to the printer. (Printers are so slow compared to the rest of the computer that PRINT can keep a printer fully occupied while you have most of the processing time for whatever you're working on.)

> Before you can use it, your printer must be cabled to the computer, plugged in, turned on, and on-line (or selected). Also, your printer must have paper, a ribbon or ink cartridge, and possibly a font cartridge or print wheel.

You can print any kind of files, but non-ASCII files tend to have bizarre effects. Many non-ASCII bytes print as graphic or foreign-language characters; others trigger printer functions such as beeping its alarm, ejecting incomplete pages, or changing fonts. This is true even in document files prepared by a word processor. The formatting codes for functions such as word wrapping and bold-faced type are usually non-ASCII codes.

To print files through the Shell:

1. Prepare the printer, if necessary.

2. Select the files you want to print.

3. Choose File.

A confirmation message appears on the screen, but you might not see anything more than a flash on a fast system. Your files should start printing shortly. If not, the printer probably isn't ready. Check that the cable is tightly connected at both ends and that your printer is turned on.

Understanding the Print Queue

PRINT maintains a print queue, which is a list of files waiting to be printed. You can line up 10 files in the queue. Every time you choose File Print, PRINT adds the selected files to the end of the queue.

Figure 10.5 shows the Print File dialog box, which opens when the print queue has no more room. PRINT continues to print while you make up your mind what to do. You can leave the message on-screen while some files finish printing and then choose option 1 to add more files to the print queue, but that ties up the computer and defeats the entire purpose of using PRINT to print in the background. Or you can choose option 3 (or press Cancel), let PRINT finish the current queue while you do other work, and then select the unprinted files and try again. (Option 2 doesn't make much sense when the print queue is full; it won't have room for the next file either.)

Figure 10.5.
The PRINT *queue*
is full *message.*

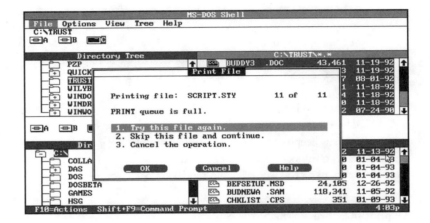

Understanding Print Formatting

As print functions go, PRINT is kind of primitive. It can't do many of the things that text editor and word processor print functions do, such as numbering pages or enabling you to print multiple copies. It does break the text into pages, but that's about it. PRINT's main advantage is that, after initialization, you don't have to load any program to use it. And it prints in the background, even when you're not using the task swapper.

For the Future

If you find that you make heavy use of PRINT, you might want to learn more about it. There's quite a bit more to the PRINT command than you have seen here. You can, for example, enlarge the print queue or allot more time to printing (giving less to your other work). When you're working at the command prompt, you can view the print queue, remove files from it, and add other files to it.

If you want to know more about PRINT, look up the PRINT command in the Command Reference at the back of the book.

Working with Programs

11

Introduction

You don't have to exit DOS Shell to run a program. In fact, it's often better to run programs from within the Shell.

Executing Programs
from the Shell

You can start a program from the Shell screen and return to the same screen when it ends. There are several ways to run a program from the Shell, and each has some advantages and some disadvantages.

Launching a Program
from the File List

One way to start a program is to open its executable file from the file list. This means you must know the name of its program file, but that's not too hard to figure out. It's usually the program name with an EXE extension, as in WORD.EXE or MEM.EXE. The extension might also be COM or BAT.

When you start a program this way, the Shell screen clears, and the program begins. Then a message asks you to press any key to return to MS-DOS Shell. If there's a final message from the program, you can take all the time you need to examine it before returning to the Shell.

> As usual, a shifting or a locking key doesn't qualify as a keystroke. You must press a character or function key to return to the Shell.

To launch a program from the file list:

1. Open the directory containing the program.

2. Double-click the program's EXE (or COM or BAT) file. Or, you can select the program's EXE (or COM or BAT) file and press Enter.

3. When you're finished with the program, press a key to return to the Shell screen.

You can't run every program this way. Windows applications, for example, can't start without Windows. You receive an error message if you try. Many programs, such as DIR and COPY, are built into DOS's command processor and don't have their own program files. Also, any program that requires a startup parameter, such as a filespec or a switch, can't be launched from the file list because there's no chance to enter the startup parameter. The FORMAT program, for example, requires a drive name. If you try to run it from the file list, you receive the error message Required parameter missing.

Dropping a File Name or a Program Name

Another way to launch a program from the file list is to use your mouse to drop a file name entry on the program file. This procedure starts the program using the dropped file as the initial file.

If, for example, you drag the file name APPNOTES.TXT and drop it on PRINT.EXE, the Confirm Mouse Operation dialog box, shown in figure 11.1, appears. When you press Yes, the PRINT program adds the APPNOTES.TXT file to its print queue. As another example, you could drop the file name MEMO.DOC on WORD.EXE to start Microsoft Word with the MEMO.DOC file open.

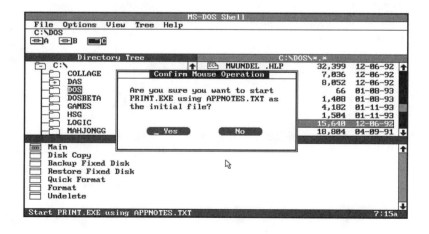

Figure 11.1.
Confirm Mouse Operation dialog box.

129

As you drag a data file around in the file list, the mouse pointer changes from the "No" symbol to a file icon when you cross over an executable program file. Don't mistake this as a signal that the program is appropriate for the data file. DOS permits you to drop a data file on any program file, regardless of appropriateness. If you drag multiple files, only the last selected file becomes the initial file for the program.

While you're dragging a file, you can scroll the file list by dragging the file on top of the scroll bar arrows. You may need to scroll to find the desired program file.

Chapter 12 shows you how to drag a data file to a program file in another directory.

To launch a program by dropping a file name on it:

1. Select the data file.

2. Drag it to the program file's entry, scrolling as necessary.

3. Drop the data file on the program file.

4. Press Yes in the confirmation dialog box.

5. When the program terminates, press a key to return to the Shell screen.

When you launch a program this way, the Shell passes the filespec to the program as an initial parameter. This procedure will not work if the program isn't designed to handle an initial file. Dropping a file name on FORMAT.COM, for example, results in an error message.

Opening an Associated File

By default, DOS Shell associates all TXT files with the EDIT program and all BAS files with QBASIC. This means that you can launch the program with an initial data file simply by opening the data file in the file list. If, for example, you open README.TXT, DOS starts EDIT with README.TXT as the initial file.

To launch a program from an associated file:

> Double-click the associated file.

> Select the associated file and press Enter (or choose File Open).

This is one of the easiest ways to run a program from the Shell. You might want to establish more file associations than the two that DOS provides. You might, for example, want to associate your document files with your word processor, your worksheet files with your spreadsheet, your databases with your database manager, and so on. Figure 11.2 shows the Associate File dialog box, which lets you associate a file extension with an application.

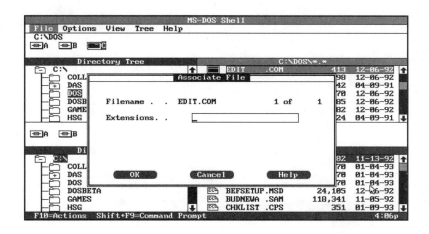

Figure 11.2.
Associate File
dialog box.

To associate a file extension with a program:

1. Select the program file.

2. Choose File Associate.

3. Add the extension to the dialog box.

4. Press OK.

You can associate as many extensions with a program as you want, but not vice versa. An extension can be associated with only one program; otherwise, DOS Shell wouldn't know what program to start when you opened the associated file.

If you use Windows, don't take the time to associate Windows applications
with their files. You can't start Windows applications under the Shell.

Launching Programs from the Program List

Another way to start programs is to open items in the program list. Opening the
Editor item, for example, starts the DOS editor. You learned in Chapter 9 how to
start the UNDELETE program from the program list.

To start a program from the program list:

1. Open the program group containing the desired item.

2. Select the program item and press Enter. Or, you can double-click the
   program item.

An item in the program list might be defined to display a dialog box so that you can
enter startup parameters, such as a filespec or drive name. Figure 11.3 shows the File
to Edit dialog box, which appears when you open the Editor item. In this dialog box,
you can enter the name of an initial file for the EDIT program.

Figure 11.3.
Starting EDIT from
the program list.

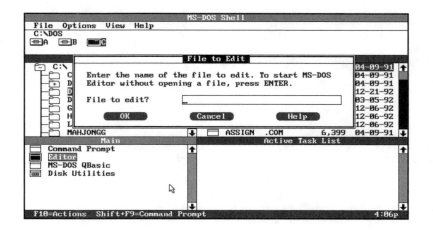

You also can request help for many program items. Just select the item (but don't open it) and press F1. The help information should explain something about the program and its parameters.

When the program terminates, you may or may not have to press a key to return to DOS Shell. Some programs return directly to the Shell. But the ones that leave a final message on the screen usually let you decide when to return.

Working at the Command Prompt

Another way to execute a program from the Shell is to go to the command prompt, enter a command, let it execute, and return to the Shell when it's done. You can read about this technique in Chapter 13 after you've seen DOS's command structure.

Task Swapping

With DOS Shell, you can start more than one program at a time. You might, for example, start a word processor, spreadsheet, database, and a drawing program. Then you can switch among them as needed to accomplish the work you're doing.

With task swapping, only one task at a time can be active. The other tasks lie dormant while you work on the active one. You don't lose your place in the dormant tasks, but they can't do any processing when they're not active (except for PRINT). This is a distinct difference from a multitasking system, such as Windows, in which several programs can be active at once, sharing processing time so that one program can be printing or calculating (for example) while you are entering data in another.

Another difference between task swapping and multitasking is that you can't copy data from one task to the other with task swapping. If you want to copy a name and address from your database into the letter that you're writing, for example, you either must memorize, print, or copy the address down on paper and then switch to the word processor and type in the data. (Windows copies the name and address for you.)

There's another major difference between Windows and task swapping. With Windows, you can see several tasks on the screen at the same time. With task swapping, you see only the active task.

But even though task swapping does not provide a true multitasking environment, it offers some real advantages over systems that do no multitasking at all. And it even has some advantages over Windows: it's cheaper, you already have it, it takes up considerably fewer system resources, and you don't have to buy special software to use with it.

To start task swapping, choose the Enable Task Swapper command from the Options menu. Your DOS Shell screen changes to show the task list (see fig. 11.4), which is empty at first. Each program you start from here on will be added to the task list. In the figure, three programs have been started.

Figure 11.4.
Shell screen with task swapping enabled.

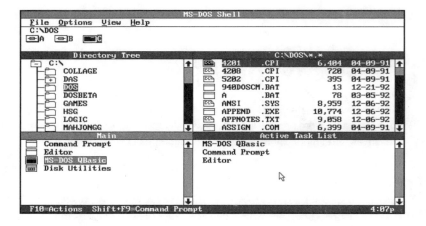

Starting Tasks

To start a task, simply start a program. The program automatically becomes a task and is added to the task list. Of course, at first you can't see the task list because you're looking at the program's screen. You learn later in this chapter how to switch back to the Shell screen from a program.

You also can start a task without leaving the Shell screen by holding down Shift while you start the program. To start DOS's EDIT program without leaving the Shell screen, for example, you could hold down Shift while you double-click Editor in the program list, or you could select Editor and press Shift-Enter. The task is added to the task list. (With some programs, including the editor, a dialog box appears first to collect initial parameters.)

You can start the same program several times, and each copy becomes a separate task. You could, for example, have one Editor task working on AUTOEXEC.BAT, another Editor task working on CONFIG.SYS, and a third Editor task working on REPORT.TXT. The first task would be displayed as `Editor` in the task list, the second as `Editor.` (with a dot), and the third as `Editor..` (with two dots).

Switching Tasks

To switch to a particular task from the Shell screen, open the task in the task list. Or, if the task has a hotkey listed next to it, press the hotkey. When you're working in a task, you can switch back to the Shell screen by pressing Ctrl-Esc.

Some programs (such as DOS 6's INTERSVR) inhibit task switching, but these always are programs for which it doesn't make sense or would be dangerous to switch away without terminating the program.

You don't have to go through the Shell screen to switch from task to task. Table 11.1 shows a set of keys you can use to switch from one task directly to another. (Unfortunately, there are no mouse equivalents for these functions.)

Table 11.1. Task Switching Hotkeys

Key Combo	Effect
Ctrl-Esc	Switch to DOS Shell
Alt-Tab	Switch to previously opened task
Alt-Tab, Tab, ...	Cycle forward through task list

continues

Table 11.1. continued

Key Combo	Effect
Shift-Alt-Tab, Tab, ...	Cycle backward through task list
Alt-Esc	Switch to next task in list
Shift-Alt-Esc	Switch to preceding task in list

Develop the habit of saving your files before switching away from a task, just in case something goes wrong and you can't get back again.

Suppose that you have started five tasks. You are now working in your word processor and want to switch to your graphics program for a moment. Your word processor is task 1, and your graphics program is task 4. Save your current file. Then press Alt-Tab. A screen appears that shows the name of the currently selected task. Continue to hold down the Alt key and press Tab twice to move to the graphics program. When you reach the desired task, release Alt, and that task is opened and moves to the top of the task list.

When you're finished with the graphics program, the fastest way to get back to your word processor is by pressing Alt-Tab, which always returns you to the previous open task (and moves that task to the top of the list). You can now switch back and forth between the word processor and the graphics program simply by pressing Alt-Tab.

DOS Shell is counted as a task even though it doesn't appear in the task list. It's always at the bottom of the list.

When your task list is long, you may be able to get where you're going faster by cycling backward through the list with Shift-Alt-Tab, Tab, and so on.

In Table 11.1, you can see that Alt-Esc and Shift-Alt-Esc also cycle through the task list, but they have two important differences from Alt-Tab and Shift-Alt-Tab:

- When you use the Esc key, each task is opened as you cycle to it so that you can see it on-screen. This takes more time, but it's nice if you can't remember which task you want, because they have similar names.

- The order of tasks is not changed by the Esc key, although the entire list is cycled so that the currently open task appears at the top. (The DOS Shell task always remains at the bottom.)

Ending a Task

When you terminate a program, DOS Shell closes its task and removes it from the task list. Terminate each program just as you would if you weren't using task swapping. But don't kill a malfunctioning program by rebooting unless you have no other choice. Rebooting kills all the current tasks, which could leave files open and unsaved. This could abandon not just your data files but also the program's support files and temporary work files.

If you really need to kill a task, you can abort it from the Shell screen. Afterwards, all other programs are suspect, and you should reboot to make a clean start.

To kill a misbehaving program:

1. Return to the Shell screen, if possible.

2. Select the misbehaving task.

3. Press Delete to abort the task. Press OK in the warning box.

4. Close all other tasks normally, if possible.

5. Exit DOS Shell.

6. Reboot.

You can exit DOS Shell with task swapping enabled, but there must not be any tasks running.

Ending the Task Swapper

Task swapping stays on until you turn it off, even if you exit the Shell and reboot. Because the Task Swapper takes up memory space, you might want to terminate it when you don't need it.

To terminate task swapping:

1. Terminate all tasks.

2. Choose Enable Task Swapper from the Options menu.

When the task swapper terminates, the task list disappears from your screen.

Customizing the Shell

12

Introduction

So far, you have been working with the standard Shell screen. But you can tailor it for yourself and others.

Managing the Program List

The program list is the easiest and most flexible way of starting programs, once you get it set up properly. When you first install DOS 6, the program list contains a number of items in the Main group and the Disk Utilities group. If the Shell is your main interface with DOS, you probably will want to add your own groups and items to the list. You may even want to redefine the items provided by DOS.

Suppose that you manage three databases: CUSTOMER.DB, ORDERS.DB, and SUPPLIER.DB. You also access several other databases on occasion. You might want to set up a separate Databases group with several items, as follows:

- Customers database (opens CUSTOMER.DB)

- Orders database (opens ORDERS.DB)

- Suppliers database (opens SUPPLIER.DB)

- Other databases (lets you enter the name of the initial database file in a dialog box)

You might create similar groups for your major word processing projects, spreadsheets, and whatever other applications you work with frequently.

Defining a Group

Figure 12.1 shows the Add Group dialog box, which you use to define a new group. You must provide a name for the group. All the other items are optional. The name can be up to 23 characters long, including spaces. Whatever you enter here appears in the program list.

You might want to provide help text if other people will be using the group you are creating. The help text can be up to 255 characters long, including spaces. DOS Shell displays the help text in a dialog box when someone selects the group name and presses F1. To start a new paragraph in the help text, type a caret (^) followed by an **M**. (Don't press Enter in the help text box to start a new paragraph; Enter closes the dialog box.)

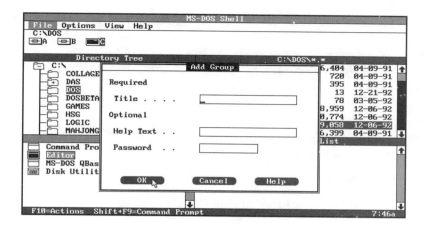

Figure 12.1.
Add Group
dialog box.

Two ^M codes in a row insert a blank line between paragraphs, which makes a paragraph break more obvious.

You also can assign a password (up to 20 characters) to the new group. When a group is password protected, DOS Shell displays the Password dialog box, shown in figure 12.2, whenever anyone tries to open or modify the group. You must enter the correct password to continue.

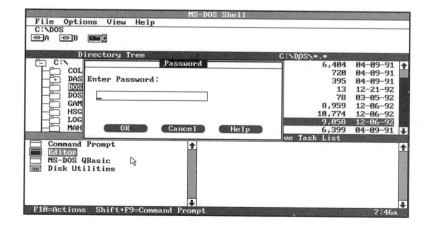

Figure 12.2.
Password
dialog box.

DOS Shell's password protection is not very powerful. A savvy user can find out the password by examining the DOSSHELL.INI file. (You can, too, if you forget a password.)

The password is case-sensitive; if you type **Jane's Coffee Shop** as your password, variations, such as "Jane's coffee shop" or "JANE'S COFFEE SHOP," won't work. This is one of the few times that DOS pays attention to case.

To create a program group:

1. Open the group that will be the parent of the new group.

2. Choose File New. (The program list must be active.)

3. In the first dialog box, choose Program Group.

4. In the next dialog box, type a title up to 23 characters long.

5. You can enter some help text (up to 255 characters long) if you want.

6. You also can define a password (up to 20 characters long).

7. Press OK.

You should see the new program group in your program list immediately.

To modify a group definition:

1. Select the program group (in its parent list).

2. Choose File Properties. You might have to enter a password. (The Program Group Properties dialog box shows your definition of the group. It looks exactly the same as the Add Group dialog box.)

3. Change the definition as desired.

4. Press OK to close the dialog box.

You can delete a program group as long as it's empty.

To delete a program group:

1. Open the group.

2. Delete all program items and subgroups. (Don't try to delete the parent group name.)

3. Return to the parent group.

4. Select the subgroup without opening it.

5. Press the Delete key.

6. Choose Delete This Item in the confirmation box and press OK.

Defining a Program Item

Now that you have a new group, you might want to add some items to it. Figure 12.3 shows the Add Program dialog box, in which you define a program item. You must define a Program Title and Commands; the other fields are optional.

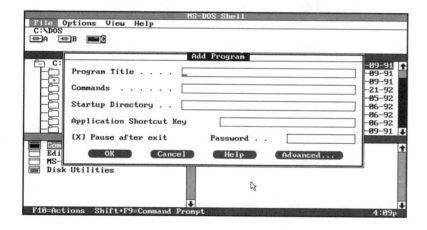

Figure 12.3.
Add Program
dialog box.

The program title can have up to 23 characters, including spaces. Whatever you type here appears in the program list. The Commands box defines the command to be submitted to DOS when someone opens the item. To start Microsoft Word, for example, you would type **WORD** in the Commands box. You can enter up to 25 characters in the box, including spaces.

If you specify a startup directory, DOS Shell switches to that directory before starting the program. This is one way of guaranteeing that DOS can find your files. But this option changes the current directory in the Shell, and some people find that annoying.

The Application Shortcut Key field is used for task swapping, as you learned in Chapter 11. To assign a hotkey to the item, place the cursor in the text box and press the key combination you want to use. The hotkey must use Ctrl or Alt; you also can use Shift. The Shell spells out the key combination you press. If, for example, you press Ctrl-E, the expression `CTRL-E` appears in the text box. If nothing appears, your key combination is not a legitimate hotkey; try again.

The Pause After Exit box is checked by default. This causes DOS Shell to display the message `Press any key to return to MS-DOS Shell` when the program terminates. If you uncheck this box, the Shell screen returns automatically as soon as the program terminates. Unchecking the box eliminates an extra step, but be sure that the program doesn't issue any kind of final message that you might want to read. If you discover that you can't read all the messages you need, check this box again.

You can password protect the program item (somewhat weakly) by entering a password of up to 20 characters in the Password box, and you can provide help text. Selecting the Advanced button opens another dialog box that contains advanced options along with the Help text box. You can enter up to 255 characters, including spaces, in this text box, and you can use ^M to start a new paragraph.

To define a new program item:

1. Open the group to contain the item.

2. Choose File New. (The program list must be active.)

3. In the first dialog box, select Program Item and choose OK.

4. In the next dialog box, enter a program title (up to 23 characters long) and startup command (up to 25 characters long).

5. If desired, enter a startup directory, define a shortcut key, uncheck Pause After Exit, or enter a password.

6. If you want to enter help text, press Advanced, enter the help text in the Advanced dialog box, and press OK to return to the Add Program dialog box.

7. Press OK to close the Add Program dialog box.

The new program item should appear in the program list immediately.

To modify the definition of a program item:

1. Select the item.

2. Choose File Properties. You might have to enter a password. (The Program Item Properties dialog box contains your definition of the item.)

3. Change the definition as needed.

4. Press OK.

To delete an item:

1. Select the item without opening it.

2. Press the Delete key.

3. Select Delete This Item in the confirmation box and choose OK.

Deleting an item doesn't delete the program itself from the disk. It merely deletes the program item from the program list.

Copying Programs to a Group

When you're setting up groups for a variety of users, it sometimes is handy to copy a program item from group to group.

To copy a program item:

1. Select the item.

2. Choose File Copy or press F8. (The program list must be active.) A note on the message line tells you to `Press F2 to complete the copy`.

3. Open the destination group.

4. Press F2.

If you want to move the item instead of copying it, simply return to its original group and delete it.

Choosing Display Options

The more information you can squeeze on your screen at once, the less you must scroll to find the items you want, and the more easily you can drag files. Figure 12.4 shows the Screen Display Mode dialog box that opens when you choose Options Display. This dialog box shows you the display options for your monitor. You can experiment with the options and select the one that works best for you.

Figure 12.4.
Screen Display
Mode dialog box.

To try various display options:

1. Choose Options Display.

2. Select an option you want to try.

3. Select Preview. (The screen changes to show what that display option looks like, but the dialog box remains open.)

4. Repeat steps 2 and 3 until you decide which option you want to use.

5. Choose OK. (The dialog box closes, and the screen changes to the new option.)

Customizing the Screen Colors

Figure 12.5 shows the Color Scheme dialog box, which opens when you choose Options Colors. The Shell offers several color schemes, including black and white. Some combinations might work better than others on your monitor. You can try them using the Preview button and select the one you like best.

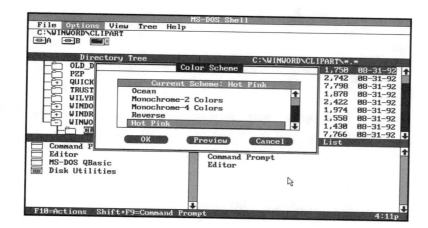

Figure 12.5.
Color Scheme
dialog box.

Customizing the File List

Even the file list can be tailored on a temporary or permanent basis. Figure 12.6 shows the File Display Options dialog box that opens when you select Options File Display Options.

Filtering the File List

You don't have to display all the files in a directory. You can enter a file name in the Name box to limit the list to files that match that name. Suppose, for example, that you want to delete all BAK files on the drive. You could enter *.BAK in the Name box and then choose View All Files to display all the BAK files on the drive.

Pressing Ctrl-/ selects them all without selecting any other files on the drive, because you can select listed files only. Then all you have to do is press Delete to erase them all.

Figure 12.6.
File Display
Options dialog box.

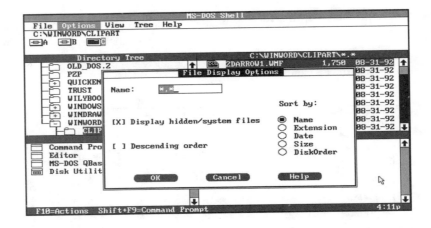

You might want to turn the Confirm on Delete option off for this operation, but if you do, turn it on again immediately afterward.

Suppose, for example, that you have misplaced the file named INTELLIG.DAT. You could enter INTELLIG.DAT in the Name box and choose View All Files. Every copy of INTELLIG.DAT would appear in the file list, and no other files would appear. You could then select each one and examine the Show Information box to see its directory.

Changing drives and views doesn't affect the filter, but the default *.* filter is restored when you terminate DOS Shell.

The title bar of the file list always shows the current file filter (along with the current path). You probably have been ignoring the title bar so far, but it's important to know when you're using a filter, because it could affect the results of your commands. If you can't find a file you're looking for, check to see whether you're filtering it out.

When a file filter causes a file list to be empty even though the directory contains files, DOS Shell displays the message `No files match file specifier` in the file list. This message tells you that the directory does contain files but they're being filtered out. When a directory is truly empty, the message says `No files in selected directory`.

Displaying Hidden and System Files

Files with hidden and system attributes should not normally be accessible for operations such as deleting, moving, and copying. For that reason, DOS Shell does not normally display hidden and system files in the file list. But you may want to display them, especially if you're trying to empty a directory so that you can remove it.

In the File Display Options dialog box, you should check the Display Hidden/System Files box to include the files in your file list. Uncheck the box again to hide them. Remember that if a file is not displayed, you can't select it. But be aware that some programs might access and process those files even if you can't see them in the file list.

The message `No files match file specifier` is displayed if files exist in the directory that you can't see. If the file filter is *.*, you can be assured that the unseen files have either the hidden or the system attribute, or both.

Sorting the File List

By default, DOS Shell displays the file list sorted by name in ascending alphabetic order. There are several other ways to arrange the file list. In the File Display Options dialog box, you can choose to sort in alphabetic order by extension (instead of file name), in chronological order by date and time, or in numeric order by file size. Even the DiskOrder option occasionally is useful. This option displays the file list in the order that the files actually appear in the directory as it is stored on the disk. (This order seems arbitrary because DOS always reuses the first deleted entry it comes to when storing a new file.)

The DEFRAG program, described in Chapter 34, can rearrange the order of the directory entries.

In the File Display Options dialog box, check the Descending Order box to reverse the order of the selected sort option. If, for example, you select Size and check Descending Order, the file list is displayed from the largest to the smallest file. If you reverse Date order, files are displayed from the newest to the oldest.

If you display two file lists with View Dual File Lists, both lists are affected by the display options. When you exit DOS Shell, the default file filter is restored, but the other display options are remembered and will be in effect the next time you start DOS Shell.

DOS Commands

Includes

Working at the Command Prompt

13

Introduction

Working at the command prompt is quite different from using the Shell screen. This chapter shows you some of the basics.

Understanding Commands

You can do many things from the command prompt that you can't do in the Shell. DOS 6, for example, includes a DELTREE command that deletes an entire directory branch without making you empty all the directories first. DOS utilities, such as FORMAT, UNFORMAT, UNDELETE, DEFRAG, and CHKDSK are started by commands. In fact, the last two programs should never be run under Windows or the Shell.

When you know how to use commands, you can create program items for the Shell's program list as well as batch programs that can be started from the Shell's file list, run at the command prompt, and passed around to other users.

When you understand commands, you can understand batch programs that you receive from other people. You will understand your own AUTOEXEC.BAT file—an important benefit. And, if you buy an application that includes batch programs, you will be able to figure out what they're doing. Whenever you're working with your PC, the less helpless you are, the better.

Getting to the Command Prompt

You can get to the command prompt in several ways, each with different effects. The primary way, of course, is to reboot. If your AUTOEXEC.BAT file doesn't start Windows or DOS Shell, the command prompt appears.

If your AUTOEXEC.BAT file does start Windows or DOS Shell, another way to get to the command prompt is to terminate that program. Press F3 to terminate DOS Shell. Choose File Exit Windows to terminate Windows.

The command prompt that you get to this way is called the *primary command prompt*. You are at the top of DOS, so to speak. You can do things at this command prompt that you shouldn't do in other command prompt situations, as you learn soon.

Secondary Command Prompts

Many programs let you access a command prompt temporarily so that you can run a command or two and then return to the program without losing your place. Many applications, for example, have a Run DOS or DOS Command command. Windows 3.1 offers an MS-DOS Prompt program item. When you go to a command prompt this way—under the wings of another program that is still open—the prompt is a *secondary command prompt*.

To access a secondary command prompt from DOS Shell:

● Open the Command Prompt item in the Main program group.

  or

● Press Shift-F9.

It is easy to remember this key combination—a reminder on the Shell message line says `Shift+F9=Command Prompt`.

In general, you can enter commands at a secondary command prompt just as at the primary one, but there are some important exceptions:

● Don't load any TSRs (terminate-and-stay-resident programs) from a secondary command prompt. Doing so could cause you to run out of memory later on or could cause a program to hang up. That's why Chapter 10 tells you to exit DOS Shell to initialize the Print program and then to restart the Shell.

● Don't run any program that deals directly with the FAT and directory structure of a disk and counts on all files being closed. The program that's paused, such as DOS Shell, might have several files open. Several DOS utilities should not be run from a secondary command prompt for this reason. The CHKDSK program (discussed in Chapter 28), for example, analyzes the FAT and directory structure for errors and inconsistencies and corrects the ones it finds; CHKDSK could damage open files. As another example, the DEFRAG program (discussed in Chapter 34) reorganizes the data in the clusters to make more efficient use of the hard disk; this program definitely will damage open files.

To return to DOS Shell from a secondary command prompt type **EXIT**.

Never shut down or reboot from a secondary command prompt. Doing so cuts off the paused program without giving it a chance to close its files properly. Be sure to exit to the paused program and end it normally before rebooting or shutting down. The general rule is reboot or shut down only from the primary command prompt.

The File Run Command

DOS Shell offers a way of accessing a secondary command prompt just long enough to run one command. Figure 13.1 shows the Run dialog box, which opens when you choose File Run. When you enter a command in the box (up to 127 characters), DOS Shell opens a secondary command prompt, executes the command, and then displays the message Press any key to return to MS-DOS Shell.

Figure 13.1.
Run dialog box with sample command entered.

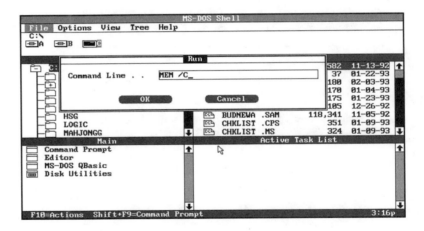

To run one command at a secondary command prompt:

1. Choose File Run.

2. Type the command in the Run dialog box.

3. Press OK.

Each method of accessing a command prompt has its advantages and disadvantages. When you use File Run, you don't have to type the EXIT command to return to the Shell. But when you use Shift-F9 (or the Command Prompt program item), you can enter as many commands as you want before returning to the Shell. And, you have learned that the major advantage of the primary command prompt is that you can start TSRs and programs that manipulate the FAT and directory structure.

Understanding Command Format

A DOS command has the following general format:

```
command-name [parameters] [switches]
```

The *command-name* is the name of the program that you want to execute. It is the executable file's file name. If, for example, the program file is named FORMAT.COM, the command name would be FORMAT. If the program file is named RUNOUT.BAT, the command name would be RUNOUT.

> In a format statement, *italics* indicate where you must substitute a word or some other data when you actually type the command.

The parameters and switches depend on the program. A *parameter* is some kind of variable information that tells the program what you want to do. When starting DOS's EDIT program, for example, you can enter a filespec as a parameter to open a document for editing, as follows:

```
EDIT README.TXT
```

When starting DOS's FORMAT program, you must include a drive name as a parameter, as follows:

```
FORMAT A:
```

Other programs have other types of parameters; a few programs have none.

A *switch* is a particular kind of parameter, usually in the form of a word or letter prefixed by a slash that selects a particular option for the program. You can, for example, make a disk bootable by adding /S to the FORMAT command, as follows:

```
FORMAT C: /S
```

DOS's DIR program displays a directory in file name order when you enter this command:

```
DIR /ON
```

As you can see in these command examples, you use spaces to separate parameters and switches from the command name and from each other.

A command is limited to 127 characters. Most commands never come near that limit.

DOS ignores case in commands; you can type them in uppercase, lowercase, or any mixture of the two. This book shows them in uppercase merely to make them stand out in the text.

Using Paths in Commands

When you enter a command, DOS makes a valiant effort to find the program that the command requests. It looks first in its own COMMAND.COM file to see if the program is there. (Programs contained in COMMAND.COM are called internal programs; they don't have their own program files.) Then it looks in the current directory for an executable file (with the extension EXE, COM, or BAT) with the correct file name.

What happens if DOS doesn't find the executable file in the current directory? DOS maintains a list of directories to search for programs, called the *program search path*. DOS looks in each directory in turn until it finds the necessary executable file.

But what if DOS reaches the end of the program search path and it still hasn't found the file? It gives up and displays this message `Bad command or file name`. DOS can't find that program file in the current directory or the program search path.

But you can override DOS's usual routine and tell it exactly where to look for a program by attaching a path to the command name. You can reach any directory this way. If, for example, UNFOLD.BAT is in directory C:\MAILING, the following command would start it up whether or not C:\MAILING is in the program search path:

```
C:\>C:\MAILING\UNFOLD [parameters] [switches]
```

Attaching a path to the command name affects only where DOS searches for the program file. It does not affect filespecs included as parameters in the command. Suppose, for example, that the complete UNFOLD command looks like this:

```
C:\>C:\MAILING\UNFOLD JUNE-AD.TXT
```

It is UNFOLD's problem, not DOS's, to find the JUNE-AD.TXT file. Where it looks depends on how it's programmed, but it probably looks first in the current directory, which is C:\ (not C:\MAILING). You might need to attach a path to the filespec to indicate where it can be found, even if it's in the same directory as the program file.

You can help DOS find a program file in other ways:

- Add the desired program's directory to the program search path.

- Switch to the desired directory (so that it's the current directory) before entering the command (the CD command is discussed in Chapter 15).

Each of these solutions has side effects that you might not find desirable. The first solution makes the search path longer, which makes DOS search more directories when it's trying to find a program file. The second changes the current directory, which could affect where the program looks for its data and support files.

Redirecting Command Output

Many DOS commands display messages. The DIR (directory) command, for example, lists the contents of a directory. The PATH command, with no parameters, displays the current search path. Under ordinary circumstances, such messages are displayed on your monitor. But you can redirect them to a file or an external device, such as a printer. The greater-than symbol (>) is used to redirect command messages. The following command saves the current directory listing in a file named DIRC:

```
DIR > DIRC
```

This command would replace an existing DIRC file.

The following command prints the current directory listing on a parallel printer attached to LPT1:

```
DIR > LPT1
```

Table 13.1 shows names of devices to which you can redirect output.

Table 13.1. Output Device Names

Name	Device
LPTn	Parallel printer port; LPT1 is the first parallel printer port.
PRN	Same as LPT1.
COMn	Serial (communications port; COM1 is the first serial port).
AUX	Auxiliary port.
NUL	Nowhere; the output is suppressed.
COM	Monitor screen.

DOS commands produce ASCII text messages. When you redirect the messages to a file, a standard ASCII file is created. When you redirect them to an output device, that device must be set up to handle ASCII text. Most devices can—but you could not, for example—redirect command messages to a PostScript printer.

Not all command messages are redirected by >; just the standard messages. Error messages are still sent to the monitor. This can create an interesting situation with a program like DIR. When DIR can't find a file to list, it normally displays a set of messages something like this:

```
Volume in drive C is MICROMATE
Volume Serial Number is 199A-59E3
Directory of C:\WILYBOOK
File not found
```

The first three lines are standard messages; the last line is an error message. If you redirect the output to a file, the first three lines are stored in the file, but the last line is displayed on your screen.

Only standard messages are redirected. Other program output goes to its normal place. The COPY program, for example, creates a file on the target directory or device. If you redirect the output of COPY, only its standard messages (such as 1 Files Copied) are redirected; the new file is not redirected.

You can redirect the output of any program that produces standard messages on the monitor. It doesn't have to be one of the DOS utilities.

Introduction to the Command Reference

The back half of this book is a complete DOS command reference, arranged in alphabetical order by command name. For each command, the Command Reference documents the command format (or formats, if the command can take more than one form), the parameters and switches, and any notes pertaining to the command. A complete set of examples also is provided.

The command reference includes all DOS commands and options, even those intermediate and advanced ones that aren't discussed in the tutorial part of this book. The command reference doesn't attempt to explain commands and options in a tutorial fashion; it just documents them.

The command reference uses several typographical conventions to portray command syntax. Words and phrases in all capital letters must be entered just as shown in the command. The VER command's format, for example, looks like this:

VER

This command displays the current DOS version number. To use it, you type the word **VER** and press Enter. (It doesn't have to be in all uppercase letters. Remember that DOS ignores case most of the time.)

Words and phrases in lowercase italics must be replaced with specific information when you enter the command. The DEL command, for example, is used to delete files. Its format looks like this:

```
DEL filespec
```

You must type the word **DEL** followed by a filespec, as follows:

```
DEL C:\CONFIG.OLD
```

Words and phrases enclosed in square brackets are optional. They make a difference in the effect of the command. The DATE and TIME commands, for example, let you examine and change the system date and time. Their formats look like this:

```
DATE [date]
TIME [time]
```

If you enter **DATE** without a date, DOS displays the current system date and asks whether you want to change it. If you add a date to the command, DOS changes the system date without asking. Similarly, TIME without a time displays the current time and asks whether you want to change it; if you specify a time, DOS changes the system time.

Sometimes options have options, causing a nest of square brackets. The DIR command can have this format:

```
DIR [/A[attributes]]
```

You use this format to list files with certain attributes. When you use the /A switch, you can add attributes to it or not. If not, files with all attributes are listed. But if you add specific attributes, only files with those attributes are listed. The following command, for example, lists only files with the read-only attribute:

```
DIR /AR
```

In some cases, a parameter can be used only with another parameter. This also causes a nest of square brackets. The DEVICEHIGH command, for example, (which loads device drivers into upper memory) looks like this:

```
DEVICEHIGH=filespec [/L:region[,min] [/S]]
```

The /L:*region* parameter is optional. If you use it, you also can add a comma and a *min* parameter, and you can follow it with the /S switch. Notice that the /S is enclosed in the brackets that contain /L:*region*. You can't use /S without /L:*region*.

Three dots (...) are used to indicate parameters that can be repeated. The PATH command, for example, looks like this:

```
PATH [path[;path]...]
```

If you specify one path parameter, you can add a second one separated by a semi-colon. The three dots indicate that you can repeat the ;*path parameter* to add directories to the command.

Sometimes you can choose between two mutually exclusive parameters, indicated by a vertical bar (|). The VERIFY command, for example, looks like this:

```
VERIFY [ON ¦ OFF]
```

This command turns controls whether DOS verifies everything it writes on disk. VERIFY ON turns verification on; VERIFY OFF turns it off. VERIFY without a parameter displays the current verification status.

When you combine several of these features, command syntax can get pretty complex. In the command reference, the notes and examples should help you understand how you can use the commands in practice.

The PATH Program

The PATH program sets the program search path. Figure 13.2 shows the format of this command. If you enter just the word **PATH** with no parameters, PATH displays the current search path, which may look something like this:

```
PATH C:\DOS;C:\;C:\WP;C:\MAILING
```

The command summary shown in figure 13.2 summarizes the PATH command. See the Command Reference section for complete command information, including advanced parameters and considerations.

Figure 13.2.
PATH command
summary.

> ## PATH
>
> Defines a search path for external executable files (including batch files).
>
> **Format:**
>
> PATH [*path* [;*path*...]]
> PATH ;
>
> **Parameters:**
>
> none   Displays the current search path.
>
> *path*   Identifies a directory to search for program files.
>
> ;   When used as the only parameter, clears the search path.

To replace the current path with a new one, follow the word PATH with a list of directories separated by semicolons. The order that you list the directories determines the order that DOS searches them when it's looking for a program. To search the DOS directory, the WP directory, and the root directory, (in that order), you would enter this command:

PATH C:\DOS;C:\WP;C:\

When you boot, there is no search path. Most users set up the path they want to use all the time in AUTOEXEC.BAT. Your AUTOEXEC.BAT file probably already contains a PATH command. When you install a new program, its INSTALL or SETUP program might add its directory to your PATH command in AUTOEXEC.BAT.

Review your AUTOEXEC.BAT file every once in a while and edit the PATH command to remove directories for programs that you no longer work with and to change the order of the directories to reflect the way you use your program.

DOS commands are limited to 127 characters, so you can't let your PATH command get too long, or the directories at the end will be ignored.

When you enter the PATH command, DOS doesn't check to make sure that the directories are legitimate. But if DOS can't find a directory, DOS displays this message:

```
Invalid directory
```

DOS doesn't stop for an answer. It continues with the next directory in the search path. You must remember that you saw an `Invalid directory` message and check your search path to figure out which one it is.

If DOS gets to the end of the search path without finding the desired program file, it displays this message:

```
Bad command or file name
```

This message doesn't necessarily mean that the program file isn't in your system. It means that DOS didn't find it in the current directory or any directory in the program search path. DOS won't look anywhere else.

The PROMPT Command

The command prompt usually takes the form of the current drive and directory followed by a greater-than sign (>). But you can set up any prompt you want. Just enter a command in this format:

```
PROMPT [text]
```

If you don't specify any text, the current prompt is removed and the default prompt is established. You have probably never seen the default prompt, which is just the drive name followed by a greater-than sign, as follows:

```
C>
```

Because most people want to know not only the current drive but also the current directory, DOS installs a PROMPT command in your AUTOEXEC.BAT file to set up the prompt you're used to, which looks like this when the current directory is the root directory of drive C:

```
C:\>
```

You can change the prompt to any text you want. You can, for example, set up the following prompt:

```
What's next?
```

165

You can accomplish this by typing:

```
C:\>PROMPT What's next?
```

DOS continues to use the new command prompt until you change it again or reboot.

> This is another place where DOS pays attention to case. It uses whatever case you specify in the PROMPT command.

Table 13.2 shows some codes you can use in your PROMPT commands.

Table 13.2. Special Prompt Command Codes

Code	Meaning
$G	Greater than (>)
$$	Dollar sign ($)
$P	The current drive and directory
$D	The current date
$T	The current time

Some of these codes insert special information into the prompt, such as the date or the current directory. Others make certain characters available in the prompt text that otherwise would be interpreted as part of the PROMPT command. You already have learned that > is the redirection symbol, so you can't use it in prompt text. But you can use $G (the G stands for "greater-than") to ask for a > symbol. The standard prompt, is expressed this way:

```
PROMPT $P$G
```

This displays the current drive and directory followed by a greater-than sign. DOS's SETUP program inserted this command into your AUTOEXEC.BAT file for you.

For the Future

You have seen how to redirect standard messages from a command using the > symbol. There are several other forms of redirection that you might want to learn about. You can, for example, append standard messages to an existing file with >>; you can redirect standard input with <; and you can pass standard output from one program to the next with |.

An advanced book, such as *Peter Norton's Advanced DOS 6* (also published by Brady Books), explains these redirection features.

DOSKEY

Introduction

Working at the command prompt used to be awkward and confusing until DOS introduced DOSKEY. Now it's simple.

Understanding What DOSKEY Does

O ften, it is handy to be able to recall and edit a former command rather than typing a new one from scratch. Earlier versions of DOS let you do this to a limited extent, but you had to work blind (you couldn't see the former command). Now you can load a terminate-and-stay-resident program (TSR) named DOSKEY that makes command editing easy.

DOSKEY does more than mere command editing. You also can

● Combine two or more commands in one.

● Create command macros — complex commands that can be executed by entering a simple name.

Figure 14.1 shows the format of the command that starts DOSKEY. If your system is set up for it, you can load DOSKEY into upper memory.

To start DOSKEY using all default parameters, type **DOSKEY** (to load it into conventional memory). Or you can type **LH DOSKEY** (to load it into an upper memory block).

> If you plan to use DOSKEY all the time and you have upper memory blocks available, place the DOSKEY command in AUTOEXEC.BAT and run MEMMAKER to optimize it for you.

The size of the DOSKEY buffer determines how many commands it can remember. With the default size (512 bytes), DOSKEY can store about 50 commands with an average length of 10 characters. Most people don't really need to recall that many commands—10 or 20 would be plenty. You probably can save some memory space by cutting the buffer down to its minimum by specifying the /BUFSIZE parameter when you load DOSKEY, as follows:

```
DOSKEY /BUFSIZE=256
```

DOSKEY

Saves and provides access to commands and macros entered at the DOS command prompt.

Format:

```
DOSKEY [/BUFSIZE=size] [/INSERT ¦ /OVERSTRIKE] [/HISTORY]
[/MACROS] [mname=text] [/REINSTALL]
```

Parameters and Switches:

none	Loads the DOSKEY TSR with default values for BUFSIZE and INSERT │ OVERSTRIKE; immediately begins recording commands in the DOSKEY buffer.
/BUFSIZE=size	Specifies the size of the DOSKEY buffer. This parameter is effective only when loading or reinstalling the DOSKEY TSR.
/INSERT	Sets default typing mode to insert.
/OVERSTRIKE	Sets default typing mode to overstrike.
/HISTORY	Lists all commands in the DOSKEY buffer; abbreviate as /H.
/MACROS	Lists all current macros; abbreviate as /M.
mname=text	Defines a macro named *mname*. *Text* defines command(s) to execute when you run *mname*.
/REINSTALL	Installs a new copy of DOSKEY.

Figure 14.1.
DOSKEY command summary (to load DOSKEY).

But don't minimize the buffer if you're going to use macros; they take up about half the buffer space. Macros are discussed in the "Using Macro Power" section later in this chapter.

You can't change the buffer size after DOSKEY is installed, but you can change the default typing mode.

If you have ever done word processing or even text editing with an editor like DOS's EDIT, you know the difference between insert and overstrike mode. And you know that you can toggle between them with the Insert key. Which mode is better? It's your preference, but be sure to set up the mode you like best as the default, because it's restored every time you press Enter. Suppose that you load DOSKEY without specifying a typing mode; overstrike mode is automatically set up as the default. You can change the default mode to insert by using this command:

```
DOSKEY /INSERT
```

The cursor takes the shape of the normal flashing underline when you're in the default typing mode. It becomes a flashing rectangle when you're in the other mode.

Using the Command History

As soon as DOSKEY is loaded, it begins recording commands. Table 14.1 shows the keys you use to recall commands from the buffer. Most often you will simply press the up-arrow key to get back to the command you want. Each time you press up arrow, DOSKEY moves back one more command in the buffer and displays it at the command prompt. If you go back too far, you can move forward again by pressing the down-arrow key. When you see the command you want, edit it as necessary and press Enter.

Table 14.1. Recalling Commands from the DOSKEY Buffer

Key	Action
Up arrow	Recalls the previous command in the buffer.
Down arrow	Recalls the next command in the buffer.
PgUp	Recalls the oldest command in the buffer.
PgDn	Recalls the newest command in the buffer
F8	Recalls the next command in the buffer that starts with the letters on the command line.

Key	Action
F7	Displays a numbered list of all saved commands.
F9	Prompts for a command number, and then recalls that command.
Alt-F7	Deletes all the commands in the buffer.

If you want to go back more than a few commands, it's often convenient to type the first few letters of the command you want and press F8. Suppose, for example, that you want to recall a DEL command you know is about 10 commands back. Type **DEL** and press F8. The most recent DEL command is recalled. If that's not the one you want, press F8 again to recall the next most recent DEL command. Keep pressing F8 until you get the one you want.

Another way to get back to an earlier command is to press F7, which displays all the commands in the buffer, assigning a number to each one. Decide which command you want and press F9. DOSKEY asks for a command number, then it displays the command associated with that number. Obviously, it's easier to just press up arrow a few times. But if you need to go back 25 or 30 commands, then the F7-F9 combination can be much faster. (If you know the command number, you just use F9; F7 is not required.)

Editing Commands

Now that you have some text on the command line, how do you edit it? Simply move the cursor back and forth and insert, delete, and overtype characters. You move the cursor just as you do with a word processor or text editor, except that you can't use a mouse. DOSKEY responds to the cursor keys and to the backspace, Ins, and Del keys. When the command is ready, press Enter to process it (and record it in DOSKEY's buffer).

Combining Commands

Suppose that you want to switch to the parent directory and list it. You could enter two separate commands, but with DOSKEY you can combine them on one command line, as follows:

```
CD .. ¶ DIR
```

Press Ctrl-T to enter the ¶ symbol.

There are two advantages to combining commands. First, it is slightly faster than entering two separate commands. Second, the commands are recorded as one command in the DOSKEY command buffer; when you recall them, you get two commands for the price of one. You're not limited to two commands. You can combine as many commands as you can squeeze into 127 characters. (The ¶ doesn't count as a character.)

Using Macro Power

Suppose that you execute the following command several times a day:

```
FORMAT A: /V:Daily Log ¶ XCOPY C:\LOGDATA\LOG*.DAT A:
```

DOSKEY lets you assign a name, such as MAKELOG, to the command and execute it simply by entering **MAKELOG** at the DOS prompt. This is called a *macro*; using macros is better than recalling the command from the history list because it doesn't get overwritten by newer commands. Figure 14.2 shows the DOSKEY command format for creating macros. You would create the MAKELOG macro using the following commands:

```
DOSKEY MAKELOG=FORMAT A: /V:Daily Log $T XCOPY
C:\LOGDATA\LOG*.DAT A:
```

Figure 14.2.
DOSKEY
command
summary (for
creating macros).

DOSKEY

Defines a macro.

Format:

DOSKEY *mname=text*

Parameters:

mname   Names the macro.

text   Defines a command to be associated with *mname*.

Notes:

Macro definitions can contain these special characters:

$G   Redirects output; equivalent to the redirection symbol for output (>).

$T   Separates commands; equivalent to the DOSKEY command separator (Ctrl-T).

$$ Specifies the dollar-sign character.

$n   Represents a parameter to be specified when the macro is run; *n* may be 1 through 9. These are similar to the batch parameters %1 through %9.

$*   Represents all parameters. $* is replaced by everything on a command line following a macro name.

Notice that the ¶ symbol has been replaced with $T. When you're defining a macro, you can't include any command symbols, such as ¶ and >, or they will be interpreted right away. When you use the special characters defined in figure 14.2 to represent these symbols, DOSKEY stores them in the macro and they're not interpreted until the macro is executed.

Suppose that you want to create a macro named PD that prints the current directory list by redirecting a DIR command to PRN. You must use the special DOSKEY symbol for redirection, because if you use >, DOS would try to redirect the output of the DOSKEY command. (Because DOSKEY issues no messages, nothing would happen.) The correct command to define the macro is as follows:

```
DOSKEY PD=DIR $G PRN
```

Using Replaceable Parameters

Sometimes you want to leave variable parameters out of a macro and supply them when you execute the macro. This makes the macro more flexible, and therefore more useful. You might, for example, want to leave the drive name out of the FORMAT and XCOPY commands in MAKELOG so that you can run it on either drive A or B, depending on the situation. (For ultimate flexibility, you also could leave out the volume label in the FORMAT command and the filespec in the XCOPY command.)

Use the symbols $1 through $9 in a macro definition to indicate where to plug in variable information. To supply the drive name when you execute MAKELOG, for example, you could define the macro as follows:

```
DOSKEY MAKELOG=FORMAT $1 /V:Daily Log $T XCOPY
C:\LOGDATA\LOG*.DAT $1
```

You use the $1 symbol twice to insert the same variable in both places. To run MAKELOG using B as the target drive, you would enter this command:

```
MAKELOG B:
```

DOSKEY replaces every instance of $1 with B: before executing the command.

It's important to remember the replaceable variables when you execute a macro like this. If you just enter the word MAKELOG without a drive name, DOSKEY replaces $1 with a null value (that is, nothing), creating this command:

```
FORMAT /V:Daily Log ¶ XCOPY C:\LOGDATA\LOG*.DAT
```

In this case, the FORMAT command fails because it must have a drive name. Then the XCOPY command copies the requested files to the current directory, because no other destination is specified. Altogether, you don't get the results you wanted.

If you see that a macro is going wrong, you can stop it by pressing Ctrl-C. If the macro contains multiple commands, you must press Ctrl-C once for each remaining command.

Understanding Macro Facts

DOSKEY stores macros in the same buffer as the command history. Every time you save a new macro, it overwrites some of the commands in the buffer—not necessarily the oldest commands, either. So you lose some of your command history. But the reverse is not true: new commands do not overwrite macros. Once you save a macro, it stays there until you reboot.

DOSKEY lets you fill about half the buffer with macros; it saves the other half for the command history. When you have reached the macro limit, DOSKEY displays an error message when you try to create a new macro. If you find that you need more macros than DOSKEY permits, use the /BUFSIZE parameter to create a larger buffer the next time you load DOSKEY.

Macros are stored in memory, not on disk, and that has both good and bad aspects to it. On the plus side, a macro runs very quickly because it doesn't have to be loaded from disk. On the minus side, all your macros are lost when you reboot or power down. But why not add your favorite macro definitions to AUTOEXEC.BAT so that they will be redefined every time you boot? There's no limit to the length of AUTOEXEC.BAT (except the size of the disk). Just be sure to put the macros after the command that loads DOSKEY in AUTOEXEC.BAT.

If you give a macro the same name as another program, the macro overrides the program. If, for example, you name a macro FORMAT, when you type **FORMAT**, you will access the macro instead of the DOS FORMAT program.

Revising Macros

Suppose that you decide you don't like a macro. You can replace it by entering another macro definition for the same macro name, or you can remove it altogether by entering a macro definition with no command. The following definition, for example, deletes the definition of MAKELOG:

```
DOSKEY MAKELOG=
```

Looking at Two More DOSKEY Features

Figure 14.3 shows two more DOSKEY switches used to review your commands and macros. The nice thing about these two switches is that you can redirect them to print. The following command, for example, prints your command list:

```
DOSKEY /H > PRN
```

Figure 14.3.
DOSKEY
command summary
(reviewing
commands and
macros).

DOSKEY

Displays the command history and macro list.

Format:

```
DOSKEY [/HISTORY] [/MACROS]
```

Parameters and Switches:

/HISTORY   Lists all commands in the Doskey buffer; abbreviate as /H.

/MACROS   Lists all current macros; abbreviate as /M.

For the Future

There are a few features of DOSKEY that you might want to explore in the future:

- You can reload DOSKEY without rebooting using the /RELOAD switch.

- You can clear out your command history by pressing Alt-F7.

- You can turn your command list or your macro list into a batch program by redirecting it to a BAT file.

- You can use macros to override DOS commands.

When you're ready to learn more about these DOSKEY features, look up DOSKEY in the Command Reference.

Managing Directories

15

Introduction

Any directory management you can do in the Shell you also can do at the DOS prompt—and more besides.

Changing the Current Directory

D OS automatically looks for files in the current directory when you don't specify otherwise. When you plan to work with files in one directory, you save time (and potential mistakes) by making that directory the current one. That way, you don't have to type paths for every filespec.

Figure 15.1 shows the CD command, which you use to change the default directory. CD also can show you the name of a default directory. (Sometimes, you may see CHDIR used as an alternative for CD. It's the same command.)

Figure 15.1.
CD command
summary.

<u>CD</u>

Changes a default directory or displays the name of a default directory.

Syntax:

`CD [drive] [path]`

Parameters:

none	Displays the name of the default directory on the current drive.
drive	Displays the name of the default directory on the specified drive.
path	Specifies the name of new default directory. *Path* must represent an existing directory.

Normally, the command prompt shows you the name of the current directory (that is, the default directory on the current drive). But what if you want to know the name of the default directory on another drive? The following commands, complete with command prompts, show how you would display the name of the default directory on drive D:

```
C:\DOS>CD D:
D:\ORDERS\BACKLOGS
C:\DOS>
```

In this case, the default directory on D is \ORDERS\BACKLOGS.

Figure 15.2 shows a sample directory tree used for the examples in this chapter.

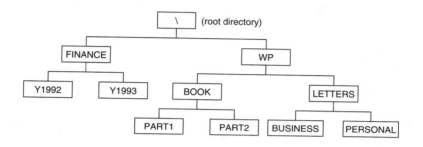

Figure 15.2.
*A directory
structure.*

Suppose that the current directory is the root directory on drive C. The following command changes to the BUSINESS directory:

```
CD \WP\LETTERS\BUSINESS
```

This command also changes to the BUSINESS directory:

```
CD WP\LETTERS\BUSINESS
```

The only difference is the backslash (\) at the beginning of the path. It tells DOS to start from the root directory instead of the current directory. But, because the root is the current directory in this case, you don't really need the initial backslash.

After changing the directory, the new prompt looks like this:

```
C:\WP\LETTERS\BUSINESS>
```

If you want to change to the PERSONAL directory, you could use this command:

```
CD \WP\LETTERS\PERSONAL
```

This time the leading backslash is necessary. Without it, DOS expects to find WP as a child of the current directory, and, of course, it's not there.

Another way exists to get from BUSINESS to PERSONAL. Remember that you can use a double dot (..) to represent the parent of the current directory. Because LETTERS is the parent of BUSINESS, you could switch from BUSINESS to PERSONAL using this command:

```
CD ..\PERSONAL
```

Changing a Default Directory

Sometimes it's convenient to change the default directory on another drive. Suppose that the current directory is the root directory on drive A. Your prompt shows the following:

```
A:\>
```

You don't want to change drives, but you are going to copy some files from A:\ to the \WP\LETTERS\BUSINESS directory on drive C. You can save time and typing if you make BUSINESS the default directory on drive C. Use this command:

```
CD C:\WP\LETTERS\BUSINESS
```

Your prompt doesn't change; the current directory is still the root directory on A. But now you can copy a file to the default directory on C using the following command:

```
COPY JUNE16.LET C:
```

(See Chapter 16 for information on using the COPY command.)

Displaying Directory Structure

When your directory structure starts to get complicated, it's easy to forget how it all fits together. You can use the TREE command (see fig. 15.3) to get a picture of a directory structure. TREE diagrams the relationships between the directories in the structure, much as they're depicted in the Shell's directory tree.

You can display the structure starting from any point on a path. To display the entire structure, you display the tree of the root directory using this command:

```
TREE \
```

The display looks like figure 15.4.

Figure 15.3.
*TREE command
summary.*

TREE

Graphically displays a directory structure.

Syntax:

```
TREE [drive¦path] [/A]
```

Parameters and Switches:

none	Displays the directory structure starting with the current directory.
drive	Displays the directory structure for the specified drive.
path	Displays the directory structure for the specified directory.
/A	Uses text characters instead of graphics characters to show the lines linking subdirectories.

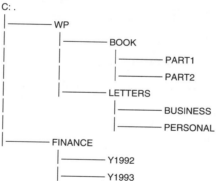

Directory PATH listing
C: .

Figure 15.4.
The TREE listing.

If the directory structure has many entries, some of the structure may roll off the top of the screen before you can read it. To see a long tree, you could redirect your output to the printer using the following command:

```
TREE > PRN
```

Suppose that you want to see just the WP branch. You can enter the following command:

```
TREE \WP
```

If you request a tree for a directory that has no subdirectories, you see the error message `No sub-directories exist`.

Listing a Directory

You can see the contents of a directory by using the DIR command (see fig. 15.5).

Figure 15.5.
DIR command
summary.

DIR

Lists a directory's files and subdirectories.

Syntax:

`DIR [filespec] [/P] [/W] [/A] [/S] [/B]`

Parameters and Switches:

none	Lists the current directory.
filespec	Identifies the directory and/or file(s) to be listed.
/P	Displays one page at a time.
/W	Displays the listing in wide format, with as many as five names per line.
/A	Displays all entries, including system and hidden ones.
/S	Lists the contents of subdirectories.
/B	Suppresses heading and summary information and lists full filespecs (including path) for all selected entries.

To list the contents of C:\WP\LETTERS\PERSONAL, for example, enter this command:

```
DIR C:\WP\LETTERS\PERSONAL
```

Or, if PERSONAL is the current directory, simply enter **DIR**.

A directory listing looks something like this:

```
Volume in drive C is MY HARDDISK
Volume serial number is 152C-B387
Directory of C:\WP\LETTERS\PERSONAL

.               <DIR>     01-17-90    6:21a
..              <DIR>     01-17-90    6:21a
SIS30222 LET     1152 02-22-93    12:08p
MOM30228 LET     3840 02-28-93    10:49a
BRO30315 FAX     1792 03-15-93    12:07p
MOM30306 LET     1787 03-06-93     9:30a
DAD30305 AIR     1659 03-04-93     9:31a
SIS30410 LET     1280 04-10-93    11:48a
MOM21210 LET     1244 02-12-92     9:30a

     9 file(s)      12754    bytes
                   318464    bytes free
```

The heading shows the volume label, the serial number, and the name of the directory being listed. The main body shows the contents of the directory. Every subdirectory contains the first two entries : **.** (which stands for the current directory) and **..** (which stands for its parent). The <DIR> shows that these are directories, not files. For directory entries, the date and time stamp shows the date and time that the directory was created. For files, it shows the date and time that the file was created or last modified. The summary lines at the end of the listing show the number of entries that are listed (including both files and directories), the number of bytes occupied by the files (the directories aren't counted in this total), and the number of free bytes on the drive.

If the PERSONAL directory had a child called FRIENDS, it also would show up in the listing (remember, the <DIR> marker identifies a subdirectory):

```
Volume in drive C is MY HARDDISK
Volume serial number is 152C-B387
Directory of C:\WP\LETTERS\PERSONAL
```

```
   .            <DIR>      01-17-90      6:21a
   ..           <DIR>      01-17-90      6:21a
SIS30222 LET     1152 02-22-93     12:08p
MOM30228 LET     3840 02-28-93     10:49a
BRO30315 FAX     1792 03-15-93     12:07p
FRIENDS      <DIR>        01-19-93      7:30p
MOM30306 LET     1787 03-06-93      9:30a
DAD30305 AIR     1659 03-04-93      9:31a
SIS30410 LET     1280 04-10-93     11:48a
MOM21210 LET     1244 02-12-92      9:30a
        10 file(s)    12754   bytes
                      318464   bytes free
```

By default, entries appear in the order that DOS finds them in the directory; you cannot count on them to be in chronological order, alphabetical order, or any other particular order.

A long directory might be difficult to see. The first entries disappear off the top of the screen before you get to the end. There are several ways around this problem:

- You could redirect the listing to the printer by using > PRN at the end of the command.

- You could use the /P switch, which pauses the display after each page and waits for you to press any key to continue the display.

- You could use the wide listing format (using the /W switch). This format doesn't show sizes and times, but most directories fit on the screen with this format. The wide format lists up to five file and directory names across each row. Directory names are enclosed in square brackets. The command DIR / W lists the directory like this:

```
Volume in drive C is MY HARDDISK
Volume serial number is 152C-B387
Directory of C:\WP\LETTERS\PERSONAL

[.]   [..]      SIS30222 LET   MOM30228 LET   BRO30315 FAX
MOM30306 LET    DAD30305 AIR   SIS30410 LET   MOM21210 LET

        9 file(s)       12754  bytes
                        318464  bytes free
```

Using Switches with the DIR Command

The DIR command, by default, doesn't list system or hidden files. If you want to see every file regardless of attributes, use the /A switch. You can't see attributes in the directory listing. Chapter 17 explains how to use the ATTRIB command to display and manage attributes at the command prompt.

Directories can have any of the attributes that files can have. A few applications (notably the Delete Sentry deletion protection utility) place hidden directories on your drive. You don't see these directories in a DIR listing unless you use the /A switch. (Hidden directories don't show up in a TREE listing either—there's no way around that.)

Filtering the List

Sometimes you want to see a directory listing of only one file. Perhaps you want to find out whether a file exists, its size, or its date and time stamp. When you add a filespec to a DIR command, DIR lists only the file(s) that match that filespec. To find out about MOM30306.LET, you could enter this command:

```
DIR C:\WP\LETTERS\PERSONAL\MOM30306.LET
```

The listing might look like this:

```
Volume in drive C is MY HARDDISK
Volume serial number is 152C-B387
Directory of C:\WP\LETTERS\PERSONAL

MOM30306 LET    1787 03-06-93    9:30a

        1 file(s)    1787   bytes
                   318464   bytes free
```

If you use a global filespec, as follows:

```
C:\WP\LETTERS\PERSONAL>DIR MOM*.*
```

you will see a group of entries:

```
Volume in drive C is MY HARDDISK
Volume serial number is 152C-B387
Directory of C:\WP\LETTERS\PERSONAL

MOM30228 LET     3840 02-28-93    10:49a
MOM30306 LET     1787 03-06-93     9:30a
MOM21210 LET     1244 02-12-92     9:30a

    3 file(s)      6871    bytes
                 318464    bytes free
```

If you use a command, such as the following, to ask for a file that's not in the directory:

```
C:\WP\LETTERS\PERSONAL>DIR POP*.*
```

you see a message like this:

```
Volume in drive C is MY HARDDISK
Volume serial number is 152C-B387
Directory of C:\WP\LETTERS\PERSONAL

        File not found
```

In this case, DIR displays the heading information but not the summary, so you don't find out how much space is available on the drive.

Listing Branches

You may want to list entries throughout a branch. A quick way is to start at the top of the branch and use the /S switch. If the current directory is C:\WP, the command DIR /S produces seven listings, one for each of the directories in the branch. Each listing has a heading, a set of entries, and a summary (unless no matching files are found). This produces a lot of output, most of which scrolls off the screen.

Using the /B switch with /S makes the listing much easier to handle because it suppresses the headings and summaries. You see just entries, including full paths so that you know where each file can be found. Suppose that you can't find one of the letters you wrote to FOB. The following command searches all of drive C for FOB*.LET files:

```
DIR C:\FOB*.LET /S /B
```

The listing would look something like this:

```
C:\FINANCE\Y1992\FOB30331.LET
C:\WP\LETTERS\BUSINESS\FOB30115.LET
C:\WP\LETTERS\PERSONAL\FOB30228.LET
C:\WP\LETTERS\PERSONAL\FOB30306.LET
C:\WP\LETTERS\PERSONAL\FOB21210.LET
```

As you can see, the display shows the path for each file but not the size or date and time stamp. It's easy to find the file you want (as long as it's on the drive) from this listing.

Creating a Directory

How do directories come about in the first place? Some of them, of course, are created when you install programs, but you will create many directories yourself. Figure 15.5 shows the command summary for the MD (Make Directory) command, which creates a directory. (MKDIR is a synonym for MD.)

Figure 15.6.
MD command summary.

MD

Creates a new directory.

Syntax:

MD [*path*]*dirname*

Parameters:

path	Identifies the parent of the new directory.
dirname	Identifies the name of the new directory.

Notes

Dirname's full path, from the root directory up to and including *dirname*, including backslashes, cannot be more than 63 characters.

Dirname must be unique to the parent. You can't duplicate a directory or file name belonging to the parent.

As you can see, it's a pretty simple matter to create a new directory. As with any other directory command, though, you need to know where you are when you issue it. Suppose that you want a TAX directory as a child of your Y1993 directory. If the current directory is C:\FINANCE\Y1993, you could enter the following command:

```
MD TAX
```

If some other directory is current, you must include the path in the command, as follows:

```
MD C:\FINANCE\Y1993\TAX
```

You also can create a directory on a drive other than the current one. Just include the drive name in the command. To create a directory named AFTER as a subdirectory of the root on drive A, enter this command:

```
MD A:\AFTER
```

Deleting a Directory

If you have an empty directory you want to delete from the structure, you can use the RD (Remove Directory) command (see fig. 15.7). RMDIR is a synonym for this command.

Figure 15.7
RD command
summary.

RD
Deletes a directory.
Syntax:
RD *path*
Parameter:
path　　　　Identifies the directory you want to delete.

Suppose that you decide you're never going to use Y1992 again. First, you must make sure that it's empty. You can't delete a directory with anything in it. Also, you can't delete the current directory, so be sure that some other directory is current before you try to remove Y1992. If the current directory is C:\FINANCE, you can delete Y1992 using this command:

```
RD Y1992
```

If the current directory is somewhere else, you need to include a path in the command, as follows:

```
RD \FINANCE\Y1992
```

RD doesn't ask you to confirm a directory deletion. If it can't delete the directory, however, you see this message:

```
Invalid path, not directory,
or directory not empty
```

You may have entered the wrong name for the directory, or you tried to delete the current directory, or possibly the directory is not empty. If DIR shows that the directory is empty but you still cannot delete it, try using the DIR /A command to see whether some hidden files, system files, or subdirectories are in the directory. In Chapter 17, you learn how to change attributes so that you can delete such entries.

Deleting a Branch

Before DOS 6, you could delete only one directory at a time, and it had to be empty. But DOS 6 has a new command, DELTREE, that deletes the whole branch, including hidden, system, and read-only entries, at one fell swoop (see fig. 15.8). You can see that this is a powerful, but dangerous, facility; if you use it, you need to exercise some caution.

If, for example, you wanted to delete the WP branch, you could use DELTREE. First make sure that the current directory is not WP or any of its descendants. Then enter this command:

```
DELTREE \WP
```

Figure 15.8.
DELTREE
command
summary.

DELTREE

Deletes a directory and all its files and subdirectories.

Syntax:

DELTREE *path*

Parameter:

path   Identifies the directory at the top of the branch that you want
              to delete.

DELTREE prompts you to confirm that you want to delete this branch, as follows:

```
Delete directory "wp" and all its subdirectories? [yn]
```

If you press N, nothing happens; you see a new prompt. If you press Y, you see the following message:

```
Deleting wp...
```

It can take a while to delete a large branch with all its files. The command prompt returns when DELTREE is done.

If you like, you can use DELTREE instead of RD to remove a single directory without first deleting its files. To delete Y1992 whether or not it is empty, you can enter the following command:

```
DELTREE C:\FINANCES\Y1992
```

Renaming Directories

Another command new to DOS 6 enables you to change the name of a directory. Before DOS 6, you had to use the Shell to rename a directory. Now you can do it at the command prompt with the MOVE command (see fig. 15.9). Chapter 16 explains more about this command.

MOVE

Renames a directory.

Syntax:

```
MOVE directory newname
```

Parameters:

directory   Identifies the directory you want to rename.

newname   Specifies the new name.

Notes:

If *directory* contains a path, *newname* should include the same path.

Figure 15.9.
MOVE command summary.

Suppose that you want to change the name of your FINANCES directory to MONEY. You can't change the name of the current directory, so be sure that some other directory is current. If the current directory is the parent of FINANCES, you could enter this command:

```
MOVE FINANCES MONEY
```

If the current directory isn't the parent of FINANCES, include a path. You could enter this command from any place except the FINANCES directory:

```
MOVE C:\FINANCES C:\MONEY
```

If you use a drive or path when describing the original directory, be sure to include the same drive or path with the new name. If you do everything correctly, you see this message:

```
c:\finance XXX → c:\money [ok]
```

If FINANCE is the current directory, or if you don't use the correct path for the new name, you see the message:

```
c:\finance XXX → c:\money [Permission denied]
```

Future Considerations

Several of the commands you have learned about in this chapter have options you might find useful some day:

- TREE can list the files in each directory as it displays the directory tree.
- DIR can sort the directory listing.
- You can set up default options for DIR.
- You can bypass the confirmation step with DELTREE.

If you want to know more about any of these options, look up the appropriate command in the Command Reference at the back of this book.

Copying and Moving Files

16

Introduction

You don't have to start up the Shell just to copy or move files. DOS includes several commands to copy and move files from the command prompt.

Using the COPY Command

DOS's original copying command was COPY (see fig. 16.1), which can be used to copy one or more files from a source to a destination.

Figure 16.1.
COPY command
summary.

> ### COPY
>
> Copies one or more files to another location.
>
> **Syntax:**
>
> COPY source [*destination*]
>
> **Parameters and Switches:**
>
> *source*   Identifies file(s) to copy.
>
> *destination*   Identifies location or name of copy.

Probably the simplest use of COPY is to make a copy of one file, keeping the copy in the same directory but giving it a new name. Suppose that you want to make a backup copy of THISYEAR.DAT in the current directory, calling the copy THISYEAR.SAV. You could enter this command:

COPY THISYEAR.DAT THISYEAR.SAV

If THISYEAR.SAV already exists, COPY overwrites it with the new files without a warning message. Otherwise, COPY creates a new file to hold the copy. In either case, you see the message `1 File(s) copied`, which indicates a successful job.

It's almost as easy to copy a file to another directory. The following command copies THISYEAR.DAT from directory \FINANCE to directory \SAVERS:

COPY \FINANCE\THISYEAR.DAT \SAVERS

Because the command doesn't specify a destination file name, the new copy also is named THISYEAR.DAT. If you want the new copy to have a different name, you could enter this command:

COPY \FINANCE\THISYEAR.DAT \SAVERS\1993.DAT

In these examples, the original file is unchanged. The copy has the same date and time stamp as the original file, the archive attribute of the copy is turned on, and the hidden, system, and read-only attributes are turned off.

When you don't specify a destination directory, COPY places the new file into the current directory. In the following command, the copy comes from the \FINANCE directory and is placed into the current directory under the original name of THISYEAR.DAT:

```
COPY \FINANCE\THISYEAR.DAT
```

Of course, if \FINANCE is the current directory, COPY displays an error message saying `File cannot be copied onto itself`.

Copying More Than One File

You can copy several files at once by using a global filespec. To copy all the files from \FINANCE to \SAVERS, for example, you enter this command:

```
COPY \FINANCE\*.* \SAVERS
```

When copying multiple files, COPY displays the name of each source file it selects. Each copy is given the same name as the original, the date and time stamp of the original, a positive archive attribute, and negative read-only, hidden, and system attributes. If some of the files already exist in \SAVERS, COPY overwrites them without warning. When the operation ends, a message tells you how many files were copied.

You can change file names when you make multiple copies by including a global filespec for the destination. The following command, for example, makes a copy of every file in the current directory with the extension BAT, giving each copy the extension SAV:

```
COPY *.BAT *.SAV
```

If you do decide to try this technique, be sure to use wildcards in the same places in both filespecs. Otherwise, the results can be unpredictable.

Copying to the Printer

The source or destination for COPY can be a device, such as COM1 (the first serial port) or PRN (the default printer). Other acceptable device names are LPT1, LPT2, LPT3 (all names of parallel printer ports), COM1, COM2, COM3, COM4 (all names of serial ports), COM, and AUX.

The most common way to use a device with COPY is to make a "quick-and-dirty" printout of an ASCII text file. This command prints a file named REPORT.DAT:

```
COPY REPORT.DAT PRN
```

A printout produced this way is completely unformatted. COPY doesn't even break it into pages like the PRINT function does; it prints over the perforated edges of continuous-form paper. The only advantage to printing files this way is that you don't load and initialize PRINT.

Understanding What Can Go Wrong with COPY

The biggest problem with COPY is that it will overwrite an existing file in the destination directory without warning. Because it doesn't actually delete the overwritten file (it just overwrites the directory entry), your deletion protection system does not capture the data necessary to undelete the file. DOS 6 doesn't offer any way to recover a file that has been overwritten by a copy operation.

> The Norton Utilities's Unerase program can recover an overwritten file's data from the unused clusters.

You can't copy a system or hidden file with COPY as you can in the Shell. If you name as a source a single file that is system or hidden, you see the message `File not found`. (This message also could mean that the file doesn't exist in the source directory.) If a destination file already exists and has a system, hidden, or read-only attribute, the copy job fails and you see the message `Access denied`. If you're copying multiple files, the `Access denied` message includes the name of the destination file that caused the problem; because the copy job fails, any remaining source files aren't copied.

There's always a chance that the destination disk doesn't have room for the new file; then the copy job fails and you see the `Disk full` error message. This error is especially likely if you're copying files to a floppy disk, but even a hard disk can run out of space. When the destination disk is full, COPY doesn't give you a chance to change disks and continue; therefore, this is an area in which the Shell offers a strong advantage over the command prompt.

Using the XCOPY Command

DOS 6 includes a newer, faster, more powerful command for copying files called XCOPY (for extended copy). Figure 16.2 shows the XCOPY command summary.

XCOPY

Copies files and subdirectories.

Syntax:

`XCOPY source [destination] [/P] [/S [/E]]`

Parameters and Switches:

source	Identifies the file(s) you want to copy.
destination	Specifies the location where the copy should be written; the default is the current directory.
/P	Prompts you for permission to copy each selected file.
/S	Extends copying to the entire branch headed by the source directory.
/E	Copies empty subdirectories when copying to the entire branch. You must use /S if you use /E.

Figure 16.2.
XCOPY command summary.

In addition to outright speed, one of XCOPY's major advantages over COPY is that it copies files and subdirectories. XCOPY can duplicate an entire branch on the target drive.

Like COPY, XCOPY overwrites a file in a destination directory without warning if it has the same name as the intended copy. You can't undelete a file overwritten this way with DOS 6's UNDELETE facility.

The following XCOPY command has a similar effect to using COPY if TEMPY is the name of an existing subdirectory belonging to the current directory. XCOPY copies the file as TEMPY\MYFILE.DAT:

```
XCOPY MYFILE.DAT TEMPY
```

This command produces these messages:

```
Reading source file(s)...
MYFILE.DAT
    1 File(s) copied
```

The first line appears while XCOPY locates and reads MYFILE.DAT; the second line appears while it writes MYFILE.DAT; and the last line appears when the job is finished. When multiple files are involved, XCOPY reads as many files as it can into memory while you see the `Reading source file(s)` message. Then it writes those files, displaying the name of each file in turn. It repeats this process as many times as necessary to complete the job. The summary line appears only once, at the end of the job.

The more memory available to XCOPY, the faster it works.

Specifying a Directory or a File

In the last example, suppose that no subdirectory is named TEMPY in the current directory. Then XCOPY doesn't know whether you intended TEMPY to be the copy's new file name or a new subdirectory. You see the following message:

```
Does TEMPY specify a file name
or directory name on the target
(F = file, D = directory)?
```

XCOPY asks this question even if the destination identifies an existing file; it suppresses the question only if the destination identifies an existing directory.

If you press F, XCOPY creates or overwrites TEMPY in the current directory. If you press D, XCOPY creates a new TEMPY subdirectory as a child of the current directory and copies MYFILE.DAT (with the original name) to it.

If you want to copy MYFILE.DAT to another directory using the original name, you can use the following command:

```
XCOPY MYFILE.DAT \SAVERS\
```

The backslash at the end of \SAVERS indicates that it's a directory, so XCOPY doesn't need to ask you the file or directory question. XCOPY creates \SAVERS, if necessary, and places a copy of MYFILE.DAT into it. If you want the copy to have a new name, such as NEWFILE.DAT, you could enter the following command:

```
XCOPY MYFILE.DAT \SAVERS\NEWFILE.DAT
```

Again, XCOPY asks you whether NEWFILE.DAT is a file or a directory (even if \SAVERS\NEWFILE.DAT already exists as a file) and proceeds according to your answer.

As with COPY, when XCOPY copies a file, the original file is unchanged; the copy receives the same date and time stamp as the original; the archive attribute of the copy is turned on; and the hidden, system, and read-only attributes are turned off. XCOPY can't copy hidden or system files.

Using XCOPY with Multiple Files

XCOPY is much faster at handling multiple files than COPY. The command formats are similar, but you need to remember to end a destination directory name with a backslash to avoid the file or directory question. To copy all the files from \FINANCE to \SAVERS, for example, you could enter this command:

```
XCOPY \FINANCE\*.* \SAVERS\
```

An XCOPY command with wildcards in both the source and destination works the same as the COPY command. In this case, XCOPY knows that the destination is a file name, so it doesn't ask the file or directory question:

```
XCOPY *.BAT *.SAV
```

Again, be sure that you use wildcards in the same places in both filespecs, or you might end up with some unexpected file names.

If you try to copy multiple files to a single destination, you might think XCOPY would realize the destination is a directory, but it doesn't. Suppose that you enter this command:

```
XCOPY *.BAT \NEW
```

XCOPY asks the familiar file or directory question. What's more, if you indicate that \NEW is a file, XCOPY copies each BAT file to \NEW in turn. The final content of \NEW is a copy of the last source file copied. This is probably not what you had in mind.

Extending XCOPY

One major advantage of XCOPY over COPY is that it works with entire branches. Figure 16.3 shows a sample directory structure.

Figure 16.3.
Sample directory structure.

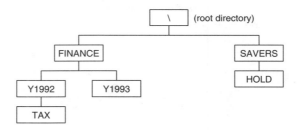

Suppose that FINANCE is the current directory, and you enter this command:

```
XCOPY MYFILE.DAT \SAVERS\ /S
```

XCOPY starts by looking for MYFILE.DAT in FINANCE. If found, it copies the file to \SAVERS. Then XCOPY goes on to look in each subdirectory of FINANCE. Because there is a MYFILE.DAT in FINANCE\Y1992\TAX, XCOPY creates the necessary subdirectories so that it can copy the file to \SAVERS\Y1992\TAX\MYFILE.DAT.

> If the command had included the /E switch along with /S, XCOPY would also have created a SAVERS\Y1992 subdirectory.

You can use wildcards in the source filespec with the /S switch. Suppose that you enter this command:

```
XCOPY \FINANCE\*.* \SAVERS\ /S
```

The entire FINANCE branch is copied to the SAVERS branch. The two branches will not be identical, though, because SAVERS has a subdirectory HOLD that FINANCE doesn't have. Also, any hidden or system files or subdirectories in the FINANCE branch are not copied.

Suppose that you're ready to put all your 1992 financial records onto a floppy disk for permanent storage and remove them from your hard disk. You can do it with only two commands, provided that the whole 1992 branch fits on one disk and that no hidden or system files or subdirectories are involved, as follows:

```
XCOPY C:\FINANCE\Y1992\*.* A:\ /S
DELTREE C:\FINANCE\Y1992
```

Understanding What Can Go Wrong with XCOPY

You can experience many of the same problems with XCOPY as with COPY. XCOPY overwrites existing destination files without warning, and DOS 6 can't undelete them. Hidden, system, and nonexistent source files produce the `File not found` message. Hidden, system, and read-only destination files produce an `Access denied` message. You can receive a `Disk full` message in mid-copy. XCOPY also quits when the target disk is full.

In addition, another error situation can arise with XCOPY. Suppose that you tell XCOPY to create a new directory but the parent directory contains a file of the same name. In DOS, a directory can't contain a file and a subdirectory with the same name, so you see an `Unable to create directory` error message. You can resolve the problem by deleting or renaming the file or by using a different subdirectory name.

Moving Files

Until DOS 6, you moved files from the command prompt by copying them, making sure that the copy was completed successfully, and then deleting the originals. This process was not as simple as it sounds; it's not easy to determine whether all requested files are successfully copied to the destination before deleting them from the source.

DOS 6 has a new command, MOVE, that accomplishes this in one step. (It's the same MOVE command that you used to rename directories in Chapter 15. Now you see why it's called MOVE.) Figure 16.4 shows the command summary for this function of MOVE.

Figure 16.4.
MOVE command summary.

MOVE

Moves one or more files and renames a file.

Syntax:

`MOVE filespec [...] destination`

Parameters:

filespec	Identifies the file(s) you want to move or rename.
destination	Identifies the file or directory to which you want to move file(s) or the new name for the file.

To move MYFILE.DAT from \FINANCE to \SAVERS, you could enter this command:

```
MOVE \FINANCE\MYFILE.DAT \SAVERS
```

If a file named MYFILE.DAT already exists in \SAVERS, it is replaced without warning; otherwise, a new file is created.

If you're moving only one file, you can assign it a new file name. If you want to move MYFILE.DAT but name the new file MYFILE.SAV, you could enter the following command:

```
MOVE \FINANCE\MYFILE.DAT \SAVERS\MYFILE.SAV
```

Unlike XCOPY, MOVE does not create a directory. The destination directory must exist already.

Moving Multiple Files

You can use wildcards in the source file name to move more than one file. The destination must be a directory, however; you can't specify a destination file name, even with wildcards. The following command moves all the files from Y1992 to Y1993:

```
MOVE Y1992\*.* Y1993
```

You also can use a list of source file names followed by a destination. The following command moves all MY*.* files from the current directory, along with YOURFIL.TXT and \OURFIL.DAT, to the \NEW directory:

```
MOVE MY*.* YOURFIL.TXT \OURFIL.DAT \NEW
```

MOVE always assumes that the last parameter on the command line is the destination; every parameter before that is a source filespec. As always, when more than one file is being moved, the destination must be a directory.

Using MOVE To Rename Files

If you move a file to its own directory, the effect is to rename it. Unfortunately, MOVE will replace an existing file of the desired name without warning, and the file can't be undeleted by DOS 6's UNDELETE facility (even if you're using Delete Sentry). This makes MOVE dangerous when compared with the REN command, which refuses to rename a file when the new name already is in use in the directory. The REN command is explained in Chapter 17.

Understanding What Can Go Wrong with MOVE

MOVE can't access a system or hidden file as a source file. It overwrites a system or hidden destination file without warning, but not a read-only one. If a file can't be moved, you see the error message `Permission denied`.

For the Future

Both COPY and XCOPY have additional features. COPY can be used to concatenate (combine) files and to update a file's date and time stamp. XCOPY can select files based on their archive attributes or their date and time stamps so that you can use XCOPY to create a backup system if you don't care for DOS 6's MSBACKUP (or MWBACKUP) program.

Another copying command, REPLACE, actually seeks out files on the destination drive and replaces them with files from the source directory. REPLACE also can compare the source and destination directories and copy only those files that are missing from the destination directory. When you're ready to find out more about these features, look up the appropriate command in the Command Reference at the back of this book.

Additional File Management

Introduction

The Shell generally manages files better than using the command prompt, but occasionally you may want to stay at the command prompt.

Deleting Files

To delete files, you are better off deleting files in the Shell. The Shell enables you to select specific files rather than use a global filespec, and it helps you protect yourself with deletion confirmation. But if you're working at the command prompt and just want to delete a file or two without starting up the Shell, you can use the DEL command (see fig. 17.1).

<u>**DEL**</u>

Deletes a file or a set of files.

Syntax:

DEL *filespec* [*/P*]

Parameters and Switches:

filespec   Identifies the file(s) to delete.

/P   Prompts for confirmation before each deletion.

Whenever you use DEL, keep its limitations in mind:

- If you don't use the /P switch, DEL deletes files without warning or confirmation; it doesn't even display the names of the files that it deletes.

- A global filespec could very likely delete more files than you intended. On the other hand, it could delete fewer files than you intended, as the following two items explain.

- DEL will not delete hidden or system files. When you use a single file name, you see a File not found message for a hidden or system file. But with a global file name, even if you use /P, DEL doesn't display any message about the files that it skips.

- DEL also will not delete a read-only file. With a specific filespec, you see an Access denied message. The same is true if you use a global filespec with /P. But if you use a global filespec without /P, you receive no warning that read-only files were skipped.

Bearing all these limitations in mind, suppose that you want to delete the file named MEMO3.TMP. You could enter the following command:

```
DEL MEMO3.TMP
```

If the next thing you see is a command prompt, the file was deleted. The message `Access denied` tells you that the file is read-only. The message `File not found` means either that it's a hidden or system file or that it's not in the current (or specified) directory.

For safety's sake, you should include the /P switch whenever you use a global filespec. /P causes DEL to prompt you for each selected file before deleting it. This slows down DEL considerably, but the safety factor is worth it. A complete interaction would look like this:

```
C:\WP\DOCS>DEL *.TMP
C:\WP\DOCS\1STTRY.TMP,      Delete (Y/N)?Y
C:\WP\DOCS\BALANCE.TMP,     Delete (Y/N)?N
C:\WP\DOCS\2NDTRY.TMP,      Delete (Y/N)?Y
C:\WP\DOCS\3RDTRY.TMP,      Delete (Y/N)?Y
C:\WP\DOCS>
```

In this example, the user deleted three of the files but saved BALANCE.TMP. Without /P, DEL would have deleted BALANCE.TMP.

Using REN To Rename Files

When you want to rename one or more files at the command prompt, use the REN command (see fig. 17.2).

Unlike the Shell, REN enables you to perform a group rename. Suppose that you want to rename all PGM files in the current directory to BAT files. You use the following command:

```
REN *.PGM *.BAT
```

You should use wild cards in the same place in both filespecs; otherwise, the results may not be what you wanted (or expected).

Figure 17.2.
*REN command
summary.*

<u>**REN**</u>

Changes the name of a file or files.

Syntax:

REN *filespec newname*

Parameters:

filespec   Identifies the file(s) to be renamed.

newname   Specifies the new name(s) for the file(s).

REN will not rename a file if the name is already in use for another file, or a subdirectory, in the same directory. You receive this message:

Duplicate file name or file not found

As you can see, this message also appears when no file matches the source filespec.

Displaying Files with the TYPE Command

The TYPE command (see fig. 17.3) displays a file on the command prompt screen.

TYPE can be handy to take a quick peek at a short ASCII text file. In other situations, you might not be so happy with the results, because TYPE simply dumps the text onto the screen with no formatting.

If a file is too long to fit on your screen, the beginning scrolls off the top of the screen before you have a chance to read it. You might be able to control the scrolling with the Pause key, but the faster your system, the harder that is. Because TYPE can't go backward, once text has disappeared off the top of the screen, you can't get it back without re-entering the command. You're better off examining longer ASCII text files in the Shell (see File View File Contents) or with EDIT (explained in Chapter 20); both these programs enable you to scroll around in the file.

TYPE

Displays the contents of a file.

Syntax:

TYPE *filespec*

Parameter:

filespec   Identifies the file that you want to view.

Figure 17.3.
TYPE command
summary.

Files that contain non-ASCII codes don't display well with TYPE. The non-ASCII codes might appear as graphics characters, might beep the computer's alarm, and might terminate the command before the entire file has been displayed. The best way to view a non-ASCII file is with the application that created it in the first place.

Printing Files with PRINT

There are several ways to print an ASCII text file with DOS. You could redirect the output of COPY or TYPE to the printer port, as follows:

```
TYPE AUTOEXEC.BAT > PRN
```

This is fine for a short file, but because TYPE doesn't do any formatting, a long file runs off the end of the page.

For longer ASCII text files, the PRINT command is the best choice. Chapter 10 explains how to initialize PRINT and use it from within the DOS Shell. Figure 17.4 shows some parameters you can use to print files and manage the print queue.

The following command adds three files to the print queue:

```
PRINT TRY.TXT SAVE.TXT PLUS.TXT
```

The following command clears the print queue:

```
PRINT /T
```

Figure 17.4.
PRINT command summary.

<u>PRINT</u>

Manages the print queue.

Syntax:

```
PRINT [/T] [filespec]
```

Parameters and Switches:

none   Displays the contents of the print queue or loads the TSR.

/T   Removes all files from the print queue.

filespec   Identifies a text file to place in the print queue.

The printer might continue printing from its own memory after you clear the print queue. Turn the printer off to clear its memory. You might also need to reset the top of form after clearing the print queue; your printer manual should explain how to do this.

You can clear the print queue and add new files to it in one command, but be sure to put the /T before the new filespecs because the parameters are processed from left to right. The following command clears the queue and adds new files to it:

```
PRINT /T TRY*.TXT SAVE*.TXT
```

Managing Attributes with the ATTRIB Command

You can examine and change file attributes at the command prompt with the ATTRIB command (see fig. 17.5).

ATTRIB

Displays or changes file and directory attributes.

Syntax:

ATTRIB [+R ¦ -R] [+A ¦ -A] [+H ¦ -H] [+S ¦ -S] [filespec] [/S]

Parameters and Switches:

None	Shows the attributes of all files in the current directory.
+R ¦ –R	Turns on or off the read-only attribute.
+A ¦ –A	Turns on or off the archive attribute.
+H ¦ –H	Turns on or off the hidden attribute.
+S ¦ –S	Turns on or off the system attribute.
filespec	Identifies the file(s) or a directory to process. You can use wildcards to identify files but not directories.
/S	Processes all files in the branch headed by the current directory.

Figure 17.5.
ATTRIB command summary.

When you enter a specific or global filespec without any switches, ATTRIB displays the attributes of those files, as shown in the following interaction:

```
C:\>ATTRIB *.SYS
    SHR     C:\IO.SYS
    SHR     C:\MSDOS.SYS
    A       C:\CONFIG.SYS
            C:\HIMEM.SYS
```

The attributes of the first two files are system, hidden, and read-only (SHR). The third file has a positive archive attribute (A), which indicates that it needs to be backed up. The fourth file's attributes are all negative.

To change attributes, you include attribute switches in the command. A switch preceded by + turns on an attribute; a switch preceded by – turns it off. Suppose that you wanted to turn off the archive attribute and turn on the hidden attribute for CONFIG.SYS in the preceding example. You can do both in one command, as follows:

```
ATTRIB CONFIG.SYS -A +H
```

Because hidden and system files are supposed to be invisible, ATTRIB will not change their attributes unless you deal with the hidden and system attribute somehow. But ATTRIB does warn you when it skips a hidden or system file. The following command, for example, produces the error message shown:

```
C:\>ATTRIB IO.SYS -R
Not resetting hidden file C:\IO.SYS
```

When both attributes are present, as in this example, ATTRIB reports the hidden attribute, but not the system one. If only the system attribute is present, the message displayed is `Not resetting system file....` The long way around this problem is to turn off the hidden and system attributes, change the attributes you want, and then turn on the attributes again. But there's an easier way. You can confirm the hidden and system attributes while changing whatever other attributes you want in the same command. The following command, for example, successfully turns off IO.SYS's read-only attribute without turning off its hidden and system attributes:

```
ATTRIB IO.SYS +H +S -R
```

If you use a global filespec, you can change several files' attributes with one command. The /S switch extends the range of the command throughout the entire branch headed by the specified directory. Unlike the Shell, other attributes are not cleared automatically when you handle files as a group. Fortunately, you receive the `Not resetting` message for each hidden or system file. You need to treat those files individually so that you can confirm each one's hidden and system attributes while you handle the attribute(s) you want to change.

Understanding Directory Attributes

Directories can have attributes just as files can. You can, for example, hide a directory and it will not show up in DIR or TREE listings. ATTRIB works with a directory only if you supply its specific name; global filespecs never access directories with ATTRIB.

Suppose that you want to hide the C:\PERSONAL directory. You could use the following command:

```
ATTRIB C:\PERSONAL +H
```

Now when you list the contents of C:\, PERSONAL does not show up (unless you use the /A switch with DIR). But DIR lists the contents of PERSONAL if you reference it directly, as follows:

```
DIR PERSONAL
```

Don't count on hiding a directory as a security measure. Most programs (including DOS Shell) ignore directory attributes.

Comparing Files with FC

The FC (file comparison) command lets you compare two files and identify exactly where they are different. FC can do two basic types of comparisons: binary and ASCII. In binary mode, FC compares the two files byte by byte, displaying any mismatched bytes. In ASCII mode, FC compares the two files line by line and displays mismatched lines. After a mismatch, FC tries to find a place where the two files match again and continues the comparison from there; this is called *resynchronization*. Binary comparisons are much simpler than ASCII comparisons, but they're also less useful when you're trying to find how two text files differ.

Making Binary Comparisons

Figure 17.6 shows the format of the FC command for binary comparisons. FC automatically uses binary mode for files that it knows to be program files; that is, for COM, EXE, BIN, SYS, OBJ, and LIB files. Any other files are compared in ASCII mode by default; you must use the /B switch if you want the comparison done in binary mode.

Figure 17.6.
FC command
summary (for
binary compari-
sons).

FC

Compares two files and displays lines or bytes that don't match.

Syntax:

`FC [/B] filespec1 filespec2`

Parameters and Switches:

filespec1	Identifies first file to compare.
filespec2	Identifies second file to compare.
/B	Compares files in binary mode, byte by byte, without attempting to resynchronize after a mismatch. This is the default mode with files having the extensions EXE, COM, SYS, OBJ, LIB, or BIN.

Suppose that you want to compare your DOS 6 COMMAND.COM with your DOS 5 COMMAND.COM. You could use the following command:

`FC C:\COMMAND.COM C:\OLD_DOS.1\COMMAND.COM`

What you would quickly find out is that these two files are vastly different. The FC messages start off this way:

```
00000002: 15 14
00000003: 60 00
```

This means that byte 2 contains 15 in C:\COMMAND.COM but 14 in C:\OLD_DOS.1\COMMAND.COM. Byte 3 of C:\COMMAND.COM contains 60, but byte 3 of C:\OLD_DOS.1\COMMAND.COM contains 00. The addresses and byte values are all reported in hexadecimal. The listing goes on like this for several hundred lines. Obviously, this is information that only a programmer could love. What it tells a normal person is that the two files different—in this case, very different. When two files are identical, FC displays the message No differences encountered.

Suppose that you have just copied a set of files and want to make sure that the copies are exact. A binary FC comparison is the perfect choice for this task.

Making ASCII Comparisons

An ASCII comparison tells you which lines in two files are different. Figure 17.7 shows the format of the FC command for ASCII comparisons. FC automatically does an ASCII comparison for any file that doesn't have one of the program extensions EXE, COM, SYS, OBJ, LIB, or BIN.

FC

Compares two files and displays lines that don't match.

Syntax:

FC [/L] [/C] [/N] *filespec1 filespec2*

Parameters and Switches:

filespec1	Identifies the first file to compare.
filespec2	Identifies the second file to compare.
/L	Compares files in ASCII mode, comparing line by line and attempting to resynchronize after a mismatch.
/C	Ignores case.
/N	Displays line numbers when showing mismatched lines during an ASCII comparison.

*Figure 17.7.
FC command summary
(for ASCII comparisons).*

ASCII comparisons can be useful to identify changes made to a file. Suppose that you have an AUTOEXEC.BAT and an AUTOEXEC.BAK file, and you want to see what the differences are. An ASCII comparison is a perfect choice for this task.

If you want to do an ASCII comparison for a file with a program extension, you must use the /L switch. Most program files are binary files and do not have lines; an ASCII comparison would make no sense on such files. But CONFIG.SYS is an ASCII text file with a program's extension, so it makes sense to use the /L switch with this file.

When FC finds a mismatch in an ASCII comparison, it displays a set of lines for each file. Each set starts with the last matching line. Next, it shows all the unmatched lines. Then it shows the first line that matches again (unless the end of the file was reached first). Here's an example using two AUTOEXEC files:

```
***** AUTOEXEC.BAT
PATH C:\DOS;C:\WINWORD;C:\NDW;C:\WINDOWS
mouse\mouse bon

***** AUTOEXEC.NDW
PATH C:\DOS;C:\WINWORD;C:\NDW;C:\WINDOWS
cls
mouse\mouse bon
*****
```

The first set of lines, identified by the header ***** AUTOEXEC.BAT, shows what's in AUTOEXEC.BAT. The lines following ***** AUTOEXEC.NDW show what's in the other file. The line starting with PATH is the last matching line. You can see it in both files. The line beginning with mouse in each set shows the first line that matches after the mismatched lines. AUTOEXEC.BAT has no lines between these two, but AUTOEXEC.NDW has a CLS command. That command is the difference between the two files; in other words, AUTOEXEC.NDW contains a line that is missing from the other file.

If two files have more than one mismatch, you will see several mismatch reports like this. Each report starts with ***** followed by the name of the first file and ends with *****.

Looking at Resync Features

By default, FC doesn't consider a single matching line enough evidence of resynchronization. It requires two matching lines in a row to continue the comparison. Look at these "files," for example:

GARDEN	*PRODUCE*
Apples	Apples
Bananas	Pears
Peaches	Plums
Tomatoes	Artichokes
Plums	Peppers
Cherries	Figs
Figs	Onions
Onions	Carrots
Carrots	

The first line matches; then a mismatch starts. Scanning down the GARDEN file, you can see that Plums on line 5 matches line 3 in PRODUCE. But the next lines don't match, so FC would not restart the comparison at that point. Further down in GARDEN, Figs on line 7 matches line 6 of PRODUCE. The next lines (Onions) also match; because two lines in a row match, FC would continue the comparison at that point. The message from FC would look like this:

```
***** GARDEN
Apples
Bananas
Peaches
Tomatoes
Plums
Cherries
Figs
***** PRODUCE
Apples
Pears
```

```
Plums
Artichokes
Peppers
Figs
*****
```

As usual, the message shows the last line that matches (Apples), the mismatched lines, and the first line that matches again (Figs).

Comparison Options

FC is sensitive to case; ordinarily, Figs does not match figs or FIGS. But you often don't care about case when comparing two files, especially if they're batch programs. If the only difference between AUTOEXEC.BAT and AUTOEXEC.SAV, for example, is that CLS is capitalized in one and lowercase in the other; the two files would produce exactly the same results. You can tell FC to ignore case with the /C switch.

In long files, seeing the mismatched lines themselves might not be enough. You can add line numbers to the display with the /N switch. This could help you identify which lines you want to edit in the files.

For the Future

Two of the commands discussed in this chapter, PRINT and FC, offer some advanced features. PRINT enables you to configure the Print TSR to control such factors as the size of the print queue and the amount of time devoted to print jobs. You also can remove individual files from the queue without clearing the entire queue.

FC includes several parameters to control how an ASCII comparison is done and how two files are resynchronized. You can, for example, tell FC not to expand tabs and to ignore differences in spacing. You can control how far FC searches for resynchronization and how many lines must match for the comparison to continue. You will need these parameters only in unusual cases, but if you're interested in learning more, look up PRINT and FC in the Command Reference at the back of this book.

Formatting and Unformatting Disks

18

Introduction

You must format every disk before you can use it. And because everyone makes mistakes, DOS also enables you to unformat a disk, if necessary.

Formatting

F ormatting prepares a disk by laying out its sectors, installing the root directory and FAT, and otherwise getting the disk ready to store files. This section explains the difference between floppy and hard disk formatting.

Formatting Floppy Disks

A disk needs two levels of formatting. First it must be physically formatted (low-level formatting), which creates the sectors. Then it must be logically formatted (high-level formatting), which installs DOS's system information on the disk: the boot record, an empty root directory, and the initial FAT. (Actually, a logical format installs two FATs for safety's sake.) It also assigns a serial number that helps DOS identify the disk internally. You also can request two optional features:

● Formatting can store an internal label to help you identify the disk. (Most people would rather deal with a label, such as FEB ORDERS, than a DOS serial number, such as 57A4-8C14.)

● Formatting can install the DOS files (IO.SYS, MSDOS.SYS, and COMMAND.COM) so that you can boot from the disk.

Not all disks are perfect, and weaknesses in the magnetic recording surface could cause problems in storing data reliably. The physical formatter tests the disk surface and makes note of any bad spots. Then the logical formatter marks the spots in the FAT so that DOS will never attempt to store data there.

DOS's FORMAT program handles both low-level and high-level formatting for common disk types. DOS 6 can handle anything from a 360K 5.25-inch disk to a 2.88M 3.5-inch disk. Version 6 can even prepare a disk for use in a system that's using an earlier version of DOS; for example, DOS 6 can format a 360K disk as a 320K disk to work with a Version 1 system. And, to a certain extent, it can prepare a lower capacity disk (such as a 720K disk) in a higher capacity drive (such as a 1.44M drive).

Formatting a New Disk

Figure 18.1 shows the FORMAT command summary to format a new, unformatted disk.

Figure 18.1.
FORMAT
command summary
(formatting a new
disk).

FORMAT

Prepares a disk for use.

Syntax:

FORMAT *drive* [*/V:label*] [*/S*] [*/U*]

Parameters and Switches:

drive   Identifies the drive to format.

/V:label   Specifies the volume label for the formatted disk. The label can be up to 11 characters long. If you omit /V, DOS prompts you for the volume label during the format process.

/S   Makes the disk bootable.

/U   Specifies an unconditional format.

The /U switch is not required, but without it FORMAT tries to perform a safe format, discovers that the disk is unformatted, and switches to an unconditional format. You can save that extra time by including /U in the command. A basic command to format a new disk in drive A is as follows:

FORMAT A: /U

This command produces the following messages:

```
Insert new disk for drive A:
and press ENTER when ready...
Formatting 1.2M
        0 percent completed.
Format complete.
```

```
Volume label (11 characters, ENTER for none)?

     1213952 bytes total disk space
     1213952 bytes available on disk
     512 bytes in each allocation unit.
     2371 allocation units available on disk.

Volume Serial Number is 2A46-17F8

Format another (Y/N)?
```

The first message gives you a chance to insert the correct disk into the drive before FORMAT goes to work. When you press Enter, format tells you what capacity it is going to use. (When the command specifies no capacity for an unformatted disk, FORMAT uses the maximum capacity of the drive, even if that's not appropriate for the disk.) Then it displays a count from 0 to 99 percent completed as it tests the surface and creates the sectors.

Understanding the Volume Label

Because the formatting command in the preceding section did not specify a volume label, FORMAT asks for one. (In the example, Enter was pressed to indicate that no label was desired.) You can bypass this step by specifying /V:label in the original command. Following are some label tips:

- Labels show up in directory listings and in messages from several other programs to help you identify which disk you're working with.

- In the /V parameter, place the label in quotation marks if it contains spaces, as in /V:"MY DISK." Without the quotation marks, a space causes an error message. Spaces count in the 11 characters, but the quotation marks don't.

- If you don't want a label, you can enter /V:"" (in other words, a null label in quotation marks).

- DOS translates labels to uppercase characters. If you specify /V:"My Disk," DOS stores the label as MY DISK.

- You can view a label with the VOL command and change it with the LABEL command, both of which are discussed in Chapter 19.

Ending the Format

After the label, FORMAT displays the disk's storage capacities for you. In addition to the lines shown in the previous example, FORMAT might tell you how many bytes are used by system files (if you used the /S switch) and bad allocation units.

FORMAT assigns the serial number, and there's nothing you can do to stop or change it. You will see the serial number in some program messages, but it's really for DOS's internal use. You can ignore it.

Finally, FORMAT asks whether you want to format another disk. If you press Y, the entire routine starts over again. You can't change any parameters (such as /S or /V), but you do get a chance to insert another disk. If you used /V, the same label is assigned to the next disk, too. To get out of the routine, press N, which terminates FORMAT and returns you to the DOS command prompt.

Installing the System Files

Include the /S (for System) switch in the FORMAT command to make the disk bootable. FORMAT copies the DOS system files and COMMAND.COM to the disk after formatting it. (If you booted from a floppy disk, FORMAT asks you to insert that same floppy disk in drive A in order to access the system files.)

Formatting Hard Disks

Hard drive formatting is a little different than formatting a floppy disk. It starts with physical formatting, just as disk formatting does, but DOS's FORMAT program can't handle this job—too many different types of hard disks exist. Low-level formatting usually is done at the factory; if you must redo it for any reason, you might have to buy a special program. (Some systems include a physical formatting program, so check your system documentation to see whether you already have one.)

For hard disks, the second formatting step is partitioning, performed by DOS's FDISK program. *Partitioning* divides the disk into separate partitions, which you can think of as separate disks even though they're located on the same physical device. You must partition a hard disk, but if you want, you can set up only one partition that contains all the sectors on the hard disk (most DOS users do this). FDISK stores a partition table in the first sector so that DOS knows what sectors belong to which partitions.

Each DOS partition can contain one or more logical drives. A logical drive behaves just like a physical drive, such as a disk unit. Each logical drive has its own boot record, root directory, and FAT, and each logical drive is referred to by a drive name, such as C or D.

Many dealers routinely partition a hard disk before delivering it to a customer. This has two benefits: it lets the dealer install software on the hard disk as part of the package, and it avoids making a new computer user perform a rather high-level procedure right off the bat. Unfortunately, if you don't like the way your dealer partitioned your hard disk, you will have a difficult time changing the partitioning once the disk contains data. Repartitioning a disk can cause you to lose access to all its data.

After you have established one or more logical drives on the hard disk, you use the FORMAT program to logically format them. The process is the same as logically formatting a disk, except that it takes considerably longer. After the logical formatting is complete, the hard disk is ready to go.

Understanding Format Levels

When reformatting a disk, you can choose from three levels of formatting: quick, safe, and unconditional. Each has its own characteristics, and each is appropriate under certain circumstances.

Using a Quick Format

A quick format simply stores the mirror file and reworks the logical format without checking the sectors for reliability. This takes almost no time at all, although it's not a good idea when you have been experiencing any kind of errors on the disk.

However, if all you want to do is reuse the disk for new data, a quick format is often the best choice.

Using a Safe Format

A safe format does the same thing as a quick format but also checks the sectors for validity. Although this is not the same as a physical formatter's surface test, it can locate and block out clusters that have been causing read-and-write errors. The disk can still be unformatted if necessary.

Using an Unconditional Format

An unconditional format performs a physical format followed by a logical format on a floppy disk. The physical format destroys all the data on a disk; the disk can't be unformatted. DOS's FORMAT program doesn't enable you to perform an unconditional format on a hard disk, of course, because DOS can't physically format a hard disk.

An expert using the right equipment can still read old data from a physically reformatted disk. To eliminate classified data, you need a program that will remove the data according to government standards (the Norton Utilities includes such a program).

You must perform an unconditional format in two cases:

● The disk has never been formatted before.

● You want to change the capacity of the disk; for example, a disk is formatted for 720K and you now want to format it for 1.44M.

If a disk has been experiencing `Sector not found` errors, its physical format has weakened. You can't access a file when any of its sectors can't be found. If you have up-to-date backups of all the files on the disk, you're in good shape. Reformat the disk, starting with a physical format to rework the sectors. Then you can restore its former files to it.

If you don't have valid backups, you might consider two solutions:

- You can buy third-party programs that refresh a disk's physical format without destroying the data. This is possible for both floppy and hard disks.

- Copy as many files as possible from the disk and then redo the formatting, starting with a physical format. Any files you can't copy will be lost.

Mixing Media

When high-density drives first came out, their manufacturers tried to make them upwardly compatible with double-density drives so that old disks would still be usable. A high-density drive can read a double-density disk with no problems. Supposedly, it also can write a double-density disk, but the results are not always reliable. The reverse is not true; a double-density drive can't read or write a high-density disk.

With DOS, it is possible to format a double-density disk in a high-density drive, but not vice versa. You also can format a disk manufactured for high-density capacity as a double-density disk, but not vice versa. You later can reformat that disk as a high-density disk. And you can reformat a disk currently formatted as high-density to be double-density.

The trouble is that all these procedures yield unreliable results. If, for example, you use a high-density drive to prepare a disk for a friend who has only a double-density drive, the odds are that the friend's drive will not be able to read it. Unless you're in a desperate situation, use disks manufactured for your drive's maximum capacity and format them for that capacity.

Understanding What Can Go Wrong with Formatting

When you're formatting a disk for the first time, manufacturing defects can disrupt the process. As you have seen, DOS can cope with bad spots in most of the sectors, but it can't handle some situations. The system information (partition table, boot record, FAT, and root directory) must go in the first track, and if bad spots exist in that track, the disk is unusable.

You also can run into problems if you try to format a double-density disk for high density. FORMAT will make a Herculean effort to accomplish this, but you will end up with much of the disk marked off as bad sectors. (You usually can hear the drive having trouble with the disk as it tests and retests each bad sector.)

When you are reformatting, you can experience the same problems as the initial format. Also, keep in mind that a quick format will not clear up any bad sector problems you might have been having.

Reformatting a Disk

Figure 18.2 shows FORMAT command parameters for reformatting a disk.

FORMAT

Prepares a disk for reuse.

Syntax:

FORMAT *drive* [*/V:label*] [*/S*] [*/Q*] [*/U*]

Parameters and Switches:

drive	Identifies the drive to format.
/V:*label*	Specifies the volume label for the formatted disk.
/S	Makes the disk bootable.
/Q	Does a quick format.
/U	Does an unconditional format.

Figure 18.2.
FORMAT command summary (reformatting a disk).

As you can see, most of the command is exactly the same as the previous FORMAT command summary, but you can add a /Q switch to request a quick format. If you don't use either /Q or /U, FORMAT does a safe format.

If you're positive that you will not want to unformat the disk, use both /Q and /U. The /Q causes FORMAT to do a quick format, and the /U keeps FORMAT from storing the unformatting file. This is the fastest possible format, but remember that a quick format doesn't check for bad sectors.

When you reformat a used disk, FORMAT uses the disk's current capacity rather than the maximum capacity for the drive.

When you don't specify /U, the message `Checking existing disk format` appears before formatting begins. Then you see the message `Saving UNFORMAT information`. When you perform a safe format, you see the message `Verifying capacity`, and then FORMAT counts up as it checks the sectors. A quick format displays the message `Quick Formatting capacity`, and there's no count because FORMAT doesn't check the sectors.

When you're doing a quick or safe format, you see the following message if no room exists on the disk for the unformatting file:

```
Drive x error. Insufficient space for the MIRROR image file.
There was an error creating the format recovery file.
This disk can't be unformatted.
Proceed with Format (Y/N)?
```

If you're sure you will not want to reformat the disk, press Y to continue. If you're not sure, press N, delete some unnecessary files to make room for the unformatting file, and try again.

Reformatting

Physical formatting eventually deteriorates, and you begin to see `Sector not found` errors when the drive controller can no longer read the sector addresses that were laid down by the physical formatter. You might also experience `Read error` or

`Write error` messages, indicating that some new bad spots have developed. In either case, you're likely to lose at least some of the data on the disk. It's time to reformat the disk.

> If you're about to lose an important file because of physical disk problems, and you don't have a good backup of the file, the Norton Utilities includes programs that might be able to rescue at least some of your data.

Many people also use reformatting simply to clean all the data off a disk. When you redo the logical formatting, you get a new root directory and FAT, as well as a new internal label, a new serial number, and a new boot record. When you redo the physical formatting, the sectors are reworked and retested. Redoing the logical format doesn't actually erase any data from the clusters; all it does is mark the clusters as available for new data. But when you redo the physical format, the surface test actually erases the existing data from the clusters; the data can't be recovered.

Unformatting a Disk

Suppose that you have formatted a disk. You take it out of the drive and see the label—uh oh! It's the wrong disk. No fear, you can reach for the UNFORMAT command (see fig. 18.3).

UNFORMAT

Restores a disk reformatted by the FORMAT command.

Syntax:

`UNFORMAT drive [/L] [/TEST] [/P]`

Parameters:

drive   Identifies the drive to be unformatted.

Figure 18.3.
UNFORMAT
command
summary.

As you can see, it's very simple. Just enter **UNFORMAT** followed by the drive name, and UNFORMAT does the rest. The messages look like this:

```
Insert disk to rebuild in drive A:
and press ENTER when ready.

Restores the system area of your disk by using the image file
created by the MIRROR command.

WARNING !!        WARNING !!

This command should be used only to recover from the inadvertent
use of the FORMAT command or the RECOVER command.  Any other use
of the UNFORMAT command may cause you to lose data!  Files
modified since the MIRROR image file was created may be lost.

Searching disk for MIRROR image.

The last time the MIRROR or FORMAT command was used was at 22:14
on 10-16-93.

The MIRROR image file has been validated.

Are you sure you want to update the system area of your drive A
(Y/N)? y

The system area of drive A has been rebuilt.

You may need to restart the system.
```

If you have specified a disk drive, UNFORMAT starts by giving you a chance to insert the correct disk into the drive. Then UNFORMAT finds the mirror file, displays the date and time it was recorded, and validates the file (which simply confirms that it is an image file, not that its data is correct). You have a final chance to change your mind. If you tell UNFORMAT to continue, it restores the root directory and FAT from the mirror file and displays the final two messages. Rebooting the system can be important to flush old directory data out of any buffers and caches. If you're not sure, reboot. (Don't forget to remove the disk from drive A to boot from the hard disk.)

Unformatting

It's easy to format the wrong disk. You might use the wrong drive name by accident, reformatting the disk in drive A instead of drive B, for example. Or you might simply put the wrong disk in the drive. DOS 6 does everything possible to protect you from accidental formats.

When you redo the logical formatting only, FORMAT stores on the disk a file containing a copy of the current root directory and FAT before it replaces them. This special file is called an unformatting file, a mirror file, or an image file. DOS 6's UNFORMAT program uses this file to recover the former data if need be.

FORMAT stores the unformatting information as close to the end of the disk as possible, where it easily can be found. Once the root directory has been replaced, the only way UNFORMAT can find the file is to search through the clusters for it.

UNFORMAT recovers the data on a disk by restoring the former root directory and FAT. As long as nothing was added to the disk after the reformatting, this should completely restore its former contents. But if anything was added, you might find that some files have been ruined. Even so, that might be better than losing all the former data on the disk.

When you redo the physical formatting, FORMAT doesn't bother to store the mirror file. It would be wiped out along with all the other data by the surface test, so unformatting is not possible.

Unformatting can cause two major problems. The first comes when UNFORMAT can't find the mirror file. DOS's FORMAT always stores the mirror file, but some third-party format programs may not. UNFORMAT can try to rebuild the disk's directory structure from scratch by searching the clusters for directory entries, but this process does not produce the best results. It's a desperation measure, at best.

The other unformatting problem comes when you have added data to the disk after formatting it. Even making a disk bootable adds several files to the disk after formatting it. That new data would have overwritten some of the former data that you're trying to rescue. You can't recover the overwritten data, of course.

For the Future

The FORMAT command has several parameters not discussed in this chapter. You can control the capacity of the disk, ask for a one-sided or eight-sector disk (to prepare the disk for a computer that's using a very early DOS), and leave room on the disk for one of the earlier DOS versions. You will not use any of these features under normal circumstances, but if you ever do need them, look up FORMAT in the Command Reference at the back of this book.

As long as UNFORMAT can find the mirror file, unformatting is easy. If you need to unformat a disk that doesn't have a mirror file, it is much more difficult, and UNFORMAT will cut off any fragmented files.

You also can use UNFORMAT to recover a deleted subdirectory in emergency situations, and if you ever make the mistake of using the RECOVER command from earlier versions of DOS (which is capable of ruining your directory structure), UNFORMAT can help you recover from that, too. All these procedures are unreliable, and you're much better off restoring lost files from their backups. But if you're stuck, check the UNFORMAT command in the Command Reference for additional details.

Additional Disk Management

19

Introduction

Occasionally, you will need to duplicate disks, and you sometimes might want to change a label that you assigned during formatting. This chapter discusses methods for accomplishing these tasks.

Copying Disks with
DISKCOPY

W henever you buy a new software program, you should protect your investment by making backup copies of all the disks. Put the originals away and use the copies to install the software. Keep the two sets in different places so that an event such as a fire or a flood doesn't destroy both sets.

Figure 19.1 shows the DISKCOPY command summary, which you use to copy disks.

Figure 19.1.
DISKCOPY
command
summary.

DISKCOPY

Copies one floppy disk to another.

Syntax:

DISKCOPY [*drive1*] [*drive2*] [/V]

Parameters and Switches:

drive1	Identifies the drive holding the source disk.
drive2	Identifies the drive holding the destination disk.
/V	Verifies that the copied data is correct.

This is a true copy, in which each track on the target disk duplicates the comparable track on the source disk. Because DISKCOPY copies the source disk's formatting along with the data, the target disk doesn't have to be formatted first. This has quite a different effect than copying all the files from one disk to another. A file-by-file copy doesn't duplicate the source disk's system area, it doesn't delete existing data from the target disk (except to overwrite destination files of the same name), and it stores the copies wherever it can find available clusters, which might fragment or defragment them. A track-by-track copy overwrites the entire target disk, including the system area, even if the source disk is not full; the clusters end up in the same order on the target disk as the source disk, reproducing any file fragmentation from the source to the target disk. When you're copying software disks, it could be important that you make a track-by-track copy so that the application's Install program works correctly.

> DISKCOPY can't be used to copy hard disks, only floppy disks. Both disks must be identical in size and capacity.

Copying a disk's formatting can create some problems. If the source disk has some bad sectors blocked out, those same sectors will be blocked out in the target disk, even though they are not bad on the target disk. This isn't a big problem; it just wastes a little space. But suppose that the reverse case is true—the target disk has bad spots that aren't on the source disk. If DISKCOPY identifies this problem, it displays an error message. If it doesn't notice the bad spots, you could end up losing some data later.

Understanding Which Drives To Use

The drive name parameters you need in your DISKCOPY command depend on your disk setup. If you have two identical drives, you can put the source disk in one drive and the target disk in the other. DISKCOPY works much faster that way. If the source disk is in drive A, the command looks like this:

DISKCOPY A: B:

If you have a high-density and a double-density drive of the same size (either 3.5 inches or 5.25 inches), you can use both drives to copy a double-density disk. Put the source disk in the high-density drive (because it reads double-density disks more reliably than it writes them). If the high-density drive is drive B, the command looks like this:

DISKCOPY B: A:

To copy a high-density disk with this setup, you can use only the high-density drive, so for the example, the correct command is as follows:

DISKCOPY B: B:

If you have only one drive, or if your drives are different sizes, then you always must perform one-drive copies.

Verifying the Copy

The verification switch (/V) can add an extra measure of protection to the copy. Your drive controller automatically verifies all the data it stores. But some errors may creep in as the data travels from memory to the drive controller. (Such errors are unusual; they are mostly a matter of power fluctuations or malfunctioning hardware.) DOS's verification feature compares the written copy to the copy in memory and corrects any errors it finds. Frankly, this type of error is so rare that you might not think it's worthwhile to slow down DISKCOPY to look for them.

If you keep DOS's general verification feature on (see the VERIFY command), you don't need the /V switch. They both have the same function.

DOS verification does not catch errors that occur before the data leaves memory. The DISKCOMP command, discussed later in this chapter, is the only way to do that.

Swapping Disks

When you perform a two-drive copy, DISKCOPY tells you to where to insert the source and target disks and then it makes the copy with no further fuss. But for a one-drive copy, you must swap the source disk with the target disk several times. DISKCOPY tells you when to insert each disk.

It's easy to get the two disks mixed up. If you write-protect the source disk, you will prevent accidentally copying the target disk to the source.

Finishing the DISKCOPY

In the process of copying tracks, DISKCOPY naturally copies the label and serial number of the source disk but, at the end of the process, it assigns a new serial number to the target disk.

When the copy is finished, DISKCOPY asks whether you want to make another copy. If you respond **Y**, DISKCOPY uses the same parameters for the next copy. You don't have to reenter the DISKCOPY command. (This feature comes in handy when copying a set of disks in a software program.)

Copying Disks in the Shell

The Shell does not have a menu command to copy disks. But DISKCOPY can be started from the Shell's Disk Utilities group. By default, the program item named Disk Copy generates this command:

```
DISKCOPY A: B:
```

A dialog box enables you to change the drive name parameters if you want.

Comparing Disks with DISKCOMP

As you have seen, DOS's verification feature doesn't really guarantee that a copy matches the original; it only verifies the written version against what's in memory. For complete verification of a copied disk with its original, you must compare them with DISKCOMP.

The DISKCOMP command has nearly the same format as DISKCOPY, but instead of copying disks, it compares them. Figure 19.2 shows the format of the command.

If you have only one disk drive and want to compare two disks, you use this command:

```
DISKCOMP A: A:
```

As with DISKCOPY, DISKCOMP tells you when to insert each disk. If the disks are identical, DISKCOMP displays the message `Compare OK`. If not, it displays a message like the following for each mismatched track:

```
Compare error on
side 1, track 79
```

Figure 19.2.
DISKCOMP
command
summary.

DISKCOMP

Compares two floppy disks.

Syntax:

DISKCOMP [*drive1*] [*drive2*]

Parameters and Switches:

drive1   Identifies one drive that holds a disk for comparison.

drive2   Identifies a second drive that holds a disk for comparison.

DISKCOMP doesn't make any effort to identify the exact byte, or even the sector, containing the error.

If DISKCOMP finds mismatches in a copy that you have just made with DISKCOPY, the problem may be due to a hardware malfunction, such as a failing memory chip, or it could have been caused by a power fluctuation during the copy process. Try making the copy again. If you can't get a perfect disk copy with your system, it probably needs repairs.

DISKCOMP compares disks track by track, not file by file. When you use COPY or XCOPY to copy all files from one disk to another, the result is not a track-by-track copy, and DISKCOMP will find many mismatches.

Managing Internal Labels with VOL and LABEL

You can create a label for a disk when you format it. The label is stored internally (in the root directory) and appears in such places as directory and tree listings. DOS does not use the label; it identifies disks by their serial numbers. The label is mostly for your use. Other programs, however, might pay attention to disk labels. Some Install or Setup programs, for example, check disk labels to make sure that the correct disks have been inserted.

You can view the label of a disk with the VOL command (see fig. 19.3).

Figure 19.3.
VOL command
summary.

VOL

Displays a disk's volume label and serial number, if they exist.

Syntax:

```
VOL [drive]
```

Parameters and Switches:

none   Displays the volume label and serial number, if any, of the current drive.

drive   Specifies a drive whose volume label and serial number you want to see.

An entire VOL interaction looks something like this:

```
C:\>VOL A:
Volume in drive A is RESERVED
Volume Serial Number is 199A-59E3

C:\>
```

To change a label, you use the LABEL command (see fig. 19.4).

You can include the new label in the command or let LABEL prompt you for it. To change the label of the disk in drive A to COLD CALLS, for example, you could enter this command:

```
LABEL A: COLD CALLS
```

You don't use quotation marks in the LABEL command like you do with FORMAT. This means that you can't eliminate a label by including a null label on the command line; without quotation marks, there's no way to specify the null label.

To remove a label:

1. Enter **LABEL D:** with no label parameter.

2. When LABEL asks for a label, press Enter.

3. When LABEL asks whether you want to delete the current label, press Y.

Figure 19.4.
LABEL command
summary.

<u>**LABEL**</u>

Displays and changes the volume label of a disk.

Syntax:

LABEL [*drive*] [*label*]

Parameters and Switches:

none Displays the volume label of the current drive and lets you change or delete it.

drive Identifies the location of the disk whose label you want to display and/or change; the default is the current drive.

label Specifies a new volume label for the disk; the label may contain up to 11 characters.

For the Future

DISKCOPY and DISKCOMP both include switches to emulate one-sided and eight-sector disks. If you need to work with disks from an older DOS SETUP, you may want to look up these switches in the Command Reference.

DOS Edit

Introduction

DOS's editor makes it easy to manage those pesky little text files that are so surprisingly hard to handle with most word processors.

Understanding the Use of Edit

DOS has always included a text editor so that people can edit simple ASCII text files, such as AUTOEXEC.BAT and CONFIG.SYS, without bothering with a word processor. But DOS's original editor was so unfriendly that only a dedicated programmer could love it. DOS 5 finally introduced an easy-to-use, full-screen, graphic-interface editor called EDIT.

EDIT makes it easy not only to create and modify ASCII files, but also to view them. With EDIT, you can open a document, such as README.TXT, scroll back and forth in it, print all or a portion of it, add your own notes, and so on.

If you use a word processor on a regular basis and you're used to its way of doing things, you might prefer it even for editing ASCII files. But there are good reasons to use EDIT. EDIT has fewer functions than most word processors, so it's smaller and takes less time to load. EDIT was designed specifically for ASCII files; most of the leading word processors do their own file formatting, which isn't compatible with ASCII standards. You have to go out of your way to store a file in ASCII format. If you forget and let your word processor format the file, DOS can't read it; if it's a BAT file or CONFIG.SYS, it will not work.

Even though EDIT is not as full-featured as the average word processor, it has many more facilities than many ASCII editors:

- EDIT's graphic user interface enables you to use your mouse or keyboard to edit text and access menus and dialog boxes.

- EDIT has a complete on-line help system to guide you through unfamiliar procedures.

- EDIT includes a Clipboard so that you can cut, copy, and paste text in a document or from document to document.

- You can search for text and replace it with other text.

DOS's EDIT is a function of the QBASIC programming system. You can't use EDIT if you delete QBASIC.EXE.

Starting Edit

You can start Edit in several ways. You can use these techniques from the Shell:

- Choose Editor (in the Main group).

- Open EDIT.COM in the DOS directory.

- Drop an ASCII text file on top of EDIT.COM.
  (Edit can open only one file at a time.)

- Open a TXT file associated with EDIT.COM.

- Use File Run to enter an Edit command at the DOS prompt.

From the DOS command prompt, you start the editor using the EDIT command
(see fig. 20.1).

EDIT

Starts DOS's full-screen editor, which creates, modifies, and displays ASCII
text files.

Format:

EDIT [*filespec*]

Parameters and Switches:

none   Starts the editor with default screen characteristics and no
startup file.

filespec   Opens an ASCII text file. If the file does not exist, creates it;
if it does exist, displays its contents.

Figure 20.1.
EDIT command
summary.

If you don't include a filespec, Edit starts with an empty, untitled document. An initial
dialog box tells you to press Enter for help or Esc for the editing screen. If you press
Enter, some initial help information is displayed. When you press Esc, you see a blank
editing screen, and you can start creating a new document.

If you do include a filespec, Edit opens that document for editing. You see the beginning of the document displayed on your screen.

Figure 20.2 shows what Edit's screen looks like when a document is open for editing. At the top is the menu bar. The main portion, in the middle, is the document editing area. The bottom line is a message line. Two scroll bars are for mouse control.

Figure 20.2.
Edit screen.

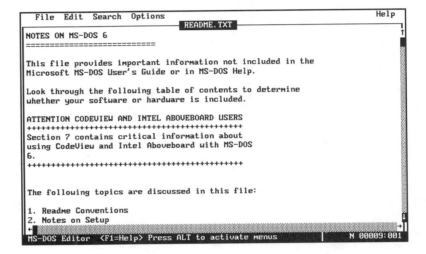

```
   File  Edit  Search  Options                                     Help
                          ┌─────────────┐
                          │ README.TXT  │
  NOTES ON MS-DOS 6
  ============================

  This file provides important information not included in the
  Microsoft MS-DOS User's Guide or in MS-DOS Help.

  Look through the following table of contents to determine
  whether your software or hardware is included.

  ATTENTION CODEVIEW AND INTEL ABOVEBOARD USERS
  ++++++++++++++++++++++++++++++++++++++++++++++++
  Section 7 contains critical information about
  using CodeView and Intel Aboveboard with MS-DOS
  6.
  ++++++++++++++++++++++++++++++++++++++++++++++++


  The following topics are discussed in this file:

  1. Readme Conventions
  2. Notes on Setup

  MS-DOS Editor   <F1=Help> Press ALT to activate menus        N 00009:001
```

Lines versus Paragraphs

If you're used to a word processor, you're used to working with paragraphs. But an ASCII editor works with lines, not paragraphs. A line is a string of up to 255 characters terminated by a carriage return. Edit does not wrap lines; if a line is longer than the viewing area, it continues off into the void. You must scroll sideways to see the entire line. Use the horizontal scroll bar (at the bottom of the editing area) to scroll sideways or move the cursor in the desired direction.

Editing Text

You edit an existing document by inserting, deleting, overtyping, copying, and moving text. This means that you need to be able to move the cursor, select text, switch between Insert and Overstrike mode, cut and paste, and search and replace. You can do much of this with your mouse; if you prefer the keyboard, Edit recognizes not only the standard keyboard cursor keys, such as the up-arrow and down-arrow keys, but also the WordStar control keys, such as Ctrl-E and Ctrl-X.

Cursor Movement

To move the cursor with your mouse, scroll as necessary and click the position you want. If you prefer the keyboard, table 20.1 shows the cursor-movement keys. Notice that the WordStar keys give you some functions that the standard keys don't. But don't worry about memorizing many weird key combinations. You can always get where you're going with the standard keys, even if it takes a little longer.

Table 20.1. Cursor-Movement Keys

Standard Key	WordStar Key	Function
Up arrow	Ctrl-E	Up one line
Down arrow	Ctrl-X	Down one line
Left arrow	Ctrl-S	Left one character
Right arrow	Ctrl-D	Right one character
Ctrl-left arrow	Ctrl-A	Left one word
Ctrl-right arrow	Ctrl-F	Right one word
Home	Ctrl-Q,S	Beginning of line
End	Ctrl-Q,D	End of line

continues

Table 20.1. continued

Standard Key	WordStar Key	Function
Ctrl-Enter	Ctrl-J	Beginning of next line
	Ctrl-Q,E	Top of window
	Ctrl-Q,X	Bottom of window
Ctrl-Home	Ctrl-Q,R	Beginning of file
Ctrl-End	Ctrl-Q,C	End of file

Inserting Text

By default, you are in Insert mode. Press the Ins key or Ctrl-V to switch back and forth between Insert and Overstrike modes. The cursor changes to a flashing rectangle when you're in Overstrike mode.

To insert text, position the cursor where you want it, make sure that you're in Insert mode, and start typing. The new characters shove the rest of the line to the right. Edit beeps and refuses to accept any more characters when the line reaches the 255 character limit.

Selecting Text

There are many occasions when you need to select text. You might, for example, select a block of text to be moved, copied, or printed. You can select part of a line, or if you want to select text from more than one line, you must select whole lines.

You drag the pointer with your mouse to select text. Drag the pointer left or right to select part of a line. If you drag the pointer up or down, you select whole lines. To select text with the keyboard, hold down the Shift key while you move the cursor. To deselect text, click somewhere, move the cursor without holding down Shift, or press Esc.

Deleting Text

You can delete text in several ways. Table 20.2 shows various keys you can use. Keep in mind that if you hold down a key, it repeats, and you can delete a string of text.

Table 20.2. Deleting Keys

Standard Key	WordStar Key	Function
Backspace	Ctrl+H	Delete one character to the left
Delete	Ctrl+G	Delete one character (or delete the selected block)
	Ctrl+T	Delete the remainder of the current word

Cutting and Pasting

When you cut a block, you delete it from where it is but save it in a special memory area called a Clipboard. You also can copy a block to the Clipboard, which saves it in the Clipboard without removing it from its present location. You can't see the Clipboard, but it always contains the last thing that you cut or copied. You can paste the contents of the Clipboard anywhere you want. Table 20.3 shows the WordStar keys that cut and copy blocks to the Clipboard and paste things from the Clipboard.

Table 20.3. Clipboard Keys

WordStar Key	Function
Shift-Del	Cut block to Clipboard
Ctrl-Y	Cut current line to Clipboard

continues

Table 20.3. continued

WordStar Key	Function
Ctrl-Ins	Copy block to Clipboard
Ctrl-Q,Y	Cut to Clipboard from cursor to end of line
Shift-Ins	Paste block from Clipboard

To copy a block of text to another location:

1. Select the block.

2. Choose Edit Copy or press Ctrl-Ins.

3. Move the cursor to the desired destination.

4. Choose Edit Paste or press Shift-Ins.

5. Repeat steps 3 and 4 as often as desired.

To move a block to another location:

1. Select the block.

2. Choose Edit Cut or press Shift-Del.

3. Move the cursor to the desired destination.

4. Choose Edit Paste or press Shift-Ins.

Finding and Replacing

Suppose that you use Edit to create a 20-page README.TXT document and then discover that you used the term "block" when you should have said "handle." You may need to make dozens of changes to correct the error. Edit's find-and-replace feature can make the changes for you. All you have to do is fill in the Change dialog box (see fig. 20.3).

You enter the string of text to be replaced in the Find What box and enter the replacement string in the Change To box.

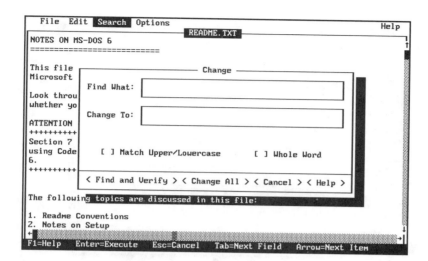

Figure 20.3.
Change dialog box.

To delete a string instead of replacing it, leave the Change To box blank.

If you don't check Match Upper/Lowercase, Edit ignores case when searching for the string; that is, *BLOCK*, *Block*, and *block* will all be found. But Edit replaces all occurrences with the exact string, including case, that you specify in the Change To box.

When you check Match Upper/Lowercase, Edit finds only those strings that match the case shown in the Find What box. Suppose that you want to change all instances of *DOSKEY* to *Doskey*, but you want to leave *DOSkey* alone. You must check the Match Upper/Lowercase box to avoid changing *DOSkey* too. Figure 20.4 shows how to set up the dialog box for this replacement task.

The Whole Word option also might be necessary. When you're changing *block* to *handle*, for example, you don't want Edit to change *blockhead* to *handlehead* or *unblocked* to *unhandled*. If Whole Word is checked, Edit finds only instances of *block* that are surrounded by spaces or punctuation marks.

When you have filled in the boxes, you must choose a command button to start the replacement. Find And Verify shows you each found string and lets you decide whether to replace it. You could call this the "tortoise" method, slow but sure. Change All makes all the replacements without asking for confirmation. This is the "hare" method; it's fast, but it can make some strange substitutions, especially if you don't check Whole Word.

Figure 20.4.
Changing
DOSKEY to
Doskey.

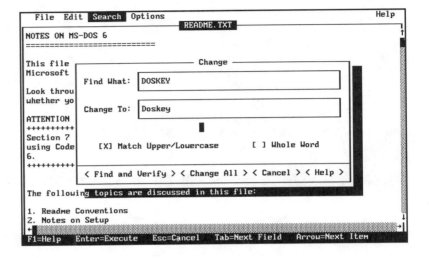

Avoid using spaces in your find string. A phrase containing spaces might be split over the end of a line in the document, and Edit wouldn't find it.

Using Find without Replace

Suppose that, instead of replacing instances of *DOSKEY*, you simply want to look at them. You could use the Search Find command, which opens the dialog box shown in figure 20.5. The Find What box and the two check boxes are the same as in the Change dialog box. When you select OK, Edit locates the next matching string, marks it as a block, and terminates the search. When you're finished working with that string, press F3 (or choose Edit Repeat Find) to find the next occurrence.

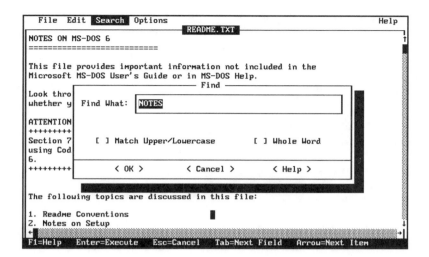

```
   File   Edit  Search  Options                              Help
                        ┌──────────┐
                        │README.TXT│
NOTES ON MS-DOS 6       └──────────┘                             ↑
============================

This file provides important information not included in the
Microsoft MS-DOS User's Guide or in MS-DOS Help.
                                ─────── Find ───────
Look thro
whether y  Find What: │NOTES                              │

ATTENTION
+++++++++
Section 7       [ ] Match Upper/Lowercase     [ ] Whole Word
using Cod
6.
+++++++++        < OK >          < Cancel >        < Help >


The following topics are discussed in this file:

1. Readme Conventions                      ■
2. Notes on Setup                                              ↓
←
 F1=Help    Enter=Execute    Esc=Cancel    Tab=Next Field    Arrow=Next Item
```

Figure 20.5.
Find dialog box.

Search Find can be a handy way to move the cursor long distances in a document, as long as you can come up with a unique text string, contained in one line, to search for.

Edit remembers the last Find What and Change To text you entered. The next time you open either dialog box, the most recent Find What text appears as the default. You can use the text as is, edit it, or replace it. When you open the Change box, the most recent Change To text appears as the default replacement text.

Saving and Opening Files

As you have seen, you can open a file when you start Edit, or you can use the empty editing space to create a new file. The File menu provides the commands that open and save files, print files, and exit Edit (see fig. 20.6).

Figure 20.6.
File menu.

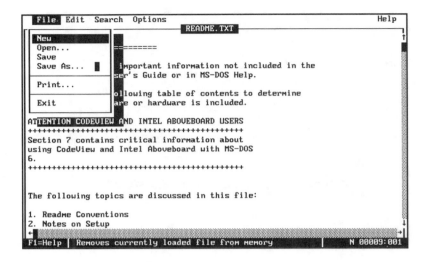

Saving a New File

When you're ready to save an untitled document—one that's never been saved before—choose File Save As. Figure 20.7 shows the Save As dialog box that opens. You select the drive and directory in which you want to save the file and then enter a name in the File Name box, or you can type the complete filespec in the File Name box.

Figure 20.7.
Save As dialog box.

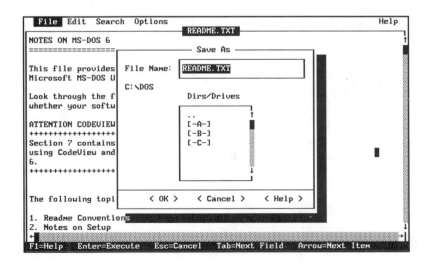

You can replace an existing file with the new file. Select the existing file's drive and directory and then enter its name in the File Name box. When Edit asks whether you want to replace it, choose Yes.

File Save As doesn't apply to new files only. You could, for example, open README.TXT, add your own comments to it, and save it as MYREADME.TXT. README.TXT would continue to exist in its unedited form. MYREADME.TXT would be a new file (unless you replaced an existing one).

Saving the Current File

The File Save command saves your current work in the open file. If, for example, you open AUTOEXEC.BAT, make some changes, and choose File Save, the changes are saved in AUTOEXEC.BAT. No dialog box is displayed.

If there is no open document—that is, if the current work is untitled—File Save works like File Save As. It opens the Save As dialog box so that you can pick a directory and type a file name.

Opening Files

You can open and work on as many documents as needed, but only one at a time. Choose File Open to open an existing document. In the dialog box displayed, you can choose the drive, directory, and file. Choose File New to clear the workspace so that you can create a new document. The document is an untitled document until you save it the first time. If the current document has been changed since the last time you saved it, Edit asks whether you want to save it before opening a new one.

Edit also asks whether you want to save the current file if there are unsaved changes when you choose File Exit.

Printing Files

Choose File Print to print the current document. In the dialog box, you can choose between printing the entire document and printing just the selected text.

Getting Help

Edit's Help system provides on-screen guidance as you work with the Edit functions. Figure 20.8 shows what the Edit screen looks like with Help activated. A Help menu or topic appears in the top window, and the open document appears in the bottom. You can keep the Help topic on-screen to guide you as you work in the document.

Figure 20.8.
Edit screen with
open Help window.

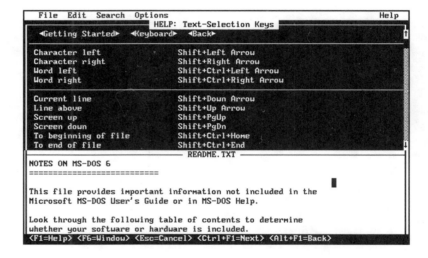

Edit's Help system has three main sections: Keyboard, Getting Started, and Survival Guide. The Keyboard section documents the keys that you can use with Edit; it offers such topics as "Text Scrolling Keys" and "Delete Keys." The Getting Started section shows you how to get started in Edit and includes general editing topics, such as "Using a Dialog Box" and "MS-DOS Editor Options." The Survival Guide is just one topic that documents a few of the most important actions, such as how to activate the menu bar and how to exit Help. The Survival Guide also enables you to link to the Keyboard and Getting Started sections.

There are several ways to start the Help system:

- Press Enter (instead of Esc) when Edit first starts without opening a document. The Survival Guide opens.

- Choose one of the commands in the Help menu.

- Press F1 to display the appropriate Help topic for the command or dialog box you're working on. (If no Help topic exists for that command or dialog box, the Getting Started topic opens.)

- Press Shift-F1 or click <Help=F1> on the message line to open the Survival Guide.

No matter how you enter the Help system, you easily can get to any topic. The labels enclosed in highlighted arrowheads, such as Using Help in the figure, are links to other topics. To use one, double-click it, click the right mouse button on it, or use the Tab key to move to it and press F1.

The message line shows other commands that you can use in the Help system. Press F6 or click <F6=Window> to toggle the cursor between the editing window and the Help window. You also can click the position where you want the cursor to be. Press the Esc key to close the Help window. Press Shift-F1 to display the next Help topic in sequence (Help decides what the sequence is). Press Alt-F1 to display the previous topic in the list of topics that you have viewed. You can back up 20 topics this way. The Back link also does this. You can print a Help topic just like a document.

To print a Help topic:

1. Place the cursor in the Help window.

2. If you don't want to print the entire topic, select the text to be printed.

3. Choose File Print.

4. Select Selected Text Only or Current Window.

Taking Care of Your Startup Files

Your startup files (CONFIG.SYS and AUTOEXEC.BAT) are so important to your system that you must take extra care to protect them. You would be wise to make backup copies before making any changes to them. You might, for example, enter the following command before editing AUTOEXEC.BAT:

```
COPY AUTOEXEC.BAT AUTOEXEC.SAV
```

After editing either startup file, reboot to try out the changes. Even if everything goes all right, keep the backup file(s) around for a few days until you're sure that you like your new setup. If you decide that you want to return to the former startup file, use COPY or XCOPY to replace the current file with the former one. To restore AUTOEXEC.BAT, for example, you could enter this command:

```
COPY AUTOEXEC.SAV AUTOEXEC.BAT
```

If you can't boot after changing one of your startup files, reboot and hold down the F5 key when you see the `Starting MS-DOS...` message. This process bypasses the startup files, so your system will be very primitive. But you will be able to enter COPY commands to restore your startup file(s). If, for example, you save AUTOEXEC.BAT as AUTOEXEC.SAV and CONFIG.SYS as CONFIG.SAV before editing both files, you could enter the following two commands to restore them:

```
COPY AUTOEXEC.SAV AUTOEXEC.BAT
COPY CONFIG.SAV CONFIG.SYS
```

Now you can reboot to restore your system to its former glory.

For the Future

If you like working with Edit, you might want to explore some of its more advanced features, such as the following:

- You can delete all spaces at the beginning of lines by pressing one key.

- You can insert special characters, such as Esc, in a document.

- You can manipulate the size of the Help window.

- Edit offers scrolling and cursor-movement keys.

- You can insert bookmarks in a document and use them to return to specific places easily.

- Edit lets you tailor the appearance of the Edit screen.

- You can control where Edit looks for its Help files.

You also can use switches for the startup command to request hardware options, such as a black-and-white color scheme. When you're ready to learn more about these features, look for them in Edit's Help system.

Batch Files

21

Introduction

You can create your own programs out of the everyday commands that you enter at the command prompt. Batch files can save you time, energy, and typing errors.

Creating Your Own Programs

Do you use certain series of commands over and over? You soon get tired of typing them repeatedly (and of making typing errors). You already have learned how to create a DOSKEY macro out of a short series of commands. Another way to store and recall commands is in a batch file, which is an ASCII text file with the extension BAT.

Batch files offer several advantages over macros:

- You can use as many lines as you need in a batch file (a DOSKEY macro must fit on one command line).

- You can include some commands and parameters that are not available in macros.

- You save batch files permanently on disk; they aren't lost when you shut down or reboot your system.

- You can distribute the batch files to other people.

The major disadvantage of a batch file compared to a DOSKEY macro is in the way you access it. Because the batch file is stored on disk, DOS must search for it and load it into memory just like any other program. Therefore, it takes longer to load, and DOS could fail to find it.

You run a batch file like other programs by typing its name, with or without the extension, at the command prompt. Suppose that you often need to display or edit the file MYTEXT.TXT in directory C:\TALLY. You could create a batch file with these commands:

```
C:
CD \TALLY
EDIT MYTEXT.TXT
```

If you call the batch file EMT.BAT, you can execute it by entering EMT at the command prompt. As you will see, many batch files are longer and more complicated than this one, but even such a short and simple program can save many keystrokes if you use it several times a day.

Locating the Batch File

When you enter a command, such as **EMT**, at the command prompt, there's a standard order of processing:

1. If any TSRs are loaded that process keyboard input, they get first access to the newly entered command (in the order they were loaded). If DOSKEY is loaded and currently has a macro named EMT, DOSKEY processes the command.

2. If no TSR claims the batch file, DOS's command processor must handle the command. First, DOS looks for an internal command named EMT.

> Internal commands are built into the command processor and reside in memory with DOS. Your most common commands, such as DIR and CD, are internal commands.

3. Because EMT isn't an internal command, DOS next looks in the current directory for a file named EMT.COM, EMT.EXE, or EMT.BAT, in that order. Notice that BAT files come at the end of the pecking order.

4. If DOS can't find an EMT program in the current directory, it looks in the first directory in the program search path. If the EMT program file isn't there, DOS looks in the second directory in the path, and so on. In each directory, it looks first for EMT.COM, then for EMT.EXE, and finally for EMT.BAT.

5. If DOS doesn't find an EMT program, you see the message `Bad command or file name` and you return to the command prompt.

As you can see, it's important to choose your batch file names carefully. For best results, don't duplicate the name of a DOSKEY macro, internal command, or COM or EXE program that exists in any program in the search path. If you're going to use the program often, keep its name short, such as D.BAT. Otherwise, make it easy to remember—for example, CFREE.BAT.

For maximum convenience, keep batch files in a single directory and include that directory near the beginning of your program search path.

Understanding How the Batch File Executes

When DOS executes a batch file, it carries out the commands in the order they appear in the file. For each command, DOS displays a blank line, displays the command prompt, fills in the command, and then executes it. Displaying the blank line, the command prompt, and the command is called *echoing the command*. At the end of the program, DOS might display one or two command prompts as it reads empty lines from the end of the file. Then DOS terminates the batch file and displays a command prompt for you to use.

All those echoed commands and terminal command prompts can be confusing to an inexperienced user. You learn how to suppress them later in this chapter.

Stopping the Batch File

Suppose that one of the commands in a batch file displays an error message, and you realize that you need to cancel the rest of the program. You can stop a batch file by pressing one of the break key combinations, Ctrl-C or Ctrl-Break. When interrupted, the batch file displays the message `Terminate batch job (Y/N)?` and waits for an answer. If you press N, the program terminates the current command but continues with the next one; if you press Y, the entire batch file ends and you return to the command prompt. Some commands can't be interrupted at all; others respond immediately to the break keys. Sometimes a break key stops the current command only; you need to repeat it to cancel each subsequent command until you see the `Terminate batch job (Y/N)?` message.

> You can interrupt programs faster when DOS's BREAKfeature is on. See
> Break in the Command Reference.

Using Special Batch Commands

Any command that you can enter at the command prompt you also can put into a batch file, except for DOSKEY macros. DOS offers several commands that are particularly useful in batch files. The CLS, REM, ECHO, PAUSE, and CALL commands are almost always used in batch files rather than at the command prompt.

Using the CLS Command

CLS (clear screen) clears the screen and puts the cursor in the top left corner. This command has no parameters. You also can enter CLS at the command prompt to clean up your screen or hide your work.

People often use CLS near the beginning of a batch file to remove any previous information from the screen before displaying messages from the batch file. You also might want to clear the output from one command in the program before starting the next command.

Using the REM Command

The REM command creates notes or comments in your program files. These notes help document what a program does, why certain commands use the options they do, and so on. Suppose that you have a batch file called FRESHA.BAT that redoes the physical format on the disk in drive A without destroying its files. FRESHA.BAT might contain these commands:

```
XCOPY A:\*.* C:\TEMPTEXT\ /S /E
FORMAT A: /U
XCOPY C:\TEMPTEXT\*.* A:\ /S /E
DELTREE C:\TEMPTEXT
```

This program would be much easier to interpret if it included a few remarks, as follows:

```
REM This program refreshes the disk on drive A
REM Copy the tree from A to temporary branch in C:
XCOPY A:\*.* C:\TEMPTEXT\ /S /E
REM Refresh the sectors:
FORMAT A: /U
REM Restore the tree:
XCOPY C:\TEMPTEXT\*.* A:\ /S /E
REM Remove the temporary branch from C:
DELTREE C:\TEMPTEXT
```

REM often is used to disable commands temporarily in a batch file. Inserting REM in front of a command turns it into a comment that DOS ignores when executing the program. If your program doesn't work quite the way you want it to, you can convert one line at a time to a remark until you find out where the problem is. It's easy to restore the command by removing the REM.

Using the ECHO Command

Use the ECHO command to turn command echoing on or off. DOS doesn't echo commands that follow ECHO OFF in a batch file. Suppressing echoing results in a much neater screen display and is much less confusing to inexperienced users.

When a batch file ends, echoing reverts to the same status it had when the program started.

The ECHO OFF command itself is echoed because DOS echoes it before processing it to turn echoing off. If you don't want to echo the ECHO OFF command, place an @ in front of it. This symbol suppresses echoing for a single command line.

> If you enter ECHO OFF at the command prompt, the command prompt disappears. Just enter **ECHO ON** to get it back.

You may want to display your own messages as the program runs. You can do this by using a command in this format:

ECHO *message*

In FRESHA.BAT, you might use ECHO to turn off command echoing and then to explain what's happening as the program progresses, as follows:

```
@ECHO OFF
REM This program refreshes the physical formatting on drive A
REM Prepared by D. Tabler, ext. 423
ECHO Copying all the files to a temporary location on drive C...
XCOPY A:\*.* C:\TEMPTEXT\ /S /E
ECHO Reformatting the disk (please don't insert a new disk)...
FORMAT A: /U /V:""
ECHO Returning the files to drive A...
XCOPY C:\TEMPTEXT\*.* A:\ /S /E
ECHO Please press Y to remove the temporary files from drive C...
DELTREE C:\TEMPTEXT
```

Notice the difference in the way this program uses ECHO and REM messages. The ECHO messages both document the program and display messages to a user. With echoing off, the REM comments don't display, so they provide documentation only when you read the program file.

The output from this batch file might look like this:

```
Copying all the files to a temporary location on drive C...
Reading source file(s)...
A:\BUDDY1.SAM
A:\BUDDY2.SAM
A:\SCRIPT.STY
A:\CHAP11.DOC
A:\NDWBOOK.STY
A:\SUMFLY2.SAM
A:\TICKETS.DRW
```

```
A:\TICKETS.WMF
A:\TICKETS.BAK
A:\TICKETS.EPS
    10 File(s) copied
Reformatting the disk (please don't insert a new disk)...
Insert new disk for drive A:
and press ENTER when ready...
Formatting 1.2M
    Format complete.
    1213952 bytes total disk space
    1213952 bytes available on disk
    512 bytes in each allocation unit.
    2371 allocation units available on disk.
Volume Serial Number is 252B-0FEA
Format another (Y/N)?N
Returning the files to drive A...
Reading source file(s)...
C:\TEMPTEXT\BUDDY1.SAM
C:\TEMPTEXT\BUDDY2.SAM
C:\TEMPTEXT\SCRIPT.STY
C:\TEMPTEXT\CHAP11.DOC
C:\TEMPTEXT\NDWBOOK.STY
C:\TEMPTEXT\SUMFLY2.SAM
C:\TEMPTEXT\TICKETS.DRW
C:\TEMPTEXT\TICKETS.WMF
C:\TEMPTEXT\TICKETS.BAK
C:\TEMPTEXT\TICKETS.EPS
    10 File(s) copied
Please press Y to remove the temporary files from drive C...
Delete directory "C:\TEMPTEXT" and all its subdirectories? [yn]Y
Deleting C:\TEMPTEXT...
```

For the sake of someone using the program, you could do a few things to emphasize its messages. You might use a CLS command so that the display starts with a clear screen. You might like to set off some of the ECHO messages with blank lines. You can use **ECHO.** to display a blank line. Be sure that the period immediately follows ECHO, with no space between. You also might like to use spaces to center a message, asterisks to highlight a message, or even to draw a box around a message to make it stand out on the screen. Combining some of these techniques, you could create a batch file like this:

```
@ECHO OFF
REM This program refreshes the physical formatting on drive A
REM Prepared by D. Tabler, ext. 423
ECHO Copying all the files to a temporary location on drive C...
ECHO.
ECHO.
XCOPY A:\*.* C:\TEMPTEXT\ /S /E
ECHO.
ECHO.
ECHO ***** Reformatting the disk (please don't insert a new disk) *****
ECHO.
ECHO.
FORMAT A: /U /V:""
ECHO.
ECHO.
ECHO Returning the files to drive A...
ECHO.
ECHO.
XCOPY C:\TEMPTEXT\*.* A:\ /S /E
ECHO.
ECHO.
ECHO Please press Y to remove the temporary files from drive C...
ECHO.
ECHO.
DELTREE C:\TEMPTEXT
```

Using the PAUSE Command

The PAUSE command, which has no parameters, stops the progress of the batch file until you press a key. Some programs have built-in pauses. The FORMAT command, for example, always gives you a chance to change disks before starting to

format. XCOPY has a special /W (wait) switch you can use to generate a pause before copying begins; this switch is useful in a batch file to give someone a chance to
change disks. Most commands, though, begin working immediately. If you need a
chance to change disks, load special paper, read messages before they scroll off the
top of the screen, or even to decide whether to continue the program, a PAUSE
command gives you the opportunity to do so.

Suppose that you want a program to delete from a directory certain file types that
you consider temporary. After the directory is cleaned up, you want the program to
print a listing of its remaining entries. You may want to include PAUSE to give you
time to make sure that the printer is ready. You might call this batch file
CLEANDIR.BAT, as follows:

```
@ECHO OFF
DEL *.BAK
DEL *.TMP
DEL TEMP.*
DEL TEST.*
ECHO ***** GET THE PRINTER READY *********
PAUSE
DIR > PRN
```

When you run this program, it deletes four types of files from the current directory
and tells you to get the printer ready. The PAUSE command then prints its own
message, telling you to press any key when ready. When you press a key, the directory starts to print. By the way, a pause is an ideal time to use Ctrl-C to cancel the
rest of a batch job.

As shown in this example, you can use command redirection in a batch file.
You can't, however, redirect the output of the batch file itself. If you enter
the command **CLEANDIR > PRN**, DOS ignores the redirection.

Using the CALL Command

You can start a batch file from another batch file. Suppose that you already have a
program, CLEANUP.BAT, that cleans up the current directory, as follows:

```
@ECHO OFF
DEL *.BAK
DEL *.TMP
DEL TEST.*
DEL TEMP.*
```

Now, suppose that you want to create a program called VAULT.BAT that copies all the files from the current directory to drive A, but first you want to delete unnecessary files. You might try this approach:

```
CLEANUP
XCOPY *.* A:\
```

Unfortunately, this will not work. When you run one batch file from another, DOS transfers to the second program and never returns to the first one. In this example, when DOS processes the CLEANUP command, it starts that program and returns to the XCOPY command.

You can use the CALL command to execute another batch file without completely transferring to it. When you call a batch file, DOS returns to the original program after finishing the called program. Using CALL to run CLEANUP from VAULT.BAT works fine, as follows:

```
@ECHO OFF
CALL CLEANUP
XCOPY *.* A:\
```

When CLEANUP is finished, DOS returns to Vault and executes the XCOPY command.

Using Replaceable Parameters

In Chapter 14, you learned how to make macros more flexible by using replaceable parameters. Batch files also use replaceable parameters, but they are coded with a percent sign instead of a dollar sign.

A program can have up to 10 replaceable parameters, from %0 to %9. %0 stands for the first word in the command, which is always the name of the batch file. (If you use %0 at all, it's usually as part of an ECHO message.)

The following batch file, DUPDEL, compares two files and gives you a chance to delete the second one:

```
@ECHO OFF
CLS
REM Compare the two files:
FC %1 %2
ECHO.
ECHO **************************************
ECHO.
ECHO    If you don't want to delete %2
ECHO    Press Ctrl-C now!
ECHO.
ECHO **************************************
PAUSE
DEL %2
```

Suppose that you enter the following at the command prompt:

DUPDEL AFILE.BAT AFILE.SAV

DOS sees this as three words divided by spaces, numbered from 0 through 2. DUPDEL is number 0; AFILE.BAT is 1; and AFILE.SAV is 2.

When DOS begins to execute the program, it replaces the numbered parameters with the comparable parameters from the command line. The program becomes the following:

```
@ECHO OFF
CLS
REM Compare the two files:
FC AFILE.BAT AFILE.SAV
ECHO.
ECHO **************************************
ECHO.
ECHO    If you don't want to delete AFILE.SAV
ECHO    Press Ctrl-C now!
ECHO.
```

```
ECHO ****************************************
PAUSE
DEL AFILE.SAV
```

You can use any two file names in the DUPDEL command line, including full filespecs if necessary, as follows:

```
DUPDEL C:\FINANCE\MYDAY.TXT A:\MYDAY.TXT.
```

Modifying CLEANUP

Suppose that you want to use CLEANUP on any directory, not just the current one. You could change the commands in the batch file to the following:

```
@ECHO OFF
DEL %1\*.BAK
DEL %1\*.TMP
DEL %1\TEST.*
DEL %1\TEMP.*
```

Now you can run CLEANUP on any directory by including the path as a parameter in the command line. To clean up the \FINANCE directory, you could enter this command:

CLEANUP \FINANCE

The command CLEANUP A: cleans the root directory on drive A.

But what happens if you enter CLEANUP without a parameter? When a command line leaves out a parameter, DOS uses a null value (nothing) as a replacement. The program becomes as follows:

```
@ECHO OFF
DEL \*.BAK
DEL \*.TMP
DEL \TEST.*
DEL \TEMP.*
```

This program cleans up the root directory on the current drive.

Understanding Your AUTOEXEC.BAT File

Almost every system has an AUTOEXEC.BAT file. When DOS boots or reboots, it looks for this file in the root directory of the boot drive. If AUTOEXEC.BAT is there, it runs immediately, before you get a chance to do anything from the command prompt.

Without AUTOEXEC.BAT, DOS asks for the date and time when you boot. But AUTOEXEC suppresses the date and time functions. If your system doesn't keep track of the date and time, you probably want to include DATE and TIME commands in AUTOEXEC.BAT so that you can set the correct date and time during booting.

At installation, DOS 6 puts several commands, including PROMPT and PATH, into your AUTOEXEC.BAT file. Most people who use DOSKEY start it with a command in AUTOEXEC.BAT. A basic AUTOEXEC.BAT file might look like this:

```
@ECHO OFF
PROMPT $P$G
PATH C:\; C:\DOS;
DOSKEY
```

Most AUTOEXEC.BAT files are much more complex than this. You may want to include commands to start anti-virus and undelete programs from AUTOEXEC. You learn more about these commands in Chapters 26 and 27.

You can add REM, ECHO, CLS, and PAUSE commands to your AUTOEXEC.BAT file to make it easier to live with.

For the Future

After you have mastered the basics of batch files, other commands (especially IF, CHOICE, and GOTO) can make your batch files more flexible. With these commands, you can skip around in the program under certain conditions. The commands also help you to build menus from which you can choose what to do next. When you're ready to try these features, look up the appropriate commands in the Command Reference at the back of this book.

In addition, there are more ways to build variable parameters into a batch file. The SHIFT command gives you access to more than nine replaceable parameters and lets you process them in a circular fashion. You also can use other types of replaceable parameters, called environment variables, in a batch file. An advanced DOS book, such as *Peter Norton's Advanced DOS 6* (published by Brady), explains how to use these features and how to redirect the output of a batch file.

Configuring Your System

22

Introduction

The CONFIG.SYS file is essential to your system, yet many DOS users have no idea what its commands do. This chapter explains some of the mysteries.

Understanding the DOS Boot Process

When you boot or reboot DOS, it loads its system files into memory. Then it looks in the root directory of the boot drive for a file called CONFIG.SYS. Commands in CONFIG.SYS help DOS set up, or configure, the system. Most of the commands are concerned with defining and managing your hardware, especially memory. Some of the commonly used commands tell DOS

- How much memory to reserve for certain functions

- Which command processor to use

- What device drivers to load

After carrying out all the commands in CONFIG.SYS, DOS looks for and runs AUTOEXEC.BAT. Then DOS turns control over to you, either from the command prompt or from a program, such as DOS Shell or Windows.

Understanding What Is in CONFIG.SYS

CONFIG.SYS is an ASCII text file, somewhat like a batch file, that contains special configuration commands. Most of these commands are unique to CONFIG.SYS; you can't use them anywhere else. Nor can you use ordinary commands, such as DIR or FORMAT, in CONFIG.SYS.

Like a batch file, you can create or modify CONFIG.SYS using an ASCII editor. Unlike a batch file, you can't run CONFIG.SYS from the command prompt. CONFIG.SYS is used only during booting.

CONFIG.SYS runs before you have a chance to establish a search path or change the current directory. You need to include in CONFIG.SYS the full path for any files or programs that aren't in the root directory of the boot drive.

The following is a sample CONFIG.SYS file:

```
DEVICE=C:\DOS\SETVER.EXE
DEVICE=C:\DOS\HIMEM.SYS
DEVICE=C:\DOS\ANSI.SYS
DOS=HIGH
BUFFERS=50
FILES=30
SHELL=C:\DOS\COMMAND.COM C:\DOS /P
STACKS=9,256
```

This example includes six different commands: DEVICE, DOS, BUFFERS, FILES, SHELL, and STACKS. These are all commands that you can use only in CONFIG.SYS. Notice their general format. In each case, an equal sign (=) follows the command name. To the right of the equal sign are filespecs, parameters, or switches.

Using Device Drivers

DOS includes built-in software to control the basic hardware components of your system: keyboards, disk drives, memory below the 1M limit, dot-matrix printers, and so on. But if you have any devices beyond the basics, such as a mouse or an expanded memory board, you probably will need to load device drivers to control them. You also might load a device driver to provide extra features for an ordinary device; for example, the DBLSPACE.SYS driver doubles the capacity of your hard disk by compressing its data.

Some device drivers simulate devices where there are none. The RAMDRIVE.SYS driver, for example, uses part of memory to simulate a hard disk, and the DRIVER.SYS driver makes one floppy disk drive look like two.

DOS 6 includes several optional device drivers; you will find full descriptions of them in the Appendix and many of them are described in the chapters. In addition, you might have device drivers that came with your hardware. You also can buy device drivers that have more features than the basic drivers provided by DOS. Many memory managers on the market, for example, have features you don't find in DOS.

You load a device driver with a DEVICE command in CONFIG.SYS. Once loaded, the driver remains in memory until you reboot the system.

Understanding the DEVICE Command

The DEVICE command takes this general format:

```
DEVICE=filespec [parameters] [switches]
```

The DEVICE command must include the device driver's filespec followed by any necessary parameters or switches. Remember that the filespec must include the drive and path names if the file isn't in the root directory of the boot drive.

The CONFIG.SYS example earlier in the chapter loads three device drivers: SETVER.EXE, HIMEM.SYS, and ANSI.SYS. Each of these drivers is explained in the following sections.

Using the Version Table and SETVER.EXE

Some programs expect to run under a particular version of DOS. Many programs use techniques that were not available in early DOS versions. A program written for DOS 3, for example, might be programmed to refuse to run under any other DOS version. It may display an error message such as Incorrect DOS Version and quit. DOS 6, however, still includes most DOS 3 techniques. Programs that require earlier versions often have no problem running under DOS 6.

The SETVER driver (called SETVER.EXE) includes a version table that lists the required version numbers for many such programs. When one of these programs checks for the current version number, SETVER lies and reports the version the program expects. Your CONFIG.SYS probably includes a DEVICE command to load SETVER.EXE, placed there by DOS 6's SETUP program. If it's there, don't delete it. Some of your DOS commands need it.

Using HIMEM.SYS

If your system includes extended memory, you need to load a device driver to manage it. HIMEM.SYS is the extended memory manager provided with DOS 6 (as well as Windows). DOS 6's SETUP may put a DEVICE command into your CONFIG.SYS file to load HIMEM.SYS.

Using ANSI.SYS

The ANSI.SYS device driver provides a set of enhanced functions for your monitor and keyboard. ANSI.SYS lets programs display color and graphics on the command prompt screen, for example, and redefines the meanings of your keyboard keys. Many applications use these functions and will not work right without ANSI.SYS. Even some DOS programs require ANSI.SYS.

Using EGA.SYS

There's one more device driver that you may need to include in CONFIG.SYS. If you use DOS Shell's task-swapping feature and you have an EGA monitor, you need to load the EGA.SYS device driver using a command like this:

```
DEVICE=C:\DOS\EGA.SYS
```

Understanding the DOS Command

Ordinarily, DOS loads itself in the first 640K of memory. (This area is called *conventional memory*.) Many programs must also use this part of memory, and you can run out of space there. If your system has extended memory, you can save some conventional memory by loading DOS into extended memory using a CONFIG.SYS command like this:

```
DOS=HIGH
```

You must load the HIMEM.SYS device driver (or an equivalent memory manager) on a line preceding the DOS command in CONFIG.SYS.

Understanding the BUFFERS Command

When an application requests data from a disk, DOS reads the data into buffers. A *buffer* is a section of memory that DOS has reserved for this purpose. Each buffer is the size of a disk sector, usually 512 bytes. DOS fills as many buffers as necessary to provide the data the program asks for. Then it passes the data to the program.

Whenever an application requests data, DOS looks in the buffers to see whether the data is already there. If it finds the data, it doesn't have to access the disk, which can save a considerable amount of time.

In the same way, DOS stores output disk data in buffers before writing it to disk. Then, if it needs to reread that data (which happens more often than you might think), it can read it from the buffers instead of the disk.

Because memory access is so much faster than disk access, buffering can save much time. The BUFFERS command tells DOS how many buffers it should use. A reasonable number, from 10 to 50, improves performance. If you use too many, searching all the buffers may take longer than accessing the disk. Too many buffers also can use more memory than you can spare.

If you have 48 or fewer read-write buffers, they're located in extended memory, if DOS is there. Otherwise, the buffers are located in conventional memory.

If you don't include a BUFFERS command in CONFIG.SYS, DOS uses default values based on how much conventional memory your system has. A system with 512K to 640K (the maximum possible) has a default of 15 buffers. You probably can benefit from more buffers than that unless you're using a hard disk-caching system such as SMARTDRV.SYS, which is explained in Chapter 32.

Some applications recommend a certain number of buffers for efficient operation. When these applications are installed, they may place a BUFFERS command into CONFIG.SYS or change the existing BUFFERS command, or their documentation may ask you to do it.

Understanding the FILES Command

DOS reserves an area of memory for a table of file handles. Each file handle contains information about an open file. The FILES command tells DOS the maximum number of files you expect to have open at one time. Some applications require a minimum number of open files. When it is installed, an application may place a FILES command into CONFIG.SYS or change the existing FILES command, or its documentation may ask you to insert the FILES command.

Understanding the SHELL Command

A command processor interprets commands entered from the command prompt or a batch program. The command processor provided with DOS 6 is COMMAND.COM. DOS expects to find COMMAND.COM in the root directory of the boot drive. If you have moved COMMAND.COM, or if you want to use a different processor, you need a SHELL command in CONFIG.SYS. The following command loads the COMMAND.COM processor from the DOS directory instead of the root directory:

```
SHELL=C:\DOS\COMMAND.COM  C:\DOS /P
```

The part of the command that follows `SHELL=` identifies the filespec of the command processor. The other parameters are unique to the command processor being loaded. The parameters in the example pertain to COMMAND.COM. The C:\DOS parameter tells DOS where to find COMMAND.COM if it needs to reload it. The /P switch tells DOS to make COMMAND.COM the primary command processor.

You can find more information about switches for COMMAND.COM in the Command Reference under COMMAND.

Understanding the STACKS Command

DOS must set aside a certain amount of memory to handle hardware functions. The reserved memory is called a *stack*. You can control how much stack space DOS allocates with a STACKS command in CONFIG.SYS. DOS usually creates enough stack space by default, but some programs might insert a STACKS command in CONFIG.SYS or modify the existing one. Unless you understand how DOS uses stacks and what your hardware and software needs are, you should leave any existing STACKS commands alone.

If you have certain programs that seem to freeze up often, or if you get occasional `Stack error` or `Stack fault` messages, talk to the Microsoft technical support team. The problem might be solved with a STACKS command.

For the Future

If your CONFIG.SYS or AUTOEXEC.BAT file is causing problems, you can bypass the whole file or individual commands during booting. Your DOS documentation shows you how.

You can modify the SETVER table to add new program entries, change an existing entry, or delete an entry. Details are included under SETVER in the Command Reference at the end of this book.

The BUFFERS command can reserve additional buffers so that DOS can actually read ahead in a file. This feature could make your system run even faster; see BUFFERS in the Command Reference for details.

Some older applications used File Control Blocks (FCBs) instead of file handles. Look up the FCBS command in the Command Reference if an application asks you to install some FCBs on your system.

All the drivers discussed in this chapter include parameters and switches to adapt them for your system. If the basic driver doesn't seem to do what you want, look up the driver in the Appendix to see what options it offers.

There are many more commands you can use in CONFIG.SYS. Most of them are used to control memory usage and are covered in Chapters 30 and 31.

Managing Your System

Avoiding Disaster: An Overview

23

Introduction

Using just the tools included with DOS 6, you can do much to protect your data from all the things that can go wrong in your system.

Understanding the Importance of Backups

As you learn in this chapter, DOS includes several facilities to help you prevent and recover from specific problems, such as FAT errors or accidental deletions. But the most important tool DOS offers—the tool that provides the best protection against data loss of any kind—is the backup system. This system, which involves several programs, helps you keep up-to-date backups of all your important files so that you can recover from any kind of loss. No matter what type of mishap you run into—if your hard drive crashes, if Delete Sentry purges a file before you realize you want to recover it, even if your computer is stolen—you can recover your data from the backups.

DOS 6 makes it easy to establish and maintain a regular backup cycle at the command prompt, in the Shell, or under Windows, whichever environment you prefer. Chapter 24 shows you how to set up and maintain your backup system, and Chapter 25 shows you how to recover files when that becomes necessary.

This chapter reads somewhat like a catalog of disaster, but keep in mind as you read that, if you have a good set of backups, you can recover from anything that can happen to your system.

Coping with Viruses

A *virus* is a program that sneaks itself into your system, hides somewhere, is triggered by an event, and does something unexpected. Some of the less harmful viruses display a silly message or play a little tune. But a truly malicious virus might trash your partition table or physically reformat your hard disk; either action wipes out all the data on your hard disk. DOS 6 includes several programs to help you protect your system against viruses.

The MSAV (Microsoft Anti-Virus) program, which runs from the command prompt or the Shell, scans memory and your drives for viruses. It can remove many viruses safely from your system; for other viruses, it deletes the infected file (the file the virus is hiding in) if you decide that's what you want to do. MWAV (Microsoft Windows Anti-Virus) is the Windows version of this program.

The VSAFE program operates as a terminate-and-stay-resident program (TSR) to monitor your system constantly for virus-like activity, such as physically reformatting the hard disk. VSAFE blocks any suspicious activity, warns you what's happening, and lets you decide what to do next. VSAFE can operate under DOS, DOS Shell, and Windows.

Chapter 26 explains DOS's anti-virus programs. If you use them regularly, your system will be nearly invulnerable to virus attack. But there's always the possibility of a new type of virus managing to sneak past all the safeguards. And, of course, if you choose not to maintain a constant watch for viruses (the anti-virus programs take up both space and time), your chances of being attacked by a virus increase dramatically. Your backup system provides the ultimate line of defense against viruses; if a virus does manage to damage some of your data, you can restore the data from your backups.

Dealing with Misbehaving Software

Any program can cause problems in your system. Back in the old days (that is, the late 1970s), when personal computers typically came with 16K of memory and could be expanded up to a whopping 64K, software was fairly simple—it had to be, or it wouldn't fit in the available memory space. But nowadays, programs can be wonderfully complex. Software, such as an animation studio, a music sequencer, even common, everyday applications like a word processor or database manager, take huge staffs to develop, perhaps with several years of effort. Unfortunately, mistakes happen, and even when the testing and debugging process is quite rigorous, a small error in some esoteric corner of a program can be overlooked. This is complicated by the fact that, in the world of IBM PC clones, so many combinations of hardware and software exist that there is no way to test a new program in every environment it's going to be used in.

Problems also can occur with programs trying to run under DOS 6 that were developed to run under an earlier version of DOS. Microsoft tested DOS 6 on thousands of systems, with every variation of hardware and software that they could get their hands on, in an effort to make it error-free. But 100-percent reliability cannot be guaranteed.

Smaller products may also have their problems. Many products developed by one or two people may not have been as rigorously tested as a program like DOS. The program may have been tested on two or three systems, perhaps even a dozen or more, but probably not 10,000. On the other hand, because such programs are smaller, they're less complex and therefore less likely to conceal problems, especially if they have a national reputation and are sold in reliable stores. Still, there's no guarantee that such a product will not trip over something in your system. But the more widespread such a program is, the less likely it is to cause problems.

And then there's the wide world of cheap software: freeware, publicware, and shareware. Part of the reason it's cheap is because the developers haven't spent money on packaging, marketing, or distribution. But they also might have cut corners during the development and testing process. A program might work fine on one system but cause problems on another.

In any of these cases, a program could malfunction in your system and cause you to lose data. It might freeze your system, forcing you to reboot at an inconvenient time. Worse, the program could actually damage the system area or the data on your hard disk.

There's very little you can do to avoid all program glitches. Certainly you should stay away from those programs most likely to bring problems with them. For the rest, your up-to-date backups are your best defense.

Coping with Hardware Failure

Any kind of hardware failure, from a momentary power fluctuation to a head crash, could damage your system areas and make your hard disk data inaccessible, or it could damage specific files.

Several hardware solutions are available to protect your system from hardware malfunctions. A surge protector, for example, prevents power surges from reaching your hardware. You can even buy a battery-powered board that swings into action when the power goes out, giving you a minute or so to save all your files and shut down your system properly. If power fluctuations and outages are a problem in your area, talk to your hardware dealer about what's available to protect your data.

But nothing can protect your system from a hard disk failure. And hard disks always fail in the end. When yours does, you will be glad you have a full set of backups to restore your files after you get the disk repaired or replaced.

Coping with Deletions

You probably know how easy it is to delete the wrong file or to change your mind after deleting a file. You have seen DOS's UNDELETE facility, which both protects files from deletion and helps you to recover them if that becomes necessary. Chapter 27 details how to set up and use UNDELETE.

But not even DOS's top level of deletion protection, Delete Sentry, can guarantee recovery of every file. Delete Sentry protects files for a while, but after a few days, or if the disk becomes too full, it purges its oldest files. The lower levels of deletion protection provide even less assurance of recovering a specific file. Again, a good set of backups can help you recover a file that cannot be recovered by any other means.

Dealing with Reformatting

You also learned how easy it is to reformat the wrong disk, and you have learned about DOS's UNFORMAT facility. But UNFORMAT counts on two factors. First, the images file must be present. Second, no new data must be added to the disk after formatting. Without these two conditions, UNFORMAT works, but not as well, so you're better off restoring the missing files from their backups.

Dealing with Problems in the FAT and Directory Structure

The directory tree and the File Allocation Table (FAT) are essential to accessing the data on a disk. If either one becomes damaged, you could lose contact with some files—perhaps even all your files. This vital system information can become damaged in many ways. Malfunctioning hardware, power fluctuations, viruses, neglecting to park your heads before powering down, and not waiting for the drive light to go out before rebooting are just some of the possibilities.

DOS includes a program called CHKDSK (check disk) that analyzes the FAT and directory structure, reports problems, and repairs many of the problems it finds. CHKDSK, which is discussed in Chapter 28, is one of the maintenance facilities that you should run on a regular basis to keep your hard disk in good running order.

CHKDSK cannot handle every problem that it finds; there are times when you must restore damaged files from their backups.

Putting It All Together

A wise person uses the preventive programs overviewed in this chapter (and described in detail in the next few chapters) on a regular basis. VSAFE and Delete Sentry should be loaded as TSRs every time you boot. MSAV or MWAV should be run daily, perhaps every time you boot. CHKDSK doesn't need to be run daily; weekly is probably good enough. Finally, you will need to use Backup daily (at least) to keep your backups up-to-date.

The DOS BACKUP Feature

24

Introduction

A good backup system is the most important way to protect your data. DOS 6 gives you a useful tool, but it's up to you to use it.

Looking at BACKUP's Features

DOS 6 includes two versions of its backup program: MSBACKUP (Microsoft Backup) runs at the command prompt or under DOS Shell, and MWBACKUP (Microsoft Windows Backup) runs under Windows. So, no matter which environment you prefer, you have a backup tool available. Both versions feature a graphic user interface to make it easy to set up and run backups. The Windows version is fancier looking than the DOS version, as you might expect, and a little bit easier to use, but the functions are the same. Figure 24.1 shows MWBACKUP's window; the figures throughout the rest of this chapter are from MSBACKUP.

Figure 24.1.
The MWBACKUP window.

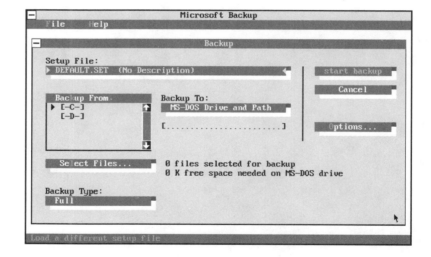

When you install DOS 6 on a system with Windows, SETUP gives you the choice of installing MSBACKUP, MWBACKUP, or both. You probably don't need both, so you can save some disk space by installing only the one you use.

Understanding Backup Functions

The backup application includes three major functions: BACKUP, COMPARE, and RESTORE. The BACKUP function archives selected files from the hard disk to a backup medium, such as disk, tape, or removable cartridge. BACKUP is capable of compressing the backed up data to save space, and you can configure it for maximum speed, maximum reliability, or somewhere between these two extremes.

The COMPARE function compares backed up files to their hard disk originals; COMPARE is useful to verify the accuracy of the backups or to identify files that have changed since they were backed up. The RESTORE function returns backed up files to the hard disk. If your hard disk fails, you can use RESTORE to place all your files on your new or repaired drive. But you also can use RESTORE to recover a file that you deleted accidentally or to return to an earlier version of a file that you trashed somehow.

COMPARE and RESTORE are explained in Chapter 25. This chapter shows you how to use the BACKUP function.

> DOS 6's BACKUP is new and can't restore files backed up by earlier DOS versions. DOS 6 includes the old RESTORE as a separate program in case you need to restore files from an earlier backup. You should back up your files with the new BACKUP as soon as possible and eliminate your old backups. Then you can delete DOS\RESTORE.EXE.

Selecting Files

Some people back up every file on their hard disk; this makes it simple to restore the entire disk, if that becomes necessary. Other people prefer to back up only those files that are created or modified after an application is installed (such as document files) but not the original program files, which never change and can be reinstalled from their original disks if necessary. Skipping program files significantly reduces backup time and media space but makes it harder to completely restore the hard disk. DOS 6's BACKUP easily can be set up for either method. And either way, you can eliminate nonessential files, such as scratch pads, personal memos, to-do lists, and so on.

Using Backup Cycles

Most people like to do their backups in cycles, starting with a full backup of all selected files, whether or not they have changed since the last full backup. You might do a full backup once a week, once a month, during a full moon, or on some other schedule.

Between full backups, perhaps on a daily basis, you back up only those selected files that have been created or modified since the last backup, using archive attributes as your guide. These partial backups take much less time and media space than full backups and, by combining the last full backup with subsequent partial backups, you have complete coverage of all your selected files. With DOS 6's BACKUP, you can switch between full and partial backups simply by selecting the type of backup you want.

BACKUP Options

BACKUP includes several options to tailor it for speed, reliability, and minimum media usage. You can, for example, choose to compress the backed up data, which not only takes up less media space but also saves backup time. You can choose to verify all written data against the original files as you go; this type of verification takes much more backup time but guarantees a restorable product. Other options let you password protect your backup files, unconditionally format all backup disks, and so on.

> The COMPARE and RESTORE functions offer their own options, which are described in Chapter 25.

BACKUP's Setup Files

When you set up a backup—selecting files, choosing a backup type, selecting options, and so on—you can save your work in a backup setup file. The next time you want to run the same backup, all you have to do is open the setup file and select Start Backup. Because you probably repeat the same backup every day, you can use the setup file to accomplish the task in just a few keystrokes.

Backup setups have other advantages. They can be handed out to other users to make sure that everyone in a work group is conforming to the same backup standards. And you can have more than one setup on your system, if that's appropriate.

Starting BACKUP

There are several ways to start BACKUP, depending on which environment you're using.

To start BACKUP from the command prompt, enter **MSBACKUP**.

To start BACKUP from DOS Shell, open the MSBACKUP.EXE file in the DOS directory. Or you can choose File Run and enter **MSBACKUP** in the Run dialog box.

To start BACKUP from Windows, open the MWBACKUP program item.

Configuring BACKUP

The first time you start either version of BACKUP, you see a message telling you that you have not yet configured BACKUP. You must do this first. During configuration, BACKUP tests your system to make sure that it can produce reliable backups. Several tests are involved:

● BACKUP tries to sense what types of hardware (video, mouse, and disk drives) you have. If it identifies them incorrectly, you have the chance to correct them.

- BACKUP checks to see whether it can sense when you have changed a floppy disk. If so, you don't have to press an OK button every time you insert a new disk, and that can save quite a bit of time in a long backup.

- BACKUP tests memory and your hard disk to make sure that it can read data at high speeds.

- BACKUP makes a practice backup; if you choose to use to a disk drive, BACKUP selects a little more than one disk's worth of data so that you must change disks once. This small backup should reveal incompatibilities with any part of your system: the drives, memory, any TSRs that conflict with BACKUP's process, and so on. BACKUP can avoid some incompatibilities by slowing itself down. Others problems (such as incompatible TSRs) you must fix yourself before you can use BACKUP.

- BACKUP does a comparison of all the files in the practice backup; again, this should reveal any problems in making reliable backups on your system.

If the comparison is successful, the tests are complete and BACKUP has been configured for your system. If you change your hardware or install a new TSR, you should rerun the configuration and compatibility tests to make sure that everything is still fine.

Running the Tests

When the initial alert box is on-screen, press Start Configuration to begin the tests. You see some dialog boxes flash past as BACKUP makes choices for you. Then BACKUP shows you its assessment of your video and mouse configuration. If it's correct, press OK. If not, you should correct it.

After the video and mouse configuration, more dialog boxes flash past. Then BACKUP is ready to do the floppy drive change test. A dialog box asks you to remove the disks from every floppy drive. Press Start Test when you're ready to continue.

The BACKUP Devices dialog box displays what BACKUP thinks your floppy drives are (see fig. 24.2).

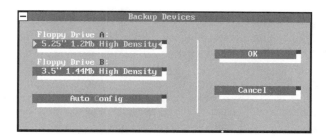

Figure 24.2.
*BACKUP Devices
dialog box.*

Each drive button is labeled with the current device setting for that drive. If correct, press OK to continue with the next test. If not, take the time to correct them now.

To correct a backup device:

1. Press the button for the drive you want to change. (A dialog box lists floppy drive types.)

2. Select the correct drive type.

3. Press OK.

Next, you see BACKUP conduct some more tests. All you can do is sit and watch until it's ready for the floppy disk compatibility test (see fig. 24.3).

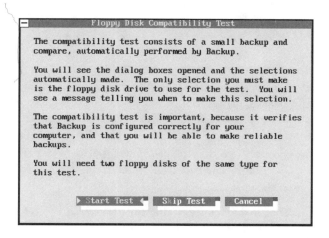

Figure 24.3.
*Floppy Disk
Compatibility
Text dialog box.*

This is the test in which BACKUP does a practice backup and compare. You have the option of skipping this test, but you shouldn't skip it, at least the first time you configure BACKUP. (If you're rerunning the configuration tests for some reason, you might not need to redo the compatibility test.)

When you press Start Test, a series of dialog boxes flash past as BACKUP goes through an automatic sequence to set up the test. (You learn how to use all these dialog boxes in this chapter, but you don't have any choices now.) Finally, BACKUP asks you to select the floppy drive and capacity you want to test. Be sure to test the one that you use for your real backups. Even if you plan to back up to a tape, a removable cartridge, or some other device, you must select a floppy drive for the compatibility test—but remember that you must provide two disks for the drive and capacity you select.

If you have two identical floppy drives, you can opt to use them both. This speeds up the entire backup process because you can prepare one drive while BACKUP writes to the other. BACKUP doesn't have to wait while you change disks.

After you select the drive, more dialog boxes flash past. Then BACKUP asks you to insert the first disk. When you press Continue, BACKUP examines the disk and displays an alert box if the disk contains data. You can replace the disk and press Retry or simply choose Overwrite to continue with the current disk.

BACKUP automatically reformats the disks during the compatibility test. Any existing data will be destroyed.

Next, you see a progress screen as the backup takes place. The progress screen is explained in the section "Using BACKUP" later in this chapter. Eventually, you are asked to insert the second disk.

If BACKUP is configured to sense disk changes, the message to insert the next disk appears directly on the progress screen, not in a dialog box. The drive light remains lit as BACKUP tests for the new disk. This is the only time while using DOS when you should change disks while a drive light is on. If you don't change disks within a few seconds, BACKUP stops testing for the changed disk and displays a dialog box. Then you must press Continue to go on.

When the backup is complete, BACKUP displays a summary dialog box. Then it starts the compare process. You must insert disks on request. At the end, BACKUP displays a Compare Summary dialog box. When you press OK, BACKUP informs you that the compatibility test is completed. Then you see BACKUP's Configure dialog box (see fig. 24.4). This dialog box enables you to reconfigure BACKUP whenever that becomes necessary.

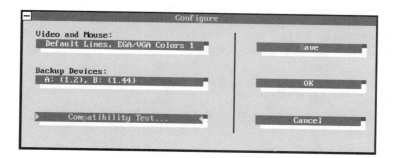

Figure 24.4.
Configure
dialog box.

It's very important at this point to press the Save button. If you don't, the results of the compatibility test are not recorded and you must rerun it the next time you start BACKUP.

Coping with Compatibility Problems

If the configuration tests produce an error message that you don't understand, copy the message down verbatim, make a note of where you were in the configuration process (such as "just about to start the practice backup"), and call Microsoft's Product Support team. They should be able to help you identify the problem and finish configuring your system for BACKUP.

If the compatibility test fails, you can go on to make backups, but you shouldn't—they will not be reliable. After you have identified and fixed the problem, you should rerun the compatibility test.

To rerun the compatibility test:

1. Start BACKUP. (A message tells you that the last compatibility test failed.)

2. Press OK to clear the alert box.

3. Press Configure to open the Configure dialog box.

4. Press the Compatibility Test button.

5. Follow the directions on your screen.

Retesting Your System

You can use the same procedure to rerun the compatibility test if you change your system configuration in any way. You should rerun the test, for example, if you install a new TSR or change the configuration of a TSR.

> BACKUP can sense many configuration changes and may insist on rerunning all the configuration tests, not just the compatibility test.

If you install a new disk drive that you want to use for backups, you should reconfigure the new drive as well as rerun the compatibility test.

To reconfigure a floppy drive:

1. Start BACKUP.

2. Press Configure.

3. For MSBACKUP, select BACKUP Devices, and then press Auto Config. For MWBACKUP, press Auto Floppy Configure.

4. Follow the directions on your screen.

5. If BACKUP mistakes any drives, correct them (as explained before).

If any other part of the configuration tests fails, you must locate and fix the problem before you can use BACKUP. The configuration alert box appears every time you start BACKUP until you have successfully passed every test except the compatibility test. A compatibility alert box warns you when your system has passed all the other configuration tests but failed the compatibility test.

Working with BACKUP Setups

A backup setup is a recorded set of backup parameters: the files to be backed up, the target drive, the backup type, and options, such as compression and verification. Once you have established a setup, you can use it over and over again. You can create several setups if you like. You might, for example, want one for each person who uses the computer, or one for each of your major applications. On the other hand, most people use one setup to back up everything.

Starting a New Setup

Each new setup must be based on an existing one. BACKUP provides one setup by default, called DEFAULT.SET, which you use to create your first setup. Don't try to adopt DEFAULT.SET as your permanent setup. Keep its default settings so that you can use it to create setups later.

By default, DOS stores the new setup file in the same directory as the current setup. If you're basing the new setup on DEFAULT.SET, C:\DOS is the default directory. If you keep all your setups in the same directory, they will all appear on one setup list, and you don't have to bother changing directories to locate and open a setup.

To start a new setup from DEFAULT.SET:

1. Start BACKUP. DEFAULT.SET is opened automatically.

2. Choose File Save Setup As. A dialog box asks for the name of the new setup.

3. Enter a name for the new setup, such as DAILY.SET or PETER'S.SET. The setup name must be a file name with extension SET.

4. If you want, enter a description of up to 31 characters for the new setup, such as "Daily backup of modified files," or "Word processed & related files."

5. If you want, select a different directory for the setup.

6. Press OK.

After you press OK, the new setup becomes the current setup.

Selecting Files

A backup setup must identify the files to be backed up. You could, for example, back up all of drive C, all nonprogram files, or all files in a specific directory. DEFAULT.SET does not select any files, so when you create a new file based on DEFAULT.SET, the new setup doesn't select any files either, at first.

Selecting an Entire Drive

In the BACKUP dialog box, the Backup From box shows all your hard drives. If you want to back up all the files on a drive, select the drive in this box. You can select as many drives as you want; potentially, you could back up every file in your system in one setup.

To select a drive:

> Double-click the drive name.

or

> Move the highlight to the drive and press the space bar.

Including and Excluding Files

Most people don't want to back up entire drives. Many files don't need to be backed up, and there's no sense in wasting time and space on them. Another way to select files in a setup is to include some and exclude others. You might, for example, want to include all DOC files but exclude MEMO*.DOC and TEMPY.DOC.

Figure 24.5 shows the dialog boxes that you use to include and exclude files in a setup.

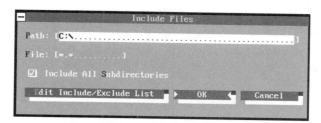

Figure 24.5
*Include and Exclude
dialog boxes.*

As you can see, you specify a path and a global or specific filespec for each type of file you want to include or exclude. You use these dialog boxes over and over again to create the complete list of inclusions and exclusions. Suppose, for example, that you want to include all files except program files but include CONFIG.SYS. You first use the Include dialog to include C:*.* and check the Include All Subdirectories box. (Or you could select the drive in the Backup From box.) Then you use the Exclude dialog box four times, to exclude C:*.EXE, C:*.COM, C:*.BIN, and C:*.SYS, checking Exclude All Subdirectories each time. Finally, you use the Include dialog to include C:\CONFIG.SYS. This time, you wouldn't need to check Include All Subdirectories. (You learn an easier way to include CONFIG.SYS shortly.)

To include or exclude files in a setup:

1. In the BACKUP dialog box, press Select Files.

2. In the Select Backup Files dialog box, press Include or Exclude.

3. In the Include Files or Exclude Files dialog box, enter the path and filespec for the file(s) to be included or excluded.

4. Check or uncheck Include All Files or Exclude All Files, as appropriate.

5. Press OK to return to the Select Backup Files dialog box.

The order of inclusions and exclusions is important. Each new specification overrides all preceding specifications. So if you include CONFIG.SYS before you exclude *.SYS, CONFIG.SYS will be excluded.

As you complete each Include or Exclude dialog box, you see the numbers in the Selected Files field change in the Select BACKUP Files dialog box (see fig. 24.6).

Figure 24.6.
Select BACKUP
File dialog box.

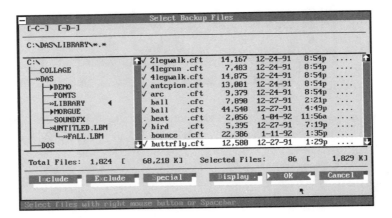

In the directory tree, directories with some selected files are marked by a chevron, whereas an arrowhead indicates that all files are selected. You can see which files in a directory are selected by moving the cursor to the directory in the directory tree. The file list shows all the files (selected or not) in the currently highlighted directory. In the file list, selected files have a check mark next to them.

You can examine and edit the entire Include and Exclude list by pressing Edit Include/Exclude List. Editing possibilities include modifying, copying, and deleting items.

Overriding the Include/Exclude List

The Include and Exclude dialog boxes create an Include/Exclude list that establishes the basic file selections for the setup. You can then override them by selecting or deselecting directories or individual files in the Select Backup Files dialog box. To toggle a directory or file's selection status, double-click it or highlight it and press the space bar.

When you override the selection of a file or directory, you permanently remove it from the Include/Exclude list. You can subsequently toggle its status between selected and deselected, but you can never return it to the control of the Include/Exclude list. If any file in a directory has been overridden, the directory name turns red in the directory tree. Unfortunately, the file name doesn't turn red, so it's sometimes hard to determine which files have been manipulated this way.

If you really goof up your file selections, you can undo them all by deleting the file named *Setup*.SLT. Then you must start your selections over from scratch.

Selecting directories and files is relatively easy, and you might be tempted to do all your file selections this way, but it's not as good a technique as building an Include/Exclude list. The Include/Exclude list affects directories and files added to the drive in the future, whereas selecting files directly affects those files only. Selecting or deselecting a directory affects all current and future files in that directory only.

Making Special Exclusions

There's one more way to exclude files that overrides any inclusion method. Figure 24.7 shows the Special Selections dialog box that opens when you press the Special button in the Select Backup Files dialog box. This feature enables you to exclude files by date, attribute, or file name.

Figure 24.7.
*Select BACKUP
File dialog box.*

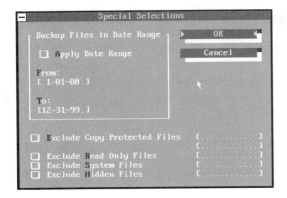

Excluding Files by Date

When you enter a date range in the Backup Files In Date Range area, you exclude all files outside that range. If you want to exclude files created or last modified before 9/10/92, you would enter **9/10/92** in the From box and any date far in the future in the To box (the maximum is 12/31/99). You also need to check the Apply Date Range box.

Excluding Files by Attribute

You can exclude hidden, system, or read-only files by checking the appropriate boxes.

Excluding Copy-Protected Files

In an effort to avoid piracy, some applications protect their files from being copied. If you try to copy them or back them up, you could invalidate the entire application. Usually the application's documentation warns you about copy protection. If you have such an application, you can prevent its files from being backed up by checking the Exclude Copy Protected Files box and entering up to five filespecs in the boxes to the right.

Understanding BACKUP Types

BACKUP offers three backup types: full, incremental, and differential. A *full backup* archives all selected files regardless of their archive attribute. It also turns off the archive attribute of every file it backs up. This begins a backup cycle. Depending on how active your system is, you might want to do this once a week, once every two weeks, or simply when the incremental or differential backups are getting too long.

Between full backups, you probably want to do incremental or differential backups. These partial backups archive only those files that have been modified since the last full backup based on their archive attributes. A *differential backup* archives only those selected files with positive archive attributes, without turning off their archive attributes. Each differential backup archives all the selected files that were backed up in the last differential backup plus any newly created or modified selected files. Thus, the last full backup together with the most recent differential backup represent the complete set of files that you need to restore the selected files to the hard disk.

An *incremental backup* archives all selected files with positive archive attributes and turns off their attributes. In other words, each incremental backup archives only those selected files that were created or modified since the last full or incremental backup. If you run an incremental backup every day, each day's run backs up only the files created and modified that day. In order to have a complete set of files, you must keep the last full backup plus each subsequent incremental backup.

Each kind of partial backup has its advantages and disadvantages. A differential backup enables you to reuse the same disk(s) every day, but backups take longer and longer as the cycle progresses. An incremental backup requires that you use a fresh disk every day, but each day's backup is relatively short. If you revise a file several times during a cycle, incremental backups save every version of the file; differential backups save only the most recent version. Unless you want to be able to fall back to earlier versions, differential backups seem to offer the advantage when you work on the same few files every day. But if you handle different files every day, especially if you work on many of them, incremental backups may be the better choice. At any rate, when the differential backup becomes too long or you have piled up too many incremental backup disks, it's time to restart the cycle with a new full backup.

Don't mix incremental and differential backups for the same set of selected files. You will end up with an incomplete set of files if you do.

Once you have created a backup setup for a group of files, use the same setup for both full and partial backups. Simply switch the Backup Type between Full and Incremental or Differential as needed. That way, you know that you're selecting the same files every day.

When the Backup Type is Incremental or Differential, only selected files with a positive archive attribute are actually backed up. If you examine the file list in the Backup File Selection dialog box, a dot appears next to those selected files that will not be backed up, either because they have been specially excluded or because their archive attributes are off. In addition, the main Backup dialog box shows the number of files that will be written; this is always one more than the number of files to be archived, as shown in the Backup File Selection dialog box. The extra file is the backup catalog file, which is explained shortly.

You will see the number of files to be written change dramatically as you switch between full and partial backups.

Identifying the Backup Drive

The Backup To box enables you to select where you want the backups written. If you're backing up to disk, be sure to select the disk drive(s) you tested in the compatibility test. (You can use them at lower densities, however.)

If you have two identical disk drives, you should choose to use them both for a speedier backup.

To back up to another type of device, it must be accessible by a DOS drive and path name. Suppose, for example, that you want to use a removable cartridge that's known as drive D. You would select MS-DOS Drive and Path in the Backup To box, and then enter **D:** in the text box underneath it.

Selecting BACKUP Options

When creating your setup, you should pay attention to the BACKUP options (see fig. 24.8). You might want to select options to emphasize maximum data protection, for example, or minimum backup time.

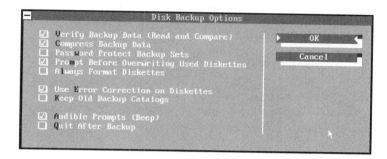

Figure 24.8.
Disk Backup Options dialog box.

Verify Backup Data

Selecting Verify Backup Data slows your backup down quite a bit but helps to ensure a perfect result. Each file is reread and compared to the original as soon as it is written. Errors are corrected immediately. If BACKUP can't write a perfect copy after several attempts because of bad spots on the target media, it asks you to change the media so that it can try again.

Another way to verify your backed up files is to compare them to the originals after the backup finishes using BACKUP's COMPARE function, explained in Chapter 25. This function also repairs errors if possible. But if you wait until the backup is completed to correct errors, you must rerun the backup if an error can't be repaired. When you verify the backup as you go, you don't have to repeat the entire backup when an uncorrectable error is encountered.

Compress Backup Data

This option saves space on the target media and backup time. BACKUP compresses the data being backed up as much as possible without actually taking extra processor time to do so. Because it doesn't take extra time to do compression, and because it ends up writing much less data, the overall result is that the backup takes less time.

315

As you know, BACKUP indicates in the Backup dialog box how many disks are needed for the backup. But this estimate does not account for compression. If you're using compression, you probably need about half the predicted number of disks. (The actual number depends on the type of files being backed up. Some types of files compress more readily than others.)

Password Protect Backup Sets

If you're backing up confidential data, you might want to password protect it so that an unauthorized person can't get at your files by gaining access to your backup disks. When you check this option, BACKUP asks you for a password of up to seven characters. You can't see the password as you type it, so you must type it twice, the second time to confirm the first. The password is case-sensitive; "Dagwood" is not the same as "DAGWOOD."

When you assign a password to a backup, you must supply the password whenever you want to access the backed up files, either to compare them or to restore them. You can, however, delete or overwrite them without the password. So the password doesn't protect you from someone who wants to sabotage your data.

Prompt Before Overwriting

It's just as easy to insert the wrong disk when making backups as it is at other times. When you check the Prompt Before Overwriting option, BACKUP warns you when a disk already contains data. You can see what data is on the disk and choose to overwrite it or change disks.

This step is time-consuming; it takes BACKUP some time to analyze each new disk; then it must wait for you to respond. If you're planning to reuse former backup disks, and you're sure that you never make a mistake, you might want to uncheck this option to take less time and less user involvement.

Always Format Diskettes

A disk with new physical formatting is always more reliable than one on which you have simply overwritten previous data. When you check the Always Format

Diskettes option, Backup unconditionally formats every disk you use. Otherwise, it formats only unformatted disks. By now you know that an unconditional format takes a long time. Imagine waiting while BACKUP formats 30 or more disks. You might not think the slight increase in reliability is worth that much extra time.

Use Error Correction

When you check the Use Error Correction option, BACKUP writes special error correction code on the backup media. This code helps BACKUP recover data even when the media is damaged. It doesn't take much additional time or space, so most people think it's worthwhile. Although it's not recommended, if you're trying to trim your backup time and media usage to a minimum, you might want to take the chance of turning this option off.

Keep Old Backup Catalogs

BACKUP records a catalog whenever it does a backup; the catalog documents the contents of the backup for the COMPARE and RESTORE functions. BACKUP automatically deletes old catalogs from your hard disk when you no longer need them. When you do a full backup, for example, BACKUP automatically deletes all former catalogs for that setup. But sometimes you want to keep old backups so that you can go back to earlier versions of files. By checking the Keep Old Backup Catalogs option, you tell BACKUP not to delete any previous catalogs when it makes a new one. You are responsible for deleting your own backup catalogs when you eliminate the backups themselves. (Backup catalogs are discussed further in the section "Using Backup Catalogs" later in this chapter.)

BACKUP stores a copy of the catalog on the backup media, too, so you can always retrieve a catalog from the media after you have eliminated it from the hard disk.

317

Audible Prompts

If you're going to sit and watch your screen while the backup progresses, you don't need BACKUP to beep when it wants you to do something (such as change disks). But if you want to wander away, check the Audible Prompts option so that BACKUP can call your attention to a message.

Quit After Backup

If you will be exiting BACKUP as soon as it completes making a backup, you can have BACKUP do it for you by checking the Quit After Backup option. If you don't check it, you return to the Backup dialog box when the backup finishes.

Managing Setup Files

Once you have tailored the setup as you want, you should save it for future use. If you already have used File Save Backup Setup to create the setup file, all you need to do is choose File Save Setup to save any changes to the setup file. Anytime you change the current setup, choose File Save Setup to make the change permanent. If you make a temporary change—changing the backup type from Differential to Full for this backup only, for example—the change will be forgotten when you exit BACKUP without saving the setup.

When you start BACKUP, DEFAULT.SET is opened by default. There are three ways to open a different setup. You can choose File Open Setup and select the setup you want to open. Or you can press the Setup File button to display a list of setup files, select the setup you want, and choose Open to open it. It's even more convenient, however, to include the setup name in the command to start BACKUP, as follows:

```
BACKUP DAILY.SET
```

If you create DOS Shell program items for your backups, you can build the setup file into the command issued by the program item.

The File menu also contains commands to print a setup file and to delete it.

Using BACKUP

When you're ready to back up files, start BACKUP, open the setup file, check to make sure that the backup type is what you want, and then press Start Backup. (If the Start Backup button is dimmed, there are no files to be backed up according to the current setup.)

Figure 24.9 shows the screen that appears while the backup is in progress.

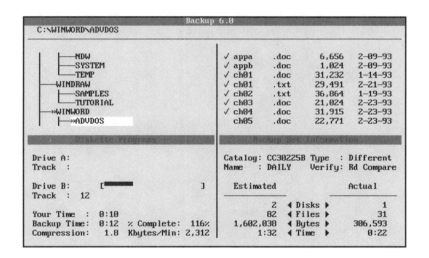

Figure 24.9.
Backup Progress
screen.

As you can see, this screen keeps you advised of how the backup is progressing. The difference between the estimated and actual time and space requirements result from backup options such as compression, the need to format disks, the amount of time that BACKUP has to wait for you to change disks, errors the BACKUP had to correct, and so on.

Using Backup Catalogs

Each time you run a backup, BACKUP creates a catalog documenting the date, time, setup, and files included in the backup. Both the COMPARE and the RESTORE functions use the catalog, as you learn in Chapter 25. BACKUP stores the catalog on the hard disk (in the DOS directory) as well as on the backup media.

319

Figure 24.10 shows how to interpret the name BACKUP assigns to each catalog. You can identify the date, the drives, and the type of backup from the catalog name. But you can't tell which setup was used. BACKUP maintains another catalog for each setup on the hard disk, called the *master catalog*, which identifies all catalogs belonging to the setup. The master catalog, named *setup*.CAT, simply lists the names of all the current catalogs belonging to the setup. Each time BACKUP creates a new catalog for a setup, it adds that catalog's name to the setup's master catalog. When BACKUP automatically deletes a catalog, it removes the name from the master catalog. Unless you check the Keep Old Backup Catalogs option, the master catalog should show at all times the catalog names of the most recent full backup plus all subsequent incremental backups or the latest differential backup.

Figure 24.10.
Anatomy of a Catalog Name.

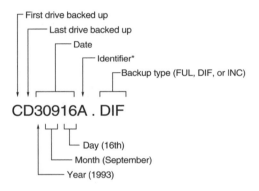

CD30916A . DIF

First drive backed up
Last drive backed up
Date
Identifier*
Backup type (FUL, DIF, or INC)

Day (16th)
Month (September)
Year (1993)

* The identifier is simply a letter that makes the catalog name unique, in case you run the same backup more than once on the same day.

Both the COMPARE and RESTORE functions use the master catalog as well as the individual backup catalogs. If you check Keep Old Backup Catalogs and manage the backup catalogs manually, be sure to maintain the master catalog, too.

Taking Care of Your Backup Disks

Once you have made your backups, you should label the backup media and put it in a safe place. The label might show the setup name and the catalog name. (If you find the catalog names hard to interpret, you might also write the date and type of backup on the label.) For a full backup, you might want to take the backup media somewhere else entirely or place it in a fireproof vault. If you believe in extra protection, you might even duplicate it and store the duplicates in different places. You might want to keep a partial backup close by for convenience, or you might want to keep it with the full backup(s) for maximum protection.

If you don't need to go back to earlier versions of files, you can reuse old backup media for newer backups. You could, for example, use last week's full backup disks for this week's full backup. You could use the same differential disk every day, overwriting yesterday's data with today's. (But don't reuse an incremental disk until after the next full backup.)

If you want to be able to restore earlier versions of files, or if you want to be able to recover deleted files from, say, a month ago, then you should keep your old backups longer. You must decide what system is best for your data. As you learn in the next chapter, even if you decide to keep old backups for a month or so, you don't need to keep their catalogs on the hard disk. Backup can retrieve catalogs from the backup media.

Reconfiguring BACKUP

BACKUP configures itself during the configuration tests, but you can reconfigure it whenever and however you want. After starting BACKUP, select the Configure button to display the Configure dialog box.

The Video and Mouse Options button opens a dialog box in which you can select the type of monitor, its resolution, its color scheme, and various mouse options, such as double-click speed. This feature isn't available with MWBACKUP because Windows configures hardware under its own Control Panel.

The Backup Devices button opens the Backup Devices dialog box, in which you can change the current settings for your drives or ask BACKUP to redo the automatic configuration. The Compatibility Test button reruns the compatibility test. If you make any changes to the configuration, be sure to press Save before exiting the Configure dialog box.

RESTORE and COMPARE

25

Introduction

You can use your backups to restore deleted files, recover from a virus attack or a hard drive crash, and much more.

Restoring Files

With a good set of backups, you are prepared for almost any kind of emergency. Suppose that you mistakenly delete a branch and can't undelete it; you can restore the entire branch—directories and files—from your backups. Suppose that you modify a spreadsheet and then decide that you want to remove the modifications; you can restore the unmodified version from its backup. Suppose that your hard disk dies, and you have to buy a new one; you can restore all the backed up directories and files to the new drive after it has been formatted.

You follow the same general steps to restore one file, a set of files, or all files in a backup: open a backup catalog, select the files you want to restore, and respond to prompts. Figure 25.1 shows the Restore dialog box.

Figure 25.1.
Restore dialog box.

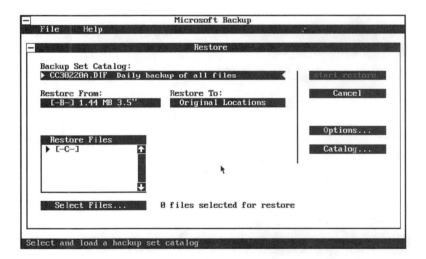

To start RESTORE:

1. Start BACKUP.

2. Press the Restore button to open the Restore dialog box.

Opening a Catalog

The Backup Set Catalog button shows the name and description of the current backup catalog. The default catalog is the most recent backup you have made. If you don't want to work with that catalog, press the button to open the dialog box shown in figure 25.2, in which you select another catalog. The descriptions next to each catalog name help you identify the catalog's setup. All master catalogs (such as JUDI.CAT) and individual backup catalogs (such as CC30108A.DIF) are available. When you select an individual catalog, only the files in that catalog can be restored. But when you select a master catalog, its individual backup catalogs become available, and you should be able to restore any file included in the setup.

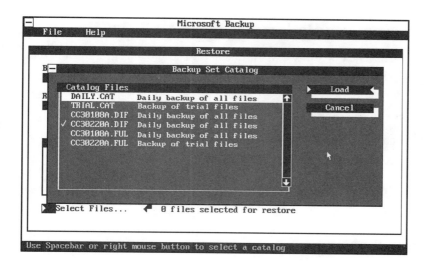

Figure 25.2.
*The Backup Set
Catalog dialog box.*

To open a catalog:

1. In the Restore dialog box, press the Backup Set Catalog button. (RESTORE lists all the available catalogs.)

2. Select a catalog by double-clicking it or by highlighting it and pressing Enter. (RESTORE puts a check mark next to the selected catalog.)

3. Press the Load button.

When you return to the Restore dialog box, the Backup Set Catalog button shows the name and description of the catalog you just opened. So far, no files are selected, and the Start Restore button is dimmed.

Selecting Files

You don't have to deal with include/exclude lists when you are selecting files to restore. You can select whole drives on the Restore screen, or you can press the Select Files button to work with a drive list, directory tree, and file list.

Selecting Whole Drives

When you select a whole drive, all the files in the backup catalog for that drive are selected. If more than one drive appears in the Restore Files box, you can select any or all of them.

To select a complete drive to be restored:

- Double-click the drive name in the Restore Files dialog box.

  or

- Highlight the drive name and press the space bar.

You should see the number of selected files change and the Start Restore button become available. You might want to press the Select Files button to view the directory tree and file list and deselect any files you don't want.

Selecting or Deselecting Individual Files

Figure 25.3 shows the dialog box that opens when you press the Select Files button. You can use this dialog box to select individual directories and files to be restored, or, if you have already selected whole drives, to deselect individual items.

```
┌─┐                Select Restore Files
│─│ [-C-]
│ C:\WINWORD\BASICDOS\*.*
│  ┌──SYSTEM          ▲█√ fig8-8  .hsg   37,951   1-13-93   6:33p  ....  ▲
│  │  └──TEMP          │ √ fig9-1  .hsg   33,535   2-03-93   9:09a  ...a  █
│  │──WINDRAW          │ √ fig9-2  .hsg   40,050   1-14-93   3:40p  ....
│  │  ├──SAMPLES       │ √ fig9-3  .hsg   34,070   1-14-93   3:40p  ....
│  │  └──TUTORIAL      │ √ fig9-4  .hsg   32,353   1-14-93   3:41p  ....
│  └──WINWORD          │   hive    .doc    6,459   2-20-93   7:40a  ...a+
│     ├──ADVDOS        │   n6outlin.doc    6,392   1-16-93   8:51a  ....
│     ├──CLIPART       │   outline .doc   15,900   1-26-93   2:09p  ...a
│     ├──»BASICDOS  ◄  │   scottmem.doc    4,194   2-17-93   1:41p  ...a
│     │  └──COMREF     │   side1-1 .doc    4,850  11-19-92   1:25p  ....
│     └──WINWORD.CBT  █▼√ tab11-1  .doc    3,341   2-03-93  10:31a  ...a  ▼
│
│ Total Files:  350 [  5,891 K]   Selected Files:  6 [    177 K]
│ ┌─────────┐ ┌───────┐ ┌─────────┐  ┌─────────┐ ┌──────┐ ┌────────┐
│ │ Version │ │ Print │ │ Special │  │ Display │ │▶. OK │ │ Cancel │
│ └─────────┘ └───────┘ └─────────┘  └─────────┘ └──────┘ └────────┘
│ Select files with right mouse button or Spacebar
```

Figure 25.3.
The Select Restore Files dialog box.

The drive list, directory tree, and file list are taken from the backup catalog. They reflect the directory structure and files that were backed up, not the current contents of your hard drives.

You select and deselect entries in the directory tree and the file list. When you select or deselect a directory, all the files in that directory are affected; you then can adjust individual selections in the file list. The Special button enables you to exclude selected files based on date, attributes, and filespec (for copy-protected files), just as you do when selecting files to back up.

To toggle the selection status of an entry, you must double-click it or highlight it and press the space bar.

Unlike the BACKUP function, RESTORE does not save your file selections. Each time you start RESTORE, you must select the files you want to restore.

Press the Print button to print a list of all the files in the catalog.

Restoring Older Versions

When you open a master catalog, a file might have several versions available. For example, suppose that you modified HIVE.DOC every day for a week, making an incremental backup each day. There would be seven versions of HIVE.DOC in the master catalog.

By default, the file list shows only the latest version of each file in the catalog, but a plus sign next to the file entry indicates that multiple versions are available (see HIVE.DOC in fig. 25.3). The Version button, which is available only for a master catalog, opens a version list for whatever file is currently highlighted in the file list, enabling you to select the version you want.

To select an older version of a file:

1. Highlight the file entry in the file list.

2. Press Version. (A Version List dialog box opens.)

3. Double-click the version you want or highlight it and press the space bar. (A check mark appears next to the selected version.)

4. Press OK. (The selected version appears in the file list.)

The RESTORE Options

RESTORE offers a number of options to ensure a successful restoration, although most of them add considerably to restoration time. Figure 25.4 shows the dialog box that opens when you press the Options button in the main Restore dialog box.

Verify Restore Data

When you turn on Verify Restore Data, RESTORE takes the time to compare each restored file to the backed up version and correct any errors it encounters.

> You also can verify the restored files after the restoration is complete by using the COMPARE function, which is explained under "COMPARE" later in this chapter.

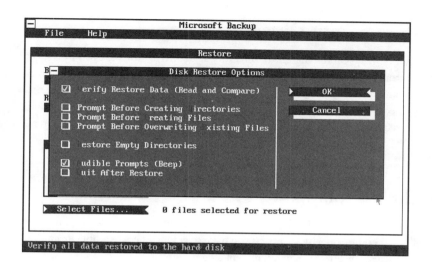

Figure 25.4.
The Disk Restore
Options dialog box.

Prompt before Creating Directories

When you restore one or more files to a directory that no longer exists, RESTORE re-creates the directory for the restored files. When Prompt before Creating Directories is unchecked, RESTORE creates directories without warning. But when you check this option, RESTORE asks you to confirm each directory it must create. If you say no, RESTORE skips any files belonging to that directory.

Prompt before Creating Files

Suppose that you want to restore a file that was deleted from a directory. By default, RESTORE returns the file to the directory with no warning. But if you select Prompt before Creating Files, RESTORE asks your permission when it must create a file in a directory. If you say no, RESTORE skips that file.

Prompt before Overwriting Existing Files

If a destination directory already contains a file of the same name as a file to be restored, RESTORE overwrites the existing file with the restored file. Unchecking Prompt before Overwriting Existing Files lets RESTORE overwrite existing files without warning. When this option is checked, RESTORE asks for permission to overwrite a file. If you say no, the backup version is not restored.

Restore Empty Directories

BACKUP always records the entire directory structure of a drive, even if some of the directories contain no files to be backed up. When you're examining the directory tree and file list in the Select Restore Files dialog box, you might come across empty directories. You can re-create a drive's former directory structure, including empty directories, by checking Restore Empty Directories. If you uncheck this item, RESTORE creates only directories for the files it is restoring.

Audible Prompts

Just like BACKUP, RESTORE prompts you for backup media. It may display other prompts, depending on which options you have selected. Check Audible Prompts if you want RESTORE to beep when it displays a prompt.

Quit after Restore

If you check Quit after Restore, the backup program terminates itself when the restoration is finished; you return to whatever program you were using when you started backup. If you don't check this option, you return to the Restore dialog box when the restoration is finished.

Saving the RESTORE Options

When you exit or cancel the RESTORE function, if you have made any changes to the options, RESTORE asks whether you want to save them. If you say yes, RESTORE saves the current option settings in the open setup file. The same options are established the next time you open that setup and select the RESTORE function.

The name of the current setup file appears in the prompt that asks whether you want to save your changes.

Keep in mind that the current setup file does not necessarily belong with the current catalog. BACKUP automatically opens DEFAULT.SET unless you include another setup filespec on the startup command. Opening a catalog does not cause its setup to be opened. For example, you might have DEFAULT.SET open as the setup file but DAILY.CAT (from the DAILY setup) open as the catalog file. In that case, any changes you make to the options are stored in DEFAULT.SET, not DAILY.SET.

If you will use the same restore options all the time, no matter what catalog is involved, store them in DEFAULT.SET. (Generally, you shouldn't modify DEFAULT.SET.) You won't have to open a different setup to reset your restore options. But, to relate the restore options to a particular setup, you must open that setup before saving the options and open it again when you want to use them. Opening a setup from the Restore dialog box is somewhat different than opening a setup from the Backup dialog box. The following procedure shows you how to do it.

To open a setup file:

1. Choose File Open Setup.

2. Select the setup file.

3. Press OK.

Running RESTORE

After you have opened the catalog, selected the files, and set (or accepted) the RESTORE options, you're ready to run the restoration. Press Start Restore to begin. RESTORE asks for the backup media by catalog name; if disks are involved, it also asks for specific disk numbers. For example, it might ask for disk #2 of backup set CC31020A.FUL.

Figure 25.5 shows the progress box that appears during the restoration. The top half shows the directory and files that RESTORE is currently working on. The bottom half shows RESTORE's progress and results.

If BACKUP stores error correction code on the backup media, RESTORE can detect and correct errors due to bad sectors, read/write errors, and other physical problems.

331

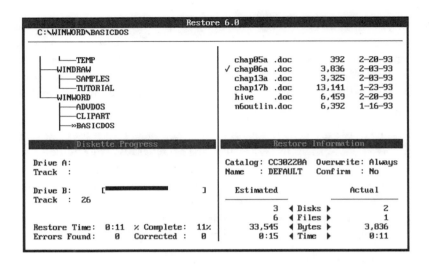

Figure 25.5.
The Restore
Progress dialog box.

At the end, a summary box shows you how many files were restored, how many files were skipped, how many errors in the backup files were detected and repaired, and so on.

RESTORE Procedures

You probably will use RESTORE most often to restore the latest versions of individual files. For example, suppose that you delete all your *.DOC files by mistake, and you can't undelete them reliably. You should be able to restore them.

To restore the latest versions of individual files:

1. Start BACKUP.

2. Press the Restore button.

3. Open the master catalog for the setup that includes the files you want.

4. Press the Select Files button.

5. Select the files to be restored and press OK to return to the Restore dialog box.

6. If desired, press Options to review and set the options for the restoration.

7. Press Start Restore.

8. Insert backup media as requested.

9. When the restoration is complete, press OK to clear the summary report.

10. Exit Restore and Backup if necessary. If you changed any restore options, you have to decide whether you want to save the changes, and if so, where.

Sometimes, you need to fall back to an earlier version of one or more files. You can use the following procedure as long as the desired version is still in a master catalog on the hard disk.

To fall back to earlier versions of individual files:

1. Start BACKUP.

2. Press the Restore button.

3. Open the master catalog for the setup that includes the files you want to restore.

4. Press the Select Files button.

5. Highlight one file to be restored and press Version to open the version list.

6. Select the desired version and press OK. (The selected version replaces the default version in the file list, and the entry is automatically selected.)

7. Repeat steps 5 and 6 for each file to be restored.

8. If desired, press Options to review and set the options for the restoration.

9. Press Start Restore.

10. Insert backup media as requested.

11. When the restoration is complete, press OK to clear the summary report.

12. Exit RESTORE and BACKUP if necessary. If you changed any restore options, you have to decide whether you want to save the changes, and if so, where.

333

COMPARE

Backup's COMPARE function notifies you when it detects a difference between the backup version and the hard drive version of a file. It's a good way to verify files if you didn't use the verification option while doing the backup or restore. In general, the verification option is a better choice because it identifies and corrects errors as it goes. COMPARE can only identify a problem; you have to take other steps—such as redoing the backup or restore—to fix it.

COMPARE also comes in handy to identify files that have been moved or deleted since the backups were made. It tells you when a backed up file no longer exists in its original hard drive directory.

Figure 25.6 shows the dialog box that opens when you select the COMPARE function. In terms of your actions, a comparison is nearly identical to a restoration. You open a catalog, select the files to be compared, set options, and respond to prompts. COMPARE offers only two options: Audible Prompts and Quit after Compare.

Figure 25.6.
The Compare
dialog box.

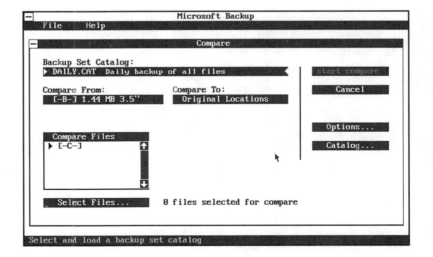

Running the Comparison

COMPARE's progress box is nearly identical to RESTORE's, which is shown in figure 25.5. COMPARE also corrects errors when it encounters physical problems on the backup media and has error correction code available. It does not correct disparities between the backup version and the hard drive version of a file; it displays alert boxes so that you know a problem exists. Make your own notes about any disparities COMPARE reports. The summary report at the end does not list the names of files that were found to be different, although it does show you how many there were.

To compare backed up files to their originals:

1. Start Backup.

2. Press the Compare button. (The Compare dialog box opens.)

3. Open the desired catalog.

4. Select the files to be compared.

5. Set up the compare options as desired.

6. Press Start Compare.

7. Insert backup media as requested.

For the Future

RESTORE and COMPARE include several features that you won't need for your everyday work but that you might find useful in unusual situations. An advanced book should explain how to handle the following procedures:

● If your computer has multiple users, you might want to store their setup and catalog files in separate directories so that they can see only their own.

● Sometimes, the backup catalog you want to work with is not on the destination hard drive. You can use the catalog stored on the backup media or, if that's also missing, rebuild it from scratch.

● You might need to restore or compare files to a different computer than you backed them up from. For example, suppose that you upgrade your computer; the disk drive might have a different name, and the hard drive might have a different directory structure. You can restore or compare using different drives and directories than you used in the backup.

● When your hard disk fails and you get it repaired or replaced, you might have to use both of the preceding techniques to restore all your files to the new hard drive.

● Backup also can be a handy tool for transferring files to another computer. Backup offers several advantages over DOS's regular copy programs: it saves disk space by compressing files; it can handle files larger than the size of one disk; and its verification facility is much more powerful. This is another case in which you might have to recover the catalog from the backup disks and compare or restore using different drives and directories.

DOS 6 also includes the RESTORE program from DOS 5 in case you need to restore files that you backed up before upgrading to DOS 6. The Command Reference at the back of this book describes this older version of RESTORE.

DOS's Anti-Virus Programs

26

Introduction

Viruses aren't just exciting stories for the six o'clock news. They are very real problems that have caused many PC users a lot of grief.

Why Virus Protection?

The following is an example of how pernicious a virus can be. Some friends had a virus in one of their computers without knowing it, and one unfortunate day, the computer wouldn't boot. When they tried to boot from an emergency boot disk, the virus installed itself on the disk—still without their realizing what was happening. They decided to see whether the boot disk would work on their other machines. Each time they tried to boot another computer, the virus immediately infected the new computer and wiped out its hard disk. In all, four hard disks were erased in just a few minutes.

When they finally realized that something extraordinary was afoot, they called a friendly expert who told them to trash the infected disk, along with all the others they had tried out. Then they reformatted their hard disks, reinstalled DOS, and— don't miss this point—restored all their files from backups. They were up and running in short order because they had a company policy of regular backups. (P.S. Now they also have a company antivirus policy.)

The virus could have invaded the original system by many routes. Perhaps it was downloaded from an on-line service or installed with some new software. It even could have been built-in when the system was new. Viruses can live in your system for a long time before doing anything except spreading themselves to other systems. Many viruses wait for some kind of triggering event, such as someone's birthday, before swinging into action.

Microsoft Anti-Virus Features

DOS 6's antivirus programs protect your system in two ways: first, they scan memory and your disks for resident viruses; second, they monitor all system activity for virus-like behavior. Both procedures take up time in your system; you can tailor antivirus options to minimize the time or maximize the protection.

The Virus Scanning Programs

The two virus scanning programs are MSAV (Microsoft Anti-Virus) and MMAV (Microsoft Windows Anti-Virus). You can install either or both programs during Setup. You probably don't need both; install the one for your preferred interface. Some minor differences exist between the two programs, but both are capable of detecting known and unknown viruses.

Known Viruses

A *known virus* is one that has already been discovered and analyzed by antivirus specialists. It has a name, such as "Stoned" or "Michelangelo." It also has a *signature*—a series of bytes contained in the virus program that serve to uniquely identify it. It might have several known *strains*—slight variations of the same basic program. More than a thousand viruses have been identified so far. Many of them haven't been seen for a while and are probably extinct, but there's no way of predicting when or where one will crop up again.

Microsoft's anti-virus programs scan for known viruses by examining memory and your disks for the thousand or so known virus signatures. This might take several minutes on a large hard drive. You can limit the search to those areas most likely to be infected by a virus: the partition tables of hard drives, the boot records of disks, and program files. Very few viruses hide themselves in other places.

Memory is automatically scanned during the first scan after starting the antivirus program. After that, only disk drives are scanned.

The scanner can remove many known viruses from a disk without damaging the infected files or system areas; this is called *cleaning* a virus. However, some viruses damage files or system areas when they invade them, and of course, the scanner can't undo the damage. Such files need to be deleted; you usually can restore them from a backup or reinstall them from their original program disks.

Microsoft's scanners can clean viruses automatically, warning you when a virus can't be cleaned. Scanners also can notify you when encountering an unknown virus.

Unknown Viruses

It's perhaps even more important to scan for unknown viruses than for known ones—because the very latest viruses are unknown for a period of time before they get detected, analyzed, named, and distributed to the virus scanners.

The scanners detect unknown viruses by looking for changes in program files indicating that they might have been infected by a virus. Most program files don't change after they're installed, so any change could indicate a virus infection.

The first time you use a Microsoft antivirus scanner on a drive, it creates a file named CHKLIST.MS in each directory, recording the size, attributes, and date/time stamps for all the program files in that directory. It also records a *checksum*, a unique value calculated from the contents of the file; if the contents change, the checksum changes, and the virus scanner knows that the file has changed, even if the size, attributes, and date/time stamp remain unchanged.

If an unknown virus already exists in your system when the scanner records the CHKLIST.MS data, it will not be identified. Fortunately, Microsoft's virus monitor (VSAFE) can block it from doing any damage.

Each subsequent scan compares the recorded data against the program files. Any difference causes the scanner to report the possibility of an unknown virus, and you must decide what to do. You could choose to ignore the change, update CHKLIST.MS with the new data, delete the infected file, or stop scanning.

Many program changes are legitimate. Some programs write in their own program files when you do such things as changing the program options or reconfiguring its screens. If you have programs like this, you will soon learn to ignore unknown virus messages for them.

If you update an application to a new version, the next scan produces unknown virus messages for the changed program files. Because you know that you updated the program, you can ask the scanner to update CHKLIST.MS with its new values.

When you get an unknown virus message for a program that you haven't upgraded or reconfigured, you should pay serious attention to it. You might choose to delete the file right away, or you might choose to stop the scan while you do some additional investigation and decide what action to take.

Monitoring for Viruses

Microsoft's antivirus monitor, called VSAFE, must be loaded as a TSR. VSAFE runs under DOS, DOS Shell, and Windows. It monitors all system activity looking for viruses. Naturally, it slows your entire system down; you're choosing security over speed when you load VSAFE. You can compromise by monitoring only for activities most likely to be undertaken by a virus, such as modifying a hard disk partition table or doing a physical format on a hard disk.

When VSAFE identifies a suspicious behavior, it blocks the activity and displays an alert box asking you whether to continue or stop. If you know that the activity is safe—perhaps you're using FDISK to rework the hard disk partition table—you can tell VSAFE to let the activity continue. If not, stop the activity, reboot to remove the potential virus from memory, and run your virus scanner immediately to locate the virus.

When To Use
the Anti-Virus Programs

If you want maximum protection, you should scan memory and your program files every time you boot. If you're using MSAV, you can set up AUTOEXEC.BAT to run a scan. For Windows, you can install MWAV in the StartUp group so that it runs every time you start up Windows.

Viruses often travel in the boot sectors of disks. When you insert a disk that comes from another system—whether it's new software or just an old disk borrowed from a friend—you should scan it before booting from it, copying from it, installing a program from it, starting up a program that's on it, or using it in any other way. In other words, scan it as soon as you insert it in the disk drive.

Scan new or rented computers as soon as you receive them, because a dealer might not scan a computer before delivering it to you. It could have been infected in the shop, or in the case of a rental, by the previous user.

You also should rescan your system when you expose it to the possibility of a virus invasion:

- If you sign on to a bulletin board service (even a nationally known one such as CompuServe or Prodigy) or any type of on-line service, especially if you download something from it

- If you link your computer to another one via INTERLNK (see the Command Reference) or similar software

- If you sign on to a network and copy anything from a network drive to one of your local drives or run a program located on a network drive

- If you restore a file from its backup after deleting an infected version of the file (The backup might also have been infected.)

- If you install or upgrade any software, but especially freeware, shareware, publicware, pirated software, or any software not sealed in its original package

Scanning when you install or upgrade software also gives the scanner an opportunity to record CHKLIST.MS data for the new files.

This calls for a lot of scanning, and most people don't care to be quite so rigorous. If you choose to scan less often, but you expose your system to viruses on occasion, be sure to install and use VSAFE regularly. You might want to insert a VSAFE command in AUTOEXEC.BAT to start it up every time you boot.

Using MSAV

The MSAV command can be entered directly at the DOS prompt, in a batch program such as AUTOEXEC.BAT or from DOS Shell using the File Run option.

Entering **MSAV** without any parameters opens the dialog box shown in figure 26.1, from which you can select the drive to be scanned, the type of scan, and the scanning options.

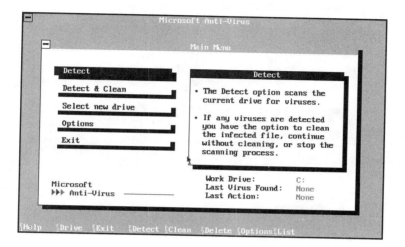

Figure 26.1.
The MSAV
dialog box.

Selecting a Drive

From the MSAV dialog box, you can scan only one drive at a time. The selected drive is always shown next to `Work Drive:` in the lower right corner of the dialog box. The drive that was current when you started MSAV is selected by default. To change the drive, press the `Select new drive` button or choose the Drive command in the menu line at the bottom of the dialog box. (You can click the command or press F2.) Any of these actions adds a drive list to the top line of the dialog box; you select the new drive in the drive list.

Selecting Options

Figure 26.2 shows the dialog box that opens when you press the Options button or choose the Options command (F8). The default settings are shown in the figure. The first group of three options controls scanning for unknown viruses. The group of two below it is miscellaneous options. The third group controls whether or not MSAV operates automatically. The final group deals with unusual situations.

343

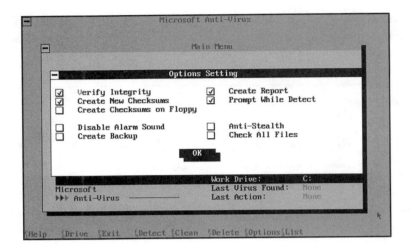

Figure 26.2.
*The MSAV
Options Setting
dialog box.*

Verify Integrity

When this option is on, MSAV checks for unknown viruses during the scan. Turning it off saves a great deal of scanning time but takes the risk of missing an unknown virus.

Create New Checksums

When this option is on, MSAV creates CHKLIST.MS entries for any new program files it finds during a scan. If you never turn this option on, you disable MSAV's capability to scan for unknown viruses right from the start, because it can't create the CHKLIST.MS files. Leaving this option on keeps your CHKLIST.MS files up-to-date as you add new software to your system.

Create Checksums on Floppy

MSAV ordinarily checks only hard drives for unknown viruses, because the CHKLIST.MS system works well only when you use the same disk over and over again. If you have floppies that you use on a regular basis and you want MSAV to scan them for unknown viruses as well as known viruses, check this option so that MSAV will create the necessary CHKLIST.MS files.

Disable Alarm Sound

Ordinarily, MSAV beeps every time it encounters a known virus or a suspected unknown virus. It's an especially annoying beep, which is meant to sound alarming. If you don't like the beep, check this option to turn it off.

Create Backup

This option is rather dangerous and causes MSAV to create a backup of an infected file. Avoid using this option unless you know exactly what you're doing.

Create Report

MSAV displays a summary report at the end of a scan. The summary contains details about how many files were scanned, how many were infected with known viruses, how many were cleaned, and so on. The summary doesn't say anything about unknown viruses, and it disappears as soon as you close its dialog box. The Create Report option causes MSAV to generate a report on disk containing summary information as well as a list of files suspected of containing unknown viruses. A sample of the disk report is shown in figure 26.3. It is stored as an ASCII text file named MSAV.RPT in the root directory of the drive that was scanned.

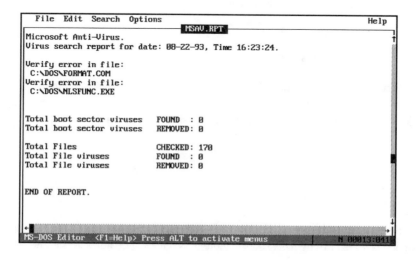

Figure 26.3.
A sample MSAV.RPT report.

Prompt While Detect

Prompt While Detect controls whether or not MSAV reports viruses to you or handles them automatically. When you check this option, MSAV displays an alert box each time it encounters a virus. If you leave this option unchecked, MSAV's behavior depends on whether you initiated the scan with the Detect or the Detect and Clean button. If you pressed Detect, MSAV merely notes viruses in its report(s) and goes on. If you pressed Detect and Clean, it also cleans whatever viruses it can.

> If the report shows that viruses were found but not cleaned, you should rerun the scan with this option turned on so that you can deal with the infected files.

Anti-Stealth

A *stealth virus* is a particularly sneaky virus that can infect a file without changing the size, date/time stamp, attributes, or checksum. MSAV can scan for stealth viruses, but it takes longer. Because stealth viruses are rare, you may want to uncheck this option if you don't care to spend the extra time. If you're going to scan anyway, a few more seconds probably won't make any difference to you, and the extra measure of protection can definitely be worth it.

Check All Files

When you check this option, MSAV scans data files as well as program files. Most of the time this is not necessary, and it makes the scan very long. If MSAV ever detects a virus known to infect data files, it suggests that you rerun the scan with this option turned on.

Running the Scan

When you're ready to start scanning, press Detect or Detect and Clean. The main dialog box (refer to fig. 26.1) acts as a progress screen. The fields in the lower right corner show the drive being scanned, the last virus that was found, and the action taken on that virus.

If you have checked Prompt While Detect, you may see some alert boxes during the scan. Figure 26.4 shows a typical alert box for an unknown virus. Choose Update if you know the file has changed legitimately and you want to update CHKLIST.MS with the new values. Choose Delete to delete the file because you suspect it contains a virus. Choose Continue to ignore the message and continue the scan; this can be a sensible choice if you have an application that frequently updates its own program files. Choose Stop to stop the scan so that you can investigate why the file has changed.

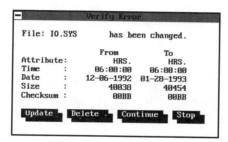

Figure 26.4.
A sample Virus Alert dialog box.

A known Virus Alert dialog box tells you the name of the virus and enables you to choose to Update the virus (if possible), Continue without handling the virus, Stop the scan, or Delete the file. If you can't clean the virus, you should delete the file and restore it from its backup. Then rescan the drive to make sure that the restored file isn't also infected.

Using MWAV

Figure 26.5 shows the MMAV dialog box, which is quite similar to MSAV's, with the following exceptions: the drive list is always available, and you can select multiple drives for one scan, but you can't generate a disk report.

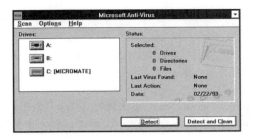

Figure 26.5.
The MWAV
dialog box.

Using VSAFE

The VSAFE command loads the VSAFE TSR. You can insert the appropriate command in AUTOEXEC.BAT to load VSAFE every time you boot.

> If your system is set up for it, you can load VSAFE into upper memory with the LH command. See Chapter 31 for an explanation of how to do this.

If you will be using VSAFE with Windows, you also need to load the MWAVTSR.EXE driver, which enables VSAFE to display alert boxes on the Windows screen. If you're using Windows 3.1 or Norton Desktop for Windows, you can add a program item for MWAVTSR.EXE to the StartUp group. You also can use the following procedure, which applies to any version of Windows.

To load MWAVTSR.EXE:

1. Edit WINDOWS\WIN.INI using an ASCII text editor.

2. Find the [Windows] section.

3. Find the load= line. (If it's not there, insert one.)

4. Add **MWAVTSR.EXE** to the end of the line.

5. Exit the editor and save the file.

6. If Windows is currently running, exit and restart it so that the new driver is loaded.

The VSAFE Options

After you have loaded VSAFE, you can view and select the VSAFE options on the DOS command prompt screen by pressing the Alt-V hotkey. If Windows is running, find the VSAFE Manager window (which should have been opened when you started Windows) and press the Options button.

Figure 26.6 shows the dialog box that appears on the Windows screen. The DOS version is similar. These options control just how much monitoring VSAFE does. The default options are shown in the figure. Any changes you make are remembered for future sessions.

Figure 26.6.
The VSAFE
Options dialog box.

HD Low Level Format

Checking this option causes VSAFE to warn you of any attempts to perform a low-level (physical) format on a hard drive.

Resident

When this option is on, VSAFE warns you when a program attempts to make itself memory-resident.

General Write Protect

This option causes VSAFE to warn you when a program attempts to write to a disk. You probably will find that this is more protection than you want on an everyday basis.

> Using this option could prevent Windows from starting up. If you encounter hard disk errors when trying to start up Windows, turn this option off.

Check Executable Files

This option causes VSAFE to check each executable file that is loaded for known and unknown viruses.

Boot Sector Viruses

This option causes VSAFE to scan for known viruses in the boot sector of every disk you insert in your system.

Protect HD Boot Sector

This option causes VSAFE to warn you when any program attempts to write to a hard disk boot sector, which includes the partition table.

Protect FD Boot Sector

This option is similar to the preceding one but applies to floppy disk boot sectors.

Protect Executable Files

When you select this option, VSAFE warns you of any attempt to change an executable file.

What Happens When VSAFE Detects a Suspicious Action?

When VSAFE detects one of the actions that it is monitoring, it blocks the action and displays an alert box similar to figure 26.7. You can choose to stop or continue the action. In this particular case, you also can choose to update the CHKLIST.MS file because VSAFE detected a change in a program file while monitoring for the Check Executable Files option.

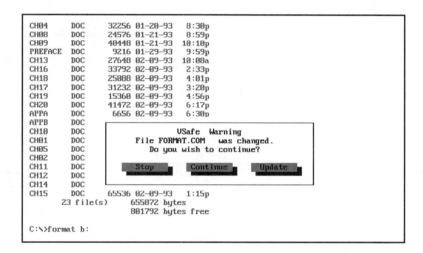

Figure 26.7.
The VSAFE
alert box.

If you press the Stop button, VSAFE blocks the action. You then might see some kind of error message from the program that was blocked, especially if it's a legitimate program. If you suspect that the action was not legitimate, close your files and programs, reboot to clear memory, and scan for viruses. If you can't find a virus but VSAFE continues to detect suspicious behavior, contact the Microsoft Product Support Team for assistance.

Unloading VSAFE

You can turn off VSAFE options to disable specific types of monitoring. For example, you might want to disable Protect HD Boot Sector when you're about to use FDISK

351

on a hard drive. To disable VSAFE entirely, you might as well unload it to free up the memory space. You must unload VSAFE to install or upgrade DOS or Windows; the SETUP program will fail if VSAFE is present.

To unload VSAFE:

1. Exit Windows if it's running.

2. Enter the following command:

   VSAFE /U

3. If a message says that VSAFE can't be unloaded because other TSRs were installed after it and if you don't load VSAFE from AUTOEXEC.BAT, reboot to unload VSAFE.

4. If the /U switch doesn't unload VSAFE, and the VSAFE command is included in AUTOEXEC.BAT, do the following:

   a. Edit AUTOEXEC.BAT.

   b. Insert the word **REM** in front of the VSAFE command.

   c. Exit the editor and save the file.

   d. Reboot.

   e. When you're ready to load VSAFE again, remove REM from the command, save the file, exit the editor, and reboot.

For the Future

New viruses become known all the time, and you're much more likely to catch a new one still making the rounds than one that's three years old. It's important for you to keep updating your known virus list. Microsoft maintains a bulletin board from which you can obtain the latest virus signatures. See your DOS documentation for information on how to contact the bulletin board. You also should periodically update your antivirus programs, which gives them the capability to do more than detect new viruses; your DOS documentation includes a coupon to obtain your first update.

When you're ready to learn more about controlling Microsoft's antivirus programs, an advanced book should explain these activities:

- Adding new virus signatures to your system

- Viewing the built-in list of known viruses

- Deleting the CHKLIST.MS files

You also can do a number of things using MSAV command parameters that you can't do from the dialog box. For example, you can scan just one directory. You can run MSAV in automatic mode so that no one needs to respond to dialog boxes and prompts. See MSAV in the Command Reference at the back of this book for more information on these options.

Using UNDELETE

27

Introduction

Undeleting is easy if you use Delete Sentry. If not, you're probably better off restoring files from their backups.

Deleting and Undeleting Files

DOS deletes a file by marking the file's directory entry as reusable. (DOS changes the first character of the file name to "s.") DOS also changes the file's FAT entries, marking each of them with zero to indicate an unused cluster.

To undelete a file, DOS must recover the file's clusters while they still contain the original data. If other files are using the clusters, DOS can't retrieve the deleted file. Deletion protection schemes try to preserve the original clusters (or at least keep track of where they were).

DOS 6 provides two levels of deletion protection. The higher level, Delete Sentry, moves a deleted file to a hidden directory, preserving all its data. The lower level, deletion-tracking, saves a list of a deleted file's clusters. The file is retrievable if the clusters haven't been reused, but it doesn't preserve the clusters. If you don't use either protection method, you might be able to undelete a file by using the information in the deleted directory entry—if it's still available—to try to recover the file's data.

Both protection methods work with DOS, DOS Shell, and Windows. The difference between DOS and Windows comes in how you undelete the files, not in how you protect them.

Using Delete Sentry

You set up Delete Sentry by loading its TSR with a command in the following format:

```
UNDELETE /S[drive]...
```

For example, the following command installs Delete Sentry to protect drive D:

```
UNDELETE /SD
```

You see a response like the following:

```
UNDELETE loaded.
Delete Protection Method is Delete Sentry.
Enabled for drives : D
```

The UNDELETE program keeps a list of protected drives. The next time you load Delete Sentry, drive D is still protected even if you don't specify it. Suppose that you include drive C the next time you load Delete Sentry:

```
UNDELETE /SC
```

The response indicates that Delete Sentry now protects both C and D:

```
UNDELETE loaded.
Delete Protection Method is Delete Sentry.
Enabled for drives : C D
```

You could have protected C and D in the first command by specifying two /S switches:

```
UNDELETE /SC /SD
```

When you specify /S without a drive name, Delete Sentry adds the current drive to its list of protected drives. If the list already includes the current drive, the following command loads Delete Sentry for all the drives in its drive list:

```
UNDELETE /S
```

If you plan to use Delete Sentry, insert in AUTOEXEC.BAT an UNDELETE command with an /S switch for each drive you want to protect. Ordinarily, you don't need to keep entering the /S switches each time you boot because Delete Sentry remembers the drive list. Including the switches in AUTOEXEC.BAT, however, makes it easy to add another drive to the list; just add the appropriate switch to the command in AUTOEXEC.BAT. Otherwise, it can be quite complicated to add on another drive.

It's also complicated to remove a drive from the list. See "For the Future" at the end of the chapter for a discussion of this problem.

Checking the Drive List

If you forget which drives Delete Sentry protects, you can enter the following command:

```
UNDELETE /STATUS
```

You should see a message something like the following:

```
Delete Protection Method is Delete Sentry.
Enabled for drives : C D
```

Listing Files Available for Recovery

You also use the UNDELETE command to recover files from Delete Sentry. You can see what files are available for undeletion in the current directory by entering a command in the following format:

```
UNDELETE /LIST
```

This command works whether or not the Delete Sentry TSR is currently loaded. As long as there is a SENTRY directory on the drive, UNDELETE shows you the files available for recovery.

If you add a filespec to the command, UNDELETE lists only the file(s) that match the filespec. Suppose that you want to see whether you can recover the file named BFUGUE.NTS. You could enter the following command:

```
UNDELETE BFUGUE.NTS /LIST
```

More than one file might be listed if you have created and deleted several files with the same name in the same directory.

You can add a path name to the command, with or without a filespec, to list a different directory. Suppose that you deleted some files from C:\TEST1 and would like to know whether they are still available. To find out, you can enter the following command:

```
UNDELETE C:\TEST1 /LIST
```

The response might look something like the following:

```
Directory: C:\TEST1
File Specifications: *.*


Delete Sentry control file contains  2 deleted files.
Deletion-Tracking file not found.
MS-DOS directory contains   3 deleted files.
Of those,   1 files may be recovered.


Using the Delete Sentry method.


TEST271   TXT   229   2-09-93   8:47a   ...A   Deleted:   2-10-93 10:35a
TEST272   TXT   1407  2-09-93   9:34a   ...A   Deleted:   2-11-93 11:13a
```

These messages include some confusing information:

- UNDELETE looks for files using every undelete method and then selects the best method—in this case Delete Sentry—to list the available files. The first part of the report shows the results of all three undelete methods.

- The Delete Sentry control file contains information about all the files in SENTRY, not just the two mentioned here. These messages indicate only the files that meet the specification C:\TEST1*.*.

- Delete Sentry displays not only the file's directory information but also the date and time it was deleted. This information comes in particularly handy if more than one file of the same name is listed.

The expression ...A indicates that the file is not system, not hidden, and not read-only, but it has a positive archive attribute.

Undeleting with Delete Sentry

Suppose that you want to undelete one or more of the files listed by UNDELETE. Enter the same command without /LIST, as follows:

```
UNDELETE C:\TEST1
```

This command produces a display with the same beginning, but it doesn't list the files. Instead, it shows one file at a time and asks whether you want to undelete it:

```
TEST271  TXT  17  1-13-93  6:42a  ...A  Deleted:  2-09-93  9:36a
This file can be 100% undeleted. undelete (Y/N)?
```

If you answer N, UNDELETE continues to the next file, if any. If you answer Y, you should see the following message:

```
File successfully undeleted.
```

But if TEST1 already contains a file named TEST271.TXT, you see the following message instead:

```
The filename already exists. Type a different filename.
Press F5 to bypass this file.
```

You can enter a new file name or decide to forget it and press F5. If you enter the file name **TEST271A.TXT**, you see the following message:

```
TEST271A TXT  17  1-13-93  6:42a  ...A  Deleted:  2-09-93  9:36a
File successfully undeleted.
```

> Press Esc to terminate UNDELETE when you have recovered all the files you want.

Windows Differences

Figure 27.1 shows the Windows version of UNDELETE. The file list shows all the files available for deletion by any method in the indicated directory. You can switch drives and directories by pressing the Drive/Dir button. To undelete files, select them and press the UNDELETE button.

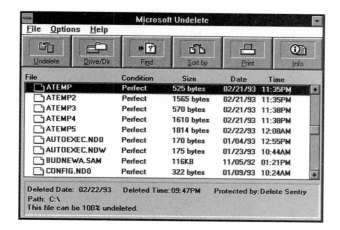

Figure 27.1.
Windows Undelete Window.

Purging the SENTRY Directory

One of the main reasons for deleting files is to free up space on your disk. You might think that Delete Sentry clogs up your drive with deleted files, but that's not completely true. Each time you load Delete Sentry, it purges any file that has been in SENTRY for at least seven days. When SENTRY takes up more than seven percent of a drive, Delete Sentry purges the oldest files until it's within that limit. (The "oldest" files are those with the oldest deletion date/time.) Also, if DOS doesn't have enough space to store a new or modified file, Delete Sentry purges the oldest files to make enough free space.

Automatic purging takes place only if the Delete Sentry TSR is loaded. If you have a SENTRY directory but don't always load Delete Sentry, you may get `Disk Full` errors when DOS tries to write files.

You can purge all the files from SENTRY by using an UNDELETE command with the /PURGE switch. To empty the current drive's SENTRY directory, you would enter the following:

```
UNDELETE /PURGE
```

You see messages like the following:

```
Delete Sentry control file contains  12 deleted files.

Confirm purging of SENTRY files on drive C (Y/N)?
```

Answer Y to empty SENTRY or N if you decide not to empty it. The file count shows all the deleted files preserved on the drive. There's no way to purge individual files or directories with the DOS version of UNDELETE. You can do it in the Windows version, however, by using the Purge Delete Sentry File command on the File menu.

What's in SENTRY?

If you view the SENTRY directory, you see some strange file names such as the following:

```
#A1B2C3E MS             17 01-13-93        6:42a
#A1B2C3F MS             89 01-13-93        5:18p
#A1B2C3G MS            339 02-09-93        9:37a
#A1B2C3H MS            421 02-09-93        9:40a
```

Delete Sentry assigns generic file names to the files it preserves. Its control file relates the original file name and directory to the name in the SENTRY directory. The control file is a system file and won't show up unless you enter **DIR \SENTRY /A**.

UNDELETE's Destination Directory

The DOS version of UNDELETE always recovers files to the same directory from which they were deleted. If you have deleted or renamed a directory, you can't recover its files until you create another directory with the same name and path. When you use DELTREE to delete a whole branch, all its files move to SENTRY. You have to remake the directories before you can recover their files.

The Windows version of UNDELETE lets you undelete directories as well as undelete files to directories that they didn't come from. See the Windows UNDELETE Help system for more information on how to accomplish these features.

When UNDELETE Can't Recover a File

You may not be able to undelete a file even though its drive is protected by Delete Sentry. Delete Sentry already may have purged it, especially if your disk is getting full. Therefore, DOS often needs to get more space from SENTRY. In addition, files with the extensions TMP, VM?, WOA, SWP, SPL, RMG, IMG, THM, and DOV are not protected by Delete Sentry. (Delete Sentry assumes that files with these extensions are temporary.)

If Delete Sentry can't find a file you want to recover, you can restore it from its backup, if you have one, or try to undelete it using the DOS directory method, described later in this chapter.

Using Deletion-Tracking

If you are upgrading from DOS 5, you probably will recognize deletion-tracking as the old DOS method of protecting deleted files. A drive protected by deletion-tracking has a system file, PCTRACKR.DEL, in its root directory. PCTRACKR.DEL keeps a list of each deleted file's clusters. Undeleting the file restores any of its clusters that DOS hasn't reused.

Because deletion-tracking can't guarantee that a file's clusters are intact, you are better off restoring a file from its backup if you haven't been using Delete Sentry. Use the deletion-tracking recovery method only for files that can't be restored from their backups for some reason.

There's almost no reason to use deletion-tracking when Delete Sentry is available. Delete Sentry does a much better job of protecting deleted files. If you load it all the time so that it can do automatic purging, you probably will never notice the disk space it uses. If you have been using DOS 5's deletion-tracking program and don't want to switch to another method, you can use deletion-tracking with DOS 6. Use /T instead of /S on the UNDELETE command to load deletion-tracking. You can't mix /T and /S switches in a command; you can load the Delete Sentry TSR or the deletion-tracking TSR. The following command loads the deletion-tracking TSR and adds drive C to its drive list:

```
UNDELETE /TC
```

Listing Files Protected by Deletion-Tracking

When you enter the **UNDELETE /LIST** command on a system that's using deletion-tracking, the messages look something like the following:

```
Directory: C:\TEST1
File Specifications: *.*


Delete Sentry control file not found.
Deletion-tracking file contains    1 deleted files.
Of those,   1 files have all clusters available,
            0 files have some clusters available,
            0 files have no clusters available.
MS-DOS directory contains    3 deleted files.
Of those,   1 files may be recovered.


Using the Deletion-tracking method.
    T4  CAT  17  1-13-93  6:42a  ...A  Deleted:  2-12-93  5:45a
```

These messages indicate that you have been using deletion-tracking, not Delete Sentry. Only one file is available for undeletion by deletion-tracking in the indicated directory. UNDELETE has compared the list of clusters in the deletion-tracking file against the FAT and determined that all the clusters belonging to this file are available. You could go on to undelete it using a command like the following:

```
UNDELETE C:\TEST1
```

UNDELETE shows one file at a time and asks whether you want to delete it, like this:

```
T4  CAT  17  1-13-93 6:42a  ...A Deleted:  2-12-93  5:45a
All of the clusters of this file are available. UNDELETE (Y/N)?
```

If you answer N, UNDELETE continues to the next file, if any. If you answer Y, you should see the following message:

```
File successfully undeleted.
```

Recovering Partial Files

Sometimes deletion-tracking can recover only part of a file. When you enter the UNDELETE /LIST command, the response might look like the following:

```
Deletion-tracking file contains    3 deleted files.
Of those,    1 files have all clusters available,
             1 files have some clusters available,
             1 files have no clusters available.
```

The list of files might show the following:

```
T4   CAT  17  1-13-93  6:42a  ...A Deleted:  2-12-93  5:45a
* BIGTIME ABC 39152 3-10-92  3:10a  ...A Deleted:  2-12-93  7:32a
**ZIGZAG  BMP  630 3-10-92  3:10a  ...A Deleted:  2-12-93  7:29a
"*" indicates some clusters of the file are available.
"**" indicates no clusters of the file are available.
```

You can't recover ZIGZAG.BMP because none of its clusters are available. Some of BIGTIME.ABC's clusters can't be recovered, but you could recover the rest. You should consider the following points when deciding whether to recover part of a file:

- The part that's available is not necessarily the beginning of the file, nor even a continuous segment. It might just be a cluster here and a cluster there.

- Restoring a file from its backup is a much better way to recover it in this case, even if the backup is slightly out-of-date.

- There's no sense in partially recovering a file that doesn't contain text, as it will be unusable.

> Never recover part of a program file. Running the program could actually do harm to your system.

- If it's a file from a word processor, desktop publisher, or database manager, it may be missing special header information that such programs build into their documents. In that case, you won't be able to open the file for editing under its original application. However, you can try to edit it as an ASCII text file, clean out any garbage, recover as much text as possible, and then insert it into another document created by the original application.

Even when UNDELETE says a file is completely available, it might not recover the correct data. Another file may have overwritten some clusters and then have been deleted. Because the clusters appear to UNDELETE to be available, it reports that the entire file can be recovered. However, it recovers the other file's data from the clusters. You may still be better off restoring it from its backup.

Recovering Files Deleted under DOS 5

If you have just upgraded from DOS 5, you may need to recover files deleted by the old deletion-tracking method for a few days. But if you have switched to Delete Sentry with DOS 6, UNDELETE won't offer to recover files by the deletion-tracking method. Adding the /DT switch to the UNDELETE command forces UNDELETE to access the PCTRACKR.DEL file. Suppose that you deleted GRFALLS.DRW a few days ago under DOS 5. The following command will recover it if the clusters are still available:

```
UNDELETE GRFALLS.DRW /DT
```

After about a week of using Delete Sentry, you can delete
PCTRACKR.DEL. Its data will be too out-of-date to be useful anymore.

Using the DOS
Directory Method

The least reliable method of undeleting files is to search a directory for deleted entries. UNDELETE uses this method only if it can't find a SENTRY directory or a PCTRACKR.DEL file. Even if you include a specific file name and that file appears in the DOS directory but not SENTRY or PCTRACKR.DEL, UNDELETE will not use the directory method if any other method is available.

If a file has been purged from SENTRY or PCTRACKR.DEL, its old directory entry may exist, and you can still recover it by the directory method. You can force DOS to use the directory method by including the /DOS switch on the UNDELETE command, as in:

```
UNDELETE \TEST1\*.* /DOS /LIST
```

If the drive has no SENTRY directory and no PCTRACKR.DEL file, you
don't need the /DOS switch.

The response to your command may look like the following:

```
Directory: C:\

File Specifications: *.*
    Delete Sentry control file not found.
    Deletion-tracking file not found.
MS-DOS directory contains    5 deleted files.
    Of those,    3 files may be recovered.
```

Using the MS-DOS directory method.

```
** ?ONFIG   TMP      778  1-05-93 10:24a  ...A
   ?OC2D31  TMP     7059 12-05-92  4:27p  ...A


** ?MF030D  TMP       18 12-05-92  4:27p  ...A
   ?OREAD   TXT    22016 12-06-92  6:00a  ....
```

"**" indicates the first cluster of the file is unavailable and can't be recovered with the UNDELETE command.

The list includes all files in the C:\TEST1 directory whose file names start with deletion characters. In the list, ? indicates that character. Even though the directory entry is still there, a file can't be undeleted if another file is using its first cluster, as indicated by ** in the list.

The list might include some unexpected file names. Delete Sentry and deletion-tracking suppress temporary files, but the directory method shows them. You might encounter a lot of temporary files made and deleted by DOS, Windows, and your applications; they tend to have generic-looking file names like MS396AX.TMP.

Suppose that you want to undelete one or more files. You can use the UNDELETE command without /LIST, as follows:

```
UNDELETE C:\TEST1\*.* /DOS
```

This command produces a display that begins the same way, but it lists one file at a time and asks whether you want to undelete it, as follows:

```
?REP     BAT     63 12-03-92  9:54a  UNDELETE (Y/N)?
```

If you answer N, UNDELETE proceeds to the next file. If you answer Y, it asks you the following:

```
Please type the first character for ?OREAD   .TXT:
```

After you type a character that creates a unique file name in the directory, you probably will see the following message:

```
File successfully undeleted.
```

UNDELETE lists files that can't be undeleted, but you don't get a chance to undelete them.

Deleted Directories

After you have deleted a directory, the DOS version of UNDELETE can never again recover its files using the directory method. Making a new directory with the same name and path doesn't help, because the old deleted directory entries will not be in the new directory. The Windows version of UNDELETE, however, may be able to recover the deleted directory as well as its files.

Problems with the Directory Method

The `File successfully undeleted` message can be deceiving with the directory method. After UNDELETE finds the directory entry and the first cluster, it still has to guess where to find the remaining clusters for the file. The longer you wait and the more work you do with the disk, the more likely it is that UNDELETE won't find the right clusters, especially if the file was fragmented.

You can be reasonably sure of getting your file back correctly with this method only if you recover it immediately after deleting it. If you have done anything else on the system, restore the file from its backup, if that's possible.

> Don't run a program recovered by the DOS directory method; if it contains the wrong information, it could damage your system.

For the Future

When you are ready to learn more about protecting and recovering files, you might want to look at the UNDELETE command in the Command Reference to find out how to undelete without prompts, how to unload the UNDELETE TSR, and how to change the number of entries in a deletion-tracking file. You also might take a look at a file called UNDELETE.INI, which contains some of the defaults for UN-DELETE. You can edit it to change the number of days a file stays in SENTRY, to remove a drive from the drive list, and to revise the list of files exempted from Delete Sentry protection.

UNDELETE for Windows can do several things that DOS UNDELETE can't do. It can undelete a directory, and it can be more selective about purging files from a SENTRY directory.

CHKDSK

28

Introduction

CHKDSK does two great things for a drive: it fixes problems that could cause data loss, and it reclaims wasted space.

What CHKDSK Does

C HKDSK examines the FAT and directory structure on a drive, looking for errors and inconsistencies that could keep you from accessing files. It can fix most of the problems that it finds. CHKDSK also finds clusters that haven't been deleted but don't belong to any file; you can convert these clusters into files or delete them. You may be able to reclaim several lost kilobytes of wasted space on your drive.

Lost Allocation Units

The most common error reported by CHKDSK is *lost allocation units*. These occur when FAT entries indicate that clusters belong to some file, but the chain cannot be traced backward to a specific file's directory entry.

Clusters get lost in a number of ways. Any type of mistake in the FAT or directory structure often creates lost clusters. Suppose that a directory entry gets damaged so that it no longer points to the first cluster of the file. That file's clusters are no longer associated with the directory entry, and CHKDSK will report them as lost allocation units. Suppose that the FAT entry for the second cluster of a file gets damaged so that it no longer points to the third cluster. The third cluster, and all subsequent clusters, are now lost. These types of mistakes happen most often because of malfunctioning hardware, power surges, and improperly parked heads.

You can have lost clusters, however, without having any other mistakes on the drive. Probably the most common way of losing clusters is to interrupt DOS when it's deleting files. If you reboot, eject a disk, or shut off the power before DOS finishes zeroing all the FAT entries belonging to a deleted file, the remaining entries become lost allocation units. Lost clusters also can occur when a program hangs up, and you have to reboot to clear it.

Lost clusters happen more often than you would expect. After you have used your system for a few months, they could be tying up many kilobytes of disk space. Those clusters are not available for new data; they're just wasted space on your drive. CHKDSK can free that space.

CHKDSK offers two ways to recover the space from lost clusters. It will convert them into files, or it will zero their FAT entries to make the space available. The choice is up to you. If you're not missing any data, and if CHKDSK doesn't report any other problems on the drive, go ahead and zero the clusters. You will recover the lost space immediately. If you are missing some data or if CHKDSK reports other types of problems, recover the lost clusters into files; you may be able to locate and rescue your missing data.

When To Use CHKDSK

You should run CHKDSK periodically to clean up any lost clusters on your drive. If you use your system full-time, you may want to run CHKDSK weekly. For less active systems, biweekly or monthly may do. You also should run CHKDSK if you see any evidence of problems, such as the following, in your FAT or directory structure:

- Data drops out of a file.

- Unexpected data appears in a file.

- A program that was working fine starts to malfunction.

- A file disappears from a directory.

- A directory contains garbage.

- A directory disappears unexpectedly.

Using CHKDSK

CHKDSK can be fooled by open files, so you must terminate all running programs (except TSRs) before starting it up. In particular, exit Windows or the DOS Shell and start CHKDSK from a primary command prompt.

Enter the following command to start CHKDSK:

```
CHKDSK [drive]
```

CHKDSK examines the requested drive (or the current drive if you omit a drive name) and produces a report. If it finds no problems, the report looks something like the following:

```
Volume MICROMATE    created 10-27-1992 10:30a
Volume Serial Number is 1A4F-4156

84768768 bytes total disk space
   88064 bytes in 6 hidden files
  126976 bytes in 41 directories
71380992 bytes in 1795 user files
13172736 bytes available on disk

    2048 bytes in each allocation unit
   41391 total allocation units on disk
    6432 available allocation units on disk

  655360 total bytes memory
  627424 bytes free
```

The memory report is left over from earlier versions of DOS. You'll see a much better way to find out about available memory in Chapter 30.

Dealing with Lost Clusters

CHKDSK reports any problems after the two heading lines. A lost clusters message looks something like the following:

```
Volume MICROMATE    created 10-27-1992 10:30a
Volume Serial Number is 1A4F-4156
Errors found, F parameter not specified
Corrections will not be written to disk

    45 lost allocation units found in 13 chains.
    92160 bytes disk space would be freed
```

```
84768768 bytes total disk space
   88064 bytes in 6 hidden files
  126976 bytes in 41 directories
71376896 bytes in 1793 user files
13084672 bytes available on disk

    2048 bytes in each allocation unit
   41391 total allocation units on disk
    6389 available allocation units on disk

  655360 total bytes memory
  627424 bytes free
```

In this example, CHKDSK found 45 lost clusters in 13 chains. If you decide to zero the clusters, you would gain 92,160 bytes (90K) of available space. If you decide to convert them into files, CHKDSK would create 13 files, one for each chain.

CHKDSK doesn't recover the lost clusters or fix any other problems in response to this command. You have to rerun it with the /F (for "fix") switch to fix any problems it finds, as in:

```
CHKDSK /F [drive]
```

When you use the /F switch, you see these messages:

```
Volume MICROMATE   created 10-27-1992 10:30a
Volume Serial Number is 1A4F-4156

  45 lost allocation units found in 13 chains.
Convert lost chains to files (Y/N)?
```

If you type **Y**, CHKDSK converts each lost chain into a file in the root directory named FILEnnnn.CHK, where nnnn is a serial number starting with 0000. You then can examine each file and decide whether to delete or keep it. Examine the files using DOS's EDIT command or your word processor. Many of the files will be unreadable, and even text files could be partially unreadable. You may have to remove some garbage from the text files that you want to keep.

If you type **N** instead of **Y**, CHKDSK deletes the lost clusters so that the space is made available for new data. If you're not missing any data and if CHKDSK doesn't report any other kind of error, this choice is best.

Cross-Linked Files

Perhaps the second most common error, and one that CHKDSK cannot fix, is cross-linked files in which two files appear to have some clusters in common. For example, suppose that the FAT shows that FILEA occupies clusters 201, 202, 203, and 204, but FILEB occupies cluster 1096, 1097, 203, and 204. Clusters 203 and 204 cannot belong to both files; one of the chains is incorrect. In all likelihood, FILEB should chain from 1097 to 1098 and beyond.

CHKDSK cannot fix this error, as it cannot guess which chain is correct and which is wrong. Your best bet to fix cross-linked clusters is to delete both files and restore them from their backups. If that's not possible, and if they are not program files, you may be able to recover at least one of them with the following procedure.

> Don't use this procedure on a cross-linked program file. Delete the file and restore or reinstall it. (This includes files with extensions COM, EXE, BIN, DLL, SYS, and OVL.)

To recover cross-linked files:

1. Recover all lost allocation units into files. Then exit CHKDSK. (You come back to the recovered files later.)

2. Make a copy of each cross-linked file, giving each copy a new name but the same extension as the original. The new files will not be cross-linked, but each one will contain a copy of the common clusters.

3. Delete the cross-linked files. These deletions clear up the problem in the FAT.

4. Examine each copy using whatever application made the original. You probably will find that one of the files is fine and that the other isn't.

5. Edit the damaged file to remove any superfluous data. Use the same application that created the file in the first place.

6. Examine the FILEnnnn.CHK files recovered by CHKDSK. If any of them contain data that belongs to the damaged file, use the file's original application to insert the data where it belongs.

7. Handle all other FILEnnnn.CHK files as you would normally.

8. Restore the original names of the files that you have recovered.

Other Types of Errors

CHKDSK can fix most of the problems it identifies. If it reports an error such as al-location error or first allocation unit is invalid, rerun it with the /F switch. It will fix the error without your being involved.

The fix might cause some files to be chopped off, so be sure to recover lost allocation units into files if you are afraid that you don't have good enough backups for all your files. If a program stops working after the fix, reinstall it. If a data file loses data or cannot be opened, restore it from its backup. If you cannot restore a text file, you can try to recover the missing text from the CHK files created by CHKDSK. Otherwise, you can delete the CHK files when you don't need them anymore.

Archaic CHKDSK Functions

CHKDSK was one of the early DOS utilities, and it includes some functions that were handy at one time but have now been replaced by better utilities. Some of its functions, besides reporting the amount of memory installed, follow:

● CHKDSK can report on file fragmentation, but DEFRAG does a better job at this.

● CHKDSK can list all the files on the disk, by directory, but DIR and TREE do it better.

Optimizing Your System

29

Introduction

DOS 6 gives you a number
of tools to improve the
overall performance of
your system.

What Can DOS Do?

O ne of the advantages of learning to use your operating system, instead of just depending on your applications, is that you can take several steps to make your system faster and more efficient. With DOS 6 utilities, you can make better use of memory so that you have more room to load and run programs. You can squeeze almost twice as much data onto your hard drive. You also can speed up all your disk drives, which improves the speed of your whole system.

Better Memory Management

Memory space in a DOS system is always tight, even if the system has many megabytes of extended or expanded memory. Traditionally, programs must run in *conventional memory*, which is limited to 640K no matter how much memory is installed on your system. After you have loaded DOS, a handful of device drivers, and perhaps some other TSRs in conventional memory, you may not have enough room left to load and run a large application such as a desktop publisher. If you have a 286-based machine, DOS 6 can provide a little relief from the conventional memory crunch. It can make a huge difference on a 386 or higher machine.

The original PCs were limited to 640K of memory unless you added an expanded memory board. 286s and higher machines, however, can extend memory for several megabytes. For any system with extended memory, DOS 6 includes HIMEM, a driver that gives DOS access to and control of the extended memory area. You can even load DOS into extended memory instead of conventional memory, freeing up about 45K of conventional memory for other programs to use. Chapter 30 explains the various types of memory, including conventional, extended, and expanded, and shows you how to load and use HIMEM.

If you have a 386 or higher machine, you can do a lot more to free up conventional memory space. The Emm386 driver enables you to load and run programs in *upper memory*, the area that comes in between conventional and extended memory. If you have any programs that need expanded memory, Emm386 also can use extended memory to emulate expanded memory. DOS 6 even includes a program called

MEMMAKER that will set up your system to use HIMEM and EMM386 so that you don't have to write the commands. Chapter 31 shows you how to use EMM386 and MEMMAKER.

Caching the Hard Drive

Your hard drive is so slow, compared to memory and the microprocessor, that your system often has to wait for data to be read and written. A *caching* program helps to ease the bottleneck by saving disk data in memory so that DOS can read from and write to memory instead of the hard disk.

DOS 6 includes a caching program named SmartDrive that creates a cache in extended memory; you should notice the difference in how fast your programs run. SmartDrive saves any data you work on in its cache. The next time you want to use the same data, SmartDrive provides the data from the cache instead of reading it from the hard drive. Reading the data from the cache is much faster than reading it from the drive. Chapter 32 explains how to load and use SmartDrive.

Using a RAM Drive

Another way to cut down on disk accesses is to create a *RAM drive*, which is like a disk drive except that it is located in memory instead of on disk, making it a hundred times faster. You can use a RAM drive just like any other drive, but it loses all its data when you reboot or shut off the power. You have to load it with data after booting and move any important data to a real drive before you reboot or shut down. Because the possibility of a power outage or system hang-up always exists, most people keep only programs and temporary files in a RAM drive; they keep their important data files in a more secure place.

With DOS 6, you can create RAM drives using the RAMDRIVE driver. You can control the size of each RAM drive and whether it is located in conventional, expanded, or extended memory. DOS assigns a drive name to each RAM drive just like it does to your real drives. Chapter 33 shows you how to create and use RAM drives.

Defragmenting

DOS is often forced to fragment files to fit them into the available space on a disk. Fragmentation doesn't hurt a file, but your drive takes longer to read a fragmented file because it has to move the read-write heads more. If you have a lot of fragmentation on your hard disk, you might notice your programs running slower.

DOS 6 includes a program called DEFRAG that defragments the files on a drive. DEFRAG moves the clusters around to bring file fragments together, adjusting the FAT and directories as necessary. Defragmenting your hard drive once a month or so is one of the steps you should take to keep your system in optimum shape. Chapter 34 shows you how to use DEFRAG.

DoubleSpace

No matter how large your hard drive, you will soon fill it up. Compressing the drive can free up a lot of space for more files. *Data compression* removes repetitious data from a file so that it takes up less room.

The amount that you can compress a file depends on how much repetitious data it contains. A program file usually contains very little repetition, and program files don't compress very much. A text file contains quite a bit of repeated information. Common strings of characters such as "the," "and," and "are" may appear hundreds of times. Text files often can be compressed to half their uncompressed size. Black-and-white bit-mapped graphic files, which consist entirely of black dots and white dots, realize the most compression of all.

In a typical system with some files of each kind, you can store roughly twice as much data on a compressed drive. Hence the name *DoubleSpace* for DOS's file compression program.

With DoubleSpace, you don't compress files individually, you create a compressed drive. Any data stored on that drive is automatically compressed as it is written and decompressed when you read it. Chapter 35 shows you how to set up and use DoubleSpace.

Managing Memory

30

Introduction

Running out of usable memory in a PC is very easy to do. DOS 6 includes several tools to help you get the most from the memory you have.

What Is Memory?

Memory is the storage device inside your computer in which programs reside while they are being executed. The basic part of memory is a set of chips located on the motherboard close to the microprocessor so that data can travel quickly between the two devices. Memory is completely solid-state; unlike a disk drive, it has no moving parts to slow it down.

You can't run programs from a disk or any other storage device; each program must be loaded into memory for execution. Therefore, the size of a computer's memory limits the size and the complexity of the programs it can run.

Even though a program must be loaded into memory, the data it processes can be stored on a slower device, such as a disk. If a program also can squeeze its data into memory, it will run much faster because it doesn't have to wait for data to be read from and written to the slower device.

The Types of Memory

In the early days of personal computers, around the mid-1970s, a new computer typically came with 16K of memory. You could expand it in 16K increments up to a maximum of 64K. Programs were necessarily limited, not only in what tasks they could accomplish, but also in how they interacted with their users. Color monitors, graphic user interfaces, and mice were unheard of. Those early programs also ran very slowly and had to keep most of their data on external storage devices.

In the late 1970s, Intel developed the 8088 microprocessor chip, which could access an incredible 1M of memory. IBM adopted the 8088 for the first IBM PCs. The PC clones soon followed, all based on the 8088 with its 1M of memory.

IBM and a new little company called Microsoft developed an operating system called the Disk Operating System (DOS) for the new machine. Intel, IBM, and Microsoft decided to divide the 1M memory area into two parts, as shown in figure 30.1. The first 640K, called *conventional memory*, is where DOS and its applications run. This area was 10 times as much memory space as previous personal computers had, and most people thought it was more than enough. The remaining 384K, called *upper memory*, was reserved for DOS's use in accessing hardware devices such as video controllers.

OK   640K   1M

conventional memory	upper memory

Figure 30.1.
Conventional and
upper memory.

Two basic types of memory devices exist, RAM and ROM. RAM, which stands for *random-access memory*, can be read from and written to. You can write to it again and again; new data replaces older data with no problems. However, RAM is *volatile*; it loses its data when you reboot or shut off the power.

ROM, which stands for *read-only memory*, has data stored in it by its manufacturer and can be read only by your computer. A ROM chip usually contains an essential program such as the basic input-output operating system (BIOS), which provides the elementary instructions to read and write data for your hardware. ROM is not volatile; it retains its memory when the power is off so that its information is available during the early parts of booting, before any programs have been loaded into RAM.

Conventional memory is always made up of RAM, because you must be able to repeatedly load programs and data there. Upper memory may contain some RAM and some ROM, depending on what devices your system has. The BIOS chip, which is usually referred to as ROM-BIOS, is located in upper memory. A lot of upper memory is empty; the space is reserved, but no memory chips support it.

Expanded Memory

As soon as 640K of memory became available, people began to think of ways to use it. Programs got fatter, faster, and fancier. Memory-resident programs began to appear—device drivers and TSRs such as ANSI.SYS and PRINT. When you load a memory-resident program, it stays in memory for the rest of the session, and any other programs you load have to fit into the remaining space. Within a few years, programs were bumping up against that 640K ceiling with no way to get around it.

An early solution to the memory crunch was called *expanded memory* (see fig. 30.2). This memory is an extra set of RAM chips, located on a separate board and treated just like any other hardware device. As indicated in the figure, expanded memory is accessed through upper memory. Notice that you can access only a portion of it at a time, but you can switch from portion to portion to take advantage of all the available space. A device driver called an *expanded memory manager* controls access to expanded memory and does the switching. Expanded memory is relatively slow compared to conventional or upper memory, but it still is considerably faster than a disk drive.

Figure 30.2.
Expanded memory.

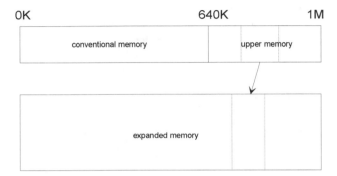

Because expanded memory is a separate device and can't be accessed directly by DOS, you can't load and run programs there. Expanded memory is useful only for data storage. Moving a program's data into expanded memory frees up that space in conventional memory, making more room for the program. Expanded memory does help to alleviate a PC's memory problems to a certain extent, but it is not an ideal solution.

Extended Memory

Intel developed another solution to the 640K ceiling. The 286 microprocessor, in addition to being a much better and faster processor, could directly access 16M of memory. Memory above the 1M mark, which is all RAM, is called *extended memory* (see fig. 30.3). The 386 and 486 have pushed the limit even further, allowing several gigabytes of memory. (A gigabyte is more than a billion bytes.) Theoretically, you could load and run programs throughout this memory space. Sadly, DOS must adhere to its original design and has no way to directly access the extra space. DOS still suffers from the 640K ceiling, with some interesting exceptions that you discover later in this book.

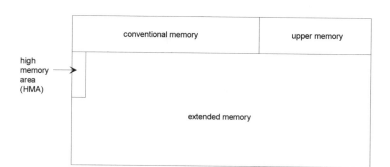

Figure 30.3.
Extended memory.

IBM and Microsoft developed a new operating system to take advantage of the full range of extended memory—OS/2. But most users preferred to hang on to the operating system they already knew. OS/2 continues to gain in popularity but has never been the success its developers expected.

In a 286 or higher machine running under DOS, the first megabyte of memory still has the same layout as before: 640K of conventional memory and 384K reserved for upper memory. Most 286 and higher machines come with at least 1M of RAM. The first 640K supplies conventional memory. The rest becomes not upper memory, which is still set aside for hardware devices, but the first part of extended memory.

DOS can't access extended memory directly, but it can treat it in much the same way as it handles expanded memory. DOS can treat extended memory as a separate device and access it through upper memory, using an *extended memory manager* to handle the details. As with expanded memory, DOS can't load and run programs in extended memory, with one exception—the high memory area.

High Memory Area

Because of a quirk in the way DOS handles memory addresses, DOS can directly access nearly 64K of extended memory. DOS's extended memory manager, named HIMEM.SYS, turns the first part of extended memory into the *high memory area* (HMA), where it can load and run one program at a time. Normally, you load DOS into the HMA, freeing up around 45K of conventional memory for other programs.

Extended memory, HIMEM.SYS, and the HMA are available only on 286s (ATs) and higher machines. The original PCs and XTs can have expanded memory boards but not extended memory.

Viewing Your Memory Layout

You can find out how much of each type of memory you have, and how it's being used, with the MEM command. When you enter the command **MEM** with no parameters, you see a message like the following:

```
Memory Type        Total =  Used  +  Free
----------------   ------   ------   ------
Conventional        640K     112K     528K
Upper                 0K       0K       0K
Adapter RAM/ROM     384K     384K       0K
Extended (XMS)     3072K    3072K       0K
----------------   ------   ------   ------
Total memory       4096K    3568K     528K
Total under 1 MB    640K     112K     528K
Largest executable program size   527K  (540096 bytes)
Largest free upper memory block     0K       (0 bytes)
```

This system has 640K of conventional memory, of which 528K is currently free. It has 384K of upper memory, which appears next to `Adapter RAM/ROM` because this system uses upper memory for its original purpose—to access RAM and ROM associated with hardware adapters; because upper memory is not available to run programs, it is not counted in the `Total under 1 MB` line.

The system has 3M of extended memory, none of which is free. It has no expanded memory. Altogether, this system has 4M of memory, of which about 528K is free. The largest executable program size is 527K because that is the largest fragment of conventional memory available. (There must be a 1K fragment somewhere.)

MEM without any switches gives you a general feel for how much memory is available, but you can't see what specific programs are loaded. Adding the /C (classify) switch to the MEM command causes MEM to add details about programs, as in the following example:

```
Modules using memory below 1 MB:

  Name         Total    =  Conventional  +  Upper Memory
  --------    ----------    ------------     ------------
  MSDOS       61037  (60K)   61037  (60K)       0  (0K)
  SETVER        784   (1K)     784   (1K)       0  (0K)
  ANSI         4208   (4K)    4208   (4K)       0  (0K)
  COMMAND      5760   (6K)    5760   (6K)       0  (0K)
  MOUSE       13616  (13K)   13616  (13K)       0  (0K)
  GRAB        23760  (23K)   23760  (23K)       0  (0K)
  GRAPHICS     5872   (6K)    5872   (6K)       0  (0K)
  Free       540208 (528K)  540208 (528K)       0  (0K)

Memory Summary:

Type of Memory        Total       =       Used      +      Free
----------------   ---------------    ---------------    ------------
Conventional          5360  (640K)     115152  (112K)    540208 (528K)
Upper                    0   (0K)           0   (0K)          0   (0K)
Adapter RAM/ROM     393216 (384K)     393216 (384K)          0   (0K)
Extended (XMS)     3145728 (3072K)   3145728 (3072K)         0   (0K)
----------------   ---------------    ---------------    ------------

Total memory      4194304 (4096K) 3654096 (3568K) 540208 (528K)
Total under 1 MB   655360  (640K) 115152  (112K) 540208 (528K)
Largest executable program size       540096   (527K)
Largest free upper memory block           0     (0K)
```

Now you can see that DOS and a bunch of drivers and TSRs are loaded into conventional memory.

If your monitor displays only 24 lines at a time, you should add the /P (page) switch to MEM to break the output into pages.

Loading HIMEM

HIMEM is a device driver that gives you access to the extended memory on your machine. HIMEM not only creates and controls the HMA, it also manages the rest of extended memory so that programs can safely store and use data there without conflicting with each other. You load HIMEM from CONFIG.SYS with a command such as the following:

```
DEVICE=C:\DOS\HIMEM.SYS
```

> Be sure to include the correct path for your DOS directory. When DOS processes CONFIG.SYS, no search path is available, so you have to tell DOS where to find the desired file.

Most people put the HIMEM.SYS command first in CONFIG.SYS so that HIMEM can seize immediate control and make extended memory available to other drivers.

Loading DOS into the HMA

HIMEM enables one program to use the HMA. If you permit a small program of 10K to load into the HMA, you do not free up much room in conventional memory. One way to guarantee that a sizable program uses the HMA is to load DOS up there, which you can do with the following CONFIG.SYS command:

DOS=HIGH

Making this the second command in CONFIG.SYS, right after you load HIMEM, guarantees that DOS gets into the HMA before some other program does. How much conventional memory space you save depends on how your DOS is configured, but it will probably be around 45K. A small portion of DOS stays in conventional memory.

The MEM summary for the system shown earlier appears as follows when you load HIMEM and place DOS in the HMA:

```
Memory Type       Total =  Used  +  Free
---------------   ------   ------    ------
Conventional       640K     68K      572K
```

```
Upper                    0K        0K        0K
Adapter RAM/ROM        384K      384K        0K
Extended (XMS)        3072K       64K     3008K
----------------      ------    ------    ------
Total memory          4096K      521K     3580K

Total under 1 MB       640K       68K      572K

Largest executable program size             572K
Largest free upper memory block               0K
```

MS-DOS is resident in the high memory area.

Notice how much more conventional memory is available, 572K as opposed to 528K. You also can see a difference in the use of extended memory. Now that HIMEM is in control, most of it is available. The HMA represents the 64K in use. The final line of the report shows that DOS is now located in the HMA.

Using LOADFIX

When you load DOS high, other programs can occupy the first 64K of conventional memory where DOS normally resides. This practice usually is not a problem, but some programs actually can't function when loaded that low. If you try to start up a program and get the message Packed file corrupt, you need to use the LOADFIX command to load the program above the 64K line. Insert LOADFIX in front of the command that starts up the program, as in the following:

```
LOADFIX EDIT README.TXT
```

This command loads the DOS editor and opens the file named README.TXT for editing. The editor is loaded above the 64K line in conventional memory.

For the Future

The MEM command can give you even more detail than the /C switch provides. The additional information is useful mostly to programmers, but if you want to know more about it, look up MEM in the Command Reference at the back of this book.

The default settings for HIMEM work on most systems, but in a few situations, you need to add some parameters to the HIMEM command to make it work. If you're having trouble loading HIMEM, see HIMEM.SYS in the Appendix for details.

Additional Memory Facilities for the 386

31

Introduction

If you have a 386 or 486, you may be able to move most of your drivers and TSRs out of conventional memory space using the tools included in DOS 6.

DOS and the 386

DOS 6 includes several programs to optimize memory in a 386 or higher machine. If you have a program that requires expanded memory, which you don't have, you can use part of extended memory to simulate the needed expanded memory. You also can load and run programs in the unused portions of upper memory, freeing up even more space in conventional memory. DOS even provides a program that will set up your CONFIG.SYS and AUTOEXEC.BAT to make the best possible use of upper memory.

Simulating Expanded Memory

DOS 6 includes a driver named EMM386 that can be used to emulate expanded memory. If you load EMM386 with no parameters or switches, it turns 256K of extended memory into expanded memory. A program can request and receive more expanded memory space on a temporary basis if enough extended memory is available. When the program is done with the expanded memory, all but the basic 256K reverts to extended memory.

Insert the following command in CONFIG.SYS to load EMM386 and set up a minimum of 256K of expanded memory:

```
DEVICE=C:\DOS\EMM386.EXE
```

EMM386 requires HIMEM, so this command must follow the command that loads HIMEM. If you put the EMM386.EXE command right after the DOS=HIGH command (or right after the HIMEM.SYS command if you're not using DOS=HIGH), EMM386 can take 256K of extended memory before some other program takes it all.

Using Upper Memory Blocks

In Chapter 30, you saw that the memory range from 640K to 1M, called *upper memory*, was traditionally reserved for DOS's use in accessing hardware devices. Very few systems, however, actually use the entire 384K. That unused space is valuable because, unlike expanded and extended memory, DOS can run programs there. EMM386 has a second function that enables you to load and run programs in unused upper memory space.

Figure 31.1 shows an example of how upper memory may be laid out in a system. Device memory and ROM-BIOS don't necessarily occupy consecutive locations; the unused space could be divided into chunks called *upper memory blocks* (UMBs). Most people manage to load all their device drivers and TSRs into upper memory, leaving more than 600K of conventional memory for applications.

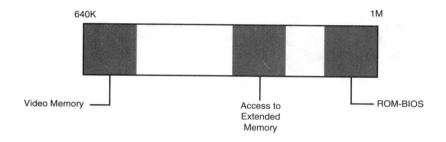

Figure 31.1.
Typical upper
memory layout.

The empty blocks in upper memory have no RAM associated with them; they are just reserved space. EMM386 takes enough RAM from extended memory to supply upper memory for the programs that you want to load. If it can't make a large enough UMB available to load a particular program, because the UMB space doesn't exist or because it can't get enough extended memory, DOS loads the program into conventional memory without warning you.

Using MEMMAKER

Setting up and using upper memory blocks require a number of commands in CONFIG.SYS and AUTOEXEC.BAT and in SYSTEM.INI if you are using Windows. Most of the commands are simple enough in their basic form, but you do not make the best use of upper memory without their advanced parameters. DOS 6 provides a program called MEMMAKER to set up upper memory for you. MEMMAKER analyzes your system, figures out the best way to use the available UMBs, and inserts the necessary commands in CONFIG.SYS, AUTOEXEC.BAT, and SYSTEM.INI.

MEMMAKER adapts any driver and TSR commands in your startup files to load those programs into upper memory. Before running MEMMAKER, edit CONFIG.SYS and AUTOEXEC.BAT to remove any unwanted commands and to insert commands that you want MEMMAKER to adapt. (Edit SYSTEM.INI only if you understand how this file works.) You can rerun MEMMAKER later if you add more drivers and TSRs to your system.

Start MEMMAKER at the DOS command prompt with this simple command:

    MEMMAKER

MEMMAKER offers you the choice of a custom or express setup. You probably want to choose an express setup, at least the first time you run MEMMAKER. (You may be able to squeeze more programs into upper memory with a custom setup, but most people don't need to do this.)

Be prepared to tell MEMMAKER whether or not any of your programs need expanded memory. If you're not sure, say "No." You can rerun MEMMAKER later if you discover that you do need some expanded memory.

MEMMAKER does a fairly good job of keeping you informed of what's happening as it works. It reboots your system several times while experimenting with the best setup, but MEMMAKER always warns you when it's about to reboot. Sometimes, your system will get stuck when MEMMAKER tries to reboot it—for example, when MEMMAKER tries out a technique that is not right for your system. If you see that your system is stuck, turn the power off and on to force it to restart. When MEMMAKER returns, it suggests that you choose the option `Try again with conservative settings`. You should choose this option unless you want to try the more aggressive settings a second time.

When MEMMAKER is ready for its final reboot using the new settings for your system, it asks you to watch for any error messages during booting. During the boot process, you can press the Pause key to give yourself time to read messages. (Press any other key to resume after a pause.) After the final reboot, you have the chance to tell MEMMAKER whether it worked or not. You also can press Esc to undo MEMMAKER's work and restore your original system.

When it has successfully reconfigured your system, MEMMAKER displays a report comparing your old memory use with the new. You see exactly how much conventional memory you're saving with the new settings. If you run MEM /C /P, you see a report something like the following:

```
Modules using memory below 1 MB:
Name             Total      =   Conventional   +   Upper Memory
--------      ------------      ---------------     ---------------
MSDOS           16621   (16K)     16621   (16K)        0     (0K)
HIMEM            1152    (1K)      1152    (1K)         0     (0K)
EMM386           3120    (3K)      3120    (3K)         0     (0K)
COMMAND          3680    (4K)      3680    (4K)         0     (0K)
SETVER            816    (1K)         0    (0K)       816     (1K)
ANSI             4240    (4K)         0    (0K)      4240     (4K)
MOUSE           13616   (13K)         0    (0K)     13616    (13K)
GRAB            23744   (23K)         0    (0K)     23744    (23K)
GRAPHICS         5872    (6K)         0    (0K)      5872     (6K)
SMARTDRV        27264   (27K)         0    (0K)     27264    (27K)
Free           713952  (697K)    630656  (616K)     83296    (81K)
Memory Summary:
Type of Memory      Total     =      Used      +      Free
------------     ------------      ---------------     ---------------
Conventional       655360  (640K)    24704    (24K)   630656  (616K)
Upper              158848  (155K)    75552    (74K)    83296   (81K)
Adapter RAM/ROM    234368  (229K)   234368   (229K)       0    (0K)
Extended (XMS)    3145728 (3072K)  1429504  (1396K) 1716224 (1676K)
-----------      ------------      ---------------     ---------------
Total memory      4194304 (4096K)  1764128  (1723K) 2430176 (2373K)
Total under 1 MB  814208  (795K)    100256    (98K)   713952  (697K)
Largest executable program size             630560   (616K)
Largest free upper memory block              67952    (66K)
MS-DOS is resident in the high memory area.
```

Compare these figures with those in Chapter 30, which are taken from the same system before running MEMMAKER. The available space in conventional memory has jumped from 572K to 616K. The programs currently in conventional memory—a small portion of DOS, HIMEM, EMM386, and COMMAND—can't be run from upper memory. All other drivers and TSRs have been loaded in upper memory, and there's still quite a bit of space left up there.

MEMMAKER's Changes

A typical CONFIG.SYS after being modified by MEMMAKER looks something like the following:

```
DEVICE=C:\DOS\HIMEM.SYS
DOS=HIGH
DEVICE=C:\DOS\EMM386.EXE NOEMS
BUFFERS=15,0
FILES=50
DOS=UMB
DEVICEHIGH /L:1,12048 =C:\DOS\SETVER.EXE
STACKS=9,256
DEVICEHIGH /L:1,9072 =C:\DOS\ANSI.SYS
SHELL=C:\DOS\COMMAND.COM C:\DOS\ /E:1024 /p
```

Loading HIMEM and EMM386

MEMMAKER inserted commands in CONFIG.SYS to load HIMEM and EMM386. If the HIMEM command already exists in the file, MEMMAKER doesn't change it, although MEMMAKER may move the HIMEM command to a better position. The EMM386 command in this example has a NOEMS ("no expanded memory") switch to request upper memory support without expanded memory support. If you tell MEMMAKER that you need expanded memory, it uses the RAM switch instead of NOEMS to request both types of support.

> If you specify neither RAM nor NOEMS, EMM386 provides expanded memory support but not upper memory support, as explained in Chapter 30.

The DOS Command

Notice that two DOS commands are in the file. The DOS=HIGH command loads DOS into the HMA, as explained in Chapter 30. MEMMAKER deals only with upper memory and does not insert DOS=HIGH in CONFIG.SYS. You must put in the command there yourself, before or after running MEMMAKER.

The DOS=UMB command makes the upper memory blocks available to DOS. This command must come after the command that loads EMM386. MEMMAKER inserts this command in CONFIG.SYS for you.

The DEVICEHIGH Commands

MEMMAKER converts all other DEVICE commands into DEVICEHIGH commands to load device drivers into upper memory blocks. The /L switch tell DOS exactly where to load the programs in upper memory to make the best use of the available space.

The AUTOEXEC.BAT File

After you run MEMMAKER, your AUTOEXEC.BAT file may resemble the following:

```
PATH C:\DOS;C:\WINWORD;C:\NDW;C:\WINDOWS;C:\HSG
CD MOUSE
LH /L:1,20304 MOUSE BON
CD \HSG
LH /L:1,23744 GRAB
CD \
PROMPT $P$G
SET TEMP=C:\WINDOWS\TEMP
LH /L:1,20560 GRAPHICS LASERJET /R
LH /L:0;1,42432 /S SMARTDRV
```

MEMMAKER converts every command that loads a TSR into an LH (Loadhigh) command, which loads the TSR into upper memory. The /L and /S switches control exactly where the program is loaded.

If you load more TSRs from the command prompt as you continue with your work, you can load them into upper memory by inserting LH in front of their usual commands. For example, suppose that you decide to use VSAFE. Instead of entering the word VSAFE, enter the following command to load VSAFE into upper memory:

LH VSAFE

Don't try to use the /L or /S switches; they're for MEMMAKER's use.

You can do the same with DOSKEY, PRINT, and any other TSR. If DOS can't find room for the TSR in upper memory, it loads it into conventional memory without warning.

Undoing MEMMAKER

If you have programs that no longer work after letting MEMMAKER reconfigure your system, you can return to your former configuration with this command:

MEMMAKER   /UNDO

You still can make use of upper memory by following these steps:

1. Insert commands to load HIMEM and EMM386 in CONFIG.SYS. (Use the NOEMS switch on the EMM386 command if you don't want expanded memory support; otherwise, use the RAM switch.)

2. Insert the DOS=UMB command in EMM386.

3. Change all other DEVICE commands into DEVICEHIGH commands. (Don't try to use the /L or /S switch.)

4. In AUTOEXEC.BAT, insert LH in front of any command that loads a TSR. (Don't try to use the /L or /S switch.)

For the Future

The EMM386 command includes a number of parameters and switches to control such things as the minimum and maximum amounts of expanded memory. If the default EMM386 setup does not provide your system with enough expanded memory, see EMM386.EXE in the Appendix for explanation of parameters and switches you can use.

If you need more upper memory space than MEMMAKER creates for you in the express setup, an advanced book should explain how to do a custom setup.

Caching the Drives

32

Introduction

Other than upgrading your hardware, the single best thing you can do to speed up your system is to cache your drives.

About Caching

A disk cache (pronounced "cash") is a memory area reserved for holding data that DOS reads from or writes to a disk. The buffers that you learn about in Chapter 22 provide a simple form of caching. SmartDrive 4.1, the disk-caching program provided with DOS 6, does more sophisticated caching than buffers do.

> SmartDrive requires extended memory. You may want to skip to Chapter 33 if you don't have extended memory.

Moving data around in memory is much faster than accessing a disk drive. Disk caching may be the best way to improve your system's performance because it dramatically reduces the number of disk accesses.

SmartDrive positions itself between DOS and your disk drives (see fig. 32.1) so that it can process read and write requests from DOS. When DOS tries to read data from a disk, SmartDrive intervenes. If the desired data is already in the cache, SmartDrive passes the data to DOS from the cache, saving the time it would normally take to read from the disk. If the desired data is not in the cache, DOS goes ahead and gets it from the disk. SmartDrive copies the data into its cache to make it available for future reads and writes. If the cache is full, the new data replaces some existing data. One of the things that makes SmartDrive so smart is that it knows how to identify and replace the least used data in its cache.

Figure 32.1.
SmartDrive, DOS,
and your drives.

SmartDrive also can do write caching. When DOS tries to write data to a disk, SmartDrive intervenes and writes it in the cache instead, replacing some existing cache data if necessary. SmartDrive does not necessarily pass the written data to the disk immediately. It holds the write-cached data until you are not typing, printing, or accessing a disk. During a pause in this kind of activity, SmartDrive writes out cached data, writing the oldest portions first. This *delayed writing* improves system performance by giving priority to reading and processing; writing takes place when the system isn't busy.

SmartDrive writes from the cache to the disk at four other times:

- When data has been delayed for five seconds.

- When SmartDrive needs room in the cache for new data.

- When you press Ctrl-Alt-Del. (SmartDrive immediately writes all delayed data before the system reboots.)

- When you enter the command SMARTDRV /C. (The /C switch forces SmartDrive to write all delayed data.)

Although some people worry that delayed writes could cause them to lose data, delayed writes to a hard disk probably will not cause any problems. If your system goes down, you are more likely to lose data by not saving your work often enough than because of delayed writes. Some programs, however, update several records from one transaction. An accounts receivable program, for example, may update a customer record, invoice due record, and accounting information when you enter a payment. If a system goes down with delayed writes pending for this kind of application, problems may occur with unsynchronized records. If you use a transaction-oriented program, you may want to turn off write-caching.

You also don't want to use delayed write-caching with a floppy drive. Losing data by changing the disk before DOS writes the delayed data is easy to do.

Caches and Buffers

Even with a caching program, DOS needs to keep some information in its buffers. Because DOS looks through all the buffers before going to SmartDrive, you will save time if you drastically reduce the number of buffers in a cached system. If you use SmartDrive, change your CONFIG.SYS Buffers command to use only 10 to 15 buffers.

Starting SmartDrive

To start SmartDrive, enter the following command:

`SMARTDRV`

You may need to include a path if SMARTDRV isn't in the current directory or the search path. For example, if you load SmartDrive from AUTOEXEC.BAT and the SmartDrive command precedes the PATH command, you have to include a path. If, like most people, you keep your DOS 6 programs in C:\DOS, you can enter the following:

`C:\DOS\SMARTDRV`

> You must load an extended memory manager such as HIMEM.SYS before you start SmartDrive.

The exact response you get depends on your system configuration. A typical response looks like this:

```
Microsoft SMARTDrive Disk Cache version 4.1
Copyright 1991,1993 Microsoft Corp.
Cache size: 1,048,576 bytes
Cache size while running Windows: 262,144 bytes
            Disk Caching Status
drive   read cache   write cache   buffering
- - - - - - - - - - - - - - - - - - - - - - - - - - - - - - - - -
A:      yes          no            no
B:      yes          no            no
C:      yes          yes           no
For help, type "Smartdrv /?".
```

The cache sizes are default values that depend on the amount of extended memory in your system. The values shown here are for a system with 1M to 2M of extended memory available when SmartDrive is loaded. SmartDrive gives up some extended memory when Windows starts because Windows works best when it has at least 2M of extended memory available.

By default, floppy drives are read cached but not write cached; whereas hard drives are both read cached and write cached. Other types of drives, such as RAM, CD-ROM, network, and compressed drives, are not cached.

In Chapter 22, you saw how to use a DEVICE command to install SmartDrive's double-buffering feature. This slower method of read and write caching is needed by some disk drives. When SmartDrive loads, it evaluates each drive to see whether it requires double-buffering. You need to install double-buffering if the SmartDrive messages show **yes** or - on any line in the buffering column. To install double-buffering, put the following command in CONFIG.SYS:

```
DEVICE=C:\DOS\SMARTDRV.EXE /DOUBLE_BUFFER
```

Changing Drives

In the SmartDrive command, you can choose the type of caching for each drive instead of settling for the defaults. Adding a *drive* parameter to the SmartDrive command turns on read caching, but not write caching, for the indicated drive. *Drive+* turns on both read and write caching for that drive. *Drive-* turns off all caching for the drive. You can't turn on write caching without read caching.

Suppose that you have two floppy drives (A and B) and three hard drives (C, D, and E). If you want drives B and C to be read-cached only, drives A and E to have read and write caching, and drive D to have no caching, you would use the following command to start SmartDrive:

```
C:\DOS\SMARTDRV A+ B C D- E+
```

You get a response similar to the following:

```
Microsoft SMARTDrive Disk Cache version 4.1
Copyright 1991,1993 Microsoft Corp.
Cache size: 1,048,576 bytes
Cache size while running Windows: 262,144 bytes
            Disk Caching Status
drive   read cache   write cache   buffering
- - - - - - - - - - - - - - - - - - - - - - - - - - - - - - - -
A:        yes           yes          no
B:        yes           no           no
```

```
C:      yes         no          no
D:      no          no          no
E:      yes         yes         no
For help, type "Smartdrv /?".
```

Because you want default caching for drives B and E, you could start SmartDrive with the following command:

```
C:\DOS\SMARTDRV A+ C D-
```

Changing Types

After SmartDrive is loaded, you can use the SmartDrive command to change the type of caching for a drive. To turn off all caching for drive A, for example, enter the following:

```
SMARTDRV A-
```

This command changes caching for drive A only; other drives are not affected. To change drives C and D so that they are read cached but not write cached and leave other drives unchanged, enter the following command:

```
SMARTDRV C D
```

SmartDrive Results

Use the SmartDrive command with the /S (for "status") switch to see the caching status of your drives:

```
SMARTDRV /S
```

The response may appear as follows:

```
Microsoft SMARTDrive Disk Cache version 4.1
Copyright 1991,1993 Microsoft Corp.
Room for 128 elements of 8,192 bytes each
There have been 5,727 cache hits
        and 3,111 cache misses
Cache size: 1,048,576 bytes
```

```
Cache size while running Windows: 262,144 bytes
            Disk Caching Status
drive   read cache   write cache   buffering
- - - - - - - - - - - - - - - - - - - - - - - - - - - - - - - - - - -
A:      yes           no            no
B:      yes           no            no
C:      yes           yes           no
For help, type "Smartdrv /?".
```

As you see, SmartDrive tells you not only the caching setup but also the latest caching statistics. A *hit* means that SmartDrive found data in the cache and avoided a disk access; a *miss* is the other way around. A hit ratio of 5,700 to 3,100 is pretty good; SmartDrive has prevented a majority of this system's disk accesses so far. Your hit ratio could reach 9 to 1 or higher, depending on the kind of processing you're doing.

Before Shutting Down

As you have seen earlier, the /C switch forces SmartDrive to write out any write-cached data. Just enter the following command:

SMARTDRV /C

Always use this command before you park your heads and turn off your system. If you are write caching a floppy drive, use it before you remove a disk.

Sometimes your system hangs up, and you can't enter the SMARTDRV /C command. If you can reboot with Ctrl-Alt-Del, you have no problem. SmartDrive senses this key combination and writes out all data immediately. If you can't reboot with Ctrl-Alt-Del, you have to use a reset button or turn off the system. When that happens, delayed data is lost.

Windows and SmartDrive

DOS and Windows come with a SMARTDRV.EXE file. If you have Windows 3.1 or later, compare the date/time stamp on SMARTDRV.EXE in your Windows directory with that of the same file in your DOS directory. Use the latest version of SmartDrive.

Do not start SmartDrive when Windows is running; do not start it from the Windows' File Manager, the Program Manager, or a DOS prompt provided by Windows. Exit Windows if you want to start SmartDrive. When SmartDrive is running, you can safely start Windows.

For the Future

The SmartDrive command includes parameters and switches to control such factors as the size of the cache and whether or not SmartDrive displays messages. When you are ready to explore SmartDrive further, look it up in the Command Reference at the back of this book.

RAM Drives

33

Introduction

If you have some memory to spare, you can speed up your system by creating a RAM drive. However, this chapter explains why you may not want to do that.

About RAM Drives

I f you create a RAM drive in memory every time you boot and copy the programs and files that you use most often into that drive, those programs will run much faster because they aren't slowed down by the drive hardware. However, you also can give yourself some major headaches. First, you have to remember to copy any modified data from the RAM drive to a real drive before shutting down. Second, should your system go down, you would lose any modified data that was not saved on a real drive.

Therefore, most people don't keep any important data on a RAM drive. The most common use of a RAM drive is to hold the temporary files created by DOS, DOS Shell, Windows, and applications such as Microsoft Word. Windows writes and deletes numerous temporary files, and letting it use a RAM drive can make a significant difference in system performance.

An additional advantage to keeping temporary files on a RAM drive is that when the system goes down, the temporary files disappear. When you keep them on a hard drive, they get abandoned, and you have to delete them manually.

Byte-for-byte, you get better performance improvement out of a SmartDrive cache than a RAM drive. Don't create a RAM drive in extended memory unless you have enough room to satisfy all other program needs and to let SmartDrive have a cache of at least 2M.

You also can create a RAM drive in conventional or expanded memory. You have only one reason to create a RAM drive in conventional memory: if you have no hard drives, you may want to use a small RAM drive to hold enough data to avoid floppy drive accesses. Otherwise, a RAM drive in conventional memory would do more harm than good.

If you have real expanded memory—not the simulated type supplied by Emm386— that isn't being used for any other purpose, it makes a perfect RAM drive. The examples in this chapter assume that you are creating a RAM drive in expanded memory.

How To Set Up
a RAM Drive

You set up a RAM drive by loading the RAMDRIVE.SYS driver from CONFIG.SYS.
To use all default settings, you don't have to include any parameters or switches in
the command. However, not including them would create the RAM drive in conventional memory. Use /A to place the RAM drive in expanded memory or /E to
place it in extended memory. The following command creates a RAM drive with
default settings in expanded memory:

```
DEVICE=C:\DOS\RAMDRIVE.SYS /A
```

The command that loads your expanded memory manager must precede
this command in CONFIG.SYS.

The default RAM drive is 64K, has 512-byte sectors, and has 64 entries in the root
directory. A 64K RAM drive is fine for some applications, such as Microsoft Word
for DOS, but it doesn't do you much good with Windows. Windows needs at least
2M for its temporary files; if 2M is not available, Windows Print Manager mixes up
the data in your print jobs.

You can include a *size* parameter on the RAMDRIVE.SYS command to control the
size of the RAM drive. Specify the amount in kilobytes, from 4 to 32767 (32M).
The following command sets up a 2M RAM drive in expanded memory. It will have
512-byte sectors and 64 entries in the root directory:

```
DEVICE=C:\DOS\RAMDRIVE.SYS 2048 /A
```

Even though the RAM drive is created in expanded memory, the RAMDRIVE
program is loaded into conventional memory, taking up about 5K. If your system is
set up to use UMBs, you can load it into upper memory by using DEVICEHIGH
instead of Device.

You can add the basic DEVICE command to CONFIG.SYS and then run
MEMMAKER to turn it into a DEVICEHIGH command.

Using the RAM Drive

Ordinarily, you use a RAM drive just like any other drive. A RAM drive shows up
in drive lists such as those for DOS Shell, MSAV, and BACKUP. Figure 33.1 shows
how the RAM drive looks on the Shell screen. You can assign a volume label to the
drive with LABEL, copy or move files to and from the drive, delete files from the
drive, and so on. DoubleSpace will even compress it.

Figure 33.1.
A RAM drive
in the Shell.

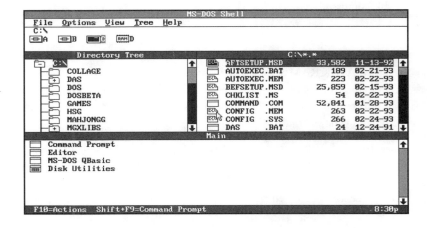

However, you shouldn't do the following to a RAM drive:

- Don't format it; it's ready to go as soon as it's created.

- Don't cache it; because it is in memory, a RAM drive already is running at
  maximum speed. Caching would actually slow it down.

- Don't scan it for viruses; it will be scanned when memory is scanned.

- Don't defragment a RAM drive; fragmentation is not much of a problem when no read-write heads are involved.

- Don't use DISKCOPY and DISKCOMP with a RAM drive; they pertain to floppy disks only.

- Don't need to protect it with Delete Sentry or deletion-tracking if you are using it solely for temporary files.

Naming the RAM Drive

After you insert the RAMDRIVE.SYS command in CONFIG.SYS, reboot and watch for a message that tells you the name of your new drive. The message looks something like the following:

```
Microsoft RAMDrive version 3.07 virtual disk D:

    Disk size: 64k
    Sector size: 512 bytes
    Allocation unit: 1 sectors
    Directory entries: 64
```

If you miss the message, you can start up DOS Shell to find out the name of the drive. Usually, the drive receives the next name after your hard drive(s), but several DOS facilities, including DoubleSpace, may take that name.

Directing Temporary Files to a RAM Drive

DOS and Windows use a variable named TEMP to tell them where to place their temporary files. You set the TEMP variable with a SET command, as follows:

```
SET TEMP=D:\
```

This command establishes the root directory of drive D as the place to write temporary files. You would place this command in AUTOEXEC.BAT to establish the RAM drive as the location for temporary files. You do not need to create subdirectories on the RAM drive.

413

For the Future

If you're interested in learning how to control the sector size, allocation unit size, and the number of entries in the root directory, look up RAMDRIVE.SYS in the Appendix.

Defragmenter

34

Introduction

About once a month or so, you should run DEFRAG to optimize your hard drives for faster access times.

About File Fragmentation

A *cluster*, or allocation unit, is the smallest unit that DOS uses for storing a file. Suppose that you have a file, UPTIME.DAT, that is 2,500 bytes. If your disk has 512 byte clusters, a 2,500 byte file requires five clusters. DOS may not store UPTIME.DAT in five contiguous (neighboring) clusters.

When you begin to use a disk, DOS writes files one after the other, each one in contiguous clusters. Deletions, however, leave "holes" in this structure—holes in which DOS can store newly written files. As the disk fills up, DOS begins to have trouble finding places to write unfragmented files; eventually it must start fragmenting them, storing data wherever a free cluster exists. Fragmentation also occurs when you expand a file so that it needs another cluster, and the next consecutive cluster is already in use by another file. DOS must search forward to find the next available cluster, and a new fragment is born. As you delete, write, and modify files on the disk, you are likely to develop more and more fragmented files.

What Fragmentation Does to Your System

DOS has no problem reading a fragmented file. The file allocation table (FAT) guides it to each cluster of the file, even if they aren't contiguous. When you access a fragmented file, however, the drive's read/write heads have to move several times to locate all the clusters of the file; once moved, they have to wait for the correct sector to roll around. Moving the read-write heads is the slowest part of accessing the drive and greatly increases the time it takes to read the file. If your hard drive has many fragmented files, your entire system suffers.

Optimizing Your Drives

You can reduce or eliminate fragmentation from a drive by using a disk optimizing program such as DOS 6's DEFRAG. An optimizer reduces fragmentation in two ways:

416

- It moves clusters around as needed to bring each file's clusters together.

- It moves clusters around so that all empty clusters are at the end of the disk. This practice creates a solid block of used clusters followed by a solid block of unused ones. When DOS adds new files to the disk, it is more likely to be able to write them in contiguous clusters. (But DOS still has problems expanding a file.)

DEFRAG can't move or rewrite system and hidden files. These files may be copy-protected program files that must not be moved after you install the program. Others are system files, such as the DOS system files, that must occupy a particular position on the disk.

When you optimize a disk with DEFRAG, you can choose to defragment files only or to reorganize empty space. Occasionally, the two goals are incompatible. When you defragment files, DEFRAG may have to leave holes around unmovable files. When you reorganize the empty space, DEFRAG may fragment a file to fit into one of these new holes. A little file fragmentation, however, will not cause much performance degradation. The purpose of defragmenting is to eliminate huge amounts of fragmentation.

You can't use DEFRAG on network or INTERLNK drives.

Using DEFRAG

You should do a few things before running DEFRAG:

1. Exit Windows or DOS Shell.

Never run DEFRAG with files open.

2. Free up as much space as possible by deleting any unneeded files.

3. If you use deletion-tracking, delete PCTRACKR.DEL from the root directory of the drive. (It will be invalid after DEFRAG moves all the clusters around.) You need to remove its hidden attribute first.

Deleting a hidden file by using DOS Shell is easy, but be sure to exit the Shell before running DEFRAG.

4. Remove any TSRs you don't absolutely need for the basic functioning of your system. Be particularly careful to disable any TSR that may write to the disk, such as one scheduled to update a file automatically. Follow these steps to remove TSRs:

   a. Open CONFIG.SYS in an ASCII editor.

   b. Insert **REM** in front of every command you want to disable.

   c. Save CONFIG.SYS.

   d. Do the same thing for AUTOEXEC.BAT.

   e. Reboot.

   f. After running DEFRAG, remove the REMs you inserted and reboot to restore your usual TSRs.

If any program writes to the disk while DEFRAG is reorganizing the clusters, some files could be damaged beyond repair.

5. Run CHKDSK /F to eliminate lost clusters. If CHKDSK reports any cross-linked files, clear them up before running DEFRAG.

Starting DEFRAG

Start DEFRAG with the following command at the primary command prompt:

```
DEFRAG  /B
```

The /B switch tells DEFRAG to reboot the system when it finishes. Some functions may be running, usually as TSRs, that maintain file location information. DEFRAG's work invalidates old location information, and if such a program tries to access the disk using out-of-date information, several files could be damaged. Rebooting clears out any buffers maintained by such programs and forces them to reread the drive.

The first thing DEFRAG does is test your system memory to make sure that it can move data around at high speeds reliably. If your system fails this test, you can't use DEFRAG until you get it fixed.

Choosing a Drive

Figure 34.1 shows the first dialog box you see after starting DEFRAG. This dialog box enables you to choose the drive you want to optimize.

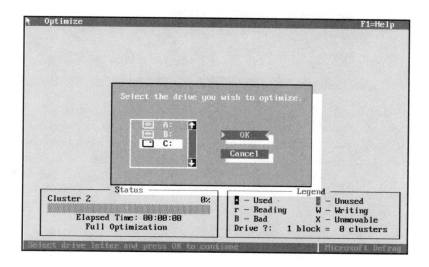

Figure 34.1.
Drive Selection
dialog box.

The Status and Legend boxes in the lower part of the screen have no meaning at this point. The middle of the screen is where the action takes place.

You can press F1 to get help information at any time in DEFRAG.

419

Choosing an Optimization Method

DEFRAG analyzes the drive you choose and recommends an optimization method (see fig. 34.2). DEFRAG may recommend no optimization, unfragment files only, or full optimization (defragment files and consolidate empty space).

Figure 34.2.
Recommendation
dialog box.

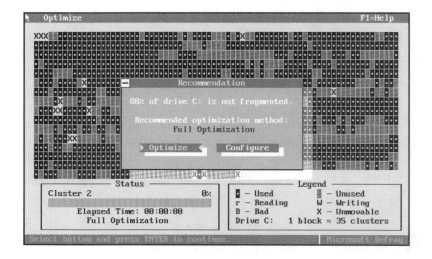

The screen background is a map of the drive. The Legend box in the lower right corner tells you how to interpret the map. In Figure 34.2, each map block represents 35 clusters. This figure varies depending on the size of the drive, because the map always represents the entire drive. After DEFRAG begins optimizing, it animates the map to show what is happening. You see blocks being read (indicated by an "r") and written (indicated by a "W"), and you see the used and unused blocks move around in the map. (The bad and unmovable blocks don't move.)

If a block contains a mixture of cluster types, DEFRAG uses the symbol with the highest priority. From high to low, the priorities are bad, unmovable, used, unused. For example, if a block contains some unmovable blocks and some unused blocks, its symbol will be X (for unmovable).

If you choose to follow the recommendation, press the Optimize button. To do anything else, such as choose a different method, choose a different drive, or exit without optimizing the selected drive, press the Configure button. If you press Configure, DEFRAG pulls down the Optimize menu, which is described later in this chapter.

If no optimization is recommended, you see an OK button instead of the Optimize and Configure buttons. When you press OK, DEFRAG pulls down the Optimize menu.

Optimization Progress

Suppose that you choose to accept the recommendation, and DEFRAG begins optimizing. You can watch DEFRAG's progress on the map and in the Status box. Figure 34.3 shows what the screen looks like during an optimization. The darkened blocks in the first and second rows are finished. You can see the "r" near the right end of the second row; DEFRAG is currently reading that block.

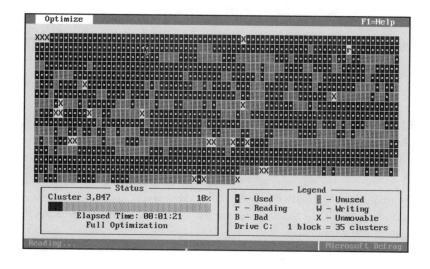

Figure 34.3.
Optimization
progress screen.

The Status box in the example shows that 10 percent of the drive has been defragmented so far, up through cluster 3,847, and 1 minute 21 seconds have elapsed. Because 10 percent of the job is done, you can predict that it will take another 10 minutes or so — enough time to take a break (unless you get hypnotized by the moving blocks). The optimization method appears at the bottom of the Status box.

When the optimization is done, the dialog box shown in figure 34.4 opens. You can choose what you want to do next— optimize another drive, go to the Optimize menu, or exit from DEFRAG.

Figure 34.4.
Optimization
Complete
dialog box.

The Optimize Menu

Figure 34.5 shows the Optimize menu. Select Drive to reopen the Drive Selection dialog box (refer back to fig. 34.1). DEFRAG analyzes whatever drive you choose and displays a recommendation for that drive.

If you don't want to use the current optimization method shown in the status box, choose Optimization Method to open the dialog box shown in figure 34.6. After you have made your choice, the Optimize menu returns. Choose Begin Optimization to start optimizing the drive.

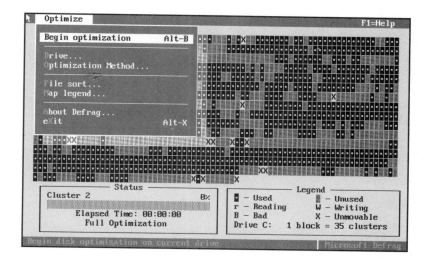

Figure 34.5.
Optimize menu.

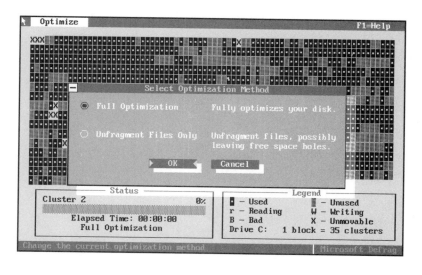

Figure 34.6.
Select Optimization Method dialog box.

For the Future

You can control most of the DEFRAG options with switches on the DEFRAG command so that you don't have to go through the menus and dialog boxes. In fact, some command-line options aren't available in the DEFRAG dialog boxes, such as the /B switch that you already have seen and a /V switch to verify the rewritten clusters. You also can ask DEFRAG to sort directory entries, although this practice doesn't make any difference in the speed or layout of the drive. See DEFRAG in the Command Reference at the back of the book for more details on these features.

DoubleSpace

35

Introduction

For many people, the most appealing feature of DOS 6 is DoubleSpace, which can double the amount of data you can store on your hard drive.

About Data Compression

Sooner or later, everyone runs short of hard drive space. Buying a new disk is expensive, and moving data from the old to the new is time-consuming. If your drive is running short on space but can be expected to last a while longer—three to five years is the average life span of a hard drive—the answer may be to compress its data. A good disk-compression program usually can double the amount of data you can store on a drive. DOS 6 includes such a program—DoubleSpace.

Data compression schemes take advantage of the fact that most files include a lot of repetition. DoubleSpace stores a string of bytes only the first time it appears in a file. It replaces other appearances of that string with a code pointing to the first occurrence. For example, if the first sentence in this paragraph were the first sentence in a file, DoubleSpace would replace each of the bracketed strings with a code pointing to an identical string earlier in the sentence:

```
Data compression schemes [ta]ke advan[ta]ge of t[he] fact[th]
[at] most fil[es] includ[e ][a ]lot[ of ] repeti[ti][on].
```

From this short example, you can see that as you continue on in a file, more strings and longer strings can be replaced with codes. When DOS needs to read the file, DoubleSpace decompresses it, replacing each code with the appropriate string of characters. This same data compression scheme is used by DOS 6's backup programs.

DoubleSpace also eliminates a lot of wasted space by allocating file space in sectors instead of clusters. A small file on a hard disk uses up only 512 bytes instead of 2,048 or more. This savings alone can be 1.5K for each of the small files on a disk.

The DoubleSpace Drive

A DoubleSpace drive is a not really a drive. It actually is a file, called a *Compressed Volume File* (CVF), residing on a real drive, known as the *host* drive. The CVF is a system, hidden, and read-only file in the root directory of the host drive. Although the CVF usually takes up most of the host drive, a little space is reserved for the host.

The CVF and the host drive each have their own drive letters, assigned by DoubleSpace. Suppose that after you compress drive C, DoubleSpace assigns the letter

C to the CVF and K to the host drive. Any time you write a file to drive C, DoubleSpace compresses the file and puts it into the CVF. When you read a file from drive C, DoubleSpace decompresses it before passing it to DOS. You can still read and write uncompressed files to any free space left on drive K.

Some files can't be compressed, and DoubleSpace stores them on the host drive. These include the Windows swap file, IO.SYS, MSDOS.SYS, DBLSPACE.BIN, and some DoubleSpace files. These files usually are system or hidden files, so your host drive looks empty if you use a DIR command on it. They are all important files, however; don't delete any of them.

DoubleSpace has many functions, but most people need to use only a few of them. In this chapter, you learn to compress one or more drives, get information about compressed drives, and run DoubleSpace's CHKDSK function.

Compressing an Existing Drive

When you compress an existing drive with DoubleSpace, it creates the CVF on the host, compresses all or most of the files on the drive, and stores them in the CVF. The CVF is always named DBLSPACE.000. Then DoubleSpace assigns the host's original drive letter to the CVF and a new letter to the host. This drive assignment process, called *mounting* the DoubleSpace drive, makes the data in the CVF available through its original drive letter. Therefore, you don't have to change the commands and path statements that you're used to using.

DoubleSpace must remount the compressed drive(s) every time you boot or reboot. You see messages from DoubleSpace during the boot process. Sometimes, after you use a DoubleSpace function like CHKDSK, you see a message saying that DoubleSpace is remounting the drive.

Setting Up DoubleSpace

DoubleSpace's setup includes the following tasks:

- Set up the core program, DBLSPACE.BIN, to be loaded every time you boot.

- Install DoubleSpace's system files in the root directory of your boot drive (regardless of which drive is being compressed).

- Install a command in CONFIG.SYS to position the core program properly in memory.

All this takes place automatically the first time you compress a drive on your hard disk. You can't set up DoubleSpace without compressing at least one hard drive.

> Don't compress a drive with DoubleSpace just to see if you like it. No simple procedure is available for removing DoubleSpace after you install it.

Don't install DoubleSpace if you're already using some other type of data compression system. You may need to uninstall the other product from your system first if you want to convert to DoubleSpace. (DoubleSpace can, however, convert Stacker compressed drives to run with DoubleSpace.)

You also should back up the drive you're going to compress. The chances of losing data during compression are small, but it's better to be safe than sorry. Even if you lose power while compressing a drive, DoubleSpace is able to take up where it left off when the system reboots. You also should run CHKDSK on the drive and fix any errors CHKDSK finds by running CHKDSK/F before compressing the drive.

Be prepared for the initial compression to take quite a bit of time. It takes about one minute per megabyte to compress a hard drive.

Getting Started

Before you start DoubleSpace to compress a hard drive, stop any other program that is running. Exit from Windows or DOS Shell. If you normally use a network, connect to the network and its drives. Because DoubleSpace is going to assign a new drive letter to the host drive, it needs to know about any drive letters you usually use.

To start the setup procedure, enter the following command:

`DBLSPACE`

DoubleSpace greets you with a `Welcome` screen and then displays the Setup selection screen (see fig. 35.1). Express setup does most of the work for you, but it always compresses drive C. In this chapter, you see how to use the Custom setup to compress the data on a different drive instead.

```
Microsoft DoubleSpace Setup

      There are two ways to run Setup:

      Use Express Setup if you want DoubleSpace Setup to compress
      drive C and determine the compression settings for you. This
      is the easiest way to install DoubleSpace.

      Use Custom Setup if you are an experienced user and want to
      specify the compression settings and drive configuration
      yourself.

      ┌─────────────────────────────────────────────────────────┐
      │ Express Setup (recommended)                             │
      │ Custom Setup                                            │
      └─────────────────────────────────────────────────────────┘

      To accept the selection, press ENTER.

      To change the selection, press the UP or DOWN ARROW key
      until the item you want is selected, and then press ENTER.

 ENTER=Continue  F1=Help  F3=Exit
```

Figure 35.1.
Setup Selection screen.

When you choose Custom setup, the screen in figure 35.2 appears. Choose the first option, `Compress an existing drive`. The other option creates an empty CVF on a drive; this option is not covered in this chapter, but you can read more about it in the Command Reference.

Figure 35.2.
Compressing an existing drive.

```
Microsoft DoubleSpace Setup
═══════════════════════════

  DoubleSpace provides two ways to create more disk space:

  To compress the files on an existing drive so that the drive
  has more free space, choose 'Compress an existing drive.'
  This method provides the most free space, and is
  particularly useful if the drive is getting full.

  To convert the free space on an existing drive into a new
  compressed drive, choose 'Create an empty compressed drive.'
  You might want to use this method if the drive has a lot of
  free space.

  ┌──────────────────────────────────────────────────────────┐
  │ Compress an existing drive                                 │
  │ Create a new empty compressed drive                        │
  └──────────────────────────────────────────────────────────┘

  To change the selection, press the UP or DOWN ARROW key
  until the item you want is selected, and then press ENTER.

 ENTER=Continue  F1=Help  F3=Exit  ESC=Previous screen
```

Selecting a Drive

The screen in figure 35.3 enables you to choose the drive you want to compress. The drives listed are the only ones you can compress. You may wonder why your other drives are not on the list. You can't compress network drives or CD-ROM drives. You can't compress floppy drives when setting up DoubleSpace, although you can do that later. You can't compress drives that are too full. DoubleSpace needs a minimum of 1.2M of free space to compress the boot drive; other drives must have at least about 665K free.

> To compress a drive that doesn't have enough free space, move some of the files to another drive or a floppy disk temporarily. After compression, there will probably be enough free space on the compressed drive to move them back.

Figure 35.4 shows the screen that appears next. By default, DoubleSpace keeps 2M of uncompressed space on the host drive to hold files that can't be compressed. You can follow the directions on the screen to request more or less uncompressed space. You also can change the drive letter that DoubleSpace assigns to the host drive. However, if you don't have a strong reason to do otherwise, you should accept the settings that DoubleSpace suggests for both parameters.

```
Microsoft DoubleSpace Setup
──────────────────────────

      Select the drive you want to compress:


                    Current          Projected
          Drive     Free Space       Free Space

           C        15.6 MB          64.2 MB
           D        12.6 MB          32.5 MB
           E        16.4 MB          58.1 MB
           F         2.0 MB           4.0 MB


      To accept the current selection, press ENTER.

      To select a different drive, press the UP ARROW or DOWN
      ARROW key until the drive you want is selected, and then
      press ENTER. If there are more drives than fit in the
      window, you can scroll the list by pressing the UP ARROW
      DOWN ARROW, PAGE UP, or PAGE DOWN key.

ENTER=Continue  F1=Help  F3=Exit  ESC=Previous screen
```

Figure 35.3.
*Selecting a drive
to compress.*

```
Microsoft DoubleSpace Setup
──────────────────────────

      DoubleSpace will compress drive D to create free space on
      it.

      Certain files, such as the Windows permanent swap file, must
      remain uncompressed. When DoubleSpace compresses drive D, it
      also creates a new uncompressed drive to contain files from
      drive D that must remain uncompressed. DoubleSpace creates
      the new uncompressed drive using the following settings:


      Free space on new uncompressed drive:    2.00 MB
      Drive letter of new uncompressed drive:  K:

                                            Continue

      To accept the current settings, press ENTER.
      To change a setting, press the UP or DOWN ARROW key to
      select it. Then, press ENTER to see alternatives.

ENTER=Continue  F1=Help  F3=Exit  ESC=Previous screen
```

Figure 35.4.
*Compression
settings.*

Although this screen mentions a new drive, it really is the original host drive with a new drive letter.

The next screen gives you a last chance to back out. If you choose to continue, DoubleSpace begins compressing the selected drive.

If you have a disk in drive A, DoubleSpace asks you to remove it so that
DoubleSpace can reboot your system as necessary.

During Compression

As DoubleSpace compresses your drive, it displays a number of messages and activity screens. All you can do is watch (or go away). Even turning off the power to your computer doesn't cancel the compression process. When you turn the power back on, DoubleSpace takes up where it left off.

First, DoubleSpace runs CHKDSK on your drive. Then it begins the actual compression. It keeps you informed about the progress of the compression—what file is currently being compressed, the time left and estimated finish time, the percentage of the drive not yet compressed, and so on.

After compression is done, DoubleSpace runs its own DEFRAG function on the compressed drive and adjusts the size of the CVF. When finished, DoubleSpace displays a final screen that contrasts the original free space on the drive and the new amount; it also shows you the compression ratio and the time that it took to compress the drive. After you have read the screen, press Enter, and DoubleSpace will reboot your computer again. Setup is now complete, and your new compressed drive is ready to be used.

A 2:1 compression ratio means that, for every 2 bytes in the uncompressed
file, only 1 byte was needed in the compressed file.

Compressing Additional Drives

From now on, whenever you start DoubleSpace, you see a screen like the one in figure 35.5.

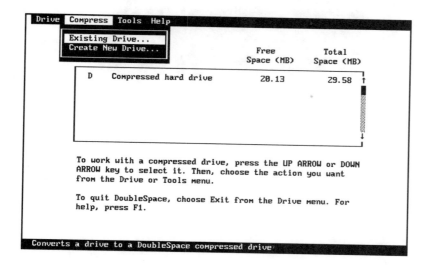

```
 Drive  Compress  Tools  Help

                                       Free          Total
        Drive  Description        Space (MB)    Space (MB)

         D    Compressed hard drive    20.13         29.58    ↑





     To work with a compressed drive, press the UP ARROW or DOWN
     ARROW key to select it. Then, choose the action you want
     from the Drive or Tools menu.

     To quit DoubleSpace, choose Exit from the Drive menu. For
     help, press F1.


 DoubleSpace  |  F1=Help  ALT=Menu Bar  ↓=Next Item  ↑=Previous Item
```

Figure 35.5.
Selecting a
compressed drive.

This screen lists all the compressed drives on your system and provides you with some pull-down menus for performing various DoubleSpace functions. To compress another drive, choose the Compress menu (see fig. 35.6).

```
 Drive  Compress  Tools  Help
     ┌──────────────────────┐
     │ Existing Drive...    │
     │ Create New Drive...  │          Free          Total
     └──────────────────────┘     Space (MB)    Space (MB)

         D    Compressed hard drive    20.13         29.58    ↑





     To work with a compressed drive, press the UP ARROW or DOWN
     ARROW key to select it. Then, choose the action you want
     from the Drive or Tools menu.

     To quit DoubleSpace, choose Exit from the Drive menu. For
     help, press F1.


 Converts a drive to a DoubleSpace compressed drive
```

Figure 35.6.
Compress menu.

Choose the Existing Drive option. From there on, the procedure is the same as the one you followed to compress the original drive.

433

Working with Compressed Drives

DoubleSpace's menus provide several commands for managing your compressed drives. You can, for example, check the directory and FAT structure and view statistical information about the compressed drive.

DoubleSpace's CHKDSK Function

You can check the structure of a compressed drive using DoubleSpace's Tools CHKDSK command (see fig. 35.7) much as DOS's CHKDSK program checks an uncompressed drive. Press Check to check the drive without fixing any errors or press Fix to check the drive and fix as many errors as possible.

Figure 35.7.
Chkdsk dialog box.

Getting Information

Choose Drive Info to display an information screen like the one shown in figure 35.8. Most of the information in this display is clear, but the free space figures need some explanation.

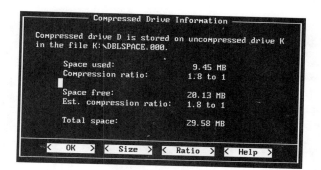

Figure 35.8.
Compressed Drive Information dialog box.

When an uncompressed drive has 2M of free space, there are 2,097,152 unused bytes on the drive, and you can add just that amount of data to it—no more. The situation isn't quite the same for a compressed drive. The dialog box in the example shows drive D with 20.13M of free space. DoubleSpace estimates that it can add to drive D files that total 20.13M when uncompressed. This estimate assumes that the new files will compress according to the estimated compression ratio for the drive (1.8 to 1 in the example), which is not always true. You may be able to add only 15M of program files to the drive because they usually can't achieve a 1.8:1 compression ratio. You also could add 50M or more of graphic files to the drive.

DIR and Compressed Drives

Other DOS programs coordinate with DoubleSpace when you use them on compressed drives. For example, if you use CHKDSK on a compressed drive, it reports the estimated amount of space available on the drive, not the actual. It also calls DoubleSpace's CHKDSK function to check the drive structure.

The DIR command also reports the estimated amount of space on the drive. You can add a /CH switch to the DIR command to display compression ratios for the files. The report looks something like the following:

```
Volume in drive D has no label
Volume Serial Number is 13EF-2218
Directory of D:\FRENCH

.             <DIR>      02-21-93   12:28p
..            <DIR>      02-21-93   12:28p
```

```
CHKLIST   MS           54 12-22-92   3:58p   4.0 to 1.0
FLASHCRD  BAS       30896 05-05-92  10:42a   2.3 to 1.0
FLASHCRD  EXE       91084 05-05-92  10:43a   1.3 to 1.0
VOCAB     BAS       31265 05-05-92  11:42a   2.2 to 1.0
VOCAB     EXE       91242 05-05-92  11:42a   1.3 to 1.0
WORK      BAS       13054 05-04-92  11:59a   1.6 to 1.0
                     1.4 to 1.0 average compression ratio
         8 file(s)       257595 bytes
                       21102592 bytes free
```

In this example, CHKLIST.MS has a 4:1 compression ratio; whereas the two EXE files have only a 1.3:1 compression ratio. The average compression ratio for this listing (not the entire drive) is 1.4:1.

DIR's /C switch also displays compression ratios, but the /CH switch produces more accurate results.

The file sizes shown in the listing are the uncompressed sizes so that you can see how much space a file would take if loaded in memory or moved or copied to an uncompressed drive.

For the Future

This discussion has scratched only the surface of DoubleSpace, just enough so that you can create and use a compressed volume. When you're ready for more, you may want to learn how to do the following:

- Create and use empty compressed volumes.
- Convert a Stacker volume to a DoubleSpace volume.
- Create and use compressed volumes on floppy disks.
- Defragment a compressed volume.
- Delete a compressed volume.

- Reformat a compressed volume.

- List information about all your drives, not just the compressed ones.

- Unmount and remount compressed volumes.

- Change the estimated compression ratio for a compressed drive.

- Change the size of a compressed drive.

All of these functions are explained under DBLSPACE in the Command Reference at the back of the book.

Putting It All Together

36

Introduction

HIMEM, SmartDrive, VSAFE, UNDELETE, BACKUP...How do you bring the DOS facilities together into a coordinated system to optimize your work and protect your data?

Setting Up a 286 System

A well-designed CONFIG.SYS for a 286 computer with two megabytes of extended memory might look something like the following:

```
DEVICE=C:\DOS\HIMEM.SYS
DOS=HIGH
DEVICE=C:\DOS\SETVER.EXE
DEVICE=C:\DOS\ANSI.SYS
BUFFERS=15
FILES=50
STACKS=9,256
```

The HIMEM.SYS driver is loaded first so that it can provide extended memory support to other programs. The second command loads DOS into the HMA before any other program tries to load in that location. The command that loads SETVER was installed by DOS's SETUP program; because DOS needs SETVER, you should not modify the SETVER command. The ANSI.SYS driver is installed because this system uses at least one program that requires that driver. (Your system probably also requires it, but if you haven't used it so far, you probably don't need it.)

The BUFFERS command requests only 15 buffers because this system uses SmartDrive, which is loaded from AUTOEXEC.BAT. The FILES command requests 50 file handles because this system uses a program that needs them. You may be able to get away with fewer file handles; retain whatever FILES command is in your current CONFIG.SYS. The STACKS command was installed by some program and should not be modified or deleted.

An AUTOEXEC.BAT file for the same system might contain at least the following commands. (Your AUTOEXEC.BAT file probably contains additional commands to set up TSRs and other features with which you want to work.)

```
@ECHO OFF
PATH C:\DOS;C:\WINDOWS;C:\
PROMPT $P$G
DOSKEY
SMARTDRV
UNDELETE /SC
VSAFE
MSAV
```

The DOSKEY command sets up the DOSKEY program to record command history. The SMARTDRV command loads the SmartDrive caching system with a 1M cache (by default) in extended memory and with default caching parameters. The UNDELETE command loads the Delete Sentry deletion protection system for drive C (and any other drives already on its list); the VSAFE command loads the VSAFE virus monitor; the MSAV command starts up the Microsoft Anti-Virus scanner so that the system is scanned for viruses right away. This command opens the first dialog box; the user must complete the scan.

Setting Up a 386 System

With a 386 or 486, you can use EMM386 to provide upper memory support and to load drivers, such as ANSI.SYS, and TSRs, such as VSAFE, into UMBs. Running MEMMAKER will set up EMM386 for you. A typical CONFIG.SYS adapted by MEMMAKER might look like the following:

```
DEVICE=C:\DOS\HIMEM.SYS
DEVICE=C:\DOS\EMM386.EXE NOEMS
BUFFERS=15,0
FILES=50
DOS=UMB
LASTDRIVE=E
FCBS=4,0
DOS=HIGH
STACKS=9,256
DEVICEHIGH /L:1,5888 =C:\DOS\RAMDRIVE.SYS 3092 /E
DEVICEHIGH /L:1,12048 =C:\DOS\SETVER.EXE
DEVICEHIGH /L:1,9072 =C:\DOS\ANSI.SYS
DEVICE=C:\DOS\DBLSPACE.SYS /MOVE
```

As with the 286 system, the first command loads the extended memory driver, HIMEM.SYS. The second command loads EMM386.EXE to provide upper memory support; the NOEMS switch suppresses its expanded memory facility. (Without the switch, EMM386.SYS converts 256K of extended memory into expanded memory.)

The DOS=UMB command makes the upper memory blocks available to DOS. The DOS=HIGH command loads DOS into the HMA.

The RAMDRIVE.SYS command creates a 3M RAM drive in extended memory. This RAM drive is used for DOS's and Windows' temporary files, as you can determine from the AUTOEXEC.BAT file. The command that loads DBLSPACE.SYS was inserted when DoubleSpace was installed.

The commands that load RAMDRIVE.SYS, SETVER.EXE, and ANSI.SYS have been modified by MEMMAKER to load these drivers in specific locations in upper memory.

The AUTOEXEC.BAT file for this system might look something like the following:

```
@ECHO OFF
PATH C:\DOS;C:\WINDOWS;C:\
PROMPT $P$G
REM Direct temporary files to the RAM drive:
SET TEMP=D:\
LH /L:1,42448 /S SMARTDRV 4096
LH /L:1,53968 UNDELETE /SC
LH /L:1,63088 VSAFE
WIN
```

The SET command, as the comment indicates, directs the DOS and Windows temporary files to RAM drive D. Because the RAM drive is 3M, it has plenty of room for the Windows' temporary files. In this 16M system, there also is plenty of extended memory left for a 4M SmartDrive cache.

MEMMAKER has adapted the SmartDrive, UNDELETE, and VSAFE commands to load their TSRs into upper memory. The final command starts up Windows. The Windows StartUp group (not shown here) loads the MWAVTSR.EXE program to support VSAFE and starts up the MWAV virus scanner so that memory and the hard drive are scanned for viruses every time the system is started up.

Daily Shutdown

You need to consider not only your startup routines but also what you want to do before shutting down. For example, you may want to run a differential or incremental backup. If you are using SmartDrive with delayed writes, you probably should force any delayed data to be written before shutting off the power.

If you use the DOS version of BACKUP, you may want to make a SHUT-DOWN.BAT file that runs these programs for you. You can use DOS's EDIT to create the file, which can be as simple as the following:

```
MSBACKUP DAILY.SET
SMARTDRV /C
```

The MSBACKUP command starts up the program and opens the first dialog box. You still have to complete the backup in the dialog boxes. When you exit BACKUP, the SmartDrive command executes. After that, you can shut down your system.

Weekly Shutdown

Once a week, you may want to run a more extensive shutdown program in which you do a full backup, run CHKDSK with the /F switch, and run DEFRAG. If you use the DOS version of BACKUP, the batch file may appear as follows:

```
MSBACKUP DAILY.SET
SMARTDRV /C
CHKDSK /F
DEFRAG /B
```

When the BACKUP program opens with the DAILY setup, be sure to reset the backup type to Full to do a full backup. When BACKUP asks whether you want to save changes to DAILY.SET, choose No and the normal Differential or Incremental type will be restored.

If you set up your startup files to establish the best configuration for your system—making sure to use all the protection features—and you decide what routines you will use when shutting down, you will be using DOS to its best advantage.

For the Future

The more you know about your operating system, the better you will use your computer. This book has covered the basic survival skills. When you feel comfortable with the basics, you may be ready to expand your DOS knowledge with an advanced book such as *Peter Norton's Advanced DOS 6*, 2nd Edition, published by Brady.

Command
Reference

Command
Reference

Throughout this reference, icons appear next to the command names. These icons represent the type of command:

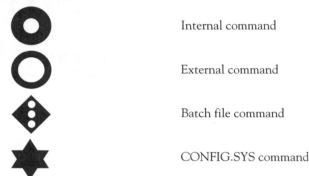

Internal command

External command

Batch file command

CONFIG.SYS command

APPEND

Enables programs to access files in specified directories as though those files were in the current directory.

Format 1

APPEND [*path*[;path...]] [/X[:ON | :OFF]] [/PATH:ON | :OFF]]

Appends *path* to the current directory.

Parameters and Switches

none	Displays list of appended directories.
path	Identifies the directory to append.
/X	Specifies whether DOS is to search appended directories for program files. The default setting is OFF. /X has the same effect as /X:ON.
/PATH	Specifies whether DOS is to search appended directories for a data file when the data filespec includes a path. The default setting is ON.

Notes

If *path* does not include a drive name, DOS assumes that the directory is on the drive that is current when it executes APPEND.

448

When /X is ON, DOS searches for programs first in the current directory, then in any appended directories, and finally in the search path.

If you are going to use /X:ON at any time during a session, you must use /X:ON the first time you use this format. After that, you can use /X:OFF and /X:ON anytime.

Each new APPEND command in this format cancels all previous APPEND commands. If you want to append more than one directory to the current directory, do them all in one APPEND command. If you want to change the setting of the /X or /PATH switch, be sure to include in the command any path that should still be appended.

If you are going to use APPEND and ASSIGN in the same session, you must use APPEND first even if none of the same drives are involved.

Using DIR for the current directory does not list appended directories.

Many application programs, when called on to save an updated file, actually create a new file rather than writing over the old one. Even if the original file was in an appended directory, the updated version is stored in the current directory—thus not replacing the earlier version. For this reason alone, APPEND can be a dangerous command. Many experts advise against using APPEND. Anything you want to do with APPEND you can do by judicious use of path names and the PATH command.

Examples

APPEND D:\MYDIR\TOKEN

Appends the specified directory.

APPEND \NEWDIR /X

Appends directory NEWDIR (on the current drive) and turns on /X so that DOS looks for program files in NEWDIR if they aren't in the current directory.

APPEND \NEWDIR;A:\BDIR /X:OFF /PATH:OFF

Appends directory NEWDIR on the current drive and directory BDIR on drive A to the current directory. Turns off /X so that DOS searches for program files first in the current directory and then in the search path. Turns off /PATH so that when a data filespec includes a path, DOS searches for the file in the specified directory only.

Format 2

APPEND /E

Assigns the list of appended directories to an environment variable named APPEND.

Notes

If used, this command must be the first APPEND command after starting your system. Notice that you can't use path with this format.

Format 3

APPEND ;

Cancels the existing list of appended directories.

ATTRIB

Displays or changes file and directory attributes.

Format

ATTRIB [+R | -R] [+A | -A] [+H | -H] [+S | -S] [*filespec*] [/S]

Parameters and Switches

none	Shows the attributes of all files in the current directory.
+R	Turns on the read-only attribute.
-R	Turns off the read-only attribute.
+A	Turns on the archive attribute.
-A	Turns off the archive attribute.
+H	Turns on the hidden attribute.

-H	Turns off the hidden attribute.
+S	Turns on the system attribute.
-S	Turns off the system attribute.
filespec	Identifies file(s) or a directory to process. You can use wild cards to identify files but not directories. When *filespec* appears with no attribute switches, ATTRIB displays the current attributes of the file(s) or directory.
/S	Processes all files in the branch headed by the current directory.

Notes

The read-only attribute prevents a file from being overwritten or deleted. The hidden attribute prevents a file from being accessed by many commands. The system attribute combines hidden and read-only characteristics. The archive attribute indicates that a file has not been backed up.

If a file has the hidden or system attribute, you can't change any of its other attributes unless you turn off the hidden or system attribute, either in a preceding command or in the same command in which you change the other attributes.

DOS automatically sets the archive attribute when it creates or modifies a file. Many backup programs can select files for processing based on their archive attributes and turn off the attribute after backing up a file.

If you use /S with *filespec*, ATTRIB ignores /S and processes the specified file(s) or directory only.

Examples

ATTRIB +H \D1

Turns on the hidden attribute for directory D1 (unless D1 is a system directory).

ATTRIB -H -S -R TESTFILE.*

Turns off the hidden, system, and read-only attributes for all files in the current directory that match the filespec.

ATTRIB +A /S

Turns on the archive attribute for all files in the current direc-tory and its subdirectories (except system and hidden files).

ATTRIB *.EXE

Displays the attributes of all files that match the filespec in the current directory.

BREAK

Controls extended break checking.

Format

BREAK [ON | OFF]

Parameters

none	Displays the current status of extended break checking.
ON	Turns on extended break checking.
OFF	Turns off extended break checking.

Notes

When BREAK is off, DOS checks for the use of the Break key (Ctrl-Break or Ctrl-C) only while reading from the keyboard, writing to the screen, or writing to the printer. When BREAK is on, DOS also checks for the Break keys during other operations, such as reading from or writing to disks. This additional checking, however, may slow down such operations.

BREAK is off by default.

You can use BREAK with one of its parameters either at the command prompt or in CONFIG.SYS. In CONFIG.SYS, you also can use the format BREAK=ON | OFF.

Examples

BREAK ON

Turns on extended break checking.

BREAK=OFF

Turns off extended break checking (in CONFIG.SYS only).

BREAK

Displays current status of break checking. Don't use this form in CONFIG.SYS.

BUFFERS

Specifies the number of disk buffers.

Format

BUFFERS=*read-write*[,*look-ahead*]

Parameters

read-write   Specifies the number of read-write buffers. The range is from 1 to 99. The default (if the BUFFERS command is omitted) depends on your system configuration.

look-ahead   Specifies the number of look-ahead buffers. The range is from 0 to 8. The default is 0. If either *read-write* or *look-ahead* is outside its range, *look-ahead* defaults to 0.

Notes

DOS uses read-write buffers to hold data while reading and writing from a disk. Before actually reading or writing on the disk, DOS looks to see whether the desired data already is in a buffer; the more buffers there are, the more likely it is that DOS can reduce the number of disk accesses.

If you also allocate some look-ahead buffers, DOS will read additional sectors whenever it reads from a disk. This increases the likelihood that the next data can be found in a buffer.

The optimum number of buffers depends on your system configuration. A reasonable number improves performance. Using too many not only takes up too much memory but actually slows down reading and writing because searching all the buffers may take longer than accessing the disk.

If you also use SMARTDRV, allocate about 15 read-write buffers and no look-ahead buffers.

Each buffer uses about .5K of memory. If DOS is loaded in the HMA (see the DOS command) and *read-write* is set at 48 or less, the read-write buffers are loaded with DOS in the HMA. Otherwise, they appear in conventional memory. The look-ahead buffers are always in conventional memory.

Examples

BUFFERS 30, 5

Allocates 30 read-write buffers and 5 look-ahead buffers.

BUFFERS 15

Allocates 15 read-write buffers and no look-ahead buffers.

CALL

Calls a second batch program without ending the first one.

Format

CALL *batch-command*

Parameter

batch-command   The command needed to start the called batch program.

Notes

The *batch-command* should be exactly the same as the command that starts the batch program from the command prompt, including any desired parameters.

After the called program ends, DOS returns to the command following CALL in the original program.

To start one batch program from another without returning to the original batch program when the second program ends, simply include *batch-command* in the original program without CALL, just as you would enter *batch-command* at the DOS prompt.

A batch program can call itself.

Examples

CALL NEWDAY

Starts a batch program called NEWDAY.BAT. When NEWDAY finishes, DOS returns to the original program on the line following this CALL command.

CALL NEWDAY JAN 1999 2

Starts a batch program called NEWDAY.BAT and passes command line parameters to it to replace %1 (JAN), %2 (1999), and %3 (3). When NEWDAY ends, DOS continues executing the original program on the line following this CALL command.

NEWDAY

Starts a batch program called NEWDAY.BAT. Because CALL has not been used, DOS does not return to the original program when NEWDAY ends.

CD

Changes the default directory or displays the name of the default directory. CHDIR is an alternate form of this command.

Format

CD [*drive*] [*path*]

CHDIR [*drive*] [*path*]

Parameters

none	Displays the name of default directory on the current drive.
drive	Displays the name of the default directory on the specified drive. *Drive* must end with a colon.
path	Specifies name of new default directory. *Path* must represent an existing directory.

Notes

DOS establishes a default directory for each drive in the system. To change the default directory for a drive that is not the current drive, include the drive name in the path.

A double dot (..) in the path specifies the next higher level of the directory tree. For example, .. represents the parent of the current directory; ..\.. represents the grandparent of the current directory.

Examples

CHDIR

> Displays the name of the current directory.

CD E:

> Displays the name of the default directory on drive E.

CD \

> Changes the current directory to the root directory of the current drive.

The following examples assume that the current drive is C: and that the current directory is \OFFICE\MYDIR.

CD NEWDIR

> Changes the current directory to C:\OFFICE\MYDIR\NEWDIR.

CD ..

> Changes the current directory to C:\OFFICE.

CD ..\YOURDIR

Changes the current directory to C:\OFFICE\YOURDIR.

CH \NEWDIR

Changes the current directory to C:\NEWDIR.

CH E:\XDIR

Changes the default directory on drive E to XDIR. The current drive
and directory are unchanged.

CHCP

Changes the code page for all devices or displays the number of the current
code page.

Format

CHCP [*page*]

Parameters

none	Displays the number of the current code page.
page	Changes to the specified code page.

Notes

A code page is a character set for a keyboard, monitor, or printer. DOS provides six
different software code pages so that you can type and display characters for languages
other than U.S. English.

The default code page for the United States is page 437. This is also the built-in
code page for most hardware sold in the U.S. The alternate code page for the U.S. is
850, which contains more international characters.

If you use the COUNTRY command in the CONFIG.SYS file, DOS establishes
default and alternate code pages appropriate for the country specified.

Before you can use CHCP to change a code page, you must take these steps:

- In CONFIG.SYS, load the proper drivers so that your monitor or printer can use software code pages.

- Run NLSFUNC to allow changing code pages with CHCP.

- Use MODE to load monitor and printer code pages.

CHCP changes code pages for all applicable devices at once and can choose between the two pages available for the current country only no matter how many code pages have been loaded. Use MODE to change to other code pages or to change the code page for one device at a time.

Examples

CHCP

> Displays the number of the current code page.

CHCP 850

> Changes the current code page to page 850.

CHDIR

> See CD.

CHKDSK

Reports disk status, reports and fixes problems in the FAT and directory structure, and reports file fragmentation.

Format 1

CHKDSK [*drive*] [/F] [/V]

> Reports disk status and reports and fixes disk structure problems.

Parameters and Switches

none	Checks the current drive.
drive	Checks the specified drive.
/F	Fixes errors in the drive's FAT and directory structure, if possible.
/V	Lists each file while checking the drive.

Notes

This format of CHKDSK automatically analyzes and reports on a drive's space usage and any errors in the FAT and directory structure. If no errors are found, the report summarizes space usage only.

CHKDSK finds logical errors in the FAT and directory structure, such as lost allocation units or cross-linked files; it does not find physical errors, such as bad sectors.

If CHKDSK /F finds lost allocation units (clusters that are marked as containing data but do not belong to any file) it asks whether you want to convert them to files. If you press Y (or Enter), CHKDSK converts each chain to a file named FILE*nnnn*.CHK. If you press N, CHKDSK immediately makes the clusters available for future use. (If you don't specify /F, CHKDSK simulates this process and tells you how many files can be recovered or how much space is freed if you run CHKDSK /F.)

Never run CHKDSK on drives on which you have used ASSIGN or SUBST or on network drives.

Do not use CHKDSK /F when files may be open. You must not start CHKDSK /F from another program (such as a word processor) or when Microsoft Windows or DOS Shell is running. You may need to reboot to eliminate TSRs before using CHKDSK /F.

Examples

CHKDSK

> Checks the current drive and reports FAT and directory structure errors and space usage.

CHKDSK E: /F

> Checks drive E, reports space usage and FAT and directory structure errors, and attempts to fix errors.

CHKDSK /V

> Checks the current drive and reports FAT and directory structure errors, reports space usage, and lists every file on the drive.

Format 2

CHKDSK *filespec*

> Reports on file fragmentation.

Parameter

filespec   Checks specified file(s) for fragmentation.

Notes

A fragmented file resides in several different areas on the disk. Such a file is *fragmented*. Excessive file fragmentation can slow down performance. You can use DEFRAG to clean up file fragmentation.

Example

CHKDSK *.*

Lists any fragmented files in the current directory.

CHOICE

Allows user to choose options during a batch program.

Format

CHOICE [/C:*list*] [/N] [/S] [/T:*char,sec*] [*text*]

Parameters and Switches

/C:*list*	Defines a list of characters that the user can type to select choices. The colon is optional.
/N	Causes CHOICE not to display any prompt.
/S	Causes CHOICE to distinguish between uppercase and lowercase; otherwise case is ignored.
/T:*char,sec*	Causes CHOICE to pause for *sec* seconds before defaulting to *char*. The colon is optional. *Char* must be a character from list. *Sec* must be between 0 and 99. Don't include any spaces in this parameter.
text	Specifies text to be displayed before the prompt.

Notes

CHOICE prompts for input by displaying list enclosed in brackets with the characters separated by commas and followed by a question mark, as in [A,B]?. Without /S, the list appears in uppercase.

If you omit /C, CHOICE uses YN as a default list.

If you use /N, CHOICE displays text with no prompt.

You must enclose text in quotation marks if it includes a slash (/).

With /T, CHOICE defaults to *char* after *sec* seconds. Otherwise, it waits for the user to type a character from list (or press Ctrl-C or Ctrl-Break). If the user enters any other response, CHOICE beeps and continues to wait.

CHOICE sets the ERRORLEVEL parameter according to the user's response: 1 for the first character in *list*, 2 for the second character, and so on. If the user presses Ctrl-C or Ctrl-Break, CHOICE sets ERRORLEVEL to 0. If an error occurs, such as a bad parameter in /T, CHOICE sets ERRORLEVEL to 255.

You can use the IF command to test the value of ERRORLEVEL and decide what to do next.

Examples

CHOICE /C:ABC /S Which do you want

> Displays `Which do you want [A,B,C]?` and waits for response. Acceptable responses are A, B, C, Ctrl-C, and Ctrl-Break.

CHOICE /C:ABC Which do you want

> Displays `Which do you want [A,B,C]?` and waits for a response. Acceptable responses are A, B, C, a, b, c, Ctrl-C, and Ctrl-Break.

CHOICE /T:y,3 Are you done

> Displays `Are you done [Y,N]?` and waits for a response. Acceptable responses are Y, y, N, n, Ctrl-C, and Ctrl-Break. If user doesn't respond within three seconds, CHOICE defaults to y and continues.

CLS

Clears the screen.

Format

CLS

Notes

CLS sets the entire screen to the current background color, with the command prompt and cursor at the top left.

COMMAND

Starts a new version of the DOS command processor COMMAND.COM.

Format

COMMAND [*path*] [*ctty*] [/C*command*] [/K*filespec*] [/E:*n*]

Parameters and Switches

path	Identifies the location of the command processor.
ctty	Identifies the device for command input and output. The default is the current device.
/C*command*	Loads a secondary command processor, performs command, and exits the secondary command processor.
/K*filespec*	Runs the specified program before displaying the DOS command prompt.
/E:*n*	Specifies the environment size in bytes for the new command processor, from 160 to 32,768.

Notes

DOS's default command processor, loaded when the system starts, is COMMAND.COM, located in the root directory of the boot drive. See the SHELL command for details about booting with other options, such as a different location or a different command processor.

COMMAND loads a new version of COMMAND.COM as a child of the current processor. This is called a *secondary command processor*. When you are through using the secondary processor, the EXIT command closes it and returns you to the parent processor.

Other programs, such as Microsoft Windows and DOS Shell, load a secondary command processor when you request a DOS prompt. The secondary processor stays loaded until you use the EXIT command to close it.

See the CTTY command for information about changing console devices.

When you specify /C*command*, DOS loads the secondary command processor, performs the specified command, and then exits to the parent command processor. When you specify /K*filespec*, DOS loads the secondary processor, runs the specified program, and prompts for more commands. It does not exit from the secondary command processor until you enter an EXIT command. Both /C and /K can run batch or other programs; only /C can perform internal commands and pass parameters.

Each version of the command processor has its own set of environment variables. When DOS loads a secondary processor, it copies the parent's environment, but you can change the child environment without affecting the parent.

If you don't use /E, DOS defaults to a request for 256 bytes for the environment. If the environment size requested (by /E or by default) is too small to contain all of the parent environment variables, DOS increases the environment to the size needed to contain all of them.

Path is used to set the COMSPEC environment variable that determines where DOS looks when it needs to reload the transient part of COMMAND.COM. When you omit path, DOS uses the parent environment's COMSPEC. If path is invalid or points to a directory that does not contain COMMAND.COM, DOS displays an error message and sets COMSPEC to \COMMAND.COM.

Path sets COMSPEC for reloading the transient portion of COMMAND.COM only. It does not tell DOS where to find COMMAND.COM to execute COMMAND. If COMMAND.COM is not in the current directory or search path, you need to specify a path with the command name, as in D:\OLDDOS\COMMAND.

Examples

COMMAND C:\DOS /E:1024

Loads COMMAND.COM from the current directory (or from the program search path), sets COMSPEC to C:\DOS\COMMAND.COM, and requests 1,024 bytes for its environment.

463

COMMAND /CFOR %X IN (C:\ D:\) DO DIR %X*.BAT > PRN

Loads the command processor, prints directory listings of all BAT files in C:\ and D:\, and returns to the parent processor. Note that the text from FOR through BAT is the command associated with /C.

C:\NEWDOS\COMMAND C:\NEWDOS COM1 /
KC:\STARTUP.COM

Loads C:\NEWDOS\COMMAND.COM, sets COMSPEC to C:\NEWDOS, changes the input/output device to COM1, runs STARTUP.COM, and then waits for new commands from COM1.

COMP

Compares two files or two sets of files.

This command is not available in DOS 6. It applies to DOS 5 and earlier versions.

Format

COMP [*filespec1*] [*filespec2*] [/D | /A] [/L] [/N=*n*] [/C]

Parameters and Switches

none	Prompts for filespecs and switches.
filespec1	Identifies the first file(s) to be compared.
filespec2	Identifies the second file(s) to be compared.
/D	Reports differences in decimal format.
/A	Reports differences is ASCII (character) format.
/L	Reports line numbers instead of offsets.

/N=n	Compares first *n* lines.
/C	Ignores case differences.

Notes

COMP compares files byte by byte. When two files are identical, COMP reports that the files compare OK.

When you compare multiple files by using wild cards, COMP compares each *filespec1* file to a *filespec2* with the same wild card characters; that is, COMP A*.* B*.* compares AFILE.DAT with BFILE.DAT, ATYPE.TXT with BTYPE.TXT, and so on.

COMP won't compare files with different file sizes unless you specify /N.

COMP stops comparing two files after finding 10 mismatches.

COMP reports each mismatched byte. By default, the report shows, in hexadecimal, the offset of the byte and the value of that byte in each file.

If you use /L or /N, COMP reports errors by line number instead of offset. This is useful in text files in which each text line ends in a carriage return. It isn't very helpful with binary files, such as graphics or executable program files, in which lines are not marked.

Use /D to force COMP to report byte values in decimal instead of hex. Use /A to force COMP to report byte values as ASCII characters (non-printable characters show up as spaces).

Microsoft is phasing out COMP in favor of the FC command, which is newer and more flexible. But COMP is still useful for a quick check to see whether files are identical.

Examples

COMP AFILE.BAT BFILE.BAT

Compares AFILE.BAT and BFILE.BAT (provided that the files are the same size) and reports up to 10 differences by showing offset and mismatched values in hexadecimal.

COMP AFILE.BAT BFILE.BAT /D

Compares AFILE.BAT and BFILE.BAT as in the previous example but reports mismatched bytes in decimal format.

COMP AFILE.BAT BFILE.BAT /A /N=19

Compares AFILE.BAT and BFILE.BAT, reporting mismatched bytes in ASCII format; compares up to 19 lines even if the files are different sizes. If one (or both) of the files is less than 19 lines, the comparison ends when COMP reaches the end of the shorter file.

COMP AFILE.* BFILE.*

Compares each file named AFILE with a file named BFILE with the same extension. COMP compares AFILE.BAT, for example, to BFILE.BAT (if it exists), and compares AFILE.D1 to BFILE.D1 (if it exists).

COPY

Copies one or more files; concatenates files.

Format 1

COPY *source* [/A] [/B] [*destination*] [/A] [/B] [/V]

Copies file(s).

Parameters and Switches

source	Identifies file(s) to copy.
destination	Identifies location and name of copies.
/A	Treats files as ASCII text files, whose sizes are determined by end-of-file markers.
/B	Treats files as binary files, whose sizes are determined by the directory entries.
/V	Verifies files after copying.

Notes

This format of COPY creates destination files with the same date/time stamp as their sources, but it sets the archive attribute for each destination file. See Format 2 to see how to assign the current date and time to the new copy.

Destination may include a path and a new file name. If *destination* does not include a path, COPY uses the current directory. If *destination* does not include a file name, COPY uses the original file name for the copy. If you omit *destination*, COPY puts the new file in the current directory using the same file name as the source file.

If the *destination* directory is the same as the *source* directory, *destination* must assign a new name to the copy. (A file can't be copied to itself.)

If *destination* already exists, COPY overwrites it. In effect, this means it deletes *destination* and creates a new file with the specified name. (You may be able to use an undelete utility to recover the data from the newly deleted file.)

If *source* identifies multiple files (by using wild cards) but *destination* provides only one file name, DOS concatenates (combines) the *source* files in *destination*. See Format 2 for more information about concatenating.

To copy multiple files from *source* to separate files with new names, you must use wildcards in destination also. If *source* is *.BAT, for example, *destination* might be *.OLD.

Source and *destination* may be device names. When *source* is CON, COPY accepts input from the keyboard until you enter an end-of-file character. (You enter this character by pressing Ctrl-Z or F6.) When *destination* is a printer port, DOS prints the *source* files.

In this format, when /A or /B follows *source*, it also applies to *destination* unless another switch follows *destination*.

COPY reads the file size in the directory entry to determine how many bytes are in the file. When /A applies to source, COPY stops copying if it finds an end-of-file marker before reaching the file size. It does not copy the marker. If /B applies to *source*, COPY continues copying until it reaches the file size. /B is the default when copying files; /A is the default when concatenating or when source is CON.

Binary files, such as EXE or COM files, may inadvertently contain end-of-file markers as data. It is important to copy them as binary files to avoid truncating them.

When /A applies to *destination*, COPY adds an end-of-file marker to the file; with /B, COPY does not add the end-of-file marker.

Examples

COPY MYFILE.DAT YOURFILE.DAT

Copies MYFILE.DAT to create (or overwrite) YOURFILE.DAT. Both files are in the current directory.

The file size of MYFILE.DAT in its directory entry determines how many bytes DOS copies. YOURFILE.DAT does not end with an end-of-file marker unless MYFILE.DAT does.

COPY MYFILE.* YOURFILE.*

Copies each file matching the *source* filespec into a file named YOURFILE with the same extension as the *source* file. MYFILE.A1, for example, is copied to YOURFILE.A1.

Format 2

COPY *source1* + [*source2*] [+...] [/A] [/B] [*destination*] [/A] [/B] [/V]

Concatenates files.

Parameters and Switches

source1	Identifies the first file(s) to be concatenated.
source2	Identifies additional file(s) to be concatenated.
destination	Identifies the file(s) to hold the concatenated data.
/A	Treats files as ASCII text files.
/B	Treats files as binary files.
/V	Verifies files after concatenation.

Notes

You can repeat *source2* as needed, but precede each filespec by with a +. Source filespecs can include wild cards.

Because the *destination* file is a new creation, COPY assigns the current date and time to it. You can use this feature to fake concatenation to assign the current date and time to a file (see the example).

If you omit *destination*, COPY concatenates all source files into the first source file that actually exists. If *source1* does not exist, but *source2* does, COPY puts the concatenated data in *source2*; if neither *source1* nor *source2* exists, but there is an existing *source3*, *source3* receives the data.

In this format, when you use wildcards in two or more *source* file names, COPY concatenates files with matching wildcard characters. COPY AFILE.* + BFILE.*

CFILE.*, for example, concatenates AFILE.DAT with BFILE.DAT to create or re-place CFILE.DAT and concatenates AFILE.NEW with BFILE.NEW to create or replace CFILE.NEW. COPY AFILE.* + BFILE.* concatenates AFILE.BAT and BFILE.BAT into AFILE.BAT (if it exists).

/A is the default for this format. An /A or /B switch applies to the preceding file name and all succeeding file names until COPY reaches a file name followed by another /A or /B switch.

As in Format 1, when /A applies to a source file, COPY stops copying if it finds an end-of-file marker without copying the marker. If there is no marker, or if /B applies, COPY determines the source file size from the directory entry. When /A applies to a destination file, COPY inserts an end-of-file marker at the end of the file; with /B, no marker is inserted unless one is copied from the source file.

When you concatenate data into one of the source files, you may receive the message `Content of destination lost before copy`. This is a normal message. It does not necessarily mean that you have lost data.

Examples

COPY C:\DS1\MYFILE.* NEWFILE.CAT

Concatenates all specified files to create (or overwrite) NEWFILE.CAT in the current directory. For each source file, COPY ends the copy if it finds an end-of-file marker. COPY also writes an end-of-file marker at the end of NEWFILE.CAT.

COPY MYFILE.DAT + YOURFILE.DAT OURFILE.DAT /V

Concatenates MYFILE.DAT and YOURFILE.DAT to create or overwrite OURFILE.DAT and verifies the result. COPY treats these files as ASCII text files and adds an end-of-file marker to the new file.

COPY MYFILE.DAT +YOURFIL.DAT +OURFILE.DAT

Concatenates MYFILE.DAT, YOURFILE.DAT, and OURFILE.DAT into MYFILE.DAT if it exists. If MYFILE.DAT does not exist, concat-enates YOURFIL.DAT and OURFILE.DAT into YOURFIL.DAT. If neither MYFILE.DAT nor YOURFIL.DAT exists, copies OURFILE.DAT to itself as though concatenating. COPY treats these files as ASCII text files and adds an end-of-file marker to the concat-enated data.

469

COPY MYFILE.DAT/B+YOURFILE.DAT OURFILE.DAT

Concatenates MYFILE.DAT and YOURFILE.DAT to create (or overwrite) OURFILE.DAT. COPY treats these files as binary files, copying all characters from the source files, and does not append an end-of-file marker.

COPY MYFILE.DAT+YOURFILE.DAT /B OURFILE.DAT

Concatenates MYFILE.DAT and YOURFILE.DAT to create (or overwrite) OURFILE.DAT. COPY treats MYFILE.DAT as an ASCII text file but YOURFILE.DAT and OURFILE.DAT as binary files.

COPY MYFILE.DAT+,, /B NEWFILE.DAT

Concatenates MYFILE.DAT with nothing (signified by the commas) to create or overwrite NEWFILE.DAT. The effect is to copy MYFILE.DAT as NEWFILE.DAT and to assign the current date and time to NEWFILE.DAT. Both files are treated as binary files. The commas mark the end of the source list; without them, COPY would consider NEWFILE.DAT a source file.

COPY MYFILE.DAT +, /B

Concatenates MYFILE.DAT with nothing to overwrite MYFILE.DAT. The effect is to update the date/time stamp for MYFILE.DAT. /B ensures that COPY copies the entire file, including end-of-file markers, but does not add a new end-of-file marker. + is necessary to indicate that this is a concatenation, not a copy.

COUNTRY

Specifies the country format for date and time displays, currency symbol, sort order, punctuation, decimal separators, and code pages.

Format

COUNTRY=*country*[,[*page*] [,*filespec*]]

Parameters

country   Specifies the code number that identifies the country.

page   Specifies a code page.

filespec   Identifies the file containing country information.

Notes

The default country (if COUNTRY is not included in CONFIG.SYS) is the United States.

Country codes, date and time formats, and appropriate code pages are documented in the on-line help for COUNTRY.

Each country has two possible code pages, or character sets, associated with it. One of them is the default code page, the other is the alternate. If you omit page, DOS uses the default code page.

Changes, such as date and time formats, take effect as soon as COUNTRY is executed in the CONFIG.SYS file; but no software code page can be used until you have followed all the steps outlined in the CHCP command. Until you load the drivers and prepare and install the code pages, DOS continues to use the default hardware page.

If you omit filespec, DOS looks for country information in COUNTRY.SYS in the root directory of your startup drive.

Examples

COUNTRY=039

Changes the country to Italy; uses default code page 850 (once all the necessary steps are taken); looks for country information in \COUNTRY.SYS on the boot drive.

COUNTRY=351,860,C:\DOS\COUNTRY.SYS

Changes the country to Portugal; uses alternate code page 860 (once all the necessary steps are taken); looks for country information in C:\DOS\COUNTRY.SYS.

COUNTRY=047,C:\OLD\SPECIAL.SYS

Changes the country to Norway; uses default code page for Norway (850) (once all the necessary steps are taken); looks for country information in C:\OLD\SPECIAL.SYS.

CTTY

Changes the console device.

Format

CTTY *device*

Parameter

device   Specifies the new console device.

Notes

The console device receives command input and displays command output. Normally, this device is CON, which represents your keyboard and monitor.

Device can be PRN, LPT1, LPT2, CON, AUX, COM1, COM2, COM3, or COM4. LPT1 and LPT2 refer to the primary and secondary parallel printer ports. PRN is the same as LPT1. COM1 through COM4 refer to serial ports. AUX refers to the auxiliary port.

If the console device is not CON, DOS can't respond to command input from your keyboard. You may need to reboot to get control back to your keyboard and monitor.

See COMMAND for another way to change your console device.

Not all input and output is transferred by this command, just standard DOS command input and output.

Examples

CTTY AUX

Uses a remote terminal connected to the auxiliary port for command input and output.

CTTY CON

Transfers input and output functions back to your keyboard and monitor (when entered from the current console device).

DATE

Displays the system date and lets you change it.

Format

DATE [*date*]

Parameters

none   Displays date in standard format and asks for a new date.

date   Changes to *date*.

Notes

The system date affects directory entries and is used by MSBACKUP, RESTORE, XCOPY, and many other applications.

When DOS asks for a new date, press Enter to retain the current date.

The COUNTRY command determines the date format. By default, the allowable date formats are the U.S. standards: mm/dd/yy, mm-dd-yy, and mm.dd.yy. In each of these, yy can be a two-digit year from 80 to 99 (interpreted as 1980 through 1999) or a four-digit year between 1980 and 2099.

DOS always computes the weekday (such as Sun or Mon) from the system date; don't try to enter the weekday.

Examples

DATE

Displays the system date and asks you to enter a new date.

DATE 12-15-97

Changes the system date to December 15, 1997.

DATE 12/15/2003

Changes the system date to December 15, 2003.

DBLSPACE

Compresses hard disk drives and floppy disks; manages compressed drives.

Format 1

DBLSPACE

> Starts the DoubleSpace setup program; compresses and mounts a drive; loads the DoubleSpace TSR.

Notes

The first time you use DBLSPACE, you must use this format. DBLSPACE sets up your system to use the program, placing the DBLSPACE kernel (DBLSPACE.BIN) and other files in the root directory of your boot drive and putting a DEVICEHIGH command into your CONFIG.SYS file so that DBLSPACE.BIN moves to upper memory, if possible; otherwise, it moves to the bottom of conventional memory. It also compresses at least one hard disk drive. You can't install DoubleSpace without compressing at least one hard disk drive.

When you use Format 1 again, it loads the DoubleSpace program and displays a dialog box with pull-down menus, from which you can compress other drives or manage compressed drives.

After installation, you can accomplish DoubleSpace functions without loading the interactive program by using other DBLSPACE formats.

When DoubleSpace compresses existing data, it creates a large file named DBLSPACE.000 that holds the compressed data. (This is a system, hidden, and read-only file.) The original drive now contains the DBLSPACE.000 file, other files that are not appropriate for compression (such as a WINDOWS swap file), and some free space. The compressed data file is called a *compressed volume file* (CVF) and is accessed and referred to by the original drive letter. The original drive, called the *host drive*, is accessed by a new letter assigned by DoubleSpace. (If you're not sure what letter DoubleSpace assigned to a host drive, use DBLSPACE /INFO or /LIST formats 9 and 10.)

Assigning drive letters to the compressed and host drives is called *mounting the compressed drive*. DoubleSpace automatically mounts all compressed hard disk drives when you boot your system. You must mount a compressed floppy disk every time you insert it (see Format 11). When a compressed drive is not mounted, you can't access it because no drive letter is assigned to it.

DoubleSpace can't compress a drive that's completely full. A hard disk drive must have at least 1M of free space before compression, and a floppy disk at least 200K.

If your drive had a SENTRY directory, there is a SENTRY directory on both the compressed and host drive after compression. Neither directory contains any recoverable files, though. Files deleted after compression can be undeleted as usual by Delete Sentry. (You need to add the new drive letter as a drive protected by Delete Sentry, however, if you want to protect the uncompressed host drive.)

If your drive had a PCTRACKR.DEL file, it is left on the host drive, but any files listed in it are probably unrecoverable because their clusters have been reused by the CVF. Files deleted after compression can be undeleted as usual by deletion-tracking. (You need to add the new drive letter as a drive protected by deletion-tracking, however, if you want to protect the uncompressed host drive.)

If you use a SMARTDRV command naming a compressed drive, you will see a message telling you that you must cache the host drive. You don't need to change the command; DoubleSpace and Smartdrive seem to work together to cache the compressed drive through the host drive. It's probably not a good idea to cache a compressed drive, though; you might want to change your SMARTDRV command to turn off caching for the host drive, and therefore the compressed drive.

Format 2

DBLSPACE /CHKDSK [/F] [*drive*]

Checks the directory structure of a compressed drive.

Parameters and Switches

/CHKDSK	Requests the CHKDSK function; abbreviate it as /CHK.
/F	Fixes errors found on the compressed drive.
drive	Identifies the compressed drive to be checked; the default is the current drive.

Notes

This command checks the internal structure of the compressed volume file. Use DOS's CHKDSK command to check the compressed drive's file allocation tables.

Examples

DBLSPACE /CHK

> Checks the internal structure of the current drive, if it's a compressed drive. Reports errors but doesn't fix them.

DBLSPACE /CHK /F D

> Checks the internal structure of compressed drive D, correcting errors if possible.

Format 3

DBLSPACE /COMPRESS *drive1* [/NEWDRIVE=*drive2*] [/RESERVE=*size*]

> Compresses the files on an existing hard disk drive, floppy drive, or other removable media, and mounts the drive.

Parameters and Switches

/COMPRESS	Identifies the DBLSPACE function desired; abbreviate as /COM.
drive1	Identifies the existing drive you want to compress.
/NEWDRIVE=*drive2*	Specifies the drive letter you want to use for the host drive; abbreviate as /NEW. (Use Format 10 to find out what drive letters are available). Without /NEW, DoubleSpace assigns an available drive letter to the new drive.
/RESERVE=*size*	Specifies, in megabytes, how much space to leave uncompressed on the host drive; abbreviate as /RES. Without /RES, DoubleSpace leaves 2M on a hard disk drive if possible.

Notes

When DoubleSpace compresses a floppy disk, it adds a file called READTHIS.TXT to the host drive. This file explains that the disk contains compressed data and how to access the data.

Whether or not you specify /RES at this point, you can increase or decrease the amount of uncompressed space later (see Format 14).

See Format 1 for more information about what happens when you compress a disk.

Examples

DBLSPACE /COM A

Compresses the floppy disk in drive A; after compression, assigns the host drive an available drive letter.

DBLSPACE /COM D /RES=2.5 /NEW=L

Compresses drive D, leaving 2.5M of free space (if possible); assigns the host drive the letter L.

Format 4

DBLSPACE /CONVSTAC=*stacvol drive1* [/NEWDRIVE=*drive2*]
[/CVF=*ext*]

Converts a STACKER compressed volume to a DoubleSpace compressed drive.

Parameters and Switches

/CONVSTAC=*stacvol*	Identifies the Stacker volume to convert, which must be on *drive1*; abbreviate as /CONVST.
drive1	Specifies the drive containing the Stacker volume.
/NEWDRIVE=*drive2*	Specifies the drive letter for the newly converted compressed drive; abbreviate as /NEW. Without /NEW, DoubleSpace assigns an available drive letter to the newly converted drive.
/CVF=*ext*	Specifies a file name extension for the new compressed volume file; must be three digits between 000 and 254; without /CVF, DoubleSpace assigns the extension.

477

Format 5

DBLSPACE /CREATE *drive1* [/NEWDRIVE=*drive2*] [/SIZE=*size1* |
/RESERVE=*size2*]

Creates a new, empty, compressed drive out of free space on an
uncompressed drive.

Parameters and Switches

/CREATE	Requests the CREATE function abbreviate as /CR.
drive1	Identifies the host drive.
/NEWDRIVE=*drive2*	Specifies the drive letter for the new CVF; abbreviate as /NEW. Without /NEW, DoubleSpace assigns an available drive letter to the new CVF.
/SIZE=*size1*	Specifies the total size, in megabytes, of the compressed volume file; abbreviate as /SI.
/RESERVE=*size2*	Specifies how many megabytes of free space to leave on the uncompressed drive; abbreviate as /RES.

Notes

You can't use /CREATE on a floppy disk.

When you create a CVF out of free space instead of existing data, DoubleSpace assigns the new drive letter to the new volume instead of the host drive (which retains its existing drive letter).

When mounting a volume, DoubleSpace uses the volume's file name extension to indicate whether it was created from existing data or free space. The extension 000 means that the volume was created from existing data and should receive the original drive letter. Any higher extension identifies a volume that should receive a new drive letter.

You can create a new, empty volume on a drive that already contains a compressed volume file. The original CVF is named DBLSPACE.000 and has the original drive letter. The new CVF is DBLSPACE.001 (assuming this is the second CVF on the drive) and receives a new drive letter. The remaining uncompressed space is on the host drive, which keeps the drive letter assigned to it when DBLSPACE.000 was created.

If you don't specify /SIZE or /RES, DoubleSpace uses all but 1M of free space.

Examples

DBLSPACE /CR E

> Creates a new, empty compressed volume file on host drive E, leaving 1M of free space; assigns an available drive letter to the new compressed volume file.

DBLSPACE /CR E /NEW=L /RES=1.5

> Creates a new, empty, CVF on host drive E, leaving 1.5M of free space on E (if possible) and assigning the drive letter L to the new CVF.

Format 6

DBLSPACE /DEFRAGMENT [*drive*]

> Defragments the compressed drive.

Parameters and Switches

/DEFRAGMENT	Requests the DEFRAGMENT function; abbreviate as /DEF.
drive	Specifies the compressed drive to defragment; the default is the current drive.

Notes

Defragmenting is not necessary to improve performance on a compressed drive. It does, however, consolidate the drive's free space. If you want to reduce the drive's size (see Format 14), you should use DBLSPACE /DEF first.

Example

DBLSPACE /DEF

> Defragments the current (compressed) drive.

Format 7

DBLSPACE /DELETE *drive*

> Deletes a compressed drive, erasing all its files.

Parameters and Switches

/DELETE   Requests the DELETE function; abbreviate as /DEL.

drive   Specifies the compressed drive to delete.

Notes

Deleting a DoubleSpace drive leaves it unmounted. If you delete DBLSPACE.000, the original drive letter is restored to the host drive. If you delete any other CVF, the drive letter from the deleted volume becomes available for other uses.

If you change your mind after deleting a DoubleSpace drive, you may be able to re-cover it using DOS's Undelete command. Look for a deleted file named DBLSPACE.*nnn* on the host drive.

If you are able to restore the file with UNDELETE, you still can't access its data until you mount it. See Format 11.

Example

DBLSPACE /DEL F

Deletes the compressed drive referred to as drive F.

Format 8

DBLESPACE /FORMAT *drive*

Formats a compressed drive.

Parameters and Switches

/FORMAT   Identifies the DBLSPACE function desired; abbreviate as /FOR.

drive   Specifies the compressed drive to format.

Notes

Formatting a compressed drive deletes all the files it contains. You can't unformat a compressed drive if you change your mind.

Example

DBLSPACE /FOR G

Formats compressed drive G, erasing all its data.

Format 9

DBLESPACE [/INFO] *drive*

Displays information about a compressed drive.

Parameters and Switches

/INFO   Identifies the DBLSPACE function desired; this is the default
             when no other DBLSPACE function is specified.

drive   Identifies the drive about which you want information.

Notes

The information displayed includes the host drive, the CVF's file name, the total
space, used space, and free space on both the CVF and the host drive, the actual
average compression ratio, and the estimated compression ratio. Free space on the
CVF is the number of uncompressed bytes DBLSPACE estimates could be compressed
into the remaining space in the CVF, based on the estimated compression ratio.

Example

DBLSPACE D

Displays information about compressed drive D.

Format 10

DBLESPACE /LIST

Lists and describes all your computer's non-network drives, include
DoubleSpace volumes.

Parameters and Switches

/LIST   Requests the LIST function; abbreviate as /L.

Notes

This format lists each available drive letter and describes its status in terms, such as Local hard drive, Compressed drive, Floppy drive, Removable media with no disk inserted, Available for DoubleSpace, and so on. (RAM drives are described as local hard drives.) Space used and free space are shown for each drive if appropriate. For each mounted compressed drive, the report shows the compressed volume name (and its host drive).

Format 11

DBLSPACE /MOUNT[=*nnn*] *drive1* [/NEWDRIVE=*drive2*]

Mounts a compressed volume.

Parameters and Switches

/MOUNT	Requests the MOUNT function desired; abbreviate as /MO.
nnn	Identifies the extension of the volume to be mounted; default is 000.
drive	Specifies the drive that contains the compressed file you want to mount.
/NEWDRIVE=*drive2*	Specifies the drive letter to be assigned; abbreviate as /NEW. Without /NEW, DoubleSpace assigns an available drive letter.

Notes

When you mount a DBLSPACE.000 file, the host's drive letter is assigned to the compressed drive, and a new letter is assigned to the host file. When you mount any other DBLSPACE.*nnn* file, the new letter is assigned to the compressed drive.

DBLSPACE automatically mounts drives when it compresses or creates them. It may unmount and mount a drive when it is performing certain functions on that drive. It automatically mounts compressed hard drives when the system boots. The only time you need to mount a hard drive is if you have unmounted it (see Format 14). You need to mount a floppy disk each time you insert it into the drive.

Examples

DBLSPACE /MO A

Mounts a disk in drive A, assigning drive letter A to DBLSPACE.000
and an available drive letter to the uncompressed portion of the disk.

DBLSPACE /MO=001 E /NEW=L

Mounts a compressed drive, assigning drive letter L to
E:\DBLSPACE.001 and retaining E as the drive letter of the host drive.

Format 12

DBLSPACE /RATIO=[r.r] [*drive* | /ALL]

Changes the estimated compression ratio of one or all compressed
drives.

Parameters and Switches

/RATIO=*r.r*	Specifies the new ratio; from 1.0 to 16.0; the default is the current overall compression ratio for the drive; abbreviate as /RA.
drive	Identifies the drive to change the estimated.
/ALL	Specifies that you want to change the ratio for all currently mounted compressed drives.

Notes

DoubleSpace uses the estimated compression ratio to estimate how many bytes of
uncompressed data would, when compressed, fit into the CVF.

If you don't specify *drive* or /ALL, DoubleSpace changes the ratio of the current drive.

Each time you reboot, DoubleSpace adjusts the estimated compression ratio of each
drive to match the current overall compression ratio of data currently stored on the
drive.

Use Format 9 to find the estimated and actual compression ratio of a drive.

Examples

DBLSPACE /RA /ALL

Changes the estimated compression ratio of all currently mounted compressed drives to match each one's average compression ratio.

DBLSPACE /RA=3 D

Changes the estimated compression ratio of compressed drive D to 3.0 to 1.

Format 13

DBLSPACE /SIZE[=*size1* | /RESERVE=*size2*] *drive*

Parameters and Switches

/SIZE	Identifies the DBLSPACE function desired; abbreviate as /SI.
size1	Specifies the new size of the CVF in megabytes. Do not use with /RESERVE.
/RESERVE=*size2*	Specifies in megabytes the amount of free space you want DoubleSpace to leave on the host drive; abbreviate as /RES; do not use if you specify *size1*. If *size2* is 0, the compressed drive is increased to its maximum possible size.
drive	Identifies the compressed drive to resize.

Notes

If you specify neither *size1* nor /RES, DoubleSpace makes the compressed drive as small as possible.

Examples

DBLSPACE /SI=30 D

Changes the size of compressed drive D to 30M (if possible).

DBLSPACE /SI /RES=10 D

> Changes the size of compressed drive D to leave 10M of free space on its host drive (if possible).

DBLSPACE /SI /RES=0 D

> Makes compressed drive D as large as possible.

DBLSPACE /SI D

> Makes compressed drive D as small as possible.

Format 14

DBLSPACE /UNMOUNT [*drive*]

> Unmounts a drive.

Parameters and Switches

/UNMOUNT	Requests the UNMOUNT function; abbreviate as /U.
drive	Specifies the drive to be unmounted; the default is the current drive.

Notes

The unmounted drive becomes unavailable until mounted again. If the host drive letter was swapped to the CVF, the original drive letter now reverts to the host drive, and the host's letter becomes available for other uses. If the letters were not swapped, the CVF's letter becomes available for other uses.

You don't need to unmount a floppy drive before removing it from the disk drive.

Example

DBLSPACE /U D

> Unmounts compressed drive D. If D was assigned to DBLSPACE.000, it now refers to the host drive. Otherwise, the host drive letter remains unchanged and D becomes an available drive letter.

DEBUG

Starts a program that lets you test and debug an executable program file.

Format

DEBUG [*filespec* [*parameters*]]

Parameters

none	Starts DEBUG without loading a program.
filespec	Loads a program for debugging. The program may include a path; it must include the extension (usually EXE or COM).
parameters	Provides any parameters for the program to be loaded.

Notes

When DEBUG starts, it displays its own command prompt, a hyphen (-). You enter DEBUG commands at the hyphen. You can exit DEBUG with the command Q (for quit).

See DEBUG online help for other DEBUG commands.

Examples

DEBUG

Starts DEBUG without loading a program.

DEBUG MYCAL.COM JAN

Starts DEBUG; loads a program called MYCAL.COM found in the current directory; passes the parameter value JAN to MYCAL.COM.

DEFRAG

Reorganizes files on a drive to optimize file performance; sorts directory entries.

Format

DEFRAG [*drive*] [/F | /U] [/S*order*] [/V] [/B] [/SKIPHIGH]

Parameters and Switches

none	Opens the DEFRAG dialog box so you can select the drive and options.
drive	Identifies the drive to optimize.
/F	Defragments files and free space.
/U	Defragments files only.
/S*order*	Sorts directory entries; *order* specifies the sort field (see Notes).
/V	Verifies data after moving it.
/B	Reboots when DEFRAG ends.
/SKIPHIGH	Loads the DEFRAG program in conventional memory.

Notes

Excessive file fragmentation can slow down system performance. DEFRAG brings a fragmented file's clusters together (if space permits).

/F also moves all empty space to the end of the drive, decreasing the likelihood of future fragmentation.

DEFRAG doesn't move hidden or system files because these files must often stay where they are. Such files can cause other files to be fragmented, especially if you have used the /F switch.

Before starting DEFRAG, do the following:

- Delete all unnecessary files from the drive.

- Delete any delete-tracking files, such as PCTRACKR.DEL. (They would not be valid after DEFRAG.)

- Purge all unneeded files from SENTRY (or other deletion protection facilities).

- Quit all programs, including Microsoft Windows. (Do not run DEFRAG from a DOS prompt provided by another program.)

- Run CHKDSK /F to clean up lost allocation units.

- Disable any program that might write to the disk while DEFRAG is running, such as a program scheduled to update a file automatically.

- Remove system and hidden attributes from files that should be defragmented and moved. (But keep in mind that many system and hidden files should not be moved.)

If you specify both drive and /F or /U in the command line, DEFRAG immediately begins defragmenting. Otherwise, the DEFRAG dialog box opens. In the dialog box, you can choose drive, defragmentation type, and sort order. You can specify /V, /B, or /SKIPHIGH only on the command line; there is no opportunity to choose them in the dialog box.

/S sorts the directory entries for each directory on the drive; but it doesn't move files around.

The values for *order* are as follows:

N   by name (alphanumeric order)

N- by name (reverse alphanumeric order)

E   by extension (alphanumeric order)

E- by extension (reverse alphanumeric order)

D   by date and time, earliest first

D- by date and time, latest first

S   by size, smallest first

S- by size, largest first

DEFRAG loads into upper memory, if possible, unless you specify Use /SKIPHIGH.

You should always reboot after DEFRAG to clear caches and buffers of old directory information. You *must* reboot if you're using Fastopen.

You can't use DEFRAG to optimize network drives or drives created with Interlnk.

DEFRAG sets an exit code as follows:

0   DEFRAG was successful.

1   An internal error occurred.

2   There was not enough free space on the disk. DEFRAG needs at least one free cluster.

3   The user pressed Ctrl-C or Ctrl-Break to stop DEFRAG.

4   A general error occurred.

5   A read error occurred.

6   A write error occurred.

7   An allocation error occurred. (Run CHKDSK /F to correct this error.)

Examples

DEFRAG

Opens the DEFRAG dialog box.

DEFRAG /B

Opens the DEFRAG dialog box; reboots when DEFRAG ends.

DEFRAG D:

Opens the DEFRAG dialog box so you can choose defragmentation type.

DEFRAG C: /F /B

Defragments files on drive C and eliminates free space between files; reboots when DEFRAG ends.

DEFRAG C: /U /SD-

Defragments files on drive C but does not eliminate free space between files. Sorts directory entries by date and time, with the latest first.

DEL

Deletes a file or a set of files. ERASE is interchangeable with DEL.

Format

DEL *filespec* [/P]

ERASE *filespec* [/P]

Parameters and Switches

filespec   Identifies file(s) to delete.

/P   Prompts for confirmation before each deletion.

Notes

DEL can't delete files with the system, hidden, or read-only attribute.

You can delete all the files in one directory (except system, hidden, and read-only files) by using *.* as *filespec* or by using a path without a file name. Without /P, DEL asks whether you really want to erase all the files.

See UNDELETE for information about possibly restoring a deleted file.

Examples

DEL OLDFILE.EXE

Deletes OLDFILE.EXE from the current directory (unless OLDFILE.EXE is a system, hidden, or read-only file).

DEL C:\OFFICE\OLDFILE.* /P

Deletes all files named OLDFILE with any extension from directory C:\OFFICE except those with system, hidden, or read-only attributes. DEL displays each file name and asks whether you want to delete it.

DEL *.*

Asks whether you really want to delete all files in the directory. If you answer Y, DEL deletes all files in the current directory except system, hidden, and read-only files.

DEL C:\OFFICE

Asks whether you really want to delete all files in the directory. If you answer Y, DEL deletes all files in C:\OFFICE except system, hidden, and read-only files.

DEL C:\OFFICE*.* /P

Displays each file name in C:\OFFICE (except system and hidden files) and asks you if you want to delete it. If you answer Y for a read-only file, DEL tells you Access denied.

DELOLDOS

Removes old version(s) of DOS from the drive.

Format

DELOLDOS

Notes

When you install DOS 6.0, Install saves any previous DOS version it finds on the boot drive in a directory called OLD_DOS.*n*. If you install DOS several times for some reason, you may have several such directories, with *n*=1 for the first, 2 for the second, and so on.

When you are sure that you can live with DOS 6.0, you can remove all these OLD_DOS.*n* directories at once by running DELOLDOS.

DELTREE

Deletes a directory and all its files and subdirectories; deletes files in a directory.

Format

DELTREE [/Y] *path* | *filespec*

Parameters and Switches

/Y	Carries out DELTREE without first prompting you for confirmation.
path	Specifies the directory at the top of the branch that you want to delete.
filespec	Specifies file(s) and directories that you want to delete.

Notes

You can't use DELTREE to delete the current directory. You can, however, delete files and children of the current directory.

DELTREE deletes files and subdirectories regardless of their attributes. When DELTREE deletes a directory, it deletes the entire branch headed by the directory with no regard to filenames or attributes within that branch.

You can use wild cards. DELTREE deletes every file and subdirectory (with all its contents) whose name matches the global name.

DELTREE always prompts you for confirmation before deleting a file or a branch. (In the prompt, it calls a file a subdirectory.)

When DELTREE is successful, it returns an exit code of 0.

Examples

DELTREE C:\TEST1

Deletes the TEST1 directory on drive C, including all its files and subdirectories and their files. Prompts before deleting the branch. (If TEST1 is a file, deletes the file.)

DELTREE C:\HOLD*.1

If C:\HOLD contains any files with names matching the filespec, deletes them, prompting before each one. If C:\HOLD has any child subdirectories with names matching the filespec, deletes them along with all their files and subdirectories; prompts before deleting each branch.

DEVICE

Loads a device driver into conventional memory.

Format

DEVICE=*filespec* [*parameters*]

Parameters

filespec	Identifies the device driver to load.
parameters	Specifies any command line parameters required by the device driver.

Notes

You must not load COUNTRY.SYS and KEYBOARD.SYS, with the DEVICE command. Use the COUNTRY command to load COUNTRY.SYS and the KEYB command to load KEYBOARD.SYS. If you try to load either of them with DEVICE, your system halts and you must bypass these commands in CONFIG.SYS to re-start it.

See on-line help for directions on loading the device drivers included in DOS. For third-party device drivers, see the manufacturer's instructions.

See DEVICEHIGH to load device drivers into upper memory instead of conventional memory.

Examples

DEVICE=C:\DOS\ANSI.SYS

Loads the device driver ANSI.SYS into conventional memory.

DEVICE=C:\DOS\DISPLAY.SYS CON=(EGA,437,3)

Loads the device driver DISPLAY.SYS into conventional memory. Note that the text from CON to the end of the command represents parameters that DISPLAY.SYS requires for its operation.

DEVICEHIGH

Loads a device driver into upper memory.

Format

DEVICEHIGH [[/L:region[,min][;region[,min]...]] [/S]] filespec [parameters]

Parameters and Switches

filespec	Identifies the device driver.
/L	Loads the device driver into specific region(s) of upper memory.
region	Identifies a region in upper memory.
min	Specifies the minimum size required in a region when the device driver is running.
/S	Shrinks the UMB to its minimum size while the driver is loading.
parameters	Specifies any command line parameters required by the device driver.

Notes

See DEVICE for information and warnings about loading device drivers.

If you have an 80386 or later processor, have loaded EMM386.EXE, and requested UMB support, you may have upper memory blocks (UMBs) available. DEVICEHIGH loads a device driver into available UMBs. If not, DEVICEHIGH loads the driver into conventional memory, if possible.

By default, DEVICEHIGH loads a driver into the largest free UMB and makes all other UMBs available for the driver's use. You can use the /L switch to load the driver into a specific region of memory and to specify other regions the driver can use. The Mem command can tell you what regions of memory are free and how many regions a given device driver needs.

Normally DOS loads a driver into a specified region only if that region contains a UMB larger than the driver's load size (usually the file size). But some drivers expand after loading. Use *min* to specify the minimum size that the driver requires in *region*.

/S shrinks the UMB to its minimum size while the driver is loading. This makes the most efficient use of memory. You can use /S only if you use /L; it affects only UMBs for which you specify *min*.

See MEMMAKER for a command that automatically converts all DEVICE commands to DEVICEHIGH, generating /L parameters and /S as needed for optimal memory configuration.

DOS 5's DEVICEHIGH command, which has a different format, still works with DOS 6.

Examples

DEVICEHIGH=C:\DOS\ANSI.SYS

> Loads the ANSI.SYS driver into upper memory if available.

DEVICEHIGH=/L:2;3 C:\DOS\DISPLAY.SYS CON=(EGA,437,3)

> Loads the device driver DISPLAY.SYS into region 2 of upper memory and allows the driver to also use region 3 if necessary. Note that the text from CON to the end of the command represents parameters that DISPLAY.SYS requires for its operation.

DEVICEHIGH=/L:1,30;3,20 /S C:\DRIVERS\NEWMS.SYS

Loads a third-party driver NEWMS.SYS found in the C:\DRIVERS directory into upper memory. Requests a minimum of 30K in region 1 and shrinks the UMB to 30K while loading. Also reserves 20K minimum in region 3 and shrinks that UMB to 20K while loading.

DIR

Displays a list of a directory's files and subdirectories.

Format

DIR [*filespec*] [/P] [/W] [/A[*attrib*]] [/O[*order*]] [/S] [/B] [/L] [/C]

Parameters and Switches

filespec	Specifies the directory and file(s) to list.
/P	Displays one page at a time.
/W	Displays the listing in wide format, with as many as five names per line.
/A[*attrib*]	Displays entries that meet the criteria in *attrib*.
/O[*order*]	Displays entries in the order specified by *order*.
/S	Lists contents of subdirectories too.
/B	Suppresses heading and summary information and lists full filespecs (including path) for all selected entries.
/L	Displays directory listing in lowercase.
/C	Displays the compression ratio of files stored on DBLSPACE volumes.

Notes

The DIRCMD environment variable establishes default switches for the DIR command (see SET). These notes describe DOS's defaults when you don't set DIRCMD.

When you use /W, the listing does not show size, date, or time. In this format, DIR encloses subdirectory names in brackets, as in [DOS].

DIR does not list system or hidden files or subdirectories unless /A requests them.

When you include the /A switch, DIR lists only those files and subdirectories that have the specified attribute(s). /A without *attrib* requests all files regardless of their attributes.

Permissible values for *attrib* are as follows:

H	Lists hidden files or subdirectories
-H	Lists nonhidden files or subdirectories
S	Lists system files or subdirectories
-S	Lists nonsystem files or subdirectories
D	Lists subdirectories (no files)
-D	Lists files (no subdirectories)
A	Lists files and subdirectories with the archive attribute
-A	Lists files or subdirectories without the archive attribute
R	Lists read-only files or subdirectories
-R	Lists nonread-only files or subdirectories

Don't put spaces between multiple values in *attrib*; /AHS-R lists files and subdirectories that are both hidden and system but not read-only.

By default, DIR lists entries in the order that they appear in the directory. /O without *order* displays directories first, sorted by name and extension, then files sorted by name and extension.

Values for *order* are as follows:

A	List entries in alphanumeric order by name
-A	Lists entries in reverse alphanumeric order by name
E	Lists entries in alphanumeric order by extension
-E	Lists entries in reverse alphanumeric order by extension
D	Lists entries by date and time, earliest first
-D	Lists entries by date and time, latest first

S   Lists entries by file size, smallest first

-S   Lists entries by file size, largest first

G   Lists all subdirectories before all files

-G   Lists all files before all subdirectories

C   Lists entries by compression ratio, lowest first

-C   Lists entries by compression ratio, highest first

Don't put spaces between multiple *order* codes. DIR sorts by the first value first; within that, by the second value, and so on. For example, if you use /OES, DIR sorts entries by extension, then by size (smallest first) within each extension.

/S produces a listing for each subdirectory in the branch (except hidden and system subdirectories). You can get a more compact listing by combining /S with /B.

/S combined with /A includes an entry for a hidden or system subdirectory in the parent directory's listing but does not list the subdirectory's contents. The only way to list the contents of a hidden or system subdirectory is to specify the subdirectory's name in *filespec*.

You can override DIRCMD settings for a single command by putting a minus sign in front of the switch letter. You can turn off the /W switch for a single DIR command, for example, by using /-W in the command line.

Examples

These examples assume that that you have not set DIRCMD.

DIR /P

Lists the current directory (except system or hidden files and subdirectories), pausing after each full screen until you press any key.

DIR E:\WIN*.BAT /S

Lists all files and subdirectories with extension BAT in E:\WIN and its subdirectories (except hidden and system files and subdirectories).

DIR MYFILE.* /OE /B > PRN

Prints a listing (with no heading and no summary) of all files and subdirectories named MYFILE with any extension in the current directory (except system and hidden ones). DIR sorts the listing alphanumerically by extension.

DIR C:\ /AD

Lists all subdirectories of the root directory on drive C, including system and hidden ones.

DIR /A

Lists all subdirectories and files in the current directory, including system and hidden ones.

DIR /A-RA /W

Lists, in wide format, all subdirectories and files in the current directory, including system and hidden ones, that have the archive but not the read-only attributes.

DIR /O-GND

Lists all subdirectories and files in the current directory except hidden and system ones. DIR displays the files first, then subdirectories. Within each of these groups, DIR sorts alphanumerically by name and within name by date and time.

DIR MYFILE.BAT /B /S

Lists all files in the current branch that have the name MYFILE.BAT except system or hidden files, or those in system or hidden subdirectories. The listing does not include headings or summaries for the directory or for any subdirectory listed, but displays the full path for each file and subdirectory. This is a good way to find a missing file on a drive.

DISKCOMP

Compares two floppy disks.

Format

DISKCOMP [*drive1*] [*drive2*] [/1] [/8]

Parameters and Switches

drive1   Identifies one drive that holds a disk for comparison.

drive2   Identifies a second drive that holds a disk for comparison.

/1   Compares only the first side of the disks, even if they are double-sided.

/8   Compares only the first 8 sectors per track, even if the disks contain 9 or 15 sectors per track.

Notes

DISKCOMP works with floppy disks only.

If you omit *drive2*, DISKCOMP uses the current drive as *drive2*. If you omit *drive1* and *drive2*, DISKCOMP uses the current drive as both *drive1* and *drive2*. When *drive1* and *drive2* are the same drive, DISKCOMP prompts you to change disks as necessary.

The disks must have the same format. The /1 and /8 switches can make certain types of disks compatible by ignoring either the second side or additional sectors per track.

DISKCOMP compares disks track by track, not file by file. When you use COPY or XCOPY to copy all files from one disk to another, the data probably does not reside in the same locations on both disks, so DISKCOMP does not recognize the disks as identical.

DISKCOMP ignores differences in volume serial numbers.

If you have just copied a disk with Diskcopy and DISKCOMP finds the copy not identical to the original, the problem may be due to bad sectors or a failing drive or memory chip.

DISKCOMP sets an exit code as follows:

    0   The disks are the same.

    1   DISKCOMP found differences.

    2   The user pressed Ctrl-C or Ctrl-Break to stop DISKCOMP.

    3   A critical error occurred.

    4   An initialization error occurred.

In a batch program you can follow DISKCOMP with an If command to test ERRORLEVEL and decide what to do next.

Examples

DISKCOMP A: B:

Compares the disk in drive A to the disk in drive B.

DISKCOMP A: A:

Compares the disk in drive A to a second disk that you will swap into drive A.

DISKCOMP

Compares the disk in the current drive to a second disk that you will swap into the same drive.

DISKCOPY

Copies one floppy disk to another.

Format

DISKCOPY [*drive1*] [*drive2*] [/1] [/V]

Parameters and Switches

drive1	Identifies the drive holding the source disk.
drive2	Identifies the drive holding the destination disk.
/1	Copies the first side only of the source disk.
/V	Verifies that copied data is correct.

Notes

DISKCOPY works with floppy disks only. If the destination disk is unformatted, DISKCOPY formats it to match the source disk.

If you omit *drive2*, DISKCOPY uses the current drive as *drive2*. If you omit *drive1* and *drive2*, DISKCOPY uses the current drive as both *drive1* and *drive2*. When *drive1* and *drive2* are the same drive, DISKCOPY prompts you to change disks as necessary.

DISKCOPY creates a new serial number for the destination disk and displays the number when the copy is complete.

DISKCOPY copies the original disk exactly. Any fragmented files on the source disk are fragmented on the destination disk. After DISKCOPY, the destination disk's FAT is identical to the source's FAT. Any bad sector markings on the source are duplicated on the destination (little harm done); but the destination's original bad sector markings, if any, are overwritten (usually causing DISKCOPY to fail).

DISKCOPY sets an exit code as follows:

0   The copy was successful.

1   A non-fatal read/write error occurred.

2   The user pressed Ctrl-C or Ctrl-Break to stop DISKCOPY.

3   A critical error occurred.

4   An initialization error occurred.

In a batch program, you can follow DISKCOPY with an If command to test ERRORLEVEL and decide what to do next.

Examples

DISKCOPY A: B:

Copies the disk in drive A to the disk in drive B.

DISKCOPY A: A:

Copies the disk in drive A to a second disk that you will swap into drive A.

DISKCOPY /V

Copies the disk in the current drive to a second disk that you will swap into the drive. Verifies that copied data is correct.

DOS

Loads DOS into the High Memory Area (HMA) and specifies that DOS manages upper memory blocks (UMBs).

Format

DOS=[HIGH | LOW] [,] [UMB | NOUMB]

Parameters

HIGH | LOW   Specifies whether DOS should load itself into the HMA; the default is LOW.

UMB | NOUMB   Specifies whether DOS should manage upper memory blocks (UMBs); the default is NOUMB.

Notes

You can use one or both parameters. When you use both, either can come first, but you must separate them by a comma.

You must install an extended memory manager, such as HIMEM.SYS before you can use either HIGH or UMB. You must install an upper-memory-block provider before you can use UMB. If you have an 80386 or higher processor, you can use EMM386.EXE to provide upper memory blocks.

When you use HIGH, DOS attempts to load part of itself into the HMA, freeing conventional space. If DOS is unable to use the HMA, it defaults to LOW.

When you load DOS in the HMA, some programs may have trouble loading in conventional memory. See Loadfix for details.

Examples

DOS=HIGH

> DOS loads itself into the HMA.

DOS=UMB

> DOS can access upper memory blocks when loading programs and device drivers.

DOS=HIGH,UMB

DOS loads itself into the HMA and can load programs and device drivers into UMBs.

DOSKEY

Saves and provides access to commands and macros entered at the DOS command prompt.

Format

DOSKEY [/BUFSIZE=*size*] [/INSERT | /OVERSTRIKE] [/HISTORY] [/MACROS] [*mname=text*] [/REINSTALL]

Parameters and Switches

none	Loads the DOSKEY TSR with default values for BUFSIZE and INSERT	OVERSTRIKE; immediately begins recording commands in the DOSKEY buffer.
/BUFSIZE=*size*	Specifies the size of the DOSKEY buffer. This parameter is effective only when loading or reinstalling the DOSKEY TSR.
/INSERT	Sets default typing mode to insert.
/OVERSTRIKE	Sets default typing mode to overstrike.
/HISTORY	Lists all commands in the DOSKEY buffer; abbreviate as /H.
/MACROS	Lists all current macros; abbreviate as /M.
mname=text	Defines a macro named *mname*. *Text* defines command(s) to execute when you run *mname*.
/REINSTALL	Installs a new copy of DOSKEY.

Notes

DOSKEY saves each command typed at the DOS prompt. When the buffer is full, each new command overlays the oldest command in the buffer. The minimum *size* for the DOSKEY buffer is 256 bytes; the default is 512 bytes.

DOSKEY lets you edit commands at the prompt using the following editing keys:

Left arrow	Moves the cursor left one character
Right arrow	Moves the cursor right one character
Ctrl-Left arrow	Moves the cursor left one word
Ctrl-Right arrow	Moves the cursor right one word
Home	Moves the cursor to the beginning of the command line
End	Moves the cursor to the end of the command line
Esc	Clears the command line
Insert	Toggles insert mode on and off
Backspace	Deletes the character to the left of the cursor
Delete	Deletes the character at the cursor
Ctrl-Home	Deletes from the cursor to the beginning of the command line
Ctrl-End	Deletes from the cursor to the end of the command line

When insert mode is on, typing inserts text at the cursor. When overstrike mode is on, typing replaces the text at the cursor. The insert key toggles between the two typing modes, but each time you press Enter, it returns to the default.

If you don't specify the typing mode when installing or reinstalling DOSKEY, /OVERSTRIKE is the default. You can change the default (without reinstalling DOSKEY) by entering a DOSKEY command with the /INSERT or /OVERSTRIKE switch.

DOSKEY lets you recall commands from the buffer. Use these keys to recall a command:

Up arrow	Recalls the previous command in the buffer.
Down arrow	Recalls the next command in the buffer.

Page Up	Recalls the oldest command in the buffer.
Page Down	Recalls the newest command in the buffer.
F7	Displays a numbered list of all saved commands.
Alt-F7	Deletes all the commands in the buffer.
F8	Recalls the next command in the buffer that starts with the letters on the command line.
F9	Prompts for a command number, then recalls that command.

To recall a command without scanning the entire list, type the first few letters and press F8. Keep pressing F8 until DOSKEY recalls the desired command.

To recall a command by number, press F7 to scan the numbered list, find the command you want, then press F9 so you can enter its number.

DOSKEY displays a recalled command at the DOS prompt. You can edit and enter the command as though you had just typed it.

DOSKEY lets you include two or more commands on a command line. Separate commands by pressing Ctrl-T, which displays as ∂. Use this feature to create more effective entries in your command history. The command DIR A: ∂ DIR B: ∂ DIR C:, for example, which displays directories for the default directories on drives A, B, and C, can be recalled and entered as a single command.

A macro consists of one or more commands that you can execute by entering the macro name. Macro definitions can contain these special characters:

$G	Redirects output; equivalent to the redirection symbol for output (>). (If you use the redirection symbol itself, it redirects the output of the DOSKEY command instead of being stored as part of the macro.)
GG	Appends output to the end of a file; equivalent to the append redirection symbol for output (>>).
$L	Redirects input; equivalent to the redirection symbol for input (<).
$B	Sends output to the next command; equivalent to the pipe symbol (	).

$T	Separates commands; equivalent to the DOSKEY command separator (Ctrl-T).
$$	Specifies the dollar-sign character.
$n	Represents a parameter to be specified when the macro is run; n may be 1 through 9. These are similar to the batch parameters %1 through %9.
$*	Represents all parameters. $* is replaced by everything on a command line following a macro name.

A macro may have the same name as a DOS command. To run the macro, type its name at the DOS prompt. To use the DOS command instead, insert one or more spaces between the prompt and the command. Use this feature to override DOS commands that you want to adapt for some reason.

DOSKEY macros and the command history share the same buffer. Newly defined macros may overlay commands in the buffer, but neither commands nor new macros ever overlay existing macros. DOSKEY limits the number of macros you can create to save about half of the buffer for the command history.

A batch program cannot execute a macro (although it can include a DOSKEY command to create one).

A macro cannot be more than 120 characters long.

/REINSTALL installs a new copy of DOSKEY with an empty DOSKEY buffer. The previous copy of DOSKEY remains in memory, although inaccessible, wasting memory space.

Examples

DOSKEY

> If this is the first DOSKEY command in a session, it installs the DOSKEY TSR with a 512-byte buffer and overstrike as the typing mode. Otherwise this command has no effect.

DOSKEY /BUFSIZE=1024 /INSERT

> If this is the first DOSKEY command in a session, it installs the DOSKEY TSR with a buffer size of 1024 bytes and a default typing mode of insert. Otherwise the command only changes the default typing mode to insert (and /BUFSIZE has no effect).

DOSKEY /H /M

> Displays the command history and lists all current macro definitions.

DOSKEY /H > TEMP.BAT

> Copies the command history to TEMP.BAT.

DOSKEY ACOPY=COPY $1 $2 $T DIR $2 $G PRN

> Defines a macro ACOPY that copies a file then prints a directory listing for the new file name.

ACOPY JUNEDAT.NEW JUNEDAT.OLD

> Executes the ACOPY macro, copying JUNEDAT.NEW to JUNEDAT.OLD and printing a directory listing for JUNEDAT.OLD.

DOSSHELL

Starts Dosshell, a graphical interface to DOS.

Format

DOSSHELL [/T[:*resolution*[n]] | /G[:*resolution*[n]]] [/B]

Parameters and Switches

/T	Starts Dosshell in text mode.
/G	Starts Dosshell in graphics mode.
/B	Starts Dosshell in black and white.
resolution	Specifies the screen-resolution category.
n	Specifies screen resolution when there is more than one choice within a category.

Notes

DOSSHELL requires at least 384K of conventional memory.

If you want to run both DOSSHELL and Microsoft Windows, start the Shell from within Windows, not vice versa.

If the file DOSSHELL.INI is not in the same directory as DOSSHELL.EXE, set the environment variable DOSSHELL to show the path for DOSSHELL.INI before you start up DOSSHELL. (See the SET command.)

Resolution can be L, M, or H for low, medium, or high resolution, respectively. The default value depends on your hardware. Possible values for *n*, as well as the default value, depend on your hardware.

If you start DOSSHELL without /T or /G and cannot read the screen, press F3 to get back to the command prompt and try using /T for text mode. Once DOSSHELL is running, you can adjust the display mode (T or G) and screen resolution by using the Options Display command. When you set values using Options Display, DOSSHELL saves them in DOSSHELL.INI and they become the default settings. (Command line switches and parameters override the default settings but do not set new defaults.)

Examples

DOSSHELL /T:L

Starts DOSSHELL in text mode with low resolution (25 lines per screen).

DOSSHELL /G /B

Starts DOSSHELL in black-and-white graphics mode with default resolution.

DOSSHELL

Starts DOSSHELL with default settings from DOSSHELL.INI.

DRIVPARM

Redefines parameters for an existing physical drive.

Format

DRIVPARM=/D:*n* [/C] [/F:*type*] [/H:*heads*] [/I] [/N] [/S:*sectors*] [/T:*tracks*]

Parameters and Switches

/D:*n*   Identifies the drive to be redefined.

/C   Indicates that the drive has change line support.

/F:*type*   Specifies the drive type.

/H:*heads*   Specifies the number of heads.

/I   Indicates an electronically compatible 3.5-inch drive.

/N   Indicates a non-removable drive.

/S:*sectors*   Specifies number of sectors per track.

/T:*tracks*   Specifies number of tracks.

Notes

Normally DOS senses block devices, such as floppy disks, hard disks, and tape drives while booting, but occasionally DOS is wrong. If DOS has trouble accessing a new block device, especially in formatting it, include the DRIVPARM command in CONFIG.SYS so that DOS always accesses the drive correctly.

In /D, *n* should be 0 for drive A, 1 for drive B, 2 for drive C, and so on.

Change-line support, indicated by /C, means that a disk drive can detect when its door is open. If you omit /C, DOS treats the drive as if it has no change-line support and checks the disk serial number every time it accesses the drive.

> Never specify that a disk drive has change-line support when it doesn't. Doing so could cause DOS to overwrite valuable data because it doesn't know you changed disks.

In /F, *type* can have one of these values:

0   360K or less
1   1.2M
2   720K
3   8-inch single density
4   8-inch double density
5   Hard disk

6	Tape drive	
7	1.44M	
8	Read/write optical disk	
9	2.88M	

If you don't use /F, disk type defaults to 2 (720K).

The following table shows the defaults for *heads*, *sectors*, and *tracks* when /F indicates a floppy disk (types 0, 1, 2, 7, or 9). To specify other values, use the /H, /S, and/or /T switches as necessary.

Type	Capacity	Heads	Sectors	Tracks
0	160K	1	8	40
0	180K	1	9	40
0	320K	2	8	40
0	360K	2	9	40
2	720K	2	9	80
1	1.2M	2	15	80
7	1.44M	2	18	80
9	2.88M	2	36	80

Use /I if the drive is a 3.5-inch floppy disk drive using your existing drive controller, but your ROM BIOS does not support 3.5-inch floppy disks.

Wrong or inconsistent values can result in erratic or bad formatting on the drive. If you must redefine a drive, get the right values from your drive's documentation or manufacturer.

If you redefine your boot drive incorrectly, your system may not boot or it may boot and destroy the root directory. Be sure to have valid backups before redefining the boot drive.

Examples

DRIVPARM /D:1 /C

Defines drive B as a 720K drive (by default) with change-line support.

DRIVPARM /D:4 /F:6 /H:1 /S:40 /T:28

Defines the fifth drive as a tape drive with one head that writes 28 tracks of 40 sectors per track.

ECHO

Turns command echoing features on or off or displays a message.

Format

ECHO [*message* | ON | OFF]

Parameters and Switches

none	Displays the current setting of ECHO.
ON | OFF	Turns command echoing on or off.
message	Displays *message* on the screen.
ECHO.	This special ECHO command displays a carriage return (a blank line). Be sure there is no space between ECHO and the period.

Notes

When command echoing is on, DOS displays the command prompt when it is ready to receive and process a command. When processing a batch program, DOS displays a command prompt line (the prompt and the command) followed by a blank line for each command in the program. Command echoing is on by default. Use ECHO ON to turn it on when it is off.

Turning off command echoing suppresses the command prompt, but you can still type and enter commands. When executing a batch program, it suppresses the command line and the blank line that normally follows it. Only command output is displayed. Use ECHO OFF to turn it off.

ECHO with *message* displays *message* as ECHO's command output, so *message* displays even when command echoing is off.

A batch program can change command echoing only for the duration of the program. If command echoing is on when a batch program starts, it is automatically turned on when the program ends; if it's off when the program starts, it's turned off when the program ends.

ECHO OFF doesn't take effect until DOS processes the next line. To suppress echoing ECHO OFF, or any other single line in a batch program, put @ in front of the line.

Examples

    @ECHO OFF
    ECHO.
    ECHO This batch program formats disks in drive A.
    ECHO You will need new 5.25 inch disks.
    ECHO.
    ECHO ON

> This sequence of commands in a batch program turns ECHO off (without displaying the ECHO command), then displays a blank line, a two-line message, and another blank line. Then it turns ECHO on again.

    ECHO. > PRN
    ECHO Beginning of weekly Report > PRN
    ECHO. > PRN

> Prints a blank line, then the message, then another blank line.

EDIT

Starts DOS's full-screen editor, which creates and changes ASCII text files.

Format

    EDIT [*filespec*] [/B] [/G] [/H] [/NOHI]

Parameters and Switches

none	Starts the editor with default screen characteristics and no startup file.
filespec	Opens an ASCII text file. If the file does not exist, creates it; if it does exist, displays its contents.
/B	Uses black-and-white screen mode.
/G	Uses fast-screen updating for a CGA monitor.
/H	Displays the maximum number of lines for your monitor.
/NOHI	Enables the use of an eight-color monitor.

Notes

EDIT does not work if QBASIC.EXE is not in the current directory, in the search path, or in the same directory as EDIT.COM. If you delete QBASIC.EXE to save space, you cannot use EDIT.

If EDIT does not display properly on your monitor, or does not display the shortcut keys, try using /B or /NOHI (or both).

Examples

EDIT ANYFILE.BAT /B

Creates or loads ANYFILE.BAT; displays black-and-white mode.

EDIT

Starts the editor in default mode without a startup file.

EMM386

Controls expanded memory support.

Format

EMM386 [ON | OFF | AUTO] [W=ON | W=OFF]

Parameters and Switches

none	Displays the status of EMM386 support.
ON	Enables the EMM386.EXE driver.
OFF	Disables the EMM386.EXE driver without unloading it.
AUTO	Lets programs control enabling and disabling of EMM386.EXE driver.
W=ON	Enables Weitek coprocessor support.
W=OFF	Disables Weitek coprocessor support. Default is W=OFF.

Notes

You must have a 386 or higher processor and must have installed the EMM386.EXE device driver before you can use this command.

You cannot turn EMM386 off when it is providing UMBs or when any program is currently using expanded memory.

Some programs, including Microsoft's Windows 3.0 in Standard mode, require that EMM386 be off.

You cannot use OFF and W=ON in the same EMM386 command.

The Weitek coprocessor support requires the HMA. If you have used DOS=HIGH, you may not be able to enable Weitek coprocessor support. (See the DOS command.)

Examples

EMM386 OFF

Disables expanded memory support without unloading the EMM386 driver.

EMM386 AUTO

Lets programs enable or disable expanded memory support as needed.

ERASE

See Del.

EXIT

Quits a secondary command processor.

Format

EXIT

Notes

In a command processor started by COMMAND without /P, EXIT closes the child version and returns to the parent. In a command processor started by another program, such as Microsoft Windows or DOS Shell, EXIT closes the command processor and returns to the starting program. In other circumstances, EXIT has no effect.

See the COMMAND command for more information about parent and child command processors.

EXPAND

Expands compressed file(s).

Format

EXPAND [*filespec* ... [*destination*]]

Parameters

none   Prompts for *filespec* and *destination*.

filespec   Identifies a compressed file that you want to expand.

destination   Specifies the location and/or name of the expanded file(s).

Notes

Use EXPAND to decompress files from DOS 6 installation disks to make them usable. Expand does not decompress files compressed by disk-compression programs, such as DoubleSpace or third-party compression programs like PKZIP.

515

You can list more than one *filespec*, but you cannot use wild cards. When the command line contains more than one *filespec*, EXPAND assumes the last one is *destination*. When expanding more than one file, *destination* must be a directory, not a file name.

For a single *filespec*, *destination* can be a directory or a file name. EXPAND prompts for *destination* if you omit it.

Most of the files on the installation disks provided with DOS 6 are compressed. You can recognize a compressed file on these disks because the last character of the name is an underscore (_). DOS 6's Setup program expands these files. If you need to get a fresh copy of one of them, look at PACKING.LST on Disk 1 to find out which disk the file is on, what its compressed file name is, and what its expanded file name should be. Then put the correct disk in a drive and use EXPAND to copy the file.

If *destination* is a directory, the expanded file's name is the same as the compressed file's name. If the name ends in an underscore, you must change it to the proper name before using it as a DOS 6 file.

Examples

EXPAND A:\SORT.EX_ C:\DOS\SORT.EXE

Expands SORT.EX_ from the disk in drive A; puts the expanded file in C:\DOS with the name SORT.EXE.

EXPAND A:\SORT.EX_

Expands SORT.EX_ from the disk in drive A; prompts you for the destination.

EXPAND CGA.IN_ CGA.VI_ C:\DOS

Expands the files CGA.IN_ and CGA.VI_ found in the current directory and puts the expanded files into C:\DOS. The expanded files have the same names as the originals; before you can use them, you need to rename them as CGA.INI and CGA.VID, respectively.

FASTHELP

Provides online information about DOS commands or lists all commands.

Format

FASTHELP [*command*]

Parameters

none   Lists commands with a short description of each.

command   Displays a format summary for command.

Notes

FASTHELP command produces a short report showing the purpose and the format of *command*, along with a description of its parameters and switches. COMMAND /? produces the same report as FASTHELP command.

FASTHELP does not provide as much information, notes, or examples as Help does.

You can customize the FASTHELP.HLP file to add information about DOS commands or to include non-DOS commands so that this information is also available through FASTHELP. The added information affects only the listing produced by FASTHELP without a specific command name.

Examples

FASTHELP

Provides a paged list of commands and a short description of each.

FASTHELP COPY > PRN

Prints a short description of COPY and its parameters and switches. You can get the same description by entering COPY /? > PRN.

FASTOPEN

Starts Fastopen, which makes it faster to open frequently accessed files.

Format

FASTOPEN *drive*[*=n*] [...] [/X]

517

Parameters and Switches

drive	Identifies drive(s) to be tracked by FASTOPEN.
n	Number of files to track for the drive, from 10 to 999; the default is 48.
/X	Stores drive information in expanded memory instead of conventional memory.

Notes

Every time you open a file, FASTOPEN records its name and location. If you re-open the file, FASTOPEN saves time by retrieving its location from the buffer instead of the disk's directory structure.

FASTOPEN works on hard disks only and does not work on networks.

The total number of files being tracked for all drives must not exceed 999. FASTOPEN requires approximately 48 bytes per file.

You must restart DOS to change the Fastopen parameters; you cannot run FASTOPEN twice in one session.

Using the FASTOPEN command from DOS Shell can lock up your system.

You can install FASTOPEN from the command prompt or from CONFIG.SYS (see INSTALL).

If you use DEFRAG while FASTOPEN is running, you must reboot after DEFRAG so that FASTOPEN doesn't try to use the original locations for relocated files.

Some experts consider FASTOPEN unreliable, and some software refuses to operate with FASTOPEN present.

Examples

FASTOPEN C:=100

> Loads FASTOPEN, tracking 100 files on drive C.

FASTOPEN C:=100 D: E:=300 /X

> Loads FASTOPEN, tracking 100 files on drive C, 48 (by default) on drive D, and 300 on drive E. Keeps FASTOPEN records in expanded memory.

FC

Compares two files and displays lines or bytes that don't match.

Format

FC [/A] [/C] [/L] [/LB*lines*] [/N │ /B] [/T] [/W] [/*resynch*] *filespec1 filespec2*

Parameters and Switches

filespec1	Identifies first file to compare.
filespec2	Identifies second file to compare.
/A	Abbreviates output by showing only the first and last line for a series of mismatched lines; the default shows all mismatched lines.
/C	Ignores case.
/L	Compares files in ASCII mode, comparing line by line and attempting to resynchronize after finding a mismatch. This is the default mode for files that do not have the extensions EXE, COM, SYS, OBJ, LIB, or BIN.
/N	Displays line numbers when showing mismatched lines during an ASCII comparison.
/B	Compares files in binary mode, byte by byte, without attempting to resynchronize after a mismatch. This is the default mode with files having the extensions EXE, COM, SYS, OBJ, LIB, or BIN. Don't use any other switches in binary mode (all other switches pertain to ASCII mode).
/LB*lines*	Specifies the number of lines in the resynch buffer; the default is 100.
/T	Does not expand tabs to spaces. The default is to expand tabs with stops at each eighth character position.
/W	Ignores white space (see notes).
/*resynch*	Specifies the number of lines that must match before files are resynchronized; the default is 2.

Notes

You can use wildcards in either filespec. If you use a wildcard in *filespec1* only, FC compares all the specified files to the file named by *filespec2*. If you use wildcards in both filespecs, FC compares files that have the same wildcard characters in their names. (See the examples.)

In ASCII mode, FC tries to find a place to continue the comparison after a mismatch. It fills its resynch buffer with lines from the second file, then searches the first file and the buffer for matching lines. If it finds a match, the files are said to be resynchronized and the comparison continues from that point; otherwise, FC gives up. (Notice that it might not search all the second file.) The */resynch* parameter determines how many lines in a row must match for resynchronization. The /LB parameter determines the size of the resynch buffer. Increasing *lines* or decreasing *resynch* can improve your chances of resynchronizing. Rerunning the FC command with *filespec1* and *filespec2* reversed also can make a difference.

Because of resynchronization, extra lines in one file don't cause FC to treat all subsequent lines as mismatches.

For an ASCII comparison, FC reports differences by displaying the name of the first file, the last line that matches in both files, the mismatched lines in the first file, then the first line to match in both files; then it lists the same information for the second file.

If *resynch* is greater than 1, some matching lines may count as mismatched and show up in the listing of mismatched lines. The files are not resynchronized until the specified number of consecutive lines match.

If you use /W, FC ignores tabs and spaces at the beginning of a line. Also, consecutive tabs or spaces (white space) anywhere count as one space. In other words, some extra spaces or tabs in a line will not cause a mismatch.

In binary mode, FC reports differences by showing, in hexadecimal, the address relative to the beginning of the file and the mismatched bytes, first from *filespec1*, then *filespec2*.

If the two filespecs default to different comparison modes and you haven't specified /B or /L, FC uses the default comparison mode for *filespec1*. When you use wildcards for *filespec1*'s extension, FC defaults to ASCII comparisons.

Examples

FC /LB200 /W JANUARY.DOC NEWYEAR.DOC

Makes an ASCII comparison of JANUARY.DOC and
NEWYEAR.DOC; stops if more than 200 consecutive lines don't
match; ignores white space. Two lines are required for resynchronization.

FC /B *.OLD EXTRA.SAV

Makes binary comparisons of each file with extension OLD in the
current directory to the file EXTRA.SAV.

FC OLD.EXE E:*.*

Makes a binary comparison of OLD.EXE in the current directory to
OLD.EXE in E:\.

FC /C /1 *.OLD *.SAV

Makes ASCII comparisons, ignoring case, of each file in the current
directory with extension OLD to the file with the same name but
extension SAV. Only one line is required for synchronization.

FCBS

Allocates file control blocks.

Format

FCBS=*n*

Parameter

n   Specifies number of FCBs to allocate; can be 1 through 255;
default is 4.

Notes

Early DOS versions used file control blocks (FCBs) for file handling. Some older
programs still control files this way; such programs may require you to use the FCBS
command in CONFIG.SYS.

See the FILES command for the newer file handling method.

Example

FCBS=8

Specifies that DOS can have up to eight file control blocks open at the same time.

FDISK

Starts the FDISK program, which partitions a hard disk for use with DOS; displays the status of hard disk(s).

Format

FDISK [/STATUS]

Parameters and Switches

none   Starts the FDISK program.

/STATUS   Displays an overview of the partition information of your hard disk(s). Does not start FDISK.

Notes

Do not experiment with partitioning. If you accidentally delete or change a drive or partition, you could lose the data from it.

Once you start it, the FDISK program prompts you for information about the tasks you want to accomplish.

FDISK does not work on a drive formed by using ASIGN, JOIN, or SUBST, on a network drive, or on an Interlnk drive.

Examples

FDISK /STATUS

Displays the status of partitions on your hard drive(s).

FDISK

Starts the FDISK program.

FILES

Sets the number of files that DOS can access at one time using file handles.

Format

FILES=*n*

Parameter

n   Specifies the number of file handles; can be 8 through 255; default is 8.

Notes

DOS uses file handles to keep track of open files. Many programs need more than eight file handles and require you to specify FILES in CONFIG.SYS.

Example

FILES=20

Allows DOS to have up to 20 files open at once.

FIND

Searches for a specific string of text in a file or files.

Format

FIND [/V] [/C] [/N] [/I] "*string*" [*filespec* ...]

Parameters and Switches

"*string*"   Specifies the group of characters you want to search for. The quotation marks are required.

filespec   Identifies a file to be searched.

/V   Displays all the lines not containing the specified string.

/C   Displays only a count of all the lines that contain the specified string.

/N	Includes line numbers in the display.
/I	Ignores case.

Notes

If you omit *filespec*, FIND takes input from the DOS standard input source, usually the keyboard or a pipe.

You cannot use wild cards in *filespec*. You can, however, list more than one *filespec*, separating them by spaces. You also can use FIND in a FOR command to search multiple files. (See FOR.)

If the search string contains quotation marks, use two quotation marks to search for one. That is, "David ""Daffy"" Jones" searches for David "Daffy" Jones.

/C and /V together display a count of the lines that do not contain the specified string. If you use /C and /N together, FIND ignores /N.

FIND considers a carriage return to be the end of a line, although many word-processing programs use them only at the ends of paragraphs. If you search for the string "no good" and one line ends with "no" while the next line begins with "good," FIND does not recognize "no good." Try to limit your search strings to ones not likely to be interrupted by carriage returns.

Examples

FIND /I /N "TENTH" TEST1.BAT TEST2.BAT

Displays every line containing the word "tenth" in files TEST1.BAT and TEST2.BAT. The search ignores case, so it will find "TENTH," "tenth," or "Tenth." The line number displays with each line.

DIR *.* | FIND /V "-93"

Displays every line from the directory listing that does not contain -93. This could produce a list of all files in the current directory not created or modified during 1993.

FOR %F IN (*.BAT) DO FIND /I "FORMAT" %F

Searches all BAT files in the current directory and lists all lines that contain the word format, ignoring case.

FOR

Repeats a command for each item in a set.

Format

FOR %*x* | %%*x* IN (*set*) DO *command*

Parameters and Switches

x   Identifies a replaceable variable which can be used in *command*. May be any non-numeric character. Use %*x* at the command prompt and %%*x* in a batch program.

(*set*)   Identifies a set of variables to replace *x*. The parentheses are required.

command   Specifies the command to repeat, including its parameters and switches.

Notes

FOR repeats *command* for each item in *set*. Use the replaceable variable (%*x* or %%*x*) in *command* to indicate where to substitute items from *set*.

Separate items in *set* by spaces.

When *set* contains a filespec with wildcards, FOR repeats *command* for each file that matches the filespec.

Command cannot be another FOR command.

You can redirect *command*'s output using > or >>, but you cannot use | to pipe its output.

Examples

FOR %R IN (A B C D) DO DIR %R:\ >PRN

Prints directory listings for the root directories of drives A, B, C, and D when used at the command prompt.

FOR %%R IN (A B C D) DO DIR %%R:\ >PRN

Prints directory listings for the root directories of drives A, B, C, and D when used in a batch program.

FOR %F IN (*.SAV *.OLD) DO FIND "ECHO" %F

> For each file with extension SAV or OLD in the current directory, displays the lines in which "ECHO" occurs; used at the command prompt.

FOR %%F IN (*.SAV *.OLD) DO FIND "ECHO" %%F

> For each file with extension SAV or OLD in the current directory, displays the lines in which "ECHO" occurs; used in a batch program.

FORMAT

Prepares a disk for use or reuse.

Format

FORMAT *drive* [/Q] [/U] [V[:*label*]] [/S | /B] [/F:*size*] [/T:*tracks* /N:*sectors*] [/1] [/4] [/8]

Parameters and Switches

drive	Identifies the drive to format.
/Q	Does a quick format.
/U	Does an unconditional format.
/V[:*label*]	Specifies the volume label for the formatted disk. *Label* can be up to 11 characters. If you omit /V, or use /V but omit *label*, DOS prompts you for the volume label after formatting is complete. Do not use with /8.
/S	Makes the disk bootable.
/B	Reserves space for system files on a newly formatted disk.
/F:*size*	Overrides the default capacity of the disk. Specify *size* in bytes, as 360K or 1.2M. Don't use this switch with /T, /N, /1, /4, or /8.
/T:*tracks*	Specifies the number of tracks on the disk; must be used with /N. Don't use with /F.

/N:*sectors*   Specifies the number of sectors per track; must be used with /T. Don't use with /F.

/1   Formats a single-sided disk. Don't use with /F.

/4   Formats a 360K disk in a 1.2M drive. If used with /1, formats 180K disk in a 1.2M drive. Don't use with /F.

/8   Formats a 5.25-inch disk with 8 sectors per track (for DOS 2.0 or earlier). Don't use with /F or /V.

Notes

If you specify /U (but not /Q), or if the disk capacity is being changed, or if the disk is unformatted, DOS performs an unconditional format. It lays out new sectors, tests the surface for bad spots, installs a boot sector, and creates the root directory and FATs. Any data already on the disk is lost. (For an unformatted disk, it's faster to specify /U than to let DOS discover that the disk is unformatted.)

If you don't specify /U or /Q for an already formatted disk, and the disk capacity is not being changed, DOS performs a safe format. It zeros the FAT, clears the root directory, checks for bad clusters, and saves information for UNFORMAT. Existing data is not destroyed. This is faster than an unconditional format, and UNFORMAT may be able to recover existing data if necessary.

If you specify /Q for an already formatted disk and the disk capacity is not being changed, DOS performs a quick format. This is the same as a safe format except that it doesn't check for bad clusters. This is even faster than a safe format, and UNFORMAT may be able to recover existing data if necessary.

For the fastest format, use both /Q and /U. DOS does a quick format, if possible, but doesn't save UNFORMAT information.

If a used disk has been producing `sector not found` errors or read/write errors, format it with /U to renew the sectors. Note that all previous data will be destroyed.

Don't format a disk at a capacity higher than it's designed for. Do not, for example, format a 360K floppy disk as 1.2M. (It's permissible to format a 1.2M disk as 360K, however.) Some 360K drives have trouble reading a disk formatted as 360K in a 1.2M drive.

When you don't use any capacity switches (/F, /T, /N, /1/, /4, or /8), an unconditional format uses the drive's capacity; a safe or quick format uses the disk's current capacity.

Permissible values for *size* and their meanings are as follows:

160 or 160K or 160KB	160K, single-sided, double-density, 5.25-inch disk
180 or 180K or 180KB	180K, single-sided, double-density, 5.25-inch disk
320 or 320K or 320KB	320K, double-sided, double-density, 5.25-inch disk
360 or 360K or 360KB	360K, double-sided, double-density, 5.25-inch disk
720 or 720K or 720KB	720K, double-sided, double-density, 3.5-inch disk
1200 or 1200K or 1200KB or 1.2 or 1.2M or 1.2MB	1.2MB, double-sided, high-density, 5.25-inch disk
1440 or 1400K or 1400KB or 1.4 or 1.4M or 1.4MB	1.44MB, double-sided, high-density, 3.5-inch disk
2880 or 2880K or 2880KB or 2.8 or 2.8M or 2.8MB	2.88MB, double-sided, extra-high-density, 3.5-inch disk

DOS versions before 5.0 required that the two DOS system files on a system disk be contiguous. If you format a disk to which you might later copy system files for a version of DOS earlier than 5.0, you need to use /B to reserve a block of space large enough for both files. (See the Sys command.) You don't need /B if you use /S or if this disk is never going to be used to hold system files for a version of DOS earlier than 5.0.

After FORMAT finishes formatting a disk, it asks you if you want to format another one. If you answer yes, DOS formats the next disk using the current options; you don't have a chance to change options.

When *drive* refers to a hard disk drive, FORMAT warns you that all data will be lost and gives you a chance to stop.

Don't use FORMAT on a drive prepared by SUBST. You cannot use FORMAT over a network or on an INTERLNK drive.

FORMAT sets an exit code as follows:

0   The format was successful.

3   The user pressed Ctrl-C or Ctrl-Break to stop the process.

4   A fatal error occurred (any error other than 0, 3, or 5).

5   The user chose not to continue after a warning message.

Examples

FORMAT A:

Formats the disk in drive A, using the default capacity. Uses safe format if disk already is formatted (you may be able to unformat the disk); otherwise, uses unconditional format.

FORMAT B: /F:360K /S /V:DATA1993 /U

Formats the disk in drive B as a 360K bootable disk, using unconditional format (you cannot unformat the disk). Assigns a volume label of DATA1993.

<u>GOTO</u>

When used in a batch program, sends DOS to a line with the specified label.

Format

GOTO *label*

Parameter

label   Identifies the line to go to.

Notes

Normally DOS processes a batch program line-by-line. GOTO changes the order of processing by directing DOS to a line that consists of a colon followed by *label*. DOS goes on to execute commands beginning on the next line after that.

Label can include spaces but not other separators, such as semicolons or equal signs. GOTO looks at the first eight characters of *label* only, so :NEXTCOMMAND and :NEXTCOMMANDS are both equivalent to :NEXTCOMM.

529

Examples

GOTO ENDPROG

Directs DOS to go to a line consisting of :ENDPROG and continue processing from that point.

GOTO %CONFIG%

Directs DOS to go to a line containing a label that matches the CONFIG environment variable.

GRAPHICS

Loads the Graphics TSR to enable DOS to print graphics screens.

Format

GRAPHICS [*type*] [*filespec*] [/R] [/B] [LCD] [/PRINTBOX:*size*]

Parameters and Switches

none	Loads the *Graphics* TSR with default values.
type	Identifies the printer type. See notes for possible values. The default is HPDEFAULT.
filespec	Identifies the printer profile file; default is GRAPHICS.PRO.
/R	Specifies that images should be printed as they appear on the screen (a postive image). Default is to print a reverse, or negative, screen image, which sometimes looks better in print (see Notes).
/B	Prints background in color for printers COLOR4 and COLOR8.
/LCD	Prints image using LCD aspect ratio instead of CGA aspect ratio. The effect of this switch is the same as /PRINTBOX:LCD.

530

/PRINTBOX:*size*　　Specifies size of printbox. You can abbreviate /PRINTBOX as /PB. *Size* may be STD or LCD. This must match the first operand of the PRINTBOX statement in your printer profile.

Notes

Valid printer types include the following:

COLOR1	IBM PC Color Printer with black ribbon
COLOR4	IBM PC Color Printer with RGB ribbon
COLOR8	IBM PC Color Printer with CMY ribbon
DESKJET	Hewlett-Packard DeskJet printer
HPDEFAULT	Any Hewlett-Packard PCL printer
GRAPHICS	IBM Personal Graphics Printer Proprinter or Quietwriter; also most Epson dot-matrix printers
GRAPHICSWIDE	Any GRAPHICS printer with a wide carriage
LASERJET	Hewlett-Packard LaserJet printer
LASERJETII	Hewlett-Packard LasterJet II printer
PAINTJET	Hewlett-Packard PaintJet printer
QUIETJET	Hewlett-Packard QuietJet printer
QUIETJETPLUS	Hewlett-Packard QuietJet Plus printer
RUGGEDWRITER	Hewlett-Packard RuggedWriter printer
RUGGEDWRITERWIDE	Hewlett-Packard RuggedWriter Wide printer
THERMAL	IBM PC-convertible Thermal printer
THINKJET	Hewlett-Packard ThinkJet printer

Choose the printer type that seems closest to your printer. GRAPHICS doesn't work with a PostScript printer, however, unless it can emulate one of the listed printers.

If you omit filespec, Graphics looks for GRAPHICS.PRO in the same directory as GRAPHICS.COM or in the current directory.

Once Graphics is loaded, you can print a graphics screen by pressing PrintScreen.

Normally a black-and-white graphics print looks best and prints fastest with black letters on a white background. With some graphics programs, such as DOS Shell, you need to use /R to get this effect.

Normally you can trust Graphics to specify the right aspect ratio for your printer (LCD or STD). If you find that the ratio is not quite right (if circles come out as ovals, for example), check the printer profile to see if your monitor can handle both LCD and STD. You can use either /LCD or /PB:LCD to specify the LCD aspect ratio. Use /PB:STD to specify a standard one.

You may need to reboot to change printer profiles if the new profile is larger than the original one.

Examples

GRAPHICS

> Loads the GRAPHICS TSR with default values: printer type HPDEFAULT, profile GRAPHICS.PRO, using negative screen image, and PB size determined by GRAPHICS.PRO.

GRAPHICS GRAPHICS

> If the GRAPHICS TSR is not already loaded, loads it for GRAPHICS type printer, with default values for printer profile, negative screen image, and PB size. If the TSR already is loaded, switches to the GRAPHICS printer type.

GRAPHICS /R

> If the GRAPHICS TSR is not already loaded, loads it with default values for printer type, printer profile, and PB size, but using a positive screen image. If the GRAPHICS TSR already is loaded, switches to a positive screen image.

 # HELP

Starts DOS's command help program.

Format

HELP [*subject*]

Parameters

none
Displays a table of contents showing subjects for which help is available.

subject
Displays the article describing syntax (format) of *subject*. *Subject* can be any subject from the Help table of contents.

Notes

HELP provides much more information than FASTHELP, but you may want to use FASTHELP for quick, compact information about command syntax.

Examples

HELP

Loads Help and displays the table of contents.

HELP COPY

Loads Help and displays the first article for the COPY command.

IF

Performs conditional processing in batch programs.

Format

IF [NOT] *expression command*

Parameters and Switches

NOT
Performs *command* only if *expression* is false. Otherwise DOS performs *command* only if *expression* is true.

expression
Identifies an ERRORLEVEL, EXIST, or equality statement that IF can evaluate as true or false.

command
Identifies a command for DOS to perform.

Notes

The expression ERRORLEVEL n is true if the previous program returned an exit code equal to or greater than n. Otherwise the expression is false. For example, ERRORLEVEL 1 is false if the exit code is 0 but true for exit codes of 1 or higher. (See Choice for a way to set ERRORLEVEL.)

The expression EXIST *filespec* is true if *filespec* identifies an existing file; otherwise it's false.

The expression *string1*==*string2* is true if *string1* is identical to *string2*. The test is case-sensitive; for example, the statement x==X is false.

One or both strings can be replaceable parameters, as in %1==Y or %FACTOR%==X. Put quotation marks around both *string1* and *string2* if either represents a replaceable parameter that might be null, as in "%1"="Y". A null string would cause a syntax error in the IF command.

Examples

```
FORMAT A:
IF ERRORLEVEL 6 GOTO UNKNOWN
IF ERRORLEVEL 5 GOTO UENDED
IF ERRORLEVEL 4 GOTO FATAL
IF ERRORLEVEL 3 GOTO INTERRUPT
IF ERRORLEVEL 1 GOTO UNKNOWN
ECHO ****FORMAT SUCCESSFUL
GOTO ENDING
:UNKNOWN
ECHO ****FORMAT ENDED WITH UNKNOWN ERROR CODE
GOTO ENDING
:UENDED
ECHO ****USER DECIDED NOT TO PROCEED WITH FORMAT
GOTO ENDING
:FATAL
ECHO ****FATAL ERROR WHILE FORMATTING
GOTO ENDING
:INTERRUPT
ECHO ****USER INTERRUPTED FORMAT
:ENDING
```

This batch program uses several IF commands to display different messages depending on which exit code Format provides.

IF NOT EXIST MAKEBAT.DAT NEWPROG.BAT
ECHO FILE ALREADY EXISTS: NEWPROG CAN'T RUN

If the file named MAKEBAT.DAT does not exist, NEWPROG runs and DOS never returns to perform the next line of the batch program. If the file does exist, DOS displays the message on the next line.

IF "%1"=="T" TYPE %2
IF "%1"=="P" PRINT %2

This program either types or prints a user-specified file. The action taken depends on the value passed by the user in %1. Notice that nothing happens if the user enters an incorrect parameter, such as t, p, X, or no parameter.

INCLUDE

Includes the contents of a configuration block at this point in CONFIG.SYS.

Format

INCLUDE=*blockname*

Parameter

blockname   Identifies the configuration block.

Notes

The INCLUDE command is used only when CONFIG.SYS contains multiple configurations. See the MENUITEM, MENUDEFAULT, Menucolor, and Submenu commands for information about setting up and using menus for multiple configurations in CONFIG.SYS.

A configuration block contains a set of CONFIG.SYS commands. A blockname enclosed in square brackets identifies the start of a configuration block. The block ends at the next [*blockname*] (or the end of the file).

DOS may need to perform the same commands for several of your configurations. Define these commands in a separate block and use Include=*blockname* to perform them within another configuration block.

Example

INCLUDE=BASIC

Processes the commands from the [BASIC] block, then continues with the rest of the current configuration block.

INSTALL

Loads a TSR from CONFIG.SYS.

Format

INSTALL=*filespec* [*parameters*]

Parameters

filespec   Identifies the memory-resident program that you want to install.

parameters   Specifies any parameters and switches needed by the program.

Notes

A program loaded with INSTALL takes slightly less memory than the same program loaded from a batch program or from the command prompt.

Some programs may not run correctly when loaded with INSTALL. Don't install programs that use environment variables or shortcut keys or that require COMMAND.COM to be present to handle critical errors.

The DOS TSRs that can safely be loaded with INSTALL are: FASTOPEN.EXE, KEYB.COM, NLSFUNC.EXE, and SHARE.EXE.

DOS processes all INSTALL commands after processing any Device commands and before loading the command processor, regardless of the order of the commands in CONFIG.SYS.

Example

INSTALL=C:\DOS\SHARE.EXE /L=25

Loads the Share TSR and passes it the /L=25 paramter.

INTERLNK

Completes an INTERLNK connection of client and server computers; redirects server drives.

Format

INTERLNK [*drive1* = [*drive2*]]

Parameters

none	Completes the link, if necessary; displays a status report, including the current drive and printer assignments.
drive1	Identifies a client drive name to be assigned to *drive2*.
drive2	Identifies a server drive to be acccessed by the name *drive1*.

Notes

You must load the INTERLNK.EXE device driver from CONFIG.SYS on the client computer, start INTERSVR on the server computer, and cable the two computers before you can use this command. See INTERSVR for more information about linking two computers.

Use this command to complete the link between the two computers, to display the status of the link, and/or to reassign a client drive name.

The INTERLNK command can reassign drive names originally assigned when the INTERLNK device driver was loaded. Both drives must be in the list of those connected by the INTERLNK device driver. If the server has drives A, B, and C assigned to the client's drive letters D, E, and F, respectively, INTERLNK can rearrange these assignments, but it cannot assign a server drive D, even if it exists, to a client drive letter.

If you omit *drive2*, the client's drive assignment is canceled.

Examples

INTERLNK

Completes the connection between a server and client computer.

INTERLNK F:=D:

Reassigns the client's drive name F to server's drive D, provided that these are both drives that were reassigned when INTERLNK.EXE was loaded.

INTERLNK F:=

Cancels the assignment of the client's drive name F.

INTERSVR

Loads the INTERLNK server software and redirects drives and printer ports; copies INTERLNK files from one computer to another.

Format 1

INTERSVR [*drive* ...] [/X=*drive* ...] [/LPT[n] | /LPT:[*address*] | /COM[n] | /COM:[*address*]] [BAUD:*rate*] [/B] [/V]

Loads the INTERLNK server software, redirecting drives and printer ports.

Parameters and Switches

none	Loads the server program and displays the server screen.
drive	Identifies server drive(s) to redirect. By default, INTERSVR redirects all the server's drives.
/X=*drive*	Identifies server drive(s) not to redirect.
/LPT	Indicates that the cable is connected to a parallel port.
/COM	Indicates that the cable is connected to a serial port.
n	Identifies the number of the port that the cable is connected to.

address	Identifies the address of the port that the cable is connected to.
/BAUD:*rate*	Sets a maximum baud rate for data transfer. Values for *rate* can be 9600, 19200, 38400, 57600, and 115200. The default is 115200.
/B	Displays the INTERLNK server screen in black and white.
/V	Prevents conflict with the server computer's timer.

Notes

To connect two computers so they can share drives and printer ports, cable either two serial ports or two parallel ports together. Then start up INTERSVR on one computer (called the *server* computer) and load the INTERLNK device driver from CONFIG.SYS on the other computer (called the *client* computer). If you load the device driver on the client computer before starting up INTERSVR, you will need to use the INTERLNK command to complete the connection. (See INTERLNK.)

When the INTERLNK device driver is installed, it assigns unused client computer drive letters to the server's drives. For example, if the client computer already has drives A, B, and C, and the server computer also has three drives, the client computer would use the letters D, E, and F to access the server computer's drives. Similarly, the client's unused parallel port names (such as LPT2) are assigned to the server's parallel ports.

The INTERSVR command can change the order of the drive assignments and/or except some drives from being accessed by the client computer. For example, INTERSVR C: B: A: causes INTERLNK to assign drive letter D to the server's drive C, E to server drive B, and F to server drive A. INTERSVR /X=A: /X=B: prevents INTERLNK from assigning drive letters to the server's floppy drives.

INTERLNK does not redirect network drives, CD-ROM drives, or any other drives that use a redirection interface. These drives cannot be accessed directly by the client.

The /LPT or /COM switch tells INTERSVR which server port is connected to the client computer. (INTERLNK has a similar switch to identify the client port.)

If you specify neither /LPT nor /COM, INTERSVR scans all parallel and serial ports for a connection with the client.

If you use /LPT without n or *address*, the INTERLNK server uses the first parallel port that it finds connected to a client.

If you use /COM without *n* or *address*, the INTERLNK server uses the first serial port that it finds connected to the client.

If you start INTERSVR from Windows and are using a serial mouse, include either /LPT or a /COM switch that designates the specific port connected to the client to avoid letting INTERSVR scan the port the mouse is attached to, which can disable the mouse driver.

Use /V if you have a serial connection between two computers and one of them stops running when you use INTERLNK to access a drive or printer port.

These commands do not work with the INTERSVR: CHKDSK, DEFRAG, DISKCOMP, DISKCOPY, FDISK, FORMAT, MIRROR, SYS, UNDELETE, and UNFORMAT.

INTERSVR assumes control of the server computer and does not permit any other program to run on that computer. (Mulitasking and task-switching are disabled.) You press Alt-F4 on the server to break the link.

Examples

INTERSVR /X=A: /COM2

Starts INTERSVR for the computer cabled to COM2; lets INTERLNK access all drives except A.

INTERSVR C: D: /LPT

Starts INTERSVR for the computer cabled to one of the parallel ports; lets INTERLNK access the server's drives C and D only.

Format 2

INTERSVR /RCOPY

Copies the INTERLNK program files from one computer to another.

Notes

This command installs INTERLNK on a computer that doesn't already have it. The two computers must be connected through serial ports by a seven-wire null-modem cable. You can use INTERLNK with earlier versions of DOS, but the target computer's DOS must include the MODE command.

If you are using a port other than COM1 on the target computer, make sure that you're not running the SHARE program on that computer. If you are, reboot without SHARE.

The INTERLNK files are copied to the current directory on the target computer.

Enter the INTERSVR /RCOPY command at the source computer's command prompt. INTERSVR displays detailed instructions telling you what to do next.

KEYB

Loads the KEYB TSR, which enables your keyboard to emulate keyboard layouts for other languages.

Format

KEYB [code [,[page] [,filespec]]] [/E] [/ID:id]

Parameters and Switches

none	Displays the current keyboard code and code page, and the current console code page.
code	Identifies the country whose keyboard you want to use.
page	Identifies the code page you want to use; the default is the current code page.
filespec	Identifies the location and name of the keyboard definition file; the default is KEYBOARD.SYS in the current directory or on the search path.
/E	Indicates that you have installed an enhanced keyboard on an 8086 computer.
/ID:id	Specifies which keyboard is in use for countries with more than one keyboard layout.

Notes

KEYB emulates another country's keyboard without physically changing the keyboard. If you have a standard US keyboard, for example, and you use KEYB to emulate a Latin American keyboard, the key marked with a semicolon produces ±.

You can change the keyboard without using Country to change other country-related information.

If you don't specify *page*, the default page for the country is used—the first value in the *Page* column in the following table. Whether or not you specify *page*, however, the characters displayed for ASCII values above 127 are those from the current console code page. (See Chcp, and MODE for more information about changing code pages for console and printer.)

If you are changing both the keyboard layout and the code page, you must prepare the code page before changing the keyboard layout (see the MODE CP PREP command).

You don't need *filespec* if your keyboard file is KEYBOARD.SYS and it's in a directory in the search path.

You can switch from the current KEYB configuration to the default keyboard configuration (US for most keyboards sold in the United States) by pressing Ctrl-Alt-F1. You can change back to the KEYB configuration by pressing Ctrl-Alt-F2. You can switch to "typewriter mode" by pressing Ctrl-Alt-F7.

Appropriate values for *code*, *page*, and *id* are as follows:

Country	Code	Page	Id		
Belgium	BE	850	437		
Brazil	BR	850	437		
Canadian-French	CF	850	863		
Czechoslovakia (Czech)	CZ	852	850		
Czechoslovakia (Slovak)	SL	852	850		
Denmark	DK	850	865		
Finland	SU	850	865		
France	FR	850	437	120	189

Country	Code	Page	Id		
Germany	GR	850	437		
Hungary	HU	852	850		
Italy	IT	850	437	141	142
Latin America	LA	850	437		
Netherlands	NL	850	437		
Norway	NO	850	865		
Poland	PL	852	850		
Portugal	PO	850	860		
Spain	SP	850	437		
Sweden	SV	850	437		
Switzerland (French)	SF	850	437		
Switzerland (German)	SG	850	437		
United Kingdom	UK	850	437	166	168
United States	US	850	437		
Yugoslavia	YU	852	850		

KEYB sets an exit code as follows:

0   Keyboard definition file was loaded successfully.

1   Invalid keyboard code, code page, or syntax was used.

2   Keyboard definition file is bad or missing.

4   An error occurred while communicating with the CON device.

5   The requested code page has not been prepared.

You can install KEYB.COM from CONFIG.SYS instead of using the KEYB command at the command prompt (see INSTALL).

Examples

KEYB

> Displays current keyboard country and code page and the current CON code page.

KEYB PO, 850

> Starts KEYB, emulating the keyboard for Portugal and using code page 850.

KEYB FR,,C:\COUNTRY\KEYBOARD.SYS /ID:189

> Starts KEYB, emulating the French keyboard with ID 189 and using the current code page; uses the keyboard definition file found in C:\COUNTRY.

LABEL

Displays and changes the volume label of a disk.

Format

LABEL [*drive*] [*label*]

Parameters

none	Displays the volume label of the current drive and lets you change or delete it.
drive	Identifies the location of the disk whose label you want to display and/or change; the default is the current drive.
label	Specifies a new volume label for the disk; the label can contain up to 11 characters (see Notes for restrictions).

Notes

If you don't specify *label*, DOS displays the disk's current label and serial number, if any, and prompts for a new label. If you press Enter, the current label is deleted.

A volume label can include spaces, but not tabs. Consecutive spaces become one space. Don't use these characters in a label:

> * ? / \ | . , ; : + = [ ] ( ) & ^ < > "

LABEL doesn't work on drives created with ASSIGN, JOIN, or SUBST.

Examples

LABEL

> Displays the volume label (and serial number, if any) of the disk in the current drive and prompts for a new label.

LABEL B:TAX 1993

> Changes the label on the disk in drive D to TAX 1993.

LASTDRIVE

Specifies the highest drive letter, and therefore the maximum number of drives, that your system can access.

Format

LASTDRIVE=*x*

Parameter

x   Specifies a drive letter, A through Z. The minimum value is the highest drive letter in use by your system.

Notes

The default number of drives is five (A through E) or the number you actually have, whichever is greater.

To allocate more drives, you can use LASTDRIVE in CONFIG.SYS with the highest drive letter that you need. DOS allocates about 100 bytes of memory per drive, so don't waste memory by making LASTDRIVE any higher than it needs to be.

Example

LASTDRIVE = K

Allows your computer to access up to 11 logical drives.

LH

Loads a program into upper memory; LOADHIGH is interchangeable with LH.

Format

LH [[/L:*region*[,*min*][;*region*[,*min*]]...] [/S]] *filespec* [*parameters*]

LOADHIGH [[/L:*region*[,*min*][;*region*[,*min*]]...] [/S]] *filespec* [*parameters*]

Parameters and Switches

filespec	Identifies the program to load.
/L:*region*	Loads the program into specific region(s) of upper memory.
min	Specifies the minimum size required in a region when the program is running.
/S	Shrinks the UMB to its minimum size while the program is loading. This switch is normally used only by MEMMAKER.
parameters	Specifies any command line parameters required by the program.

Notes

If you have an 80386 or later processor, have loaded EMM386.EXE, and have requested UMB support (see the DOS command), you can have upper memory blocks (UMBs) available. LH loads a program into upper memory if available. If not, LH loads the program into conventional memory, if possible.

By default, LH loads a program into the largest free UMB and makes all other UMBs available for the program's use. You can use the /L switch to load the program into a specific region of memory and to specify other regions the program can use (to restrict the program to smaller UMBs, for example). The MEM command can tell you what regions of memory are free and how much space a given program needs.

Use *min* to specify the minimum size that the program requires in *region* for programs that expand after loading.

/S shrinks the UMB to its minimum size while the program is loading. This makes the most efficient use of memory. You can use /S only if you use /L; it affects only UMBs for which you specify *min*.

See MEMMAKER for a command that automatically converts appropriate commands in AUTOEXEC.BAT to LH, generating /L and /S as needed for optimal memory configuration.

Examples

LH C:\TEST1\NEWDATA

Loads the NEWDATA program into upper memory if available. Otherwise, loads it into conventional memory if possible.

LH /L:1 C:\DOS\DOSKEY /BUFSIZE=1024

Loads the Doskey TSR into region 1 of upper memory, using a buffer of 1,024 bytes, if possible. Otherwise, loads it into conventional memory if possible.

LH /L:1,30;3,20 /S C:\PROGRAMS\NEWMS.EXE

Loads NEWMS.EXE found in the C:\PROGRAMS directory into upper memory if possible. Requests a minimum of 30K in region 1 and shrinks the UMB to 30K while loading. Also requests 20K minimum in region 3 and shrinks that UMB to 20K while loading.

LOADFIX

Loads and runs a program above the first 64K of memory.

Format

LOADFIX *command*

Parameter

command   Specifies a command that starts a program, including any desired parameters and switches.

Notes

If you load DOS or device drivers into the HMA, other programs might be loaded into the low parts of conventional memory where DOS and device drivers normally reside. A few programs don't work well when loaded in the first 64K of memory. If you receive the message `Packed file corrupt` when starting a program, try forcing it to load above the 64K mark by using LOADFIX.

Example

LOADFIX DREPORT JAN /C

Loads a program named DREPORT above the 64K mark. JAN /C represent information passed to the DREPORT program from the command line.

LOADHIGH

See LH.

MD

Creates a new directory. Can be used interchangeably with MKDIR.

Format

MD [*path*]*dirname*

MKDIR [*path*]*dirname*

Parameters

path	Identifies the parent of the new directory.
dirname	Identifies the name of the new directory.

Notes

Path can include a drive name. If not, DOS creates *dirname* on the current drive.

Without *path*, DOS creates *dirname* as a subdirectory of the current directory.

Dirname's full path, from the root directory up to and including *dirname*, including backslashes, can't be more than 63 characters.

Dirname must be unique within the parent. You can't duplicate a directory or file name belonging to the parent.

Examples

MD NEWSTUFF

> Creates directory NEWSTUFF as a subdirectory of the current directory.

MD E:\NEWSTUFF

> Creates directory NEWSTUFF as a subdirectory of the root directory on drive E.

MD \NEWSTUFF

> Creates directory NEWSTUFF as a subdirectory of the root directory on the current drive.

MD ..\NEWSTUFF

> Creates directory NEWSTUFF as a subdirectory of the parent of the current directory.

MEM

Displays current memory use.

Format

MEM [/CLASSIFY | /DEBUG | /FREE | /MODULE *program*] [/PAGE]

Switches

none   Displays summary information about your system's used and free memory.

/CLASSIFY	Lists currently loaded programs and their memory usage along with summary information. Abbreviate as /C. May be used with /PAGE, but not with any other switches.
/DEBUG	Lists programs and drivers currently loaded into memory. For each module, shows size, segment address, and module type. Displays summary information also. Abbreviate as /D.
/FREE	Lists the free areas of memory; shows the segment address and size of each free area of conventional memory and the largest free UMB in each region of upper memory. Displays summary information also. Abbreviate as /F.
/MODULE	Shows how a program is currently using memory. Lists the memory areas the program occupies and shows the address and size of each. Abbreviate as /M.
program	Identifies a program currently loaded in memory.
/PAGE	Pauses after each screen. Abbreviate as /P.

Notes

MEM displays the status of extended memory if installed.

MEM displays the status of expanded memory only if your system has expanded memory that conforms to LIMS 4.0 EMS standards.

MEM displays the status of upper memory only if a UMB provider, such as EMM386 is installed and DOS=UMB is included in CONFIG.SYS. MEM does not display the status of upper memory if you run MEM under Windows 3.0.

Examples

MEM /C /P

Lists programs currently loaded and shows memory usage of each; pauses after each screen.

MEM /M DOSKEY

Shows the segment address, size, and module type of each area of memory being used by Doskey. If any portion of Doskey is in upper memory, shows the region of each UMB being used by Doskey.

MEMMAKER

Optimizes memory by moving device drivers and TSRs to upper memory.

Format

MEMMAKER [/B] [/BATCH] [/SWAP:*drive*] [/T] [/UNDO]
[/W:*size1, size2*]

Parameters and Switches

none	Starts MEMMAKER.
/B	Runs MEMMAKER in black-and-white mode.
/BATCH	Runs MEMMAKER in batch mode, using default values at all prompts. If an error occurs, MEMMAKER restores your CONFIG.SYS, AUTOEXEC.BAT, and if necessary Windows SYSTEM.INI files. Puts all status messages into MEMMAKER.STS file.
/SWAP:*drive*	Identifies your startup drive; see Notes.
/T	Disables the detection of IBM Token-Ring networks. Use this switch if your computer has such a network and you have problems running MEMMAKER.
/UNDO	Undoes MEMMAKER's most recent changes, restoring your previous CONFIG.SYS, AUTOEXEC.BAT, and if necessary, Windows SYSTEM.INI files.
/W:*size1, size2*	Specifies, in kilobytes, how much upper memory to reserve for Microsoft Windows' translation buffers. (Windows needs two areas of memory for translation buffers.) The default value is 12, 12.

Notes

You must have a 386 (or higher) processor to run MEMMAKER.

MEMMAKER inserts commands in CONFIG.SYS, AUTOEXEC.BAT, and SYS.INI that count on UMB support provided by EMM386.EXE and DOS=UMB. Don't use MEMMAKER unless you use these commands in your CONFIG.SYS file.

Don't use MEMMAKER if you use Windows applications only.

You can't run MEMMAKER from another program, such as Microsoft Windows or Dosshell. Before you start MEMMAKER, exit from any other program you may be running. Also, be sure that your CONFIG.SYS and AUTOEXEC.BAT files do not start any unnecessary programs but that they do load any hardware devices or TSRs that you normally use.

Unless you use /BATCH, MEMMAKER's dialog boxes prompt you for options, such as whether to use express or custom optimization. Custom optimization requires many choices from the user.

If you use a disk-compression program, the drive letter of your startup disk may change after your computer starts. You must then use /SWAP to let MEMMAKER know where to find your CONFIG.SYS and AUTOEXEC.BAT files (and, if necessary, Windows' SYSTEM.INI). You don't need this switch with Microsoft DoubleSpace or Stacker 2.0.

If you do not use Windows, you can save upper memory space by specifying /W:0,0.

If your system doesn't work properly after MEMMAKER runs, or if you don't like the new memory configuration, you can return to your previous configuration by starting MEMMAKER with the /UNDO switch.

When you use /UNDO, MEMMAKER restores CONFIG.SYS, AUTOEXEC.BAT, and SYSTEM.INI from its backup versions of these files. If you have made any changes to these files since running MEMMAKER, your changes are lost.

Examples

MEMMAKER

> Starts MEMMAKER; displays the Welcome screen and begins prompting for options.

MEMMAKER /SWAP:D

> Starts MEMMAKER and specifies that the current drive D was the original boot drive.

MENUCOLOR

Sets the colors for a startup menu.

Format

MENUCOLOR *text*[,*background*]

Parameters

text	Specifies the text color.
background	Specifies the background color; default is 0 (black).

Notes

You can use MENUCOLOR in a main menu block or a submenu block of a multiple configuration CONFIG.SYS file only.

If you leave a space after the comma, MENUCOLOR ignores *background*.

Values for *text* and *background* are as follows:

0	Black
8	Gray
1	Blue
9	Bright blue
2	Green
10	Bright green
3	Cyan
11	Bright cyan
4	Red
12	Bright red
5	Magenta
13	Bright magenta

6	Brown
14	Yellow
7	White
15	Bright white

The effect of using a value higher than 7 for *background* can vary with different monitors or display cards. When *background* = 12, for example, you may get a blinking red background instead of a bright red background.

Example

MENUCOLOR 9

> Produces a menu with bright blue text on a black background.

MENUCOLOR 10,7

> Produces a menu with bright green text on a white background.

MENUDEFAULT

Specifies the default menu item on a CONFIG.SYS startup menu and sets a time-out value.

Format

MENUDEFAULT=*blockname*[,*time*]

Parameters

blockname   Identifies the default menu item.

time   Specifies the number of seconds DOS waits for user to choose a menu item; can be 0 to 90.

Notes

You can use MENUDEFAULT only in a main menu block or a submenu block of a multiple configuration CONFIG.SYS.

When you use MENUDEFAULT, DOS displays the menu with the default item highlighted and the number corresponding to *blockname* already inserted at the prompt.

When you use *time* in a main menu block, DOS also displays a countdown from *time* to 0. When the countdown reaches 0, DOS proceeds to *blockname*. In a submenu block, DOS currently ignores *time*.

When you don't use MENUDEFAULT, the menu screen is displayed with the first item highlighted and 1 already inserted at the choice prompt, there is no countdown, and DOS waits until the user presses Enter before proceeding.

Setting *time* to 0 effectively cancels the user's ability to choose; the startup menu goes directly to *blockname* whenever the system boots.

Examples

MENUDEFAULT WINDOW,10

Goes to configuration block [WINDOW] if the user doesn't make a choice within 10 seconds.

MENUITEM

Defines an item on a CONFIG.SYS startup menu.

Format

MENUITEM *blockname*[,*text*]

Parameters

blockname	Specifies the name of the configuration block associated with this item.
text	Specifies the text to be displayed for this menu item; default is *blockname*.

Notes

You can use MENUITEM only in a main menu block or submenu block of a multiple configuration CONFIG.SYS.

A menu block can contain up to nine items. DOS numbers the items in the order of their appearance in the menu block. You can replace MENUITEM by Submenu (see the Submenu command) for one or more items if you want more, or more detailed, choices.

There must be a block named *blockname* defined elsewhere in CONFIG.SYS. If DOS can't find *blockname*, the item is not included in the menu.

Blockname can be up to 70 characters long and can include any printable characters except spaces, backslashes (\), slashes (/), commas (,), semicolons (;), equal signs (=), and square brackets ([]).

Text can be up to 70 characters long and can contain any printable characters.

Examples

    [MENU]
    MENUITEM BASIC, BASIC STARTUP
    MENUITEM WINDOWS, GO DIRECTLY TO WINDOWS
    MENUITEM NETWORK

This menu block produces this startup menu:

    1.   BASIC STARTUP
    2.   GO DIRECTLY TO WINDOWS
    3.   NETWORK

MKDIR

See MD.

MODE

Configures system devices.

Format 1

    MODE LPTn [COLS = cols] [LINES = lines] [RETRY = retry]

    MODE LPTn [cols][,[lines][,retry]

Configures a printer attached to a parallel printer port.

Parameters

LPT*n*   Identifies the parallel port; *n* can be 1 to 3.

cols   Specifies the number of characters (or columns) per line; can be 80 or 132; the default is 80.

lines   Specifies the number of lines per inch; can be 6 or 8; the default is 6.

retry   Specifies the action to take if a time-out occurs when DOS attempts to send output to a parallel printer. See Notes.

Notes

See Format 6 for MODE LPT*n* without any other parameters.

You can use PRN interchangeably with LPT1.

If you use the first, fuller version of this format, the parameters can be in any order.

If you use the second, abbreviated, version of this format, you must use the parameters in the order shown, with the accompanying commas. If you leave out a parameter, be sure to indicate its place by the appropriate commas (trailing commas can be omitted).

Values for retry are as follows:

E Returns an error if the port is busy.

P Continues retrying until the printer accepts output.

R Returns ready if the port is busy.

N Takes no retry action.

Do not use any value for *retry* if you use MODE over a network.

If you omit a parameter, MODE uses the most recent value as the default. If no previous MODE command has specified a value, MODE uses 80 for *cols*, 6 for *lines*, and N for *retry*.

Examples

MODE LPT1 132, 8, P

Configures LPT1 with 132 columns and 8 lines per inch; tells MODE to continue to retry if the port is busy when trying to access the printer.

MODE PRN ,,E

> Configures LPT1 with default column and line values; returns an error if the port is busy when trying to access the printer.

Format 2

> MODE COMn BAUD = *baud* [PARITY = *parity*] [DATA = *data*] [STOP = *stop*] [RETRY = *retry*]
>
> MODE COMn *baud*[,*parity*][,*data*][,*stop*][,*retry*]
>
> Configures a serial port.

Parameters

COMn	Identifies the serial port; *n* can be 1 to 4.
baud	Specifies the transmission rate in bits per second (baud rate). (See Notes for values.)
parity	Specifies how the system uses the parity bit to check for transmission errors. (See Notes for values.)
data	Specifies the number of data bits per character. Values can be 5 through 8; the default value is 7.
stop	Specifies the number of stop bits that identify the end of a character. Values can be 1, 1.5, or 2. If the baud rate is 100, the default is 2; otherwise, the default is 1.
retry	Specifies the action to take if a time-out occurs when MODE attempts to send output to the port. (See Notes.)

Notes

See Format 6 for MODE COMn without any other parameters.

If you use the first, fuller version of this format the parameters can be in any order.

If you use the second, abbreviated, version of this format, you must use the parameters in the order shown, with the accompanying commas. If you leave out a parameter, be sure to indicate its place by the appropriate comma (trailing commas can be omitted). (See Examples.)

Values for *baud* rate are as follows:

11 or 110	110 baud
15 or 150	150 baud
30 or 300	300 baud
60 or 600	600 baud
12 or 1200	1200 baud
24 or 2400	2400 baud
48 or 4800	4800 baud
96 or 9600	9600 baud
19 or 1920	19200 baud

Values for *parity* can be N for no parity, E for even parity, O for odd parity, M for mark, or S for space. E is the default.

Values for retry are as follows:

E   Returns an error if the port is busy

B   Returns "busy" if the port is busy

P   Continues retrying until the port accepts output

R   Returns "ready" if the port is busy

N   Takes no retry action (default value)

Do not use any value for retry if you use MODE over a network.

Some values that are valid for MODE are not supported by all computers. These include: BAUD = 19; PARITY = S; PARITY = M; DATA = 5; DATA = 6; and STOP = 1.5.

If you omit any parameter except *baud*, MODE defaults to the most recent value for this port. If no previous MODE command has specified a value, MODE uses the default values shown above. There is no default value for *baud*; you must specify this parameter.

Examples

MODE COM1 24, O, 8, 2, P

> Configures COM1 as 2400 baud, odd parity, 8 data bits per character, and 2 stop bits; continues trying to access the port if it is busy.

MODE COM2 96,,,,,E

> Configures COM2 with 9600 baud, using default values for parity, data bits, and stop bits; returns an error if port is busy.

Format 3

MODE [*display*][,*shift* [,T]]

MODE [*display*][,*lines*]

MODE CON [COLS = *cols*] [LINES = *lines*]

> Selects and configures the active display adapter.

Parameters

none	See Format 6.
display	Specifies a display category, including color characteristics and characters per line. (See notes.)
shift	Shifts screen to left or right; valid values are L and R.
T	Provides a test pattern to be used in aligning screen correctly.
lines	Specifies the number of lines per screen; can be 25, 43, or 50. Not all monitors support 50. The ANSI.SYS device driver must be installed before you can set the number of lines.
cols	Specifies the number of columns per screen (characters per line); can be 40 or 80.

Notes

Not all monitors permit shifting and/or test patterns.

Valid values for *display* are as follows:

40 or 80	Characters per line

BW40 or BW80	CGA adapter with color disabled, 40 or 80 characters per line
CO40 or CO80	Color monitor with color enabled, 40 or 80 characters per line
MONO	Monochrome adapter with 80 characters per line

This format of the MODE command controls the display for the DOS command prompt screen and some others; but many applications such as DOS Shell override them with their own settings.

Examples

MODE 40, 43

Sets monitor to 40 characters per line, 43 lines per screen.

MODE BW80, 25

Sets monitor to black-and-white with 80 characters per line, 25 lines per screen.

MODE ,43

Leave color and characters per line unchanged; sets monitor to 43 lines per screen.

Format 4

MODE CON RATE=*rate* DELAY=*delay*

Sets the keyboard typematic rate.

Parameters

rate   Specifies the rate at which a character repeats when you hold down a key; can be 1 to 32. These correspond to about 2 to 30 characters per second respectively. For IBM AT-compatible keyboards, the default value is 20. For IBM PS/2-compatible keyboards, the default value is 21.

delay   Specifies how long you press a key before repeat begins. Values are 1, 2, 3, and 4, representing 0.25, 0.50, 0.75, and 1 second respectively; default is 2.

Notes

If you use this format, you must specify both *rate* and *delay*.

Example

MODE CON RATE = 32 DELAY = 3

Specifies that, when you hold down a key for 0.75 seconds, the character begins repeating at approximately 30 times per seconds, until you release the key.

Format 5

MODE LPTn[= COMm]

Redirects output from a parallel port to a serial port.

Parameters

LPTn Identifies the parallel port; n can be 1 to 3.

COMm Identifies the serial port; m can be 1 to 4.

Notes

When LPTn has been redirected, any output sent to LPTn goes instead to COMm; presumably a serial printer is connected to COMm.

To end redirection, use MODE LPTn without =COMm.

If n = 1, the COM port becomes the system's default printer port, PRN.

Be sure to configure COMm, using Format 2, before issuing this command.

Format 6

MODE [*device*] [/STATUS]

Displays the status of one or all of the devices installed on your system or ends redirection.

Parameters and Switches

none   Displays the status of all devices installed on your system.

device   Identifies a device whose status you want to display. Device can be CON, LPTn, or COMm.

/STATUS   Requests the status of a device; abbreviate as /STA.

Notes

Without /STA, if *device* is a parallel printer that has been redirected (see Format 5), the redirection is canceled. With /STA, the status of the redirected printer is shown and it remains redirected.

If *device* is not a redirected parallel printer, the status of the device is displayed with or without /STA.

Without *device*, the status of all devices is shown and any redirection is not affected.

Examples

MODE CON

> Displays the status of the console device.

MODE LPT1

> If LPT1 has been redirected to a serial port, ends the redirection. Otherwise, displays the status of LPT1.

MODE LPT1 /STA

> Displays the status of LPT1.

Format 7

> MODE *device* CODEPAGE PREPARE = ((*page* [...]) *filespec*)
>
> MODE *device* CODEPAGE SELECT = *page*
>
> MODE *device* CODEPAGE REFRESH
>
> MODE *device* CODEPAGE [/STATUS]

Parameters and Switches

device	Identifies the device to which the command applies.
CODEPAGE	Identifies this as a codepage command; abbreviate as CP.
PREPARE	Prepares *page*(s) for *device*; abbreviate as PREP.
page	Specifies a code page; can be 437 (US), 850 (Multilingual or Latin I), 852 (Slavic or Latin II), 860 (Portuguese), 863 (Canadian-French) or 865 (Nordic).

filespec	Identifies the name and location of the code page information file for *device*. (See Notes.)
SELECT	Loads a code page for use; page must already be prepared with a MODE CP PREP command; abbreviate as SEL.
REFRESH	Reinstates the prepared code pages if they are lost as the result of a hardware or other error; abbreviate as REF.
/STATUS	Displays the numbers of the current code pages prepared or selected for device; abbreviate as /STA.

Notes

Using this format without PREPARE, SELECT, REFRESH, or /STATUS has the same effect as using /STATUS.

The code page information files provided by DOS are as follows:

EGA.CPI	For EGA or VGA monitor, or IBM PS/2
4201.CPI	For IBM Proprinters II and III Model 4201
	For IBM Proprinters II and III XL Model 4202
4208.CPI	For IBM Proprinter X24E Model 4207
	For IBM Proprinter XL24E Model 4208
5202.CPI	For IBM Quietwriter III printer
LCD.CPI	For IBM PC Convertible liquid crystal display

You must load the device driver(s) DISPLAY.SYS (for the console) and/or PRINTER.SYS (for printers) to reserve buffer space before MODE can prepare or select code pages. You can't prepare more pages for *device* than you specified when loading the device driver.

You can use a combination of COUNTRY, NLSFUNC, and CHCP to select a code page for both console and printer(s) at once.

Examples

MODE CON PREP = ((850 437) C:\DOS\EGA.CPI)

Prepares code pages 850 and 437 for the console, using information found in C:\DOS\EGA.CPI.

MODE LPT1 SEL = 852

Loads previously prepared code page 852 for LPT1.

MORE

Displays a file or output from a program pausing after each screen.

Format

MORE < *filespec*

command | MORE

Parameters

filespec   Identifies an ASCII text file whose contents you want to display one screen at a time.

command   Specifies a command (including any necessary switches and parameters) whose output you want to display one screen at a time.

Notes

Before using a pipe (|), you should set the TEMP environment variable.

You can pipe output to More from commands such as DIR, SORT, and TYPE, or with other programs that produce ASCII text as standard output, but not from a command that runs a batch program.

Examples

MORE < TESTA.BAT

Displays the contents of TESTA.BAT, pausing after each screen.

TYPE TESTA.BAT | MORE

Displays the contents of TESTA.BAT, pausing after each screen.

TYPE TESTA.BAT | SORT | MORE

Sorts the contents of TESTA.BAT and displays them, pausing after each screen.

MOVE

Moves one or more files to another location; renames a file or directory.

Format 1

MOVE *filespec* [...] *destination*

Moves and renames a file.

Parameters

filespec	Identifies the file(s) you want to move or rename.
destination	Identifies the file or directory to which you want to move file(s) or the new name for the file.

Notes

MOVE assumes that the last entry on the command line is *destination*. Any other entries on the line are *filespecs*. *Filespec* can include wild cards.

If you move more than one file, *destination* must be a directory, not a file name. *Destination* can't include wild cards.

If you move only one file, *destination* can be (or include) a new file name; in that case, the file is moved and/or renamed. If the *destination* file already exists, MOVE overwrites it without warning you. (Notice the difference from RENAME, which will not give a file a name already in the directory and will not move a file to a new directory.)

MOVE will not process system or hidden files. It does move read-only files, but it will not overwrite one in *destination*. The read-only and archive attributes of the source files are copied to the *destination* files.

When moving one or more files to a directory, *destination* must be an existing directory.

When moving a file to the same drive, MOVE moves only the directory entry; this is much faster than copying and deleting the file. When moving to a different drive, of course, MOVE must copy the file and delete the original.

If the move is unsuccessful, because the destination is a read-only file or the destination drive is full, MOVE doesn't delete the original file. MOVE tells you when a move is unsuccessful.

Example

> MOVE AFILE.* *.BAT C:\ACCOUNT

> From the current directory, moves all files named AFILE with any extension and all files with extension BAT to directory ACCOUNT on drive C. No system or hidden files are moved. If the destination files already exist and are not read-only, they are overwritten by the new versions.

Format 2

> MOVE *directory newname*

> Renames a directory.

Parameters

directory　　Identifies the directory you want to rename.

newname　　Specifies the new name.

Notes

You can't rename the current directory.

You don't need to indicate a path in *directory* if you are renaming a child of the current directory.

Newname must produce a unique name for the new directory. You can't duplicate the name of a file or subdirectory of the parent.

If *newname* includes a path (which is not necessary) it must not specify a new parent for the directory.

Examples

> MOVE C:\T1 C:\ACCOUNT

> If T1 is a directory name, renames directory T1 on drive C; the new name is ACCOUNT. (If T1 is a file name, see Format 1.)

MOVE T1 TESTING

If T1 is a child of the current directory, renames it as TESTING. (If T1 is a file name, see Format 1.)

MSAV

Scans memory and disks for viruses; removes viruses when found.

Format

MSAV [*drive ...* | *path* | /A | /L] [/S | /C] [/R] [/A] [/L] [/N] [/P] [/F] [/VIDEO] [/*videomouse ...*]

Parameters and Switches

none	Opens the MSAV dialog box so that you can select drives and options.
drive	Identifies a drive to scan; all files on the drive are scanned.
path	Identifies the top of a branch; all files in the branch are scanned.
/A	Scans all drives except A and B.
/L	Scans all drives except A, B, and network drives.
/S	Scans without removing viruses.
/C	Scans and cleans any viruses found.
/R	Creates a report file (MSAV.RPT) that lists the number of files checked, number of viruses found, number of viruses removed, and names of files suspected of containing unknown viruses.
/N	Turns off the information display while scanning.
/P	Runs MSAV in non-graphic, command-line mode.
/F	Turns off the display of file names being scanned. Use this switch only with the /N or /P switch.

/VIDEO	Displays a list of video and mouse options. This option does not perform any virus scan or load the dialog box; to scan for viruses you must enter MSAV again after you see the list.
/videomouse	Uses *videomouse* option (see Notes for values).

Notes

MSAV identifies more than 1,000 known viruses and also can detect unknown viruses. It maintains a CHKLIST.MS file in each scanned directory to help it identify unknown viruses by changes in the directory's files. It can't clean unknown viruses; some known viruses also can't be cleaned.

The first scan you run after starting up MSAV also scans memory for viruses.

From the MSAV dialog box, you can choose options that are not on the command line, such as scanning for stealth viruses or turning off the beep. Also, from the dialog box you can see a list of known viruses and read about particular ones.

If you specify *drive* without /N or /P, the dialog box appears and you can, if you want, select options and even choose to scan a different drive. After a drive is scanned, you have another opportunity to choose options and drives for another scan.

If you use *path* without /N or /P, the dialog box appears and the scan begins immediately. When it ends, the dialog box closes. You don't have a chance to choose other options or to continue to scan another *path* or *drive*.

Values for *videomouse* are as follows:

25	Sets screen to 25 lines; this is the default value.
28	Sets screen to 28 lines. Use this switch with VGA display adapters only.
43	Sets screen to 43 lines. Use this switch with either EGA or VGA display adapters.
50	Sets screen to 50 lines. Use this switch with VGA display adapters only.
60	Sets screen to 60 lines. Use this switch with Video 7 display adapters only.
IN	Uses a color scheme even if a color display adapter is not detected.

569

BW	Uses a black-and-white color scheme.
MONO	Uses a monochrome color scheme.
LCD	Uses an LCD color scheme.
FF	Uses the fastest screen updating with CGA display adapters; can cause snow.
BF	Uses the computer's BIOS to display video; try this switch if the quality of the display is poor.
NF	Disables the use of alternate fonts.
BT	Allows use of a graphics mouse in Windows.
NGM	Uses default mouse character instead of graphics character. Try this if snow appears on the screen.
LE	Exchanges left and right mouse buttons.
IM	Disables the mouse.
PS2	Resets the mouse if the mouse cursor disappears or locks up.

/VIDEO overrides any other parameters or switches and displays only the video/mouse option list.

A summary report is displayed every time you use MSAV, whether or not you use /R to generate MSAV.RPT. MSAV.RPT is more detailed because it contains the names of files suspected of containing unknown viruses; the summary report does not include this information. Sometimes the summary report flashes on the screen too rapidly to be read; if you have a problem with this, be sure to use /R to get a readable report.

MSAV.RPT is saved in the root directory of the scanned drive. If you name more than one drive to be scanned, an MSAV.RPT is generated for each drive.

Examples

MSAV /A

Starts MSAV, scanning memory and all drives except A and B.

MSAV C: D: /BW /43

Starts MSAV in black-and-white mode with 43 lines per screen, scanning memory and drives C and D.

MSAV C:\DOS /C /R

Scans memory and the files in the branch headed by C:\DOS, removing any viruses found; stores a report in C:\MSAV.RPT.

MSBACKUP

Backs up and restores data on your computer.

Format

MSBACKUP [*setup*] [/BW | /LCD | /MDA]

Parameters and Switches

none	Opens the main MSBACKUP dialog box and loads DEFAULT.SET.
setup	Specifies a setup file to load when opening MSBACKUP dialog box; the file's extension must be SET; default is DEFAULT.SET.
/BW	Uses a black-and-white color scheme for the MSBACKUP dialog boxes.
/LCD	Uses a video mode compatible with laptop displays.
/MDA	Uses a monochrome display adapter.

Notes

You create a *setup* file using the MSBACKUP dialog boxes.

Even though you specify *setup*, you have a chance to modify settings and file selections in the MSBACKUP dialog box before starting the backup. Opening the dialog box also gives you access to configuration, backup, compare, and restore functions.

MSBACKUP can't restore files backed up by earlier versions of DOS. (See RESTORE.)

Examples

MSBACKUP

Opens the MSBACKUP dialog box and loads DEFAULT.SET.

MSBACKUP DAILY

Opens the MSBACKUP dialog box and loads DAILY.SET.

MSD

Displays or reports technical information about your computer.

Format

MSD [/F *filespec* | /P *filespec* | /S [*filespec*] | [/I] [/B]]

Parameters and Switches

filespec	Specifies a file to hold the MSD report.
/F	Prompts for identification information, then writes a complete MSD report to *filespec*; do not use with any other switch.
/P	Writes a complete MSD report to *filespec* without any prompting; do not use with any other switch.
/S	Writes a summary MSD report. If *filespec* is present, writes report to *filespec*. If *filespec* is absent, writes report to screen. Do not use with any other switch.
/I	Specifies that MSD should not initially detect hardware; use this switch if you have problems starting MSD or MSD does not run properly; do not use with any other switch except /B.
/B	Runs MSD in black-and-white instead of color; do not use with any other switch except /I.

Notes

MSD provides information about your computer's model and processor, memory, video type, DOS version, mouse, other adapters, disk drives, LPT ports, COM ports, IRQ status, TSRs, and device drivers

If /F, /P, and /S are all omitted, MSD opens a dialog box where you can select the information you want to view and displays the information online.

Examples

MSD

> Opens MSD's dialog box that lets you access data about your computer.

MSD /F MYSYSTEM.TXT

> Prompts you for name, company, address, and other identification information. Creates a report in MYSYSTEM.TXT that includes the identification data and the technical information about your computer.

NLSFUNC

Starts the program that loads country-specific information for national language support (NLS).

Format

NLSFUNC [*filespec*]

Parameters

none
: Uses the default file for country-specific information (see Notes).

filespec
: Identifies the file containing country-specific information.

Notes

If CONFIG.SYS contains a COUNTRY command, it defines the default file; otherwise, the default file is COUNTRY.SYS in the root directory of your startup drive.

There is no error message if the country-specific information file is missing, because NLSFUNC doesn't access the file until DOS requires information from it. The error message shows up later, when Chcp tries to use information from the file.

You also can load NLSFUNC by installing NLSFUNC.EXE in CONFIG.SYS. (See INSTALL.)

Examples

NLSFUNC

> Starts the national language support TSR using a default file for country-specific information.

NLSFUNC C:\OLDDOS\COUNTRY.SYS

> Starts the national language support TSR using the COUNTRY.SYS file from C:\OLDDOS for country-specific information.

NUMLOCK

Specifies whether the NumLock setting of the numeric keyboard is initially on or off.

Format

NUMLOCK=ON | OFF

Parameters

ON   Turns on the NumLock setting.

OFF   Turns off the NumLock setting.

Notes

You can use NUMLOCK only in a menu block of CONFIG.SYS.

When the NumLock setting is on, the numeric keypad produces numbers. (This can also affect the duplicate keys on an enhanced keyboard. If you have this problem, try loading ANSI.SYS with /X in CONFIG.SYS.) When the NumLock setting is off, the numeric keypad produces alternate functions (cursor movement, insert, and delete).

Without the NUMLOCK command, most computers start up with the NumLock setting off. Pressing the NumLock key toggles the NumLock setting on and off.

Example

NUMLOCK=ON

Turns NumLock on during booting, so that typing on the numeric keypad produces numbers.

PATH

Defines a search path for external executable files (including batch files).

Format

PATH [*path* [;*path*]...]

PATH ;

Parameters

none	Displays the current search path.
path	Identifies a directory to search for program files.
;	When used as the only parameter, clears the search path.

Notes

When a command name includes a path, as in C:\DOS\FORMAT A:, DOS looks for the program only in the specified directory.

When a command name does not include a path, DOS looks for the program first in the current directory, then in the directories on the search path, if any. It searches the directories in the order shown on the search path. DOS stops searching when a specified program is found even though another program with that name may exist in another directory on the search path.

If it can't find the program in the current directory or any directory on the search path, DOS displays a `bad command or file name` error message.

DOS doesn't search for internal programs, which are part of COMMAND.COM, or for Doskey macros, which are stored in memory.

Be sure that *path* is an absolute path (one that starts from a drive letter).

PATH doesn't produce an error message if *path* isn't valid. DOS displays an "invalid directory" error message when it encounters an invalid *path* while searching.

The search path created by PATH is assigned to an environment variable named PATH. You can use the SET command to create or change the environment variable PATH instead of using the PATH command.

Each time the PATH command defines a search path, it completely replaces the former search path. If you want to add another directory to the search path, be sure to include the original search path in the command, or use SET PATH=%PATH%;*path*.

The PATH command can't be more than 127 characters long, with the search path to 122 characters.

Examples

PATH C:\;C:\DOS;D:\BOOK\APPS

> Sets a search path so that DOS looks for programs first in the current directory, next in the root directory on drive C, then in C:\DOS and finally in D:\BOOK\APPS.

PATH ;

> Clears the search path. After this, DOS looks for programs in the current directory only.

PAUSE

Temporarily suspends processing of a batch program and prompts the user to press any key to continue.

Format

PAUSE

Notes

The user's response to PAUSE is not meaningful unless it is one of the break keys (Ctrl-C or Ctrl-Break). Any other response simply continues the batch program. See CHOICE for a command that lets users enter a meaningful response.

Example

ECHO Load the forms in the printer
PAUSE

After displaying the message from ECHO, the program pauses until the user presses a key, giving the user as much time as necessary to load the forms.

POWER

Reduces power consumption in laptops when applications and devices are idle.

Format

POWER [ADV:*option* | STD | OFF]

Parameters and Switches

none	Displays the current power setting.
ADV:*option*	Conserves power when applications and hardware drivers are idle; *option* can be MAX, REG, or MIN (see Notes).
STD	Uses only the power-management features, if any, of your computer's hardware.
OFF	Turns off power management.

Notes

You must install POWER.EXE as a device driver from CONFIG.SYS before you can use the Power command.

The power manager conforms to the Advanced Power Management (APM) specification.

If your computer does not support the APM specification, STD turns off power management.

Use ADV:MAX for maximum power conservation. Use ADV:REG to balance power conservation with application and device performance. If performance is not satisfactory with MAX or REG, try ADV:MIN.

Examples

POWER ADV:MIN

> Sets power conservation to a minimum to improve performance.

POWER OFF

> Turns off power conservation.

PRINT

Manages background printing.

Format

PRINT [/D:*device*] [/B:*buffer*] [/U:*ticks1*] [/M:*ticks2*] [/S:*ticks3*] [/Q:*qsize*] [/T]
[*filespec* ...] [/C] [/P]

Parameters and Switches

none	Displays the contents of the print queue or loads the TSR.
/D:*device*	Identifies the printer port on which to print. Valid values are LPT1, LPT2, LPT3, COM1, COM2, COM3, and COM4. LPT1 is identical to PRN. If used, /D must precede *filespec* on the command line.
/B:*buffer*	Sets the size, in bytes, of the buffer used to store data before printing; can be 512 to 16384; 512 is the default.
/U:*ticks1*	Specifies the maximum number of clock ticks to wait for a printer to be available; can be 1 to 255; the default is 1. If the printer is not available in *ticks1* clock ticks, the job is not printed. (There are about 18 clock ticks per second.)
/M:*ticks2*	Specifies the maximum number of clock ticks to print a character on the printer; can be 1 to 55; the default value is 2. If a character takes longer than *ticks2* clock ticks to print, DOS displays an error message.

/S:*ticks3*	Specifies the number of clock ticks the DOS scheduler allocates for background printing before returning to foreground work; maybe 1 to 255; the default value is 8.
/Q:*qsize*	Specifies the maximum number of files in the print queue; can be 4 through 32; the default value is 10.
/T	Removes all files from the print queue.
filespec	Identifies a text file to place in the print queue; can be up to 64 characters.
/C	Removes file(s) from the print queue.
/P	Adds file(s) to the print queue.

Notes

The first time you use the PRINT command after booting, DOS loads a memory-resident portion of the PRINT program to retain the print parameters. You can use the /D, /B, /U, /M, /S, and /Q switches only the first time you use the PRINT command. To change values for any of these switches, you have to reboot and issue a new PRINT command.

If you don't specify /D when loading the memory-resident program, PRINT prompts you for the name of the printer.

The actual printing occurs in the background—that is, DOS continues processing other applications while taking small blocks of time (defined by /S) to print the contents of the queue.

Increasing *buffer* decreases the amount of memory available for other purposes but speeds up printing. Increasing any of the *ticks* values speeds up printing but may slow down other work.

/P applies to the filespec preceding it, if any, and all following filespecs until it reaches a filespec controlled by /C, if any. /C applies to the filespec preceding it, if any, and all following filespecs until it reaches a filespec controlled by /P, if any.

When neither /C nor /P applies to a filespec, /P is assumed.

/T empties the queue. If any *filespecs* precede /T, they are removed from the queue. If any follow /T, they are added or canceled depending on whether /P or /C applies to them.

Examples

PRINT /D:LPT2 /B:2048

> If this is the first PRINT command, loads the PRINT TSR with a buffer of 2048 bytes. All subsequent PRINT commands will send prints to the LPT2 queue.

PRINT LETTER1.TXT

> Adds LETTER1.TXT to the print queue; if PRINT is not yet loaded, loads PRINT with the default values but prompts for printer name.

PRINT /C LETTER1.TXT LETTER2.TXT LETTER3.TXT /P

> Removes LETTER1.TXT and LETTER2.TXT from the print queue and adds LETTER3.TXT to the queue.

PRINT /T

> Removes all files from the print queue.

PROMPT

Changes the command prompt.

Format

PROMPT [*text*]

Parameters

none	Resets the prompt to the current drive letter followed by >.
text	Specifies text and information to be shown as the prompt.

See Notes for special prompt codes.

Notes

Special codes you can use in the prompt are as follows:

$Q	= (equal sign)
$$	$ (dollar sign)

$T	Current time
$D	Current date
$P	Current drive and path
$V	DOS version number
$N	Current drive
$G	> (greater-than sign)
$L	< (less-than sign)
$B	| (pipe)
$_	Enter (line feed)
$E	ASCII escape code (code 27)
$H	Backspace (deletes a character already written in the prompt)

The default prompt is equivalent to NG. However, DOS Setup inserts PROMPT PG into AUTOEXEC.BAT because most people want the current directory in the prompt.

When you include $P in a prompt, DOS has to determine the current drive and path before each prompt; this can slow down system response, especially when the current drive is a floppy disk drive.

$_ lets you define a multiple-line prompt. T_PG, for example, displays the current time on one line, then goes to the beginning of the next line to display the path followed by >.

$E, the ASCII escape code, lets you code ANSI.SYS escape sequences as part of your prompt. $E[2J, for example, clears the screen and places the cursor in the upper left corner (with no prompt text). You must load the ANSI.SYS driver in CONFIG.SYS before you can use ANSI.SYS escape sequences in a prompt.

You could use $H, the backspace character, to erase unwanted characters from $D or $T. THHH, for example, displays the time as hh:mm:ss instead of the usual hh:mm:ss.nn.

You can combine these special characters with text and spaces to define a prompt.

Examples

PROMPT USING VG

> Defines a prompt that says "USING" followed by the DOS version number and >.

PROMPT T_TIME$Q$$

> Defines a two-line prompt. The first line shows the time; the second line says "TIME=$". (The cursor follows $.)

PROMPT

> Sets the prompt to the default value: the current drive followed by >.

PROMPT PG

> Sets the prompt to the current directory followed by >.

QBASIC

Starts the QBASIC programming environment, which allows the writing, testing, and running of QBASIC programs.

Format

QBASIC [/B] [/EDITOR] [/G] [/H] [/MBF] [/NOHI] [[/RUN] *filespec*]

Parameters and Switches

none	Loads the QBASIC environment.
/B	Displays QBASIC in black and white.
/EDITOR	Invokes the DOS text editor instead of the QBASIC program editor.
/G	Provides the fastest update of a CGA monitor.
/H	Displays the maximum number of display lines possible on your screen.

/MBF	Converts the built-in functions MKS\$, MKD\$, CVS, and CVD to MKSMBF\$, MKDMBF\$, CVSMBF, and CVDMBF, respectively. This provides compatibility with data files written in some earlier versions of BASIC.
/NOHI	Allows the use of a monitor that doesn't support high-intensity video. Do not use this switch with Compaq laptop computers.
/RUN	Runs *filespec* before displaying the file. Don't use this switch without *filespec*.
filespec	Specifies a QBASIC program to load; without /RUN, displays the program; with /RUN, runs the program before displaying it.

Notes

/EDITOR has the same effect as starting the DOS text editor with the EDIT command.

If your monitor does not display shortcut keys when you run QBASIC, use /B (for CGA monitors) and/or /NOHI (for systems that do not support bold or high-intensity characters).

Examples

QBASIC TESTPROG

> Starts the QBASIC environment, loading and displaying the file TESTPROG.BAS.

QBASIC /B

> Starts the QBASIC environment with a black-and-white color scheme. No file is loaded.

QBASIC /RUN TESTPROG

> Starts the QBASIC environment, loading and running TESTPROG.BAS. When the program ends, it is displayed in the QBASIC editor.

RD

Deletes a directory. You can use RMDIR interchangeably with RD.

Format

> RD *path*
>
> RMDIR *path*

Parameter

> *path*   Identifies the directory you want to delete.

Notes

Before you can delete a directory using RD, you must delete all its files and subdirectories. The directory must be empty except for the . and .. entries.

If a DIR command shows that the directory is empty but you still can't delete it, use DIR /A (or DOS Shell) to see whether there are hidden or system files or subdirectories.

RD will not delete the current directory; make some other directory current before entering the RD command.

To delete a directory along with all its files, its subdirectories, and their files and subdirectories, see DELTREE.

Examples

> RD \DDIR
>
>> Deletes directory DDIR, a subdirectory of the root directory on the current drive.
>
> RD DDIR
>
>> Deletes directory DDIR, a subdirectory of the current directory.

REM

Identifies a comment, or remark, in a batch file or CONFIG.SYS.

Format

REM [*comment*]

Parameter

comment   Specifies text you want to include in the batch file or in
                 CONFIG.SYS without affecting operations.

Notes

You can use REM commands to provide documentation or notes in a batch file or in
CONFIG.SYS. Sometimes it is convenient to put REM in front of a command that
you want to disable temporarily. You then can easily restore the command by removing REM from the line.

Examples

REM Next run the daily backup.

> A note to remind yourself (and others) of the purpose of the next
> several commands.

REM DEL TEMP.*

> This DEL command has no effect; no TEMP files are erased by this
> command when the batch program runs.

REN

Changes the name of a file or files. You can use RENAME interchangeably with
REN.

Format

REN *filespec newname*

RENAME *filespec newname*

585

Parameters

filespec   Identifies the file(s) to be renamed.

newname   Specifies the new name(s) for the file(s).

Notes

Filespec can include a drive and/or path, but *newname* can't.

REN doesn't work if *newname* already exists (as a file or subdirectory) in the same directory as the file being renamed. (For a command that clobbers an existing *newname*, see MOVE).

If you use wild cards in both names, the wild card characters from the original name replace the wild cards in *newname*. In REN A*.* B*.*, for example, AFILE.DAT becomes BFILE.DAT, ACCOUNT.EXE becomes BCCOUNT.EXE, and so on.

Filespec can't identify a directory; for a command that renames directories, see MOVE.

Examples

REN JET.NEW JET.SAV

Changes the name of JET.NEW (in the current directory) to JET.SAV.

REN D:\YEARDATA\NEWDATA.* OLDDATA.*

For each file in D:\YEARDATA that has the name NEWDATA (with any extension), changes the name to OLDDATA (with the same extension).

RENAME

See REN.

REPLACE

Replaces or adds files from one directory to another.

Format 1

REPLACE *filespec path* [/P] [/R] [/W] [/S] [/U]

Overwrites files in the target directory with matching files from the source directory.

Parameters and Switches

filespec	Identifies the source file(s).
path	Identifies the target directory.
/P	Prompts for confirmation before replacing a file.
/R	Replaces files that are read-only in the target directory as well as nonread-only files.
/W	Waits for you to press a key before beginning to search for source files.
/S	Searches all subdirectories of *path* to find files to be replaced.
/U	Examines the date/time stamps of source and target files and replaces (updates) files in the target directory only if they are older than the source files that replace them.

Notes

REPLACE ignores system and/or hidden files in both the source and target directory.

Without /R, an attempt to replace a read-only target file produces an error message and terminates REPLACE.

If you use wildcards in *filespec*, each file matching the specification replaces file(s) with the same name in the target directory or branch.

With /U, you can be sure that you will not overwrite a more recent version. If you want to be sure that both JOHN and MARY have the latest version of TILE.DAT, for example, use REPLACE JOHN\TILE.DAT MARY /U, followed by REPLACE MARY\TILE.DAT JOHN /U.

The add function, using /A, makes it easy to ensure that every file from one directory exists in the other one without clobbering existing files in the target directory (as COPY or XCOPY, for example, might do).

REPLACE sets an exit code as follows:

0	Successful completion
1	Computer's DOS version not compatible with REPLACE
2	Source files not found

3 Source or target path not found

5 Target file(s) not accessible (read-only)

8 Insufficient memory

11 Incorrect syntax on command line

Examples

In these examples, assume that neither the source files nor the target files are system or hidden files.

REPLACE NEWDATA.921 \DIR92

If \DIR92\NEWDATA.921 exists and is not read-only, replaces it with NEWDATA.921 from the current directory.

REPLACE DONNA\NEWDATA.* JUDI /R

Copies NEWDATA.BAT from DONNA to JUDI if NEWDATA.BAT exists in both directories; copies NEWDATA.COM from DONNA to JUDI if NEWDATA.COM exists in both directories; copies NEWDATA.EXE from DONNA to JUDI if NEWDATA.EXE exists in both directories; and so on. Makes the replacement even when a JUDI file is read-only.

REPLACE A:\BUDGET.LST C:\ /S /R /W

Waits for you to press a key before beginning and then looks in every directory in the branch headed by C:\ for a file named BUDGET.LST; each occurrence of this file (even if it's read-only) is replaced by BUDGET.LST from the root directory of drive A.

Format 2

REPLACE *filespec path* /A [/P] [/W]

Replaces files missing from the target with files from the source directory.

Parameters and Switches

filespec	Identifies the source file(s).
path	Identifies the target directory.

/P   Prompts for confirmation before replacing a file.

/A   Copies source files not in the target directory, thus adding new files to the target. This function does not replace any existing files.

/W   Waits for you to press a key before beginning to search for source files.

Notes

With /A, REPLACE adds each file matching the specification to the target directory unless there's already a file with that name in that directory.

Example

REPLACE \DONNA\NEWDATA.* \JUDI /A /P

For each NEWDATA file (with any extension) in DONNA, if a file with the same name does not exist in JUDI, copies the DONNA file to JUDI, prompting for confirmation before adding each file.

RESTORE

Restores files backed up by BACKUP from previous DOS versions (DOS 2.0 through 5.0).

Format

RESTORE *drive1 target* [/S] [/P] [/B:*date*] [/A:*date*] [/E:*time*] [/L:*time*] [/M] [/N] [/D]

Parameters and Switches

drive1   Identifies the drive containing the backup files.

target   Identifies the files to be restored, and the drive to which they are to be restored. *Target* must include a drivename; it may specify files by including a path and/or file name(s).

/S   Restores files to all subdirectories.

/P	Prompts for permission to restore read-only files or those changed since the last backup.
/B:*date*	Restores only those files last modified on or before *date*.
/A:*date*	Restores only those files last modified on or after *date*.
/E:*time*	Restores only those files last modified at or earlier than *time*.
/L:*time*	Restores only those files last modified at or later than *time*.
/M	Restores only those files modified since the last backup.
/N	Restores only those files that no longer exist on the destination.
/D	Displays a list of files that would be restored but does not restore any. Even though no files are restored, you must specify *target* when you use /D.

Notes

RESTORE does not restore the system files IO.SYS and MSDOS.SYS. RESTORE does not work with drives that have been redirected with ASSIGN or JOIN.

RESTORE prompts you to insert disks from a backup set in the order in which they were created. It searches each disk for files that match the specifications.

If you know which disks contain the files you want, you can skip disks by confirming when RESTORE asks if it is OK.

You can cancel the RESTORE operation before it reads all the disks by pressing Ctrl-C.

A file can be spanned across two (or even more) disks. If you cancel RESTORE, be sure you don't do so when it has restored only part of a spanned file.

Files are restored to the directory with the same path that they were backed up from, but it doesn't have to be on the same drive. For example, if you backed up files from drive D, you can use RESTORE to put them on drive E. RESTORE will create any directories needed on E in order to restore the files.

When you specify a date or time switch, RESTORE looks at the date/time stamp on the *target* file. Suppose you want to restore any BANDLIST.* file that you modified after 4/15/93. Use RESTORE A: C:\BANDLIST.* /A:4/16/93.

Use time switches carefully. The times apply to every day, not just the day specified in a date switch. /A:4/16/93 /L:3:00P restores files modified on 4/16/93 after 3:00 p.m., on 4/17/93 after 3:00 p.m., on 4/18/93 after 3:00 p.m., and so on.

/M restores files modified since the last backup, according to the archive attribute. Files deleted since the last backup are not re-created. Files unchanged since the last backup are not restored. This could shorten restore time by not bothering to restore unmodifed files.

RESTORE sets an exit code, as follows:

0 Successful completion

1 RESTORE could not find files to restore

3 User stopped the operation by pressing Ctrl-C or Ctrl-Break

4 RESTORE stopped because of an error (such as disk full)

Examples

RESTORE A: C:*.BAT

Restores all files with extension BAT that were originally in the root directory to the root directory on C.

RESTORE A: C:*.BAT /S

Restores all files with extension BAT to drive C, including those backed up from subdirectories; each file is restored to a directory with the same name as the one from which it was backed up.

RESTORE A: C:\PROWORD*.DOC /M

Looks for any file with the extension DOC backed up from directory PROWORD. When RESTORE finds such a file both in the backup set and in C:\PROWORD, and the target file has been modified since backup, the modified version is replaced by the backup version. (Note that files created or deleted since the backup are not affected.)

RMDIR

See RD.

SET

Sets or changes values of environment variables or displays current values.

Format

SET [*variable*=[*string*]]

Parameters and Switches

none   Displays the current values of all environment variables.

variable   Identifies the environment variable to be set.

string   Specifies a new value for an environment variable; if
omitted, the current value is cleared.

Notes

When you use SET, you may get an error message saying that you are out of environment space. See SHELL and COMMAND for commands that can increase your environment space.

DOS sets some environment variables without the SET command. For example, it sets CONFIG, which keeps track of which option was chosen in a multiple configuration file, when you make that choice; the PATH command creates PATH, which contains your search path; the Prompt command sets PROMPT, which specifies the content of the command prompt; COMSPEC, which identifies the location of your command processor, is set by SHELL or COMMAND. You can change the values of these and other environment variables, or create new ones, with SET.

DOS also uses some environment variables that you create with SET. These include TEMP, which specifies a directory in which temporary files are kept, and DIRCMD, which provides a set of default options for the DIR command.

You can use environment variables in batch programs but not in Doskey macros. Surround the variable name by percent signs. %CONFIG%, for example, refers to the current value of CONFIG, which is set by a choice made in a multiconfiguration CONFIG.SYS. A command such as GOTO %CONFIG% in a batch program branches to a heading that matches the current value of CONFIG. This allows you to customize AUTOEXEC.BAT (or other batch files) to perform different actions depending on which configuration you chose when starting DOS.

When you use an environment variable in an If equality condition, you usually need to surround the entire variable, including the percent signs, with quotation marks to account for a null value, as in IF "%CONFIG%"=="SHORT". (Don't put quotation marks around environment variables in other settings, however.)

When you clear an environment variable, it may still show up (with no value) when you use SET to display the environment variables. You'll get an error message if you use the variable in a batch file GOTO, among other places.

You can use the existing value of an environment variable in a SET command. The command SET PATH=%PATH%;C:\PROGS, for example, adds the directory C:\PROGS to the end of the current search path.

Examples

SET

> Displays the current values of all environment variables.

SET TEMP=F:\TEMP

> Sets the value of TEMP to F:\TEMP. DOS commands, Windows, and some application programs use the directory specified by TEMP for storing temporary files.

SET DNT=C:\OLD_DOS

> Creates (if it doesn't already exist) an environment variable named DNT and gives it the value C:\OLD_DOS. After this command, any time %DNT% is encountered in a batch file, it is replaced by C:\OLD_DOS.

SET TEMP=

> Clears the environment variable TEMP. (When TEMP is cleared, DOS stores temporary files in the root directory of the current drive.)

SETVER

Sets the version number DOS reports to a program or device driver; displays version table.

Format

SETVER [*path*] [*filename.ext version*]

SETVER [*path*] *filename.ext* /DELETE [/QUIET]

Parameters and Switches

none	Displays the version table from SETVER.EXE in the current directory or search path.
path	Identifies the location of SETVER.EXE.
filename.ext	Identifies a program file.
version	Specifies a DOS version number to be reported to the specified program.
/DELETE	Deletes *filename* from the version table; abbreviate as /D.
/QUIET	Omits the standard warning message when deleting a program from the version table.

Notes

A version table, consisting of a list of programs and the version numbers DOS reports to them, is maintained in SETVER.EXE. If DOS 5 still exists on your system (usually in OLD_DOS.1), it may have a SETVER.EXE with a different version table. It's possible, by using *path*, to access the older version table.

When you omit *path*, DOS looks for SETVER.EXE in the current directory and then in the search path. If you include *path*, DOS looks for SETVER.EXE only in *path*.

When a program listed in the table runs, and the SETVER.EXE device driver has been loaded in CONFIG.SYS, DOS tells the program that it is running under the DOS version specified in its table entry.

The Setup program for DOS 6 usually inserts a command in CONFIG.SYS to load SETVER.EXE, including a version table provided by Microsoft. If you want to delete this command from CONFIG.SYS, first use SETVER to see if any of the programs in the table are ones that you use or that support ones you use. (The list is long; send the output to More or a file.) If you're not sure, don't delete the command that loads SETVER.

Some programs check the DOS version when they start up; when you run them, you get a message saying you are using an incorrect version of DOS. Some of these programs run correctly with DOS 6; you can safely add them to the version table. Some other programs might not run correctly with DOS 6; fooling them through the version table may lead to errors or data loss. When you add a program to your version table, be sure you back up your hard disk before you run the program for the first time.

If you add the DOS 6 command interpreter (COMMAND.COM) to your version table, you may not be able to boot your system.

Some programs that were part of earlier DOS versions but are not in DOS 6 (such as ASSIGN, Edlin, and JOIN) are in the version table provided by Microsoft; you won't get an error message if you use them.

When you use SETVER to add to or delete from your current version table, the change does not take effect until you reboot, which loads the revised table into memory.

SETVER sets an exit code, as follows:

0   Successful completion

1   Invalid command switch

2   Invalid file name

3   Insufficient memory

4   Invalid version number format

5   File name not in version table

6   SETVER.EXE file not found

7   Invalid drive (for *path*)

8   Too many command-line parameters

9   Missing command-line parameter(s)

10   Error reading SETVER.EXE file

11   SETVER.EXE file corrupt

595

12   Specified SETVER.EXE file does not support a version table

13   Version table full

14   Error writing to SETVER.EXE file

Examples

SETVER MYPROG.EXE 5.0

Adds an entry to the current version table so that MYPROG.EXE can be told that you are running DOS 5.0.

SETVER MYPROG.EXE /DELETE

Removes MYPROG.EXE from the version table.

SETVER E:\ | SORT | MORE

Displays the version table from the SETVER.EXE file found in the root directory of E; sorts the entries and pauses after each page.

SHARE

Starts the SHARE program, which installs file-sharing and locking capabilities on your disks and network drives.

Format

SHARE [/F:*space*] [/L:*locks*]

Parameters and Switches

none   Loads SHARE with the default values.

/F:*space*   Allocates space (in bytes) to record file-sharing information; default value is 2048.

/L:*locks*   Sets the number of files that can be locked at one time; default is 20.

Notes

SHARE loads the code that supports file-sharing and locking in network or multi-tasking environments in which programs share files. DOS uses this code to validate all read and write requests from programs so that, for example, two programs can't both write to the same file at the same time.

Each open file requires enough space for the length of the full path and file name. The average length of a path and file name is 20 characters.

You can load SHARE.EXE using Install in CONFIG.SYS instead of by the SHARE command, if you prefer.

Examples

SHARE

    Loads SHARE with default values.

SHARE /F:4096 /L:30

    Loads share with space for 4096 bytes of file information and allowing up to 30 open files.

SHELL

Specifies the command interpreter you want DOS to use.

Format

    SHELL=*filespec* [*parameters*]

Parameters

filespec	Identifies the command interpreter.
parameters	Specifies command-line parameters or switches for the requested command interpreter.

Notes

Without SHELL, the default command interpreter is COMMAND.COM in the root directory of the startup drive. You must use SHELL in your CONFIG.SYS file if you want to use another command interpreter, or to use COMMAND.COM from some other directory, such as C:\DOS.

See Command for parameters and switches than can be used with COM-MAND.COM. If you use some other command interpreter, see its documentation for appropriate parameters and switches.

Examples

SHELL=C:\DOS\COMMAND.COM C:\DOS /E:2048 /P

Installs COMMAND.COM from C:\DOS as the permanent command processor and specifies an environment size of 2048 bytes.

SHIFT

Changes the position of replaceable parameters in a batch file.

Format

SHIFT

Notes

The SHIFT command changes the values of replaceable parameters %0 through %9 so that the parameter that was %1 becomes %0; the parameter that was %2 becomes %1; and so on.

Examples

:LOOPER
IF "%1" == "" GOTO ENDING
DEL %1
SHIFT
GOTO LOOPER
:ENDING

Deletes one or more files; you supply the file names on the command line that executes this batch program. Each time SHIFT executes, a new name from the command line replaces %1. When there are no names left on the command line, %1 becomes a null value, so IF sends the program to :ENDING.

```
:COMPARE
IF "2"=="" GOTO ENDING
FC %1 %2
SHIFT
SHIFT
GOTO COMPARE
:ENDING
```

Lets you compare one or more pairs of files, the names to be supplied from the command line. Two Shifts are needed so that both %1 and %2 are replaced by totally new values.

SMARTDRV

Starts or configures SmartDrive, which creates a disk cache in extended memory; writes cached data.

Format 1

SMARTDRV [*drive*[+ | -]...] [/E:*element*] [InitCache] [WinCache] [/B:*buffer*] [/R] [/L] [/Q]

Starts or configures SmartDrive.

Parameters and Switches

none	If SmartDrive is not already loaded, loads the TSR portion of the program with default values. Displays caching status of drives.
drive	Identifies a disk drive for which you want to control caching (do not follow the drive letter with a colon).
+	-	+ enables both read and write caching for *drive*; - disables both read and write caching for *drive*. See Notes for defaults.
/E:*element*	Specifies in bytes the amount of the cache that SmartDrive moves at one time; may be 1024, 2048, 4096, or 8192; the default is 8192. The larger the value, the more conventional memory SmartDrive uses.

InitCache	Specifies in kilobytes the size of the cache when SmartDrive starts and Windows is not running. The default depends on your system's memory (see Notes).
WinCache	Specifies in kilobytes the smallest size to which SmartDrive reduces the cache when Windows starts. The default depends on your system's memory (see Notes).
/B:*buffer*	Specifies the size of the read-ahead buffer; may be any multiple of *element*; the default is 16K.
/R	Clears the contents of the cache.
/L	Prevents SmartDrive from automatically loading into upper memory, even if there are UMBs available.
/Q	Prevents SmartDrive from displaying error and status messages.
/S	Displays additional information about the status of SmartDrive.

Notes

SmartDrive keeps its cache in extended memory. Before using a SMARTDRV command, you must install an extended memory manager such as HIMEM.SYS.

Do not use the SMARTDRV command after Windows has started; Windows does its own cache management.

Default caching for drives not included in the initial SMARTDRV command depends on the drive type. Floppy drives and drives created by Interlnk are read- but not write-cached. Hard disk drives are both read- and write-cached. CD-ROM, RAM, network, compressed, and Microsoft Flash memory-card drives are ignored. For drives included in the command but without a trailing + or -, read caching is enabled and write caching is disabled.

Although SmartDrive by default does not cache compressed drives, it does cache their host drives. You can specify a compressed drive for caching in the SMARTDRV command, but doing so slows down your system, which is not the intent of SmartDrive.

/E, /B, /L, *InitCache*, and *WinCache* can be used only with the command that installs SmartDrive. Using /C or /S with an initial command prevents SmartDrive from loading and may produce a "help" message.

The larger the values of *element* and *buffer*, the more conventional memory SmartDrive uses.

The larger the cache size, the fewer disk accesses and the more efficient your system.

When SmartDrive loads, the size of the cache is InitCache. When Windows starts, it reduces the cache size to *WinCache* to allow more room for Windows operations. When Windows ends, the cache size returns to *InitCache*.

If you include only one cache size on the SMARTDRV command line, it is used for both *InitCache* and *WinCache*. That is, Windows can't reduce the cache size.

If you don't specify any cache size, SMARTDRV uses default values for both *InitCache* and *WinCache*, as shown in the following table:

Extended Memory	InitCache	WinCache
Up to 1M	All extended memory	0
Up to 2M	1M	256K
Up to 4M	1M	512K
Up to 6M	2M	1M
6M or more	2M	2M

SmartDrive automatically loads into upper memory if any is available (unless you use /L). You don't need to use LH with SMARTDRV.

SmartDrive also comes as a device driver to be loaded from CONFIG.SYS. If you use EMM386.EXE or run Windows in 386-enhanced mode, you may need the SmartDrive device driver also. The device driver does not enable or manage disk caching; you can do that only with the SMARTDRV command.

Examples

SMARTDRV

If SmartDrive is not yet loaded, loads it with default values for cache, element, and buffer sizes, and default caching status for all drives and displays a status report for SmartDrive. If SmartDrive is loaded, displays the status report.

SMARTDRV A- B- C 2048 512 /E:2048

If SmartDrive is not yet loaded, loads it with a cache size of 2048K; allows the cache to be reduced to 512K when Windows is running; uses the default value (16K) for *buffer*; specifies that SmartDrive should access data in blocks of 2048 bytes; turns off caching for drives A and B; enables read-caching only for drive C.

If SmartDrive is already loaded, ignores *InitCache*, *WinCache*, and *element*; changes the caching status for drives A, B, and C; caching status for other drives is unchanged.

SMARTDRV /S

If SmartDrive is already loaded, displays an extended status report.

Format 2

SMARTDRV /C

Writes all write-cached information from memory to the disk.

Notes

If you're using write caching on any of your drives, it's a good idea to write out any write-cached data before turning off the system or pressing a reset button. It's not necessary to do this before pressing Ctrl-Alt-Del; SmartDrive automatically writes cached data when it detects this sequence.

SORT

Sorts ASCII data and displays results.

Format

SORT [/R] [/+n] [< *source*] [> *destination*]

Parameters and Switches

source Identifies a file or device containing data you want to sort; the default is CON, which accepts input from the keyboard until you type Ctrl-Z.

destination Identifies a file or device to which you want to send sorted data; default is CON, which displays sorted data on the screen.

/R Reverses the sort order.

/+*n* Starts sorting in column *n*; default is column 1.

Notes

SORT does not distinguish between uppercase and lowercase letters in the data to be sorted.

SORT can handle files as large as 64K.

Normally, characters are sorted according to the ASCII code sequence; numeric digits 0–9 sort before letters A–Z. The placement of special or nonprinting characters depends on their ASCII codes.

If there is a COUNTRY command in CONFIG.SYS, SORT uses the collating-sequence table corresponding to the country code and code-page settings.

You can pipe output from other commands, such as TYPE or DIR, to sort for sorting, but not if you specify *source*. You can pipe output from SORT to MORE for a paged display, but not if you specify *destination*.

Examples

SORT

Accepts input from the keyboard until you press Ctrl-Z (or its equivalent, F6); sorts the input; then displays the sorted data on the screen.

SORT /+2 < ADDRESS.LST > LPT1

Sorts the data in ADDRESS.LST, starting with characters in column 2 of each line, and sends the output to the printer.

TYPE ADDRESS.LST | SORT /+2 > LPT1

Has the same effect as the previous example.

DIR C:\ /B /S | SORT | MORE

Creates a directory listing of all entries in C:\ and its subdirectories, sorts the items in the listing, and sends the results to the screen, pausing after each page.

STACKS

Supports the dynamic use of data stacks to handle hardware interrupts.

Format

STACKS=*number,size*

Parameters

number   Specifies the number of stacks; valid values are 0 or 8 through 64. For an IBM PC, IBM PC/XT, and IBM PC-Portable, the default value is 0; for all other computers, the default is 9.

size   Specifies the size (in bytes) of each stack. Valid values are 0 or 32 through 512. For an IBM PC, IBM PC/XT, and IBM PC-Portable, the default value is 0; for all other computers, the default is 128.

Notes

You can use the STACKS command in CONFIG.SYS only.

DOS allocates one stack when it receives a hardware interrupt. But if you specify 0 for both number and size, DOS allocates no stacks and each program must have enough stack space to accommodate the computer's hardware interrupt drivers. Many programs operate correctly with *number* and *size* set to 0.

If your computer operation becomes unstable when you set *number* and *size* to 0, return to the default values.

If *number* and *size* are not set to 0, and you get a `Stack Overflow` or `Exception error 12` message, increase *number* or *size*.

Example

> STACKS=12, 512
>
> Allocates 12 stacks of 512 bytes each for hardware interrupt handling.

SUBMENU

Defines an item on a startup menu that, when selected, displays another set of choices.

Format

> SUBMENU=*blockname*[, *text*]

Parameters

blockname	Identifies the name of the configuration block associated with this item.
text	Specifies the text to be displayed for this menu item; default is *blockname*.

Notes

You can use SUBMENU only in a main menu block or submenu block of a multiple configuration CONFIG.SYS. See Menuitem for a description of a menu block.

There must be a block named [*blockname*] defined elsewhere in CONFIG.SYS. If DOS can't find [*blockname*], the item is not included in the menu.

Blockname may be up to 70 characters long and can include any printable characters except spaces, backslashes, slashes, commas, semicolons, equal signs, and square brackets.

Text may be up to 70 characters long and can contain any printable characters.

Examples

> [MENU]
> SUBMENU BASIC, BASIC STARTUP
> MENUITEM WINDOWS
> [BASIC]

MENUITEM JOE

MENUITEM MARY

...

This startup menu block produces this startup menu:

1.   `BASIC STARTUP`

2.   `WINDOWS`

When a user chooses 1, another menu is produced:

1.   `JOE`

2.   `MARY`

SUBST

Reassigns a drive name to refer to a path.

Format 1

SUBST [*drive: path*]

Causes future references to *drive* to access *path* instead; displays current substitutions.

Parameters

none	Displays substitutions currently in force.
drive	Identifies drive name to be reassigned.
path	Specifies path to be referred to by *drive*.

Notes

Drive does not need to be an existing drive, but it must be within the range of possible drive names for the system (see LASTDRIVE). *Drive* can't be the current drive.

Path must refer to a path on an existing drive. *Path* may include a drive name; if it does not, DOS assumes that *path* is on the drive current at the time SUBST is executed.

Once a substitution is made, any reference to *drive* is redirected to *path*. If *drive* actually exists, you will not be able to access it until you cancel the substitution. (If *drive* contains your DOS commands, you will not be able to use any external DOS commands, including SUBST.)

Do not use the following commands on a substituted drive name: ASSIGN, MSBACKUP, CHKDSK, DISKCOMP, DISKCOPY, FDISK, FORMAT, LABEL, MIRROR, RECOVER, RESTORE, and SYS.

Examples

SUBST F: C:\DATADIR

> Causes any future reference to drive F to access the DATADIR directory on drive C.

SUBST A: MYDIR\D1

> Causes any future reference to drive A to access subdirectory D1 of directory MYDIR on the current drive.

SUBST A: \B:

> Causes any future reference to drive A to access the root directory of the disk in drive B.

SUBST

> Lists all current substitutions.

Format 2

SUBST *drive1*: /D

> Cancels the current substitution for *drive1*.

Example

SUBST A: /D

> Cancels any substitution for drive A. Future references to drive A will access drive A.

SWITCHES

Provides special options.

Format

SWITCHES=[/W] [/K] [/N] [/F]

Switches

/W	Specifies that WINA20.386 is in a directory other than the root directory of the boot drive.
/K	Forces an enhanced keyboard (101-key) to behave like a conventional keyboard (84-key).
/N	Prevents a user from using the F5 or F8 key to bypass startup commands.
/F	Skips the two-second delay after displaying the "Starting MS-DOS..." message during startup.

Notes

Use SWITCHES in CONFIG.SYS only.

Use /W if you are using Windows 3.0 in enhanced mode and have moved the WINA20.386 from the root directory of the boot drive to another directory. You must also add a Device command under the [386Enh] heading in your SYSTEM.INI file, specifying the new location of WINA20.386. If you do not use Microsoft Windows 3.0, do not use the /W switch.

Use /K if you have a program that does not correctly interpret input from an enhanced keyboard. If you install the ANSI.SYS device driver, use the /K switch on the DEVICE command that loads ANSI.SYS also.

Example

SWITCHES=/F /N

> Forces DOS to skip the two-second delay after the Starting MS-DOS... and prevents users from bypassing startup commands.

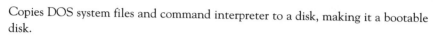

SYS

Copies DOS system files and command interpreter to a disk, making it a bootable disk.

Format

SYS [*path*] *drive*

Parameters

path	Identifies the location of the system files; the default is the root directory of the current drive.
drive	Specifies the drive to which you want to copy the system files.

Notes

Sys copies IO.SYS and MSDOS.SYS and marks them as system files. If SYS finds COMMAND.COM in *path*, it copies the file; otherwise, SYS displays a message saying that COMMAND.COM could not be copied. If SYS finds DBLSPACE.BIN along the search path, it copies this file also and marks it as system, hidden, and read-only. If SYS doesn't find DBLSPACE.BIN, there is no warning message.

All four files occupy about 197K.

SYS always copies these system files to the root directory of *drive*.

DOS no longer requires the two SYS files to be contiguous. This means you don't need to reformat a disk containing data to make it a bootable disk.

SYS does not work on drives that have been redirected by ASSIGN, JOIN, or SUBST. It also does not work on network drives or drives redirected by Interlnk.

Example

SYS A:

Copies the system files and command interpreter from the current drive's root directory to the root directory of the disk in drive A.

TIME

Displays the system time and lets you change it.

Format

TIME [*time*]

Parameters

none   Displays system time in standard format and asks for new time.

time   Changes system time to *time*.

Notes

The system time affects directory entries, MSBACKUP, RESTORE, and many applications.

When you display the time, DOS asks for a new time. To retain the current time, press Enter. To change the time, type the new time and press Enter. You can also change the time in one step by entering the new time as *time*.

By default, the standard display format is the US standard, *hh:mm:ss.nnx* where:

- ● *hh* represents hours in 12-hour format

- ● *mm* represents minutes

- ● *ss* represents seconds

- ● *nn* represents hundredths of a second

- ● *x* is A (for a.m.) or P (for p.m.)

When entering a time, you may omit the A or P designation and use the 24-hour format, where hours are 0 (midnight) through 23 (11 PM); or you may use A or P with the 12-hour format. Case is ignored in the A or P designation. Do not enter hundredths of seconds.

When setting time to an exact hour, you can omit the zeros for minutes and seconds. Similarly, when setting time to an exact hour and minute, you do not need to enter seconds.

To change to other time formats, such as *hh.mm.ss.nn*, use the COUNTRY command in your CONFIG.SYS file to specify the country whose date and time formats are to be used as standards.

Examples

TIME

>Displays the system time and asks you to enter a new time.

TIME 3:15P

>Changes the system time to 3:15:00.00PM.

TIME 15:15:30

>Changes the system time to 3:15:30.00PM.

TIME 2:12

>Changes the system time to 2:12:00.00AM.

TIME 0

>Changes the system time to 12:00 AM (midnight).

TIME 12:15P

>Changes the system time to 12:15 PM (15 minutes past noon).

TREE

Graphically displays a directory structure.

Format

>TREE [*drive* | *path*] [/F] [/A]

Parameters and Switches

none
: Displays the directory structure starting with the current directory.

drive
: Identifies the drive for which you want to display the directory structure.

path	Identifies a branch for which you want to display the directory structure.
/F	Displays the names of the files in each directory.
/A	Specifies that TREE is to use text characters instead of graphics characters to show the lines linking subdirectories. Use this switch with code pages that do not support graphics characters and to send output to printers that don't properly interpret the graphics characters.

Examples

TREE

> Displays the directory structure beginning with the current drive; does not show files; uses graphics characters for lines connecting directories.

TREE A: /F | MORE

> Displays the directory structure of the disk in drive A, showing all files in all directories and pausing after each page.

TREE C:\BOOK /A >LPT1

> Prints a directory structure of C:\BOOK and its subdirectories, using ASCII text characters instead of graphics characters for lines.

TRUENAME

Identifies the true location of a directory or file.

Format

TRUENAME [*drive* | *path* | *filespec*]

Parameters

none	Displays the true name of the current drive and directory.
drive	Displays the true name of *drive*.

path	Displays the true name of the indicated directory.
filespec	Displays the true filespec of the indicated file.

Notes

Use TRUENAME when a directory structure has been masked by ASSIGN or SUBST.

TRUENAME doesn't check to make sure a file exists. It merely inserts the correct path for the redirected one.

TYPE

Displays the contents of a file.

Format

TYPE *filespec*

Parameter

filespec	Identifies the file that you want to view.

Notes

If *filespec* is not an ASCII text file, the display will probably not be readable; it might beep several times or stop before displaying the entire file.

You can pipe the output of TYPE to SORT or MORE or redirect it to a printer.

Examples

TYPE REPORT.TXT

    Displays the contents of REPORT.TXT on the screen.

TYPE AFILE.BAT | SORT >LPT1

    Prints the sorted contents of AFILE.BAT.

TYPE MYLIST | MORE

    Displays the contents of MYLIST, pausing after each page.

UNDELETE

Enables deletion protection or restores files previously deleted.

Format 1

UNDELETE /LOAD | /U | /S[*drive*] ... | /T[*drive*[-*entries*] ... | /STATUS

Enables or disables deletion protection; reports protection status.

Parameters and Switches

/LOAD	Loads the UNDELETE TSR with the default protection method.
/U	Unloads the UNDELETE TSR.
/S[*drive*]	Loads the UNDELETE TSR, setting the current and default method of deletion protection to Delete Sentry; adds *drive* to the list of drives protected by Sentry.
/T[*drive*]	Loads the UNDELETE TSR, setting the current and default method of deletion protection to deletion-tracking; adds *drive* to the list of *drives* protected by Tracking.
entries	Specifies the maximum number of entries in the deletion-tracking file for *drive*; may be 1 to 999. The default depends on the drive size.
/STATUS	Displays the drives protected by the current protection method.

Notes

DOS 6 offers three levels of deletion protection. The highest level, Delete Sentry, and the second highest, deletion-tracking, operate only if the UNDELETE TSR is loaded at the time you delete a file. (The lowest level, DOS deletion protection, is always available.)

The UNDELETE.INI file (usually in the same directory as UNDELETE) contains default values for such things as how long a file should remain available (usually 7 days); which files are protected (often *.TMP, *.VM?, and other files are left unprotected); which drives are protected by which method; and which is the default method of protection.

You can change values in UNDELETE.INI using a text editor such as Edit.

The Delete Sentry method moves a deleted file to a special hidden directory (SENTRY). UNDELETE can easily restore the file because its clusters have not been reused. Each drive protected by Delete Sentry has a SENTRY directory once files are deleted on that drive.

Delete Sentry removes (purges) from the SENTRY directory after a length of time specified in UNDELETE.INI, or when the directory takes up more than about 7 percent of the drive, or if necessary to make room for new data on the drive. The oldest files are removed first. If Delete Sentry is not loaded, files can't be purged from the SENTRY directory unless you use /PURGE (see format 2). If your SENTRY directory is fairly large, you may easily get a "disk full" message when you disable Delete Sentry.

The deletion-tracking method places an entry describing a deleted file into PCTRACKR.DEL. UNDELETE can usually restore the file if its clusters have not been reused. Each drive protected by the deletion-tracking method has a PCTRACKR.DEL file in its root directory.

For deletion-tracking, the default value for *entries* depends on the disk size, as shown in the following table.

Drive	Entries
360K	25
720K	50
1.2M	75
1.44M	75
20M	101
32M	202
More than 32M	303

Do not use the deletion-tracking method on a drive redirected by JOIN or SUBST. If you intend to use ASSIGN, you must do so before installing deletion-tracking.

Examples

UNDELETE /SC /SD

> Loads the UNDELETE TSR using the Delete Sentry method; adds C
> and D to the list of drives protected by this method. (Any drives
> previously protected by this method remain protected).

UNDELETE /U

> Unloads the UNDELETE TSR.

Format 2

UNDELETE [*filespec*] [/DT | /DS | /DOS] [/LIST | /ALL]
[/PURGE[*drive*]]

> Recovers deleted files; lists recoverable files; clears a SENTRY directory.

Parameters and Switches

none	Offers to recover all deleted files in the current directory that can be recovered using the highest available method for the current drive.
filespec	Identifies the file(s) that you want to recover; the default is all deleted files in the current directory.
/DT	Recovers only those files listed in the deletion-tracking file, prompting for confirmation on each file.
/DS	Recovers only those files listed in the SENTRY directory, prompting for confirmation on each file.
/DOS	Recovers only those files found in the DOS directory, prompting for confirmation on each file.
/LIST	Lists recoverable files, but does not offer to recover them. The files listed depend on *filespec* and the recovery method.
/ALL	Recovers files without prompting. The files recovered depend on filespec and the recovery method.

/PURGE[*drive*]   Empties the SENTRY directory on *drive*; the default is the current drive.

Notes

You don't need to load the UNDELETE TSR to use these file functions.

When you don't specify a method switch, the method used is the highest available method for the drive.

No matter which protection method is being used for recovery, UNDELETE displays the number of Delete Sentry, deletion-tracking, and DOS entries available for *filespec*, but it recovers those available using the current method only.

When DOS deletes a file, it overwrites the first character of the file name. When you recover a deleted file by the DOS method, UNDELETE prompts you for a first character for the file name. But /ALL dispenses with prompting, so UNDELETE provides a first character (#). If the first attempt at providing an initial letter creates a nonunique name, UNDELETE substitutes another character (%), and so on. Characters are substituted in this order:

#%&0123456789ABCDEFGHIJKLMNOPQRSTUVWXYZ

Examples

UNDELETE C:\ /DT

Undeletes files deleted from the root directory on the C drive and protected by the deletion-tracking method; prompts before each file.

UNDELETE C:\WORDS /CD /ALL

Undeletes files deleted from directory C:\WORDS and protected by the Sentry method; undeletes without prompting.

UNDELETE D:\ACCOUNT /LIST

If D is protected by the Sentry method, lists files deleted from D:\ACCOUNT that are recoverable by Sentry; otherwise, if D is protected by Tracking, lists files deleted from D:\ACCOUNT that are recoverable by Tracking. If D is not protected by Sentry or Tracking, lists files deleted from D:\ACCOUNT that are recoverable from DOS.

UNFORMAT

Restores a disk reformatted by the FORMAT command; undeletes deleted directories.

Format

UNFORMAT *drive* [/L] [/TEST] [/P]

Parameters and Switches

drive   Identifies the drive to be unformatted.

/L   Lists every file and subdirectory found by UNFORMAT; without this switch, only fragmented files and directories are listed.

/TEST   Shows how UNFORMAT would re-create the information on the disk, but does not actually unformat the disk.

/P   Sends output messages to LPT1.

Notes

If an unconditional format was done, UNFORMAT can't restore the disk.

When you unformat a hard disk, the sectors must be 512, 1024, or 2048 bytes.

FORMAT (without /U) stores information about the root directory and file allocation table in a mirror file. When used with no switches, UNFORMAT uses information from this file to re-create the former data.

With /L, /TEST, or /P, UNFORMAT bypasses mirror information and searches the clusters (very slowly) for subdirectories.

When used with /L or /P, UNFORMAT may be able to restore a deleted directory, even if the disk has not been reformatted. This method of re-creating directories, however, is slow and uncertain; sometimes it creates strange directories and it truncates fragmented files, even in existing directories.

Examples

UNFORMAT A:

Unformats the disk in drive A using unformat information created by Format.

UNFORMAT B: /TEST

Simulates rebuilding the disk in drive B, searching for subdirectories and files, showing how UNFORMAT /L would re-create the disk.

VER

Displays the DOS version number.

Format

VER

VERIFY

Turns write verification on or off.

Format

VERIFY [ON | OFF]

Parameters

none	Displays the status of write verification.
ON	Turns write verification on, so that DOS verifies that files are written correctly to a disk.
OFF	Turns write verification off.

Notes

You can use VERIFY either in CONFIG.SYS or at the command prompt.

When verification is on, DOS verifies that any data written to a disk matches the copy of the data in memory. This can reassure you that no errors have been introduced during writing, but it doesn't verify that the data was correct in memory; it also slows down all disk writing slightly.

Examples

VERIFY

> Displays the status of the verify switch.

VERIFY ON

> Turns on write verification.

VOL

Displays the disk volume label and serial number, if they exist.

Format

VOL [*drive*]

Parameter

none   Displays the volume label and serial number, if any, of the disk in the current drive.

drive   Specifies a drive whose volume label and serial number you want to see.

Example

VOL A:

> Displays the volume label and serial number of the disk in drive A.

VSAFE

Loads (or unloads) the VSAFE TSR, which continuously monitors your computer for virus-like activity.

Format

VSAFE [/*option*+ |] - [...] [/NE] [/NX] [/A*key* | /C*key*] [/N] [/D] [/U]

Parameters and Switches

/*option*+ | -	Specifies how VSAFE monitors for viruses; use + or - following an option to turn it on or off. See Notes for the options.
/NE	Prevents VSAFE from loading into expanded memory.
/NX	Prevents VSAFE from loading into extended memory.
/A*key*	Sets the hotkey that displays the VSAFE options dialog box as Alt-*key*; the default is Alt-V.
/C*key*	Sets the hotkey that displays the VSAFE option dialog box as Ctrl-*key*.
/N	Allows VSAFE to monitor network drives.
/D	Turns off checksumming.
/U	Removes VSAFE from memory; don't use with any other switches.

Notes

Don't install Windows when VSAFE is running. To use VSAFE with Windows, add the command LOAD=MWAVTSR.EXE to your WIN.INI files; this allows VSAFE to display messages in Windows.

You can use LH with VSAFE.

Valid options are as follows:

1   Warns of low-level formatting that could completely erase the hard disk; default is ON

2   Warns of an attempt by a program to establish memory residence; default is OFF

3   Prevents programs from writing to disk; default is OFF

4   Scans executable files for viruses as DOS loads them; default is ON

5   Checks all disks for boot sector viruses; default is ON

6   Warns of attempts to write to the boot sector or partition table of the hard disk; default is ON

7   Warns of attempts to write to the boot sector of a floppy disk; default is OFF

8   Warns of attempts to modify executable files; default is ON

The VSAFE options list, accessed by the hotkey, shows you the status of each option, lets you change options, and lets you unload VSAFE.

Example

VSAFE /7+ /AX

Loads VSAFE, turning on the option to warn of attempts to write to the boot sector of a floppy disk; sets the hotkey to Alt-X.

XCOPY

Copies files and subdirectories.

Format

XCOPY *source* [*destination*] [/A | /M] [/D:*date*] [/P] [/S [/E]] [/V] [/W]

Parameters and Switches

source	Identifies the file(s) you want to copy.
destination	Specifies the location where the copy should be written; the default is the current directory.
/A	Copies only source files with positive archive attributes; does not change the archive attributes.
/M	Copies only source files with positive archive attributes; turns off the archive attributes.
/D:*date*	Copies only source files created or modified on or after *date*.
/P	Prompts you for permission to copy each selected file.
/S	Extends copying to the entire branch headed by the source directory (see Notes).
/E	Copies empty subdirectories when copying to the entire branch (see Notes). You must use /S if you use /E.

/V   Verifies each copy.

/W   Displays a message and waits for you to press a key before beginning to copy files.

Notes

When copying multiple files, XCOPY is considerably faster than COPY.

XCOPY copies empty files (unlike COPY) but not system or hidden files.

XCOPY turns on the archive attribute of each copy but copies the source files' date/time stamps.

When *source* includes a file name, *destination* can include a file name, and the two files can be in the same directory. When the *source* filespec includes wild cards and *destination* is a directory, XCOPY selects each file matching the specification. It looks for and replaces *destination* files with the same file names, creating new files when matching names can't be found. For example, in XCOPY CHAP*.DOC A:, XCOPY copies CHAP1.DOC to A:CHAP1.DOC, creating A:CHAP1.DOC if necessary.

If both *source* and *destination* include global filespecs, XCOPY looks for and replaces destination files with the same wild card characters in their file names, creating new files as necessary. For example, in XCOPY CHAP*.DOC A:CHAP*.BAK, XCOPY copies CHAP1.DOC to A:CHAP1.BAK, creating A:CHAP1.BAK if necessary.

If *source* is global and *destination* is a single file, XCOPY copies each file in turn to the same *destination* file; *destination* ends up as the last *source* file copied.

If *destination* does not identify an existing directory and does not end with \, XCOPY asks you whether *destination* is a directory or a file. (If it ends with \, XCOPY knows that the *destination* is a directory.)

With /S, XCOPY selects files matching the source filespec (if any) from the entire branch headed by the source directory, and copies them to comparably named subdirectories in the branch headed by the destination directory, creating destination subdirectories as needed.

With /S but without /E, XCOPY creates a destination subdirectory only if it's needed to hold a copied file. With /E, XCOPY duplicates all of the source branch's subdirectories in the target branch, even if no files are copied to some of the new subdirectories. (Note that the destination branch does not necessarily match the source branch even after XCOPY with /S and /E; the destination may have some previously existing subdirectories that are not in the source branch.)

If you use XCOPY in a batch file or Doskey macro to copy files to or from a floppy disk, you can use /W to provide time for someone to insert a disk in the drive before XCOPY starts processing files.

You can create a backup system using XCOPY. Use XCOPY without the /A, /M, or /D switches to do a full backup. Use XCOPY with /M for incremental backups or /A for differential backups. /D with an appropriate date could also be used for an in-between backups; use the date of the last full backup for a differential backup, or the date of the last incremental backup for another incremental backup.

If *date* is the day of the previous backup, you might end up with duplicate copies of files created on the date before you backed up, one in the previous backup, and one in this backup. If *date* is the day after the previous backup, you might miss files created on the day of the previous backup but after you backed up.

XCOPY sets an exit code as follows:

0   Successful completion.

1   No source files were found.

2   The user pressed Ctrl-C to terminate XCOPY.

4   Initialization error. There is not enough memory or disk space, or you entered an invalid drive name or invalid syntax on the command line.

5   Disk write error occurred.

Examples

XCOPY J*.* A:\NEWDIR\K*.*

Copies all files (except hidden and system ones) whose names start with J from the current directory to A:\NEWDIR; each destination file has the same name as the source file except that the first letter is replaced by K. If NEWDIR does not exist on drive A, XCOPY creates it.

XCOPY D:\ACCOUNT E:\ /S

If D:\ACCOUNT is a subdirectory, the branch headed by D:\ACCOUNT is copied to a branch headed by the root directory of drive E, with new subdirectories created under E:\ as needed. All files (except system or hidden ones) are copied. No empty subdirectories are created in the new branch.

If D:\ACCOUNT is a file, every file named ACCOUNT on drive D (except hidden and system ones) is copied to a comparably named directory on drive E, with new subdirectories created under /E as needed to hold the new files.

XCOPY *.COM A:\ /S /E /W

Waits for you to press a key (giving you time to insert a disk in A). After the keypress, each COM file (except system or hidden ones) from the branch headed by the current directory is copied (with the original name) to a comparably named directory on drive A, with new subdirectories created on A as needed. Source directories that don't contain a COM file are also created on drive A if they don't already exist there.

XCOPY *.DAT \SAVE /A /S

Each DAT file with a positive archive attribute from the branch headed by the current directory (except hidden or system ones) is copied (with its original name) to a comparably named subdirectory in the branch headed by \SAVE. New subdirectories are created as needed to hold the copied files. The archive attributes of the source files are unchanged.

Appendix

Device Drivers

ANSI.SYS

Provides functions that control screen colors, cursor position, and key assignments.

Format

DEVICE[HIGH]=[*path*]ANSI.SYS [/X | /K]

Parameters and Switches

path   Identifies the location of the ANSI.SYS file. The default is the root directory of the boot drive.

/X   With a 101-key (extended) keyboard, forces DOS to recognize that the extended (gray) cursor control, deletion, and insert/overlay keys have different scan codes than the numeric keypad keys for the same functions.

/K   Causes ANSI.SYS to treat a 101-key keyboard like an 84-key keyboard. Use this if you have a program that does not recognize the extended keys on the 101-key keyboard. If you use the /K switch with the SWITCHES command, use /K with ANSI.SYS also.

Notes

After ANSI.SYS has been loaded, any program can use its features by issuing escape sequences that act as commands to ANSI.SYS. (A program's documentation should tell you if it requires ANSI.SYS to be loaded.)

You also can enter an ANSI.SYS escape sequence by including it in a PROMPT command, by putting it in an ASCII text file and displaying the file with TYPE, or by inserting it in an ECHO command in a batch file and running the batch program.

All ANSI.SYS escape sequences begin with the escape character. The Esc key types the escape character, but because that key normally acts to terminate a command or program, you can't type it directly at the command prompt or in a file. You can, however, generate an escape character in a PROMPT command by typing $E. In DOS's EDIT and WordStar, you can type an escape character by pressing Ctrl-P followed by the Esc key; it shows up on the screen as a left arrow. In Microsoft Word, you can type an escape character by holding the Alt key while typing 27 on the numeric keypad. Other editors and word processors may use other techniques; some are not able to do it.

There are hundreds of ANSI.SYS escape sequences to control such things as the colors of the screen's background and text, what happens when you press Ctrl-Shift-X, and so on. They are documented in DOS 6's on-line Help system; look up the ANSI.SYS topic.

Example

DEVICEHIGH=C:\DOS\ANSI.SYS

Loads the ANSI.SYS device driver found in C:\DOS into upper memory, if available; otherwise, loads it into conventional memory, if possible.

PROMPT $E[34;57m$P$G

Sets up the command prompt screen with blue characters on a white background and displays the normal command prompt. The escape sequence $E[34;57m defines the screen colors.

CHKSTATE.SYS

Used by MEMMAKER to control the optimization process.

Notes

MEMMAKER temporarily adds the CHKSTATE.SYS command to your CONFIG.SYS file. When optimization is complete, MEMMAKER deletes it again.

DBLSPACE.SYS

Moves DBLSPACE.BIN to an appropriate memory location.

Format

DEVICE[HIGH]=[*path*]DBLSPACE.SYS /MOVE

Parameter

path Identifies the location of the DBLSPACE.SYS file. The default is the root directory of the boot drive.

Notes

DoubleSpace adds this command to CONFIG.SYS. If your system is set up to access UMBs, you may replace "DEVICE" with "DEVICEHIGH" to load the DoubleSpace driver into upper memory.

DBLSPACE.BIN manages compressed drives. DOS loads DBLSPACE.BIN into the top of conventional memory at boot time before carrying out any commands in CONFIG.SYS. This may cause conflict with other programs that require the use of this area. The DBLSPACE.SYS driver moves DBLSPACE.BIN to another location in memory to avoid this conflict.

When loaded by a DEVICE command, DBLSPACE.SYS moves DBLSPACE.BIN to the bottom of conventional memory. When loaded by a DEVICEHIGH command, DBLSPACE.SYS moves DBLSPACE.BIN to upper memory, if available; otherwise, to the bottom of conventional memory.

Example

DEVICEHIGH=C:\DOS\DBLSPACE.SYS /MOVE

> Moves DBLSPACE.BIN to upper memory or to the bottom of conventional memory.

DISPLAY.SYS

Supports code-page switching for your screen and keyboards.

Format

DEVICE[HIGH]=[*path*]DISPLAY.SYS CON=([*type*][,*codepage*] [,*max* | ,(*max, sub*)])

Parameters

path	Identifies the location of the DISPLAY.SYS file. The default is the root directory of the boot drive.
type	Specifies the display adapter in use. Valid values are EGA and LCD. EGA includes both EGA and VGA adapters. If you don't specify type, DISPLAY.SYS checks the hardware to determine the display adapter in use.

code page	Specifies the code page built into your hardware.
max	Specifies the number of code pages the hardware can support besides the one built into the hardware. Valid values are 0 through 6 for EGA, 0 through 1 for LCD.
sub	Specifies the number of subfonts the hardware supports for each code page.

Notes

See the CHCP and MODE commands for more information about code pages.

Although TYPE accepts the values CGA and MONO, DISPLAY.SYS has no effect with these values because CGA and MONO adapters don't support multiple character sets.

Code page values supported by DOS are as follows:

437	United States
850	Multilingual (Latin I)
852	Slavic (Latin II)
860	Portuguese
863	Canadian-French
865	Nordic

Most hardware sold in the U.S. uses code page 437.

If you install both DISPLAY.SYS and a third-party console driver in CONFIG.SYS, install the third-party console driver first. Otherwise, the third-party console driver may disable DISPLAY.SYS.

Example

DEVICE=C:\DOS\DISPLAY.SYS CON=(EGA,437,(2,1))

Loads DISPLAY.SYS for an EGA (or VGA) console with hardware code page 437, permitting two additional code pages, each with 1 subfont. Loads DISPLAY.SYS into conventional memory.

DEVICEHIGH=C:\DOS\DISPLAY.SYS CON=(LCD, 437, 1)

Loads DISPLAY.SYS for an LCD console with hardware code page 437, permitting one additional code page. Loads DISPLAY.SYS into upper memory, if available; otherwise, into conventional memory.

DRIVER.SYS

Creates a logical drive assigned to a physical floppy drive.

Format

DEVICE[High]=[*path*]DRIVER.SYS /D:*physical* [/C] [/F:*type*] [/H:*heads*] [/S:*sectors*] [T:*tracks*]

Parameters and Switches

path	Identifies the location of the DRIVER.SYS file. The default is the root directory of the boot drive.
/D:*physical*	Specifies the number of the physical floppy drive. Valid values are 0 through 127.
/C	States that the drive has change-line support. (See the DRIVEPARM command for information about change-line support.)
/F:*type*	Identifies the type of drive. (See Notes for values.)
/H:*heads*	Specifies the number of heads for the disk drive. Valid values are 1 through 99. The default is 2.
/S:*sectors*	Specifies the number of sectors per track. Valid values are 1 through 99. (See Notes for default values.)
/T:*tracks*	Specifies the number of tracks per side. Valid values are 1 through 999. (See Notes for default values.)

Notes

Drive name A is always assigned to physical drive 0. If the system has a second drive, it is physical drive 1 and is assigned the drive name B; otherwise, drive name B is also assigned to physical drive 0.

If you put a new floppy drive on your system and can't get DOS to recognize it, use DRIVER.SYS to assign a drive letter to it. If this is the third floppy drive for your system, its number is 2; if the fourth, its number is 3; and so on.

If you want to assign two drive names to the same drive, use DRIVER.SYS to assign the second drive name. One reason for doing this is to make it possible to use COPY or XCOPY to copy files from one disk to another in the same drive.

DOS assigns the next available drive name to a drive defined by DRIVER.SYS. If you add a DEVICE=DRIVER.SYS command to a CONFIG.SYS that also defines a RAM drive, DOS may assign a different letter to your RAM drive than it did previously. It's possible that drive names assigned by DoubleSpace may also change if you add DRIVER.SYS to your CONFIG.SYS file.

Default values for sectors and tracks depend on type. Valid values for type and the defaults associated with each type are as follows:

Type	Drive	Sectors	Tracks
0	160K/180K or 320K/360K	9	40
1	1.2M	15	80
2	720K or other (Default)	9	80
7	1.44M	18	80
9	2.88M	36	80

If you specify /H, /S, and /T, you can omit the /F switch. Usually, if you specify /F, you can omit /H, /S, and /T, but check the disk-drive manufacturer's documentation to be sure the default values for these switches are correct for your drive.

If you create two logical drives for the same physical drive, be sure that they have the same parameters and switches.

Examples

DEVICEHIGH=C:\DOS\DRIVER.SYS /D:1 /C

Loads DRIVER.SYS into upper memory if possible; otherwise into conventional memory. Assigns the next available drive name to the second floppy drive, using values appropriate for a 720K 3.5-inch floppy disk drive (by default) and specifying that the drive has change-line support. If DOS has already assigned a name to the second floppy drive during booting, this assigns an additional name to the drive.

DEVICE=C:\DOS\DRIVER.SYS /D:2 /F:7

DEVICE=C:\DOS\DRIVER.SYS /D:2 /F:7

Each of these commands loads the DRIVER.SYS file and assigns the next available drive name to the third floppy drive, using values appropriate to a 1.44M 3.5-inch floppy drive (by default). The effect is to assign two drive names to the drive.

EGA.SYS

Saves and restores the display when DOS Shell's task swapper is used with EGA monitors.

Format

DEVICE[HIGH]=[*path*]EGA.SYS

Parameter

path   Identifies the location of the EGA.SYS file. The default is the root directory of the boot drive.

Notes

If you have an EGA monitor, you must install EGA.SYS before using DOS Shell's task swapper.

If you are using a mouse on a system that has an EGA monitor, you can save memory by installing EGA.SYS before you install your mouse driver.

EMM386.EXE

Provides access to the upper memory area and uses extended memory to simulate expanded memory.

Format

DEVICE=[*path*]EMM386.EXE [ON | OFF | AUTO] [*expanded-memory*]
[MIN=*size*] [W=ON | W=OFF] [M*x* | FRAME=*address1* | /P*address1*]
[P*n*=*address2*] [[X=*mmmm1-nnnn1*]...] [[I=*mmmm2-nnnn2*]...] [B=*address3*]
[L=*minXMS*] [A=*altregs*] [H=*handles*] [D=*nnn*] [RAM[=*mmmm3-nnnn3*]]
[NOEMS] [NOVCPI] [NOHIGHSCAN] [/VERBOSE] [[WIN=*mmmm4-
nnnn4*]...] [NOHI] [ROM=*mmmm5-nnnn5*]

Parameters and Switches

path	Identifies the location of the EMM386.EXE file. The default is the root directory of the boot drive.
ON	OFF	AUTO	ON loads and activates the EMM386 driver; OFF loads the driver but deactivates it; AUTO places the driver in automatic mode, which enables expanded-memory support and upper memory block support only when a program calls for it. Use the EMM386 command to change this value after the driver has been loaded.
expanded-memory	Specifies (in kilobytes) the maximum amount of extended memory that you want EMM386.EXE to provide as expanded memory. Values are 64 through 32768 (or the amount of free extended memory). The default value is the amount of free extended memory unless you specify NOEMS. EMM386.EXE rounds the value down to the nearest multiple of 16.
MIN=*size*	Specifies (in kilobytes) the minimum amount of expanded memory that EMM386.EXE will provide. Values are 0 through *expanded-memory*. The default value is 256 unless you specify NOEMS.

W=ON | W=OFF	Enables or disables support for the Weitek coprocessor. The default is W=OFF.
M*x*	Specifies the base address of the expanded-memory page frame. Valid values are 1 through 14. If your computer has less than 512K of memory, *x* must be less than 10. See Notes for the address associated with each value of *x*.
FRAME=*address1*	Specifies the page-frame base address directly. Valid values are 8000H through 9000H and C000H through E000H, in increments of 400H. You may specify FRAME=NONE, but this could cause some programs to malfunction.
/P*address1*	Specifies the page-frame base address directly. Valid values are 8000H through 9000H and C000H through E000H, in increments of 400H.
P*n*=*address2*	Specifies the base address of page *n*. Valid values for *n* are 0 through 255. Valid values for address are 8000H through 9C00H and C000H through EC00H, in increments of 400H. The addresses for pages 0 through 3 must be contiguous to maintain compatibility with Version 3.2 of LIM EMS. If you use M*x*, FRAME, or /P*address1*, you can't specify addresses for pages 0 through 3 with the /P*n* switch.
X=*mmmm1-nnnn1*	Prevents EMM386.EXE from using a particular range of segment addresses for an EMS page or for UMBs. Valid values for *mmmm1* and *nnnn1* are in the range A000H through FFFFH and are rounded down to the nearest 4-kilobyte boundary. This parameter takes precedence over the I parameter if two ranges overlap.

I=*mmmm2-nnnn2*

Specifies a range of segment addresses to use for an EMS page or for UMBs. Valid values for *mmmm2* and *nnnn2* are in the range A000h through FFFFh and are rounded down to the nearest 4-kilobyte boundary. The X parameter takes precedence over the I parameter if two ranges overlap.

B=*address3*

Specifies the lowest segment address available for EMS bank-switching. Valid values are in the range 1000H through 4000H. The default value is 4000H.

L=*minXMS*

Ensures that *min* kilobytes of extended memory will still be available after you load EMM386.EXE. The default value is 0.

A=*altregs*

Specifies how many fast alternate register sets (used for multitasking) you want to allocate to EMM386.EXE. Valid values are in the range 0 through 254. The default value is 7. Every alternate register set adds about 200 bytes to the size of EMM386.EXE in memory.

H=*handles*

Specifies how many handles EMM386.EXE can use. Valid values are in the range 2 through 255. The default is 64.

D=*nnn*

Specifies how many kilobytes of memory to reserve for buffered direct memory access (DMA). Discounting floppy-disk DMA, this value should reflect the largest DMA transfer that will occur while EMM386.EXE is active. Valid values for *nnn* are in the range 16 through 256. The default value is 16.

RAM [=*mmmm3-nnnn3*]

Requests both expanded memory and UMB support and specifies a range of segment addresses in extended memory to use for UMBs. If you do not specify a range, EMM386.EXE selects the addresses.

NOEMS	Provides UMB support but not expanded memory support.
NOVCPI	Disables support for VCPI (Virtual Control Program Interface) applications. This switch may be used only with the NOEMS switch. When you specify both switches, EMM386.EXE disregards the *expanded-memory* and MIN parameters.
NOHIGHSCAN	Limits scanning of the upper memory area for available memory. Specify this switch only if you have trouble using EMM386.EXE.
/VERBOSE	Directs EMM386.EXE to display status and error messages while loading. By default, EMM386.EXE does not display these messages. You can abbreviate /VERBOSE as /V.
WIN=*mmmm4-nnnn4*	Reserves a range of segment addresses for Windows instead of for EMM386.EXE. Valid values for *mmmm4* and *nnnn4* are in the range A000H through FFFFH and are rounded down to the nearest 4 kilobytes. The X parameter takes precedence over the WIN parameter if two ranges overlap. The WIN parameter takes precedence over the RAM, ROM, and I parameters if their ranges overlap.
NOHI	Prevents EMM386.EXE from loading into the upper memory area. Normally, a portion of EMM386.EXE is loaded into upper memory. Specifying this switch decreases available conventional memory and increases the upper memory area available for UMBs.

ROM=*mmmm5-nnnn5*   Specifies a range of segment addresses that EMM386.EXE uses for shadow RAM. Valid values for *mmmm5* and *nnnn5* are in the range A000H through FFFFH and are rounded down to the nearest 4 kilobytes. Specifying this switch may speed up your system if it does not already have shadow RAM. (See HIMEM.SYS for an explanation of shadow RAM.)

Notes

You must load this device driver with a DEVICE (not DEVICEHIGH) command in CONFIG.SYS. You can use this driver on computers with a 386 or higher processor only.

You must install HIMEM.SYS before loading EMM386.SYS. The DEVICE command that loads EMM386 must come before any DEVICEHIGH commands in CONFIG.SYS.

EMM386 can provide expanded memory to programs by using extended memory to simulate expanded memory. To use EMM386 for this purpose, you don't usually need to specify any of the memory parameters; EMM386 normally runs properly with the default parameters. Extended memory reserved for this purpose (by the MIN parameter or its default) is no longer available for use as extended memory. If EMM386 uses additional extended memory, up to the *expanded-memory* maximum, the additional memory returns to extended memory use when it is no longer needed as expanded memory.

To provide access to upper memory, you must use either the RAM or NOEMS switch. (You must also include DOS=UMB in CONFIG.SYS.) NOEMS gives access to upper memory while suppressing expanded memory support. RAM provides both upper memory and expanded memory support.

When EMM386.EXE is used with Windows 3.1, the I, X, NOEMS, M*x*, P*address1*, and FRAME parameters have precedence over the EMMINCLUDE, EMMEXCLUDE, and EMMPAGEFRAME settings in the Windows SYSTEM.INI file.

If you have a small computer system interface (SCSI) or enhanced system device interface (ESDI) hard disk or other device, you may have to use SmartDrive double buffering (see SMARTDRV.EXE) with EMM386.

Values for Mx, and the base addresses associated with them, are as follows:

x	Base Address
1	C000H
2	C400H
3	C800H
4	CC00H
5	D000H
6	D400H
7	D800H
8	DC00H
9	E000H
10	8000H
11	8400H
12	8800H
13	8C00H
14	9000H

Examples

DEVICE=C:\DOS\HIMEM.SYS

DEVICE=C:\DOS\EMM386.EXE OFF

The first command loads the HIMEM.SYS extended memory manager using all default values; this is a prerequisite to the second command. The second command loads the EMM386.EXE device driver to provide a minimum of 256K of expanded memory, which is "borrowed" from extended memory. Additional expanded memory support can be allocated to a program upon request, up to the amount of available extended memory. All other parameters—such as page frame addresses, alternate registers, and handles—use their default values. The driver is disabled after loading, so no expanded memory is provided until an EMM386 command enables it or places it in automatic mode.

DEVICE=C:\DOS\HIMEM.SYS

DEVICE=C:\DOS\EMM386.EXE NOEMS

DOS=UMB

> The first command loads the HIMEM.SYS extended memory manager using all default values; this is a prerequisite to the second command. The second command loads the EMM386.EXE device driver to provide upper memory blocks only. (Memory for the UMBs is "borrowed" from extended memory.) The third command is required to make the UMBs available to DOS.

DEVICE=C:\DOS\HIMEM.SYS

DEVICE=C:\DOS\EMM386.EXE MIN=1024 2048 RAM

DOS=UMB

> The first command loads the HIMEM.SYS extended memory manager using all default values; this is a prerequisite to the second command. The second command loads the EMM386.EXE device driver to provide both expanded memory and upper memory support. A minimum of 1M of expanded memory is "borrowed" from extended memory; this can be expanded up to 2M on individual program request. All other expanded memory parameters use their default values. The third command makes the UMBs available to DOS.

HIMEM.SYS

Manages extended memory, including the high memory area (HMA).

Format

DEVICE=[*path*]HIMEM.SYS [/A20CONTROL:ON | OFF]
[/CPUCLOCK:ON | OFF] [/EISA] [/HMAMIN=*size*] [/INT15=*x*]
[/NUMHANDLES=*n*] [/MACHINE:*machine*] [/SHADOWRAM:
ON | OFF] [/VERBOSE]

Parameters and Switches

path	Identifies the location of the HIMEM.SYS file. The default is the root directory of your boot drive.
/A20CONTROL:ON | OFF	Specifies whether HIMEM is to take control of the A20 line even if A20 is already on. If you specify /A20CONTROL:OFF, HIMEM takes control of the A20 line only if A20 is not already in use when HIMEM loads. The default setting is /A20CONTROL:ON.
/CPUCLOCK:ON | OFF	Specifies whether HIMEM can affect the clock speed of your computer. If your computer's clock speed changes when you install HIMEM, /CPUCLOCK:ON may correct the problem but slow down HIMEM. The default setting is /CPUCLOCK:OFF.
/EISA	Specifies that HIMEM.SYS should allocate all available extended memory. This switch is necessary only on an EISA (Extended Industry Standard Architecture) computer with more than 16M of memory; on other computers, HIMEM automatically allocates all available extended memory.
/HMAMIN=*size*	Specifies (in kilobytes) how large a program must be to use the HMA. Valid values are 0 through 63; the default is 0, which forces HIMEM to give the HMA to the first program that requests it. This switch has no effect when Windows is running in 386 enhanced mode.

/INT15=*x*   Allocates (in kilobytes) extended memory for the interrupt 15h interface. Valid values are 64 through 65535 but not more than your system's available memory. The default value is 0. If *x* is less than 64, *HIMEM* uses 0.

/NUMHANDLES=*n*   Specifies the maximum number of extended memory block handles that can be used simultaneously. Valid values are 1 through 128; the default value is 32. Each handle requires an additional 6 bytes of memory. This switch has no effect when Windows is running in 386 enhanced mode.

/MACHINE:*machine*   Specifies which A20 handler to use. See Notes for valid values.

/SHADOWRAM:ON | OFF   Specifies whether or not to enable shadow RAM. If your computer has less than 2M of memory, the default is OFF (disabled).

/VERBOSE   Directs HIMEM.SYS to display status and error messages while loading. By default, HIMEM.SYS does not display these messages. You can abbreviate /VERBOSE as /V.

Notes

You must load this device driver with a DEVICE (not DEVICEHIGH) command in CONFIG.SYS. The DEVICE command must come before any commands that start applications or device drivers that use extended memory; for example, you must load HIMEM.SYS before EMM386.

In most cases, you will not need to specify command-line options. The default values for HIMEM.SYS work with most hardware.

In a 286 or newer machine, the 21st address line (named A20) gives DOS access to the high memory area (HMA), which is the first 64K (almost) of extended memory.

The HMA can be used to execute programs just like conventional memory, but you must load special software to manage the A20 line.

Usually, HIMEM detects the computer type successfully and loads the correct A20 handler, but there are a few computers that HIMEM can't detect. On such systems, HIMEM uses the default A20 handler (#1, for the IBM AT or compatible). If HIMEM does not work properly on your system, you might need to use /MACHINE to specify the A20 handler. Systems that may require this option include Acer 1100, Wyse, and IBM 7552. HIMEM's startup message shows which handler has been loaded.

With /MACHINE, you can specify either the machine code, as in /MACHINE=WYSE, or the number of the A20 handler, as in /MACHINE=8.

Machine can be any of these codes or their equivalent A20 handler numbers as follows:

Machine Code	A20 Handler	Computer Type
AT	1	IBM AT or 100% compatible
PS2	2	IBM PS/2
PTLCASCADE	3	Phoenix Cascade BIOS
HPVECTRA	4	HP Vectra (A & A+)
ATT6300PLUS	5	AT&T 6300 Plus
ACER1100	6	Acer 1100
TOSHIBA	7	Toshiba 1600 & 1200XE
WYSE	8	Wyse 12.5 Mhz 286
TULIP	9	Tulip SX
ZENITH	10	Zenith ZBIOS
AT1	11	IBM PC/AT (alternative delay)
AT2	12	IBM PC/AT (alternative delay)
CSS	12	CSS Labs
AT3	13	IBM PC/AT (alternative delay)
PHILIPS	13	Philips

Machine Code	A20 Handler	Computer Type
FASTHP	14	HP Vectra
IBM7552	15	IBM 7552 Industrial Computer
BULLMICRAL	16	Bull Micral 60
DELL	17	Dell XBIOS

Some computers "shadow" ROM by copying its information into RAM at startup. This can make ROM code run faster, but it uses some extended memory. If a computer has less than 2M of RAM, HIMEM usually attempts to disable shadow RAM to recover additional extended memory for other uses. (HIMEM can disable shadow RAM only on certain types of systems.) When HIMEM disables shadow RAM, your computer might run slightly slower than it did before. (See EMM386.EXE for a means of providing shadow RAM if you computer does not have it built-in.)

Some older applications use the interrupt 15h interface to allocate extended memory rather than using the XMS (eXtended-Memory Specification) method provided by HIMEM. If you use such an application, you can make sure that enough memory is available to it by making x 64K larger than the amount the application requires.

Examples

    DEVICE=C:\DOS\HIMEM.SYS

    Loads the HIMEM.SYS driver using all default values.

    DEVICE=C:\DOS\HIMEM.SYS /MACHINE=6 /INT15=64

    Loads the HIMEM.SYS driver with the Acer 1100 A20 handler and
    reserves 64K of memory for processing old-style extended memory
    requests.

INTERLNK.EXE

Links a client computer to a server computer and redirects drive and printer port names.

Format

DEVICE[HIGH]=[*path*]INTERLNK.EXE [/DRIVES:*n*] [/NOPRINTER]
[/COM[*n* | *address*]] [/LPT[*n* | *address*]] [/AUTO] [/NOSCAN] [/LOW]
[/BAUD:*rate*] [/V]

Parameters and Switches

path	Identifies the location of the INTERLNK.EXE file. The default is the root directory of the boot drive.
/DRIVES:*n*	Specifies the number of server drives to be redirected to the client computer. The default is 3. If *n* = 0, INTERLNK redirects only printers.
/NOPRINTER	Inhibits redirection of printers. By default, INTERLNK redirects all available parallel printer ports.
/COM[*n*	*address*]	Specifies the port by which the client computer is cabled to the server computer; if neither *n* nor *address* is specified, INTERLNK scans all serial ports for the connection.
/LPT[*n*	*address*]	Specifies the port by which the client computer is cabled to the server computer; if neither *n* nor *address* is specified, INTERLNK scans all parallel ports for the connection.
/AUTO	Installs INTERLNK.EXE in memory only if it can establish an immediate link with the server computer. By default, INTERLNK.EXE is installed even if the connection can't yet be completed.
/NOSCAN	Installs INTERLNK.EXE in memory but prevents it from establishing a connection. By default, INTERLNK tries to establish a connection with the server as soon as you install it.
/LOW	Loads the INTERLNK.EXE driver into conventional memory, even if upper memory is available. By default, INTERLNK.EXE loads into upper memory if available.

/BAUD:*rate*	Sets a maximum baud rate for serial communication. Valid values are 9600, 19200, 38400, 57600, and 115200. The default is 115200.
/V	Prevents conflicts with a computer's timer. Specify this switch if you have a serial connection between computers and one of them stops running when you use INTERLNK to access a drive or printer port.

Notes

The INTERLNK driver can establish a link and redirect a server's drives and printer ports if the two computers are cabled and the INTERSVR program has already been loaded on the server computer. Otherwise, you'll need the INTERLNK command to complete the connection after these conditions have been met.

If you don't specify /LPT or /COM, the client scans all serial and parallel ports.

> Scanning a serial port that is attached to a mouse can disable the mouse driver. If you are using a serial mouse, either specify /LPT (and not /COM) or specify /COM*n*, where COM*n* is not the port the mouse is using.

The position of the DEVICE command that loads INTERLNK.EXE can affect future drive assignments. To make sure that all drives have the same letter assignments as they did before putting this DEVICE command in CONFIG.SYS, be sure that it is the last one in CONFIG.SYS.

You can save memory space by using switches to load only the portions of INTER-LNK.EXE that you need. If you specify /NOPRINTER, INTERLNK.EXE doesn't load the code that handles printers. If you specify /LPT, the program does not load the code that supports serial ports. If you specify /COM, the program doesn't load the code that supports parallel ports.

If you redirect LPT1 or LPT2 and print from Microsoft Windows, use Control Panel to assign the printer to either LPT1.DOS or LPT2.DOS.

Some features of DOS may not be available to the client computer if you are running different DOS versions on the server and client. For example, if you have large partitions on your server computer and are running DOS 3.0 on your client, the partitions will not be available to the client because DOS 3.0 doesn't support them.

If you use INTERLNK to run an application located on the server computer, be sure the application is configured for the client computer.

These commands do not work with the INTERLNK.EXE device driver: CHKDSK, DEFRAG, DISKCOMP, DISKCOPY, FDISK, FORMAT, SYS, UNDELETE, and UNFORMAT (and any other programs that bypass DOS's normal file-handling routines and deal directly with the system areas, tracks, or sectors).

Examples

DEVICE=C:\DOS\INTERLNK.EXE /COM2

> Loads the INTERLNK.EXE device driver for the client computer's COM2 port. If a connection can be established, redirects all of the server's parallel printers and three drives.

DEVICE=C:\DOS\INTERLNK.EXE /DRIVES:5 /NOPRINTER

> Loads the INTERLNK.EXE device driver and scans all the client computer's serial and parallel ports for a connection. If a connection can be established, redirects five drives and no printers.

POWER.EXE

Reduces power consumption in a laptop computer when applications and devices are idle.

Format

DEVICE[HIGH]=[*path*]POWER.EXE [ADV[:*advtype*] | STD | OFF] [/LOW]

Parameters and Switches

path	Identifies the location of POWER.EXE; the default is the root directory of the boot drive.
ADV[:*advtype*]	Conserves power when applications and hardware devices are idle. *Advtype* may be MAX, for maximum power conservation, REG to balance application and device performance with power conservation, or MIN to minimize power conservation if performance is

unsatisfactory when using REG or MAX. ADV:REG is the default setting.

STD If your computer supports the Advance Power Management (APM) specification, STD conserves power by using only your computer's power-management features. If your computer does not support the APM specification, STD turns off power management.

OFF Turns off power management.

Notes

POWER.EXE loads into upper memory, if available; otherwise, it loads into conventional memory.

The power manager conforms to the APM specification.

See the POWER command for more information about power management.

Example

DEVICE=C:\DOS\POWER.EXE

Loads the POWER.EXE file found in C:\DOS into upper memory, if available, otherwise into conventional memory. Uses the default setting ADV:REG.

RAMDRIVE.SYS

Uses an area of your computer's random-access memory (RAM) to simulate a hard disk drive.

Format

DEVICE[HIGH]=[*path*]RAMDRIVE.SYS [*DiskSize* [*SectorSize* [*NumEntries*]]] [/E | /A]

Parameters and Switches

path Identifies the location of the RAMDRIVE.SYS file. The default is the root directory of the boot drive.

DiskSize	Specifies, in kilobytes, how much memory to use for the RAM drive. Valid values are 4 to 32767, or available memory, whichever is smaller. The default is 64.
SectorSize	Specifies disk sector size in bytes. May be 128, 256, or 512 (the default). Microsoft recommends that you use 512. If you include *SectorSize*, you must include *DiskSize*.
NumEntries	Specifies the number of files and directories you can create in the root directory of the RAM drive. May be 2 to 1024; the limit you specify is rounded up to the nearest sector size boundary. The default is 64. If you include NumEntries, you must also include *SectorSize* and *DiskSize*.
/E	Creates the RAM drive in extended memory.
/A	Creates the RAM drive in expanded memory.

Notes

DOS allocates the next available drive letter to the RAM drive.

RAM drives are much faster than hard disk drives and blindingly fast compared to floppy drives, because your computer can access memory faster than it can a disk; but you lose all the data in a RAM drive when you turn off or restart your computer. RAM drives are especially suitable to use for temporary files; many people set the TEMP environment variable to a directory on a RAM drive, both for speed and to avoid possibly filling up a hard drive with temporary data.

It's best to create a RAM drive in extended memory if possible.

To use /A, your system must have expanded memory, and you must load an expanded memory manager such as EMM386 before creating the RAM drive.

If you omit /E and /A, the RAM drive uses conventional memory. This is recommended only on a system with no extended memory, no expanded memory, and no hard disk.

If you use Windows and set TEMP to a directory on a RAM drive, be sure that *DiskSize* is at least 2048 (2M) to allow enough space for Windows' temporary print files.

If there is not enough room to create the RAM drive as specified, RAMDRIVE.SYS tries to create a drive with a limit of 16 entries in the root directory.

Watch your boot messages for the names of the new RAM drives.

Examples

DEVICEHIGH=C:\DOS\RAMDRIVE.SYS 2048 /E

> Loads the RAMDRIVE.SYS file into upper memory, if available; otherwise, loads it into conventional memory. Creates in extended memory a 2048K (2M) RAM drive with 512-byte sectors and a maximum of 64 entries in the root directory.

DEVICE=C:\DOS\RAMDRIVE.SYS 2048 512 128 /A

> Loads the RAMDRIVE.SYS file and creates in expanded memory a 2048 (2M) RAM drive with 512-byte sectors and a maximum of 128 entries in the root directory.

SETVER.EXE

Loads the DOS version table into memory.

Format

DEVICE[HIGH]=[*path*]SETVER.EXE

Parameter

path	Identifies the location of the SETVER.EXE file. The default is the root directory of the boot drive.

Notes

The SETVER.EXE device driver uses the version table to report appropriate DOS version numbers to programs that require this information. The SETVER command allows you to display and edit the version table. See the SETVER command for more details about the version table.

If you are using SETVER to report a different DOS version to a device driver, the DEVICE (or DEVICEHIGH) command loading SETVER.EXE must appear in CONFIG.SYS before the DEVICE (or DEVICEHIGH) command loading the other device driver.

Examples

DEVICEHIGH=C:\DOS\SETVER.EXE

> Loads the SETVER.EXE file found in C:\DOS into upper memory if available, rather than conventional memory.

SIZER.SYS

> Used by MEMMAKER to determine the size in memory of device drivers and TSRs.

Notes

MEMMAKER temporarily adds SIZER.SYS to your CONFIG.SYS and AUTOEXEC.BAT files. When optimization is complete, MEMMAKER deletes the SIZER.SYS commands again.

SMARTDRV.EXE

Provides compatibility for hard-disk controllers that can't work with memory provided by EEMM386.EXE or Windows running in 386 enhanced mode.

Format

DEVICE=[*path*]SMARTDRV.EXE /DOUBLE_BUFFER

Parameter

path	Identifies the location of the SMARTDRV.EXE file; the default is the root directory of the boot drive.

Notes

If you don't use EMM386.EXE and don't run Windows in 386 enhanced mode, you don't need double-buffering.

If you do use EMM386.EXE or run Windows in 386 enhanced mode, you probably need double-buffering if you have an SCSI (small computer system interface) device, and you may need it if you have an ESDI (enhanced system device interface) or MCA (microchannel architecture) device.

When the device driver is loaded for double-buffering, it requires about 2K of conventional memory.

The SMARDRV.EXE driver does not provide disk caching. You must use the SMARTDRV command to do that.

Follow the following steps to determine whether your system requires double-buffering. (Your system must be set up to use upper memory blocks.)

1. Load the SMARTDRV.EXE device driver for double-buffering.

2. Insert a SMARTDRV command in AUTOEXEC.BAT (unless it already contains one). If your system seems to be running slowly after you start using SMARTDRV, add the /L switch to this SMARTDRV command.

3. Run MEMMAKER.

4. At the command prompt, enter SMARTDRV to display information about your system.

5. Look at the column labeled "Buffering." If any line in this column reads "yes," you need double-buffering.

6. If every line in the "Buffering" column says "no," you don't need double-buffering, and you can remove the command from CONFIG.SYS.

7. If any line in the "Buffering" column says "-," SmartDrive can't detect whether double-buffering is needed.

Glossary

.	A code that represents the current directory.
..	A code that represents the parent of the current directory.
Absolute path	A path that starts from the root directory.
Address	A number that identifies a location in memory or on a disk.
Allocation unit	The smallest unit in which DOS stores a file or part of a file. Also referred to as a cluster.
Alphanumeric data	Data made up of letters, digits, and printable special characters.
ANSI	American National Standards Institute, which has established standards for data storage and communication. The standard 256-character ANSI code includes ASCII characters and others.
Anti-virus	A program designed to detect the presence of a virus in a system, prevent the virus from functioning, and remove it if possible. See *Virus*.
Archive	To make a copy of a file for safekeeping in a different location, usually on removable media. Same as *Back up*.
Archive attribute	An attribute indicating whether a file has changed since it was last backed up. The archive attribute is turned on when a file is first created and when it is modified.
ASCII	American Standard Code for Information Interchange. A standard 128-character code that represents letters, digits, printable special characters, and some control codes.
Associated file	A file with an extension that DOS associates with a particular program. If the file is selected in the DOS Shell, the program starts.

Attribute	One of four characteristics that can be assigned to a file or directory and recorded in its directory entry. They include the archive, hidden, read-only, and system attributes.
AUTOEXEC.BAT	A batch file that is executed when the system boots, immediately after CONFIG.SYS is processed.
Back up	To copy a file for safekeeping to another location, often on removable media. The copy also is called a *backup*.
BAT	An extension that indicates a batch file.
Batch file	A file that contains a series of commands to be executed like a program.
Baud rate	An indication of the speed at which data can be communicated between a computer and other equipment. Also referred to as bits per second or BPS.
BBS	See *Bulletin board system*.
Binary	A numbering system that uses only two digits, 0 and 1. All data in a computer or on a disk is handled and stored in binary.
BIOS	Basic Input Output System. See *ROM BIOS*.
Bit	The smallest unit of information handled by a computer. A bit can have one of two values, usually represented by 0 and 1. Bit stands for Binary digIT.
Boot	To start up a computer system.
Boot record	A program found in the boot sector. The boot record on the boot drive loads the operating system when you start up the computer or reboot.
Boot sector	The first sector of a disk.
Branch	A directory and all its descendants. See *Child directory*.
Buffer	A memory area that holds data temporarily.

657

Bulletin board system A computer system running software that allows access to many people at one time through their modems. Such systems typically enable you to carry on a "conversation" by reading and posting messages and to send and receive files. Abbreviated as BBS.

Byte A series of eight bits, which can form 256 unique combinations. The term *byte* is often used as equivalent to one character.

Cache A memory location used to store data for rapid access. A disk cache holds data read from or written to a disk. It is similar to, but more intelligent and efficient than, a read-write buffer.

CD-ROM A drive that holds read-only data on a medium similar to that of an audio CD.

Check box A dialog box option marked by a small box. When the option is turned on, the box contains a checkmark or an X. When the option is off, the box is empty.

Checksum A number obtained by performing a calculation on the contents of a sector or a file. Checksum is usually used to validate the data.

Child directory A subdirectory subordinate to another directory, called the parent (see *Parent directory*). DOS looks in the parent directory to find the location of the child.

Click To press and release a mouse button without moving the mouse.

Cluster See *Allocation unit*.

CMOS Complementary Metal-Oxide Semiconductor. In 286 and higher machines, a battery-powered module that retains information about the computer's hardware for booting purposes.

COM An extension used to identify a file as an executable program file. See also *EXE* and *BAT*.

Command	An instruction processed by DOS's command interpreter (or perhaps an alternative command interpreter).
Command button	A dialog box item that initiates an immediate action when you press it. Examples may be an OK button to proceed with a program or a Cancel button to cancel the dialog.
Command processor	A program that can interpret commands entered from a command prompt or a batch file. The command processor carries out internal commands and passes external commands to the proper program.
COMMAND.COM	The command processor included in DOS.
Compressed drive	See *Compressed volume file*.
Compressed volume file	CVF or compressed drive. A file that acts like a drive. The CVF is created and managed by a disk compression program such as DoubleSpace to contain compressed files.
Compression	Reducing the size of a file or files by eliminating repetition and/or waste space.
CONFIG.SYS	A file that contains commands necessary to configure the system and load device drivers. CONFIG.SYS is executed immediately after the operating system files are loaded during booting.
Console	The standard input/output device, usually a keyboard and monitor combination.
Conventional memory	RAM in the range of 0K to 640K. In versions of DOS before DOS 5, programs had to be loaded into conventional memory for execution.
Cross-linked allocation unit	An allocation unit, or cluster, that appears to belong to two files in the FAT.
CVF	See *Compressed volume file*.

DBLSPACE.BIN	One of DOS's core program files. DBLSPACE.BIN manages DoubleSpace CVFs.
Default	An item, option, or value used if you don't specify otherwise.
Deletion protection	A program that tracks deleted files to assist in undeleting them.
Device driver	A file that contains information used to control hardware devices such as memory, a monitor, a keyboard, a printer, and so on. Some device drivers create and control logical devices such as RAM drives.
Dialog box	A box displayed by a graphical program that enables you to select options and provide information needed by the program.
Directory	A data structure that contains information about the location, sizes, attributes, and so on of files and other directories. Any directory not a root directory is a subdirectory.
Directory tree	The entire set of directories on a drive, from the root directory down through its children and their children to the lowest level on the drive.
Disk	See *floppy disk* and *hard disk*.
DOS	The Disk Operating System. An operating system designed for the IBM line of personal computers and their compatibles.
Double-click	To press a mouse button twice in rapid succession without moving the mouse.
Drag	To hold down a mouse button while moving the mouse.
Drive name	A letter assigned to a physical or logical drive.
EXE	An extension used to identify a file as an executable program file. See also COM and *BAT*.

Executable file

A file containing instructions that control the computer. Also known as a program file. Executable files usually have the extension EXE or COM.

Expanded memory

Also called EMS. An external memory device managed by an expanded memory manager in accordance with Lotus-Intel Microsoft Expanded Memory Standards (LIM EMS).

Extended memory

Also called XMS. In a 286 or higher machine, RAM at addresses beyond 1M.

Extension

A suffix for a file name. An extension can be one to three characters. Extensions are connected to the file name by a period.

FAT

See *File allocation table*.

Field

A data item in a dialog box or database record; for example, a ZIP code or a name.

File

A collection of related data stored and handled as a single entity by DOS.

File allocation table

A table maintained by DOS on every floppy disk or hard drive, used to track the locations of files and empty space.

File handle

A memory area that contains the information that DOS needs to access an open file.

Filespec

An expression that identifies a file or files. A filespec may include a drive name, path, file name, and extension. The file name and extension may include wildcards.

Floppy disk

A small removable magnetic disk. The most common are 5.25-inch flexible disks and 3.25-inch hard-body disks.

Floppy drive

A drive that uses floppy disks.

Fragmentation

Storing a file in nonadjacent clusters.

Global filespec

A filespec containing wildcard characters in the file name and/or extension.

661

Hard disk	A nonremoveable storage medium.
Hard drive	A logical drive on a hard disk.
Hardware	The physical equipment that makes up a computer system, including boards, monitor, keyboard, disk drives, printer, modem, mouse, and other possible items.
Hexadecimal	Hex. A number system based on the number 16; hexadecimal numbers have 16 digits, from 0 through F. Computers often turn the binary numbers used internally into hexadecimal numbers for display purposes.
Hidden attribute	An attribute that, when turned on, indicates that a file or directory should not be casually accessible by DIR or other commands.
Hidden file	A file with the hidden attribute turned on.
High memory area	The first 65,520 bytes of extended memory.
HMA	See *High memory area*.
Host drive	The drive on which a compressed volume file resides.
Hotkey	A key or key combination that activates a TSR or command.
I/O	See *Input/Output*.
Icon	A small drawing used instead of words by a graphical program to label an item's type or to represent a command or function that can be invoked by clicking the icon.
Input	Information entered into a computer by a keyboard, mouse, or other input device.
Input/Output	Often abbreviated I/O. Input and output operations or devices.
Interface	A connection between any two parts of a system, for example, between a computer user and a program.

Interrupt	A signal sent to a computer to interrupt its current activity and request immediate processing. An *external interrupt* is from the outside world, such as a disk drive. An *internal interrupt* reports that an unusual situation has arisen, usually an error condition. A *software interrupt* is a request from a program for a service.
IO.SYS	One of DOS's system files that contains the core of the DOS program.
K or KB	See *Kilobyte*.
Kilobyte	1024 bytes. Abbreviated as K or KB.
Logical drive	An area of a disk or of memory treated as a separate drive although it has no separate physical existence.
Lost allocation unit	An allocation unit that is marked in the FAT as used but does not seem to belong to a file.
M or MB	See *Megabyte*.
Megabyte	A kilobyte squared (1,048,576 bytes). Abbreviated as M or MB.
Memory	An internal storage device used to store the programs currently being executed and their data.
Memory-resident	Also called TSR. A program that remains loaded in memory until the end of the session (or until you specifically unload it). It usually monitors input and/or processing looking for specific events that it is designed to handle.
Menu	A list of commands for you to choose from. Menus usually appear in graphical programs, which enable you to select items by using the mouse or the keyboard.
Modem	A hardware device that enables communication between two computers over a telephone line.
MSDOS.SYS	One of DOS's system files that contains the core of the DOS program.

Numeric keypad	A set of keys arranged like those on a 10-key adder and used to enter numeric data. The numeric keypad often shares the same functions as the cursor-movement keys, with the Shift and NumLock keys used to select between the two functions.
Operating system	A program that manages all of a computer's operations, controlling other programs' access to the computer's basic resources such as memory and the disk drives. The operating system also provides the user interface.
Output	Data sent from a program to a storage or output device, such as a printer, a monitor, a disk, and so on.
Parallel port	A port through which data passes eight bits (one byte) at a time. Frequently used to communicate with printers.
Parameter	A variable data item entered as part of a command. The parameter provides information to a program, such as a filespec that tells a copy command what files to copy.
Parent	A directory that contains an entry for a subordinate directory (see *Child directory*).
Partition	A division of a hard disk.
Partition table	A table stored at the beginning of a hard disk that identifies the partitions on the disk.
Path	A list of directories that DOS must go through to find a directory or file.
Pipe	Using the output from one program as input to another.
Port	An address used to communicate with another device such as a printer, modem, or mouse.
Processor	The hardware device that carries out program instructions.
Program	See *Executable file*.

Program group	A list of programs that can be opened from the DOS Shell screen.
Program search path	See *Search path*.
Prompt	A message from a program requesting input from a user.
Queue	A list of items waiting for attention; particularly, a list of files waiting to be printed by the Print command.
Radio button	A list of items in which one, and only one, item is always selected. Radio buttons usually appear in dialog boxes.
RAM	Random-access memory. Memory that can be written to and read from. Data stored in RAM is not permanent but disappears when the system is turned off or rebooted.
RAM disk	A logical drive created in RAM to provide rapid access to data that would otherwise require disk access. Data in a RAM drive disappears when the system is turned off or rebooted.
Read-only attribute	An read-attribute that indicates whether a file or directory can be written to. When the read-only attribute is turned on, programs are not supposed to modify or delete the file.
Read-only file	A file with the read-only attribute turned on.
Read-write head	The physical device that reads and writes data on a disk or tape drive.
Reboot	To reload the operating system; in DOS, you normally reboot by pressing Ctrl-Alt-Del.
Relative path	A path that starts from a drive's current directory.
ROM	Read-only memory. A type of memory in which data is permanently stored; the data cannot be erased or replaced. ROM retains its data even when the power goes out.

ROM-BIOS	A collection of programs stored in ROM that DOS uses to perform the basic input and output operations of the computer.
Root directory	The primary directory on a disk; the top level of the directory tree.
Scroll	To move data on the screen or within a box or window.
Scroll bar	A bar at the right side or bottom of a screen, box, or window that enables you to use a mouse to move data up or down or from side to side.
Scroll box	A box in the scroll bar that indicates the position of the displayed data relative to the entire file or list; you usually can move the data by dragging the scroll box.
Search path	A list of directories that DOS should scan when looking for a program file that is not in the current directory. Some newer DOS programs also use the search path to look for data files.
Sector	A portion of a track on a disk, usually 512 bytes. A sector is the smallest amount that can be read or written at one time.
Serial port	A port through which data passes one bit at a time. Usually used to connect with a modem, a mouse, or some special type of printer.
Shell	A program that replaces DOS's basic command prompt and command processor. DOS's Shell program provides a graphic interface from which you can perform many DOS functions.
Software	Computer programs.
Stack	A memory area used to store temporary information. Stacks often hold information needed to return to a program after an interrupt.
Subdirectory	Any directory on a disk except the root directory.

Switch	A parameter included in a command to turn a program feature on or off. Most switches begin with a slash (/).
SYS	An extension often used for device drivers and other programs loaded in CONFIG.SYS.
System attribute	An attribute that tells DOS whether a file or directory should be both hidden and read-only.
System file	A file with the system attribute turned on; one of the files that contain DOS's core program—IO.SYS, MSDOS.SYS, and DBLSPACE.BIN.
Task swapping	Switching between two or more programs without losing your place in any of the programs.
Telecommunications	Communication between two computers over a phone line.
Track	On a disk, one of the set of concentric circles on which the drive writes data.
Tree	See *Directory tree.*
TSR	See *Memory resident.*
Undelete	To recover data that has been deleted.
Unformat	To restore data removed from a disk by the FORMAT command.
Upper memory	The area of memory from 640K to 1024K (1M). In earlier versions of DOS, upper memory was reserved for DOS's system use, but it now can be used to load and execute programs in 386 and higher machines.
User interface	The way in which a user and a program communicate with each other. DOS provides two interfaces, the command prompt and the graphical DOS Shell.
Utility program	A program that helps to manage the computer and its data. Anti-Virus, UNDELETE, and BACKUP are examples of utility programs provided with DOS 6.

Virtual disk

See *RAM disk*.

Virus

A computer program that can duplicate and spread itself from computer to computer, usually without a user's knowledge. Viruses often hide in a system area or program file; they may do harm to a system and its data, intentionally or unintentionally.

Wildcard character

A nonspecific character in a filespec. The question mark (?) is matched by any single character. The asterisk (*) is matched by any number of characters or even no characters.

Window

A rectanglular area on a screen that displays program output independent of that displayed in other areas of the screen.

WORM

Write Once, Read Many. Similar to a CD-ROM except that the user may write the original data on the disk. Once written, it cannot be overwritten, only read.

Write protection

A physical mechanism that prevents a disk from being modified. On a 5.25-inch disk, activating this protection usually involves placing a tab over a notch. On a 3.5-inch disk, it usually involves sliding a tab to unblock a cutout on the disk.

Write-delayed cache

A caching system that delays writing data to a disk until system resources are not otherwise occupied so that reading and other processing have priority.

Index

G

H

X—Y

W